DATE DUE

NOV 7 07		

DEMCO 38-296

Insider/Outsider

Insider/Outsider:

UNIVERSITY OF CALIFORNIA PRESS

American Jews and Multiculturalism

Edited by David Biale,
Michael Galchinsky,
and Susan Heschel

BERKELEY / LOS ANGELES / LONDON

An earlier version of "The Paradox of Jewish Studies in the New Academy" by Sara R. Horowitz appeared as "Jewish Studies as Oppositional?" in *Styles of Cultural Activism,* ed. Philip Goldstein (Newark: University of Delaware Press, 1994), 152–164. It appears here in revised form by permission.

University of California Press
Berkeley and Los Angeles, California

University of California Press
London, England

Library of Congress Cataloging-in-Publication Data

Insider/outsider : American Jews and multiculturalism / edited by
    David Biale, Michael Galchinsky, and Susannah Heschel.
        p.   cm.
    Includes bibliographical references and index.
        ISBN 0-520-21108-1 (cl : alk. paper).—ISBN 0-520-21122-7 (pbk :
    alk. paper)
        1. Jews—United States—Intellectual life.   2. Jews—Cultural
    assimilation—United States.   3. Multiculturalism—United States.
    I. Biale, David, 1949-   . II. Galchinsky, Michael.   III. Heschel,
    Susannah.
    E184.J5147   1998
    305.892'4073—DC21

                                                          97-2508
                                                            CIP
                                                            r97

Printed in the United States of America

1 2 3 4 5 6 7 8 9

The paper used in this publication meets the minimum requirements of
American National Standard for Information Sciences—Permanence of
Paper for Printed Library Materials, ANSI Z39.48-1984 ∞

Contents

Introduction

The Dialectic of Jewish Enlightenment

David Biale, Michael Galchinsky, and Susannah Heschel

"It is necessary to refuse everything to the Jews as a nation and grant the Jews everything as individuals."[1] So declared Count Stanislas de Clermont-Tonnerre in 1789 during the debate in the National Assembly over the emancipation of the French Jews. To enter modern society the Jews were confronted with a demand to surrender their collective identity in exchange for full rights as individual citizens. Although they were not the only group whose emancipation was made dependent on dissolution of their medieval corporate status, it was the Jews who seemed to pose the most intractable problem for the European states.

Today's struggle, over two centuries later, to create a multicultural society in the contemporary nation-state has its historical origins in the very issue posed by Clermont-Tonnerre for the Jews. What can and should be the role of religious, ethnic, and cultural groups in a state whose theory of citizenship is based on individuals rather than collectivities? How are the identities of such groups to be defined and understood in a world that has undermined all traditional identities, in which terms like *religion, ethnicity,* and *culture* are constantly being torn apart and refashioned?

In Europe the Jews were one of the first of marginalized groups to confront these questions, and in the Holocaust they paid the highest of prices for the inability of the European states to give them satisfactory answers. If the European Enlightenment promised full equality to individuals, its own internal dialectic, as Max Horkheimer and Theodor Adorno showed half a century ago,[2] undermined the promise in a number of inescapable ways. The Enlightenment's doctrine of universal rationality offered a new doctrine of human rights and individual liberties, but this very universalist rationality also prepared the ground for the bureaucratic state and mass society, whose logic contradicted those rights and liberties. The Enlightenment could be seen as simultaneously the source of liberation and totalitarian oppression, both produced from the same principles. Side by side with the presumed equality of citizenship came the romantic idea of the nation, a new construct that mobilized historical traditions in the service of a new, homogeneous community, frequently hostile to recently emancipated groups like the Jews. What the modern state gave to such groups with one hand it took away with the other.

Even today many European states remain caught on the horns of this dilemma. Throughout Europe immigrant communities and ethnic minorities are challenging the old ideal of the homogeneous nation-state. Yet between the ideal of citizenship proclaimed during the French Revolution and the ethnic chauvinism renewed after the breakup of the Communist bloc, multiculturalism in Europe remains a dim promise at best. In France liberals invoke "Republicanism" to reject the multicultural demands of North African Muslims, such as the wearing of a chador by Muslim schoolgirls.[3] And in Bosnia ethnic "cleansing" appears to have defeated the attempt to create a multiethnic state.

The United States, heir to the same Enlightenment as the European states, exhibits a very different tension between a monolithic national identity and ethnic diversity. Lacking the corporate traditions of European monarchies and the state-sponsored churches of many European nations, the U.S. had less difficulty in absorbing religiously and ethnically different groups like the Jews, comprehending them as one among many waves of European immigrants to a nation increasingly imagining itself as a "melting pot." The overwhelming impact of immigration on the formation of the American state stretched the definition of the nation in ways unimaginable in Europe.

Although the absorption process for marginalized European immigrants like Italians, Irish, and Jews was not always painless in America, these immigrants were not usually the Other around which the majority defined its identity and consolidated its power. Rather, the majority primarily defined itself—indeed, became "white"—in relation to blacks, Native Americans, and other "peoples of color." One might argue that the Americanization of immigrants has involved a historical process of enlarging the definition of "whiteness" to include groups like the Jews who were initially considered "nonwhite." Yet a contrary process has obtained for Hispanics, who, despite their European origins, came increasingly to be considered "colored." The shifting meaning of these terms suggests how historically constructed they are in American culture and how central racial categories have been in creating the fault lines of American society.[4]

As a land of immigrants, America has always struggled with conflicting self-definitions, between what is today called "monoculturalism" and "multiculturalism." As some of the essays in the first section of this volume suggest, "melting pot," "cultural pluralism" and "ethnic diversity" were slogans hotly debated at the beginning of this century, with Jews often leading the way in challenging a monolithic American identity. These debates certainly foreshadow the current question of multiculturalism. Yet multiculturalism, as it is now invoked and as we shall use it in this book, has arisen in a specific historical context and has a set of meanings at once more focused and different from the simple affirmation of diversity. While cultural pluralism affirmed privately held ethnic identities as long as groups publicly affirmed the Anglo-Saxon character of America, multiculturalism challenges the priority of this monolithic identity in American history, highlighting racial as well as ethnic diversity and claiming public resources on behalf of these groups.

In its present theoretical and political forms, multiculturalism is a product of the civil rights movement of the 1960s. It emerged out of the tension between the demand for race blindness and the simultaneous recognition that race hatred would necessarily prevent realization of that goal. At just the moment when the political struggle for integration achieved legal successes, it became increasingly evident that this political achievement left unsolved the equally vexing problems of social, cultural, and economic integration. Political emancipation was not the same as social emancipation.

Multiculturalism arose to question whether in fact such social integration was achievable or even desirable. If the civil rights movement of the 1960s was a quintessentially Enlightenment project, its failure to achieve full social integration suggested to many an inherent flaw in the Enlightenment vision itself. The universalism of the Enlightenment appeared to be an ideological illusion, the imposition of the consciousness and experience of history's victors on its victims. The Enlightenment promised liberty for all, but its own view of reason frequently limited liberty to white men. From this perspective the Western cultural canon reflected not so much universal values as the particular values of a certain elite—white, propertied, Christian, straight, and male—in a certain time and place. The

Enlightenment belief in one, universal human nature seemed itself the creation of the same elite, a creation that failed to take into account the real differences in the cultures and experiences of non-Western peoples as well as, in the West, of groups of color, women, and gays, lesbians, and bisexuals. In this light the full liberation of women, for example, does not require the fulfillment of the Enlightenment but rather its replacement with a new philosophy of human beings that recognizes difference in place of sameness.

All of these issues resonate with Jews, for they are versions of the nineteenth-century "Jewish question" translated into an American idiom at the end of the twentieth century. Yet it is no secret that Jews confront contemporary multiculturalism with great ambivalence, trepidation, and even hostility. In part this is so because the Jewish question as it existed in Europe before the Holocaust has never existed in quite the same form or with quite the same intensity in America. Since World War II Jews in America have to a remarkable degree achieved that social emancipation that had eluded them in Europe. Judaism as a religion came to be accepted as one of the three great American religions—Protestantism, Catholicism, and Judaism—as if Jews were a third of the American population.[5] Moreover, American Jews were able to make social and political gains in such an environment because they were now seen and were willing to be seen as "white" themselves, as part of a majority whose very self-definition as a majority was based on the exclusion of those termed "nonwhite."[6] As a result of the structural racism in American society that favors "white" skin, Jews were no longer marginalized in the same sense as they were in Europe or in the sense that groups of color or sexual minorities often are in contemporary America.

But neither are the descendants of other European immigrant groups such as Irish, Poles, or Italians. They too have shed this stigmatized status and largely entered the "white" majority. Yet no one evidently feels the pressing need to write a book entitled "Multiculturalism and the Italians" or "Multiculturalism and the Irish." Why is it that only the Jews experience multiculturalism with such a special ambivalence? In part, the answer has to do with the vexed relationship between Jews and African Americans, a history that is much more complex than the prevailing myth suggests. To put the matter more bluntly, there are some extreme advocates of multiculturalism, especially in the African American community, who have singled out the Jews among the generalized category of "whites" for special criticism, criticism that is sometimes hard to distinguish from anti-Semitism.

Yet it is not only real and imagined anti-Semitism that makes Jews anxious about multiculturalism. As important is the consciousness Jews have of themselves as occupying an anomalous status: insiders who are outsiders and outsiders who are insiders. They represent that boundary case whose very lack of belonging to a recognizable category creates a sense of unease. This is not, of course, the first moment in Jewish history in which the Jews have occupied this liminal zone. Indeed, one might argue that the Jews succeeded in surviving for so many centuries as a marginalized group precisely because they were able to establish themselves close to centers of power and negotiate between competing elite and popular forces.[7]

In contemporary America this historical dualism has reached its greatest extremes. Never before have so few barriers existed to Jews' entering the corridors of political, cultural, and economic power. Yet the path to integration has also created enormous contradictions in Jewish self-consciousness. Identification and integration with the majority stands at odds with the Jews' equal desire to preserve their identity as a minority. Never before have Jews confronted so powerfully the tension between maintaining continuity with tradition and reinventing Jewish life so that it fully meets women's needs for justice and equity. At a time when Jews are enjoying their greatest acceptance as part of the majority, never before has Jewish identity been founded so centrally on a history of victimization, consisting primarily in the memory of the Holocaust. Even the relationship of American Jews to Israel expresses an ambiguity in Jews' sense of themselves as powerful and powerless: should they identify with Israel as a small, threatened state standing for centuries of Jewish vulnerability or as a regional military and economic power?

Standing somewhere between the dominant position of the white majority and the marginal position of peoples of color, Jews respond with ambivalence to the attack of multiculturalism on the Enlightenment. For two centuries Jews have staked their position in Western society on the promise of the Enlightenment. When given the chance, they used emancipation to enormous benefit and they came to repay the Enlightenment with almost excessive gratitude, rushing to adopt political liberalism and cultural rationalism to a much greater degree than any other group.[8] At the same time, the Jewish embrace of the Enlightenment reflected the limitations within the Enlightenment itself: it was Jewish men, much more than Jewish women, who realized the benefits of the Enlightenment, so the very enthusiasm for the Enlightenment needs to be qualified to some degree along gender lines.[9] And Jews also recognize that the very failure of the Enlight-

enment led to Auschwitz. The dialectic of Jewish Enlightenment therefore oscillates between these two poles of enthusiastic celebration of modern Western culture and awareness of its most horrific results.

Having finally reaped the fruits of the promise of the Enlightenment,
American Jews sometimes ask why liberalism can't do for other marginalized American groups what it has done for them. This is the source of
the conflict among Jews about affirmative action, a policy often associated with multiculturalism. If Jews historically associate quotas with barriers to opportunity, it is then particularly difficult for some to accept such
quotas (or similar vehicles) as just means for American society to redress
inequities. As beneficiaries, for whatever historical and cultural reasons,
of the Enlightenment's equality of opportunity, some Jews find it hard
to understand why such slogans might be inadequate in dealing with the
long-term consequences of slavery. At the same time, however, since probably the proportionally greatest beneficiaries of affirmative action have
been Jewish women, Jews have just as many self-interested reasons to see
the virtues of preferences.

A similar ambivalence can be seen in the relationship of Jewish studies
in American universities to ethnic studies. Emerging at about the same
time, the late 1960s and early 1970s, these disciplines owe their origins to
very different circumstances. Jewish studies in America developed precisely
at the moment when Jews felt themselves fully integrated and the field
became a vehicle for establishing their right to be considered part of the
Western canon. Ethnic studies often took the opposite tack, criticizing the
Western canon for its exclusionary practices and promoting ethnic and racial
particularism. Jewish studies typically subscribed to an Enlightenment
vision of the university while ethnic studies often challenged this vision.

Yet Jews are not immune to the notion that Jewish studies might affirm
ethnic identity. A recent controversy at Queen's College (City University
of New York) highlighted these issues. A non-Jew was appointed to head
the college's Jewish studies program and a Jewish faculty member questioned whether a non-Jew should direct a program one of whose purposes was to foster ethnic identity. This professor pointed out that no one
would entertain appointing a non-African American to head the African
American program or a man to head the women's studies program. But
the almost universal condemnation of this argument by other Jews suggested that most see Jewish studies as differing qualitatively from other
ethnic studies programs.

The differences between Jewish studies and ethnic studies are not always
as stark as this case might indicate. Jews have not always promoted inte-

gration with the Western canon. In fact, Jewish studies emerged as a discipline in the nineteenth century in order to criticize the Christian bias inherent in the term *Judeo-Christian* and to suggest Jews' distinct contributions to Western philosophy and history. Jewish studies in America can learn from ethnic studies to remember and value this strand of its own past. Perhaps women's studies presents a good model for what Jewish studies should attempt to achieve: the use of methods and insights from many disciplines to rigorously articulate what makes Jews distinct while showing the ways in which Jewish history and thought contribute to the humanities at large.

As examples like these demonstrate, Jews are often caught between fervent affirmation of the Enlightenment and criticism of it. Many Jews believe that the replacement of the Enlightenment ideal of universalism with a politics of difference and a fragmented "multiculture" would constitute a threat to Jewish achievement. At the same time, they recognize the dangers of a homogeneous "monoculture" for Jewish particularity. As insiders who are also outsiders, they seek to rescue the virtues of the Enlightenment from the shards of its failures and salvage an inclusive vision from multiculturalism, where fragmentation and divisiveness now reign.

How to save multiculturalism from some of its own excesses and weaknesses is a question that has begun to preoccupy critics increasingly uneasy with what is sometimes caricatured as a "culture of complaint."[10] In the effort to restore the voices of history's victims, these critics wonder if the status of the victim hasn't become valorized for its own sake. They also question whether an exaggerated politics of identity doesn't preclude solidarity between groups with different experiences. If understanding requires one to have personally experienced a certain history, then others must accept the insider's account of that history on faith. With the breakdown in communication and even in the belief in the universality of language, all that is left sometimes seems to be dogmatic political correctness.

Many of these arguments have been made by neoconservatives who oppose multiculturalism out of indifference or even hostility to the claims of the marginalized. But these points have also been raised by those with a great deal of sympathy for the goals of multiculturalism, some of whom have tried to articulate what they call a "critical multiculturalism."[11] Todd Gitlin, writing from a progressive political position, argues that the Enlightenment desire to establish a common polity need not contradict the equally valid quest to honor cultural difference.[12] David Hollinger challenges the assumption that identity is fixed and argues instead for a "postethnic America" in which such identities would be freely chosen rather than forcibly inherited.[13] Works such as these do not reject the desire to create a true multiculture but instead try to see beyond present multicultural politics toward a more inclusive vision of an America in which particularity and universalism are not contradictory goals but rather poles in a fruitful dialectic.

The present book is intended to contribute to this recent literature, which challenges and enriches the theories of multiculturalism. It is neither a complaint against multiculturalism by Jews who feel somehow excluded nor, from the other side, a celebration of multicultural theory as a potential savior.[14] Instead of bemoaning the Jews' anomalous status, we have sought to turn it into a productive virtue. In this spirit the contributors to this volume were asked to consider how the Jewish experience might challenge the conventional polar opposition of a majority "monoculture" and a marginalized "multiculture." Precisely because we believe that the Jews constitute a liminal border case, neither inside nor outside—or, better, both inside and outside—they have the capacity to open up multicultural theory in new and interesting ways that may help it overcome some of the deficiencies that theorists of multiculturalism have begun themselves to see.

One such area explored in this book is the politics of identity, which too often assumes that a monolithic and inherited identity should dictate political action. Multicultural theorists have begun to recognize that no modern identity is stable and transmissible. Ethnicity is itself a modern construct, not an eternal given.[15] Similarly, race is a homogenizing term that conceals the diversity within any so-called racial group.[16] Feminist theory began by suggesting that the very category "woman" is a social construct, and more recently feminist theorists stress gender as "performance" to call attention to its radically unstable, constructed nature.[17]

Here the Jewish experience has much to contribute and also much to learn.[18] The Jews are perhaps the longest-standing case of a group whose self-definition was always a part of a multicultural context. For much of Jewish history, what it meant to be a Jew was to be multilingual and multicultural and never to live in splendid isolation from interaction and struggle with other cultures. Moreover, Jewish identity was always an indeterminate composite of what we would today call religious, ethnic, and national dimensions. In the modern and postmodern periods this identity has become even more unstable since it has interacted with other equally strong national identities: Jew and German, Jew and American, Jew and Israeli. Like women, African Americans, or just about any other grouping in society one can imagine, the Jewish community is in no sense homogeneous. Rather, the word *Jew* has multiple and contradictory meanings: Orthodox, Reform, secular, Ashkenazi, Sephardi as well as male and female.

In a variety of ways, then, to be a Jew, especially at this historical juncture, means to lack a single essence, to live with multiple identities. Perhaps the Jews are even emblematic of the postmodern condition as a whole. If identity politics means to base one's political activity on one particular identity, then the Jews' experience of multiple identities suggests that identity politics conceived as monolithic or total needs serious rethinking. Many of the contributors to this volume argue instead for a politics that acknowledges the multifaceted nature of identity without abandoning the importance of identity altogether.

Multiculturalists have also begun to explore and embrace the implications of composite identities such as the mestizo or creole. Some argue that these hybrid and "impure" identities are representative rather than monstrous and that because of the increase in global migrations these hybrid identities will continue to characterize marginalized and majoritarian communities alike in the future.[19] Here is an area where the Jewish subculture and other American subcultures can begin to learn from one another, both in terms of their respective historical experiences and in terms of contemporary sociology.

In a similar way, the category of diaspora, which has become increasingly important in postcolonial theory, has critical resonance for Jews, whose history and religion have required a constant dialectic between "homeland" and "exile."[20] In the contemporary world more and more people are said to live in diaspora and the creation of a true multiculture requires devising ways of negotiating between one's home and one's homeland. For Jews, this is an old problem and a new one. On the one hand, the Holocaust has destroyed what was the ancestral homeland for most American Jews. On the other, the state of Israel has provided a new homeland, although a paradoxical one since most American Jews neither come from there nor intend to live there. The complex ways in which collective identities are formed in the tensions between homeland and diaspora are common to Jews as well as other migrant groups (contrary to the assumptions of many American Jews).[21]

Yet another question where we believe the Jewish experience may shed new light on multicultural theory is the debate about the canon. Multiculturalists have typically sought to open the Western canon to suppressed or forgotten literatures, while opponents of multiculturalism have lamented the loss of critical standards of culture and of a shared heritage.

Yet the very concept of a canon as used by both sides of this debate may be rigid and narrow, based perhaps too heavily on the Christian notion of dogma. For Jews, the canon means not only a sacred scripture but also a tradition of commentary that almost infinitely expands that scripture, often in radical and unexpected directions. The Talmud, based in some very loose sense on the Bible, is at once canonical and also the site for a remarkable polyphony of contradictory opinions. This type of sacred literature suggests that a canon need not reflect a monolithic set of doctrines but might instead involve an ever expanding and transforming culture composed of creative contradictions. Indeed, this Jewish concept of a canon is increasingly being accepted for the study of Western literature and it is one that is much more open to interaction with non-Western culture.[22]

In addition, the Jews' own relationship to the Western canon betrays the same insider-outsider relationship that increasingly characterizes that of other marginalized groups living in the West. The Bible is the quintessential Jewish book, yet the way Jews read the Bible is not necessarily that of Christian culture. But if the Bible is one of the classic canonical texts of the West, the Talmud and other rabbinic literature remain very much on the margins. Here is a literature that at once resisted Hellenistic-Christian culture yet also absorbed and interacted with it in a variety of creative ways.[23] This model of resistance and adaptation has much to teach contemporary multiculturalists about the relationship of a subculture to the dominant culture, just as American Jews can profitably learn from the experiences of the members of other subcultures.

These are only a few of the issues this volume attempts to address. We have arranged the essays in one of many possible coherent sequences, and we invite readers to take their own paths through it. In the first section, "American Symphony or Melting Pot?" the reader will encounter several essays devoted to tracing the history of varying definitions of America and the place of Jews in those definitions. How did these various definitions contribute to or detract from Jews' relationships with the majority and with other subcultures, particularly African Americans? How might the Jewish experience suggest new definitions of multicultural theory and politics?

The relationship of the Jewish experience to the definition of the cultural canon is the subject of the second section, "Canons and Counter-histories." What does the discipline of Jewish studies have to offer to the humanities as a whole? How might the way in which Jews have interpreted the Bible constitute an alternative to the traditional idea of canon as a set of monolithic texts? Alternatively, how might Jewish studies reconceptualize itself, using other multicultural models, as a form of "counterhistory" to challenge the canon and historical assumptions of Western Christianity? And, finally, how does Judaism function in the very different counterhistories of Afrocentrism and feminism?

The final section, "Diaspora Negotiations," addresses the complex ways in which Jews have defined, adapted to, and resisted exile. What is the relationship of the Jewish experience to postcolonial diaspora theory? How has the particular form of Jewish multilingualism in America served to construct a kind of homeland? How does modern Hebrew literature challenge the privileging of exile in modernism and postmodernism? And, finally, what is the meaning and what are the implications of the peculiarly "Jewish" form of vicarious politics which seems as prevalent in multiculturalism today as it was in earlier political movements in the Jewish diaspora?

This selection of articles follows no single ideological line or definition of multiculturalism. Each of the authors has been encouraged to advance his or her own point of view rather than one that we have imposed at the outset. Yet we would be disingenuous to pretend that we have no underlying agenda in undertaking this book. For too long, we believe, relations between Jews and other groups in the emerging multiculture have been marked by discomfort, suspicion, and even overt hostility. It is our hope that this effort to bring multicultural theory into conversation with Jewish experience and Jewish studies will promote real conversation outside of these pages.

We are also fully cognizant of the way history has been used to advance the claims of some groups against those of others. We acknowledge that different kinds of oppression have damaged communities in different and to some degree incommensurable ways. By acknowledging these disparities of experience at the outset, we hope to transcend the trend toward comparative victimology which has distracted Jews and other groups from more important questions. Perhaps the most urgent of these questions is whether American subcultures can construct a collective American history that gives due recognition to the oppressions of the past without permitting those oppressions to dictate the narratives of the future. We believe that the future lies in a shared commitment to writing a new narrative rather than in the competition between histories of persecution.

Our aim in this volume is not to overcome difference or erase past inequities in favor of some homogenized culture. In the final analysis, we seek ways to negotiate between marginalized groups and the majority culture, between "minor" and "master" narratives, so that the Enlightenment ideal of the universal and the multicultural vision of difference can be brought under the same roof. We seek alliances with other subcultures so that each can define its own uniqueness. At the same time, we seek a common civic discourse, a truly democratic process in which all ethnic, racial, and religious subcultures are represented. For Jews, as well as all of American society, this should be the challenge of multiculturalism: to create a community of communities and a culture of cultures.

Notes

1. Clermont-Tonnerre quoted in Paul Mendes-Flohr and Jehuda Reinharz, *The Jew in the Modern World*, 2d ed. (New York and Oxford: Oxford University Press, 1995).

2. See Max Horkheimer and Theodor Adorno, *The Dialectic of Enlightenment* (New York: Continuum, 1990). Horkheimer and Adorno focused primarily on the rationality and commodification inherent in the technology of late capitalism and their role in producing genocidal anti-Semitism.

3. It is interesting that the French prime minister declared that while the chador is disruptive because it is "ostentatious," the yarmulke is acceptable since it is so small. Thus does the size of head covering draw the line between those accepted in the French republican consensus and those excluded.

4. See Ruth Frankenburg, *The Social Construction of Whiteness: White Women, Race Matters* (Minneapolis: University of Minnesota Press, 1993), and Ronald Takaki, *A Different Mirror: A History of Multicultural America* (Boston: Little, Brown, 1993).

5. For the most famous formulation of this vision of the three great religions of America, see Will Herberg, *Protestant, Catholic, Jew: An Essay in American Religious Sociology* (Garden City, N.Y.: Doubleday, 1955).

6. For the "whiteness" of Jews before 1880, see Stephen Jay Gould, *The Mismeasure of Man,* rev. and expanded ed. (New York: Norton, 1996), and Michael Galchinsky, *The Origin of the Modern Jewish Woman Writer: Romance and Reform in Victorian England* (Detroit: Wayne State University Press, 1996). For Jews as "whites" in twentieth-century American culture, see Michael Rogin, *Blackface/White Noise: Jewish Immigrants in the Hollywood Melting Pot* (Berkeley and Los Angeles: University of California Press, 1996). For the post-World War II period, see Karen Brodkin Sacks, "How Did Jews Become White Folks?" in Steven Gregory and Roger Sanjek, eds., *Race* (Rutgers, N.J.: Rutgers University Press, 1994), 78–102.

7. For more on the historical relationship of Jews to centers of power, see David Biale, *Power and Powerlessness in Jewish History* (New York: Schocken Books, 1986).

8. See David Sorkin, *The Transformation of German Jewry* (New York: Oxford University Press, 1987), for an account of how the German Jews adopted the Enlightenment value of *Bildung* (cultural education) long after other Germans had abandoned it.

9. See Marion Kaplan, *The Making of the Jewish Middle Class: Women, Family and Identity in Imperial Germany* (New York: Oxford University Press, 1991), for the relationship of Jewish women in Germany toward the Enlightenment.

10. See Robert Hughes, *Culture of Complaint: The Fraying of America* (New York: Oxford University Press, 1993).

11. See the essay on critical multiculturalism by the Chicago Cultural Studies Group in David Theo Goldberg, ed., *Multiculturalism: A Critical Reader* (Oxford: Basil Blackwell, 1994), 107–139.

12. Todd Gitlin, *The Twilight of Common Dreams: Why America Is Wracked by Culture*

Wars (New York: Metropolitan Books, 1995). See also Michael Lind, *The Next American Nation: The New Nationalism and the Fourth American Revolution* (New York: Free Press, 1995).

13. David Hollinger, *Postethnic America* (New York: Basic Books, 1995). Also see Werner Sollors, *Beyond Ethnicity: Consent and Descent in American Culture* (New York: Oxford University Press, 1986).

14. For examples celebrating multiculturalism, see Marla Brettschneider, *Cornerstones of Peace: Jewish Identity Politics and Democratic Theory* (New Brunswick, N.J.: Rutgers University Press, 1996), and Brettschneider, ed., *The Narrow Bridge: Jewish Views on Multiculturalism* (New Brunswick, N.J.: Rutgers University Press, 1996).

15. The argument for ethnicity as a modern construct was presented long before multiculturalism in Frederik Barth, ed., *Ethnic Groups and Boundaries* (Oslo: Oslo University Press, 1969). It has been argued more recently by the contributors to Werner Sollors, ed., *The Invention of Ethnicity* (New York: Oxford University Press, 1989), and in Benedict Anderson, *Imagined Communities: Reflections on the Origin and Spread of Nationalism* (London: Verso, 1991).

16. See Michael Eric Dyson, "Essentialism and the Complexities of Racial Identity," in Goldberg, ed., *Multiculturalism: A Critical Reader*, 218–229.

17. See the illuminating collection of essays in Judith Butler and Joan W. Scott, *Feminists Theorize the Political* (New York and London: Routledge, 1992).

18. See David Theo Goldberg and Michael Krausz, eds., *Jewish Identity* (Philadelphia: Temple University Press, 1993).

19. On composite identities see, for instance, Gloria Anzaldúa, *Borderlands/La Frontera: The New Mestiza* (San Francisco: Aunt Lute Books, 1987).

20. See Arnold Eisen, *Galut: Modern Jewish Reflection on Homelessness and Homecoming* (Bloomington: Indiana University Press, 1986).

21. See, for example, Paul Gilroy, *The Black Atlantic: Modernity and Double Consciousness* (Cambridge: Harvard University Press, 1993), for a very interesting discussion of these issues of home and homeland for African Americans as well as some illuminating comparisons between African Americans and Jews.

22. One of the earliest critical works to develop and use the Jewish concept of the canon was Geoffrey H. Hartman and Sanford Budick, *Midrash and Literature* (New Haven: Yale University Press, 1986). More recent contributions have been Norman Finkelstein, *The Ritual of New Creation: Jewish Tradition and Contemporary Literature* (Albany: State University of New York Press, 1992), and Daniel Boyarin, *Intertextuality and the Reading of Midrash* (Bloomington: Indiana University Press, 1990).

23. For two different points of view on the relationship of talmudic culture to its surroundings, see Daniel Boyarin, *Carnal Israel: Reading Sex in the Talmud* (Berkeley and Los Angeles: University of California Press, 1993), and David Biale, *Eros and the Jews* (Berkeley and Los Angeles: University of California Press, 1997), chapter 2.

PART ONE

American Symphony
or Melting Pot?

CHAPTER I

The Melting Pot and Beyond

Jews and the Politics of American Identity

David Biale

As the recent controversy over national standards for the teaching of American history attests, the multicultural debate frequently revolves around the struggle between two narratives: America as the site for the realization of freedom and America as the site for oppression, persecution, and even genocide. These stories divide substantially along racial lines in which "white" ethnicities tend to emphasize the narrative of freedom while "colored" ethnicities focus on narratives of oppression.

In this essay I wish to take up the curious position that Jews occupy along this narrative divide, a position that has caused them much angst as they confront multiculturalism. Jews came to America, in large measure from eastern Europe, with a kind of double consciousness. On the one hand, millennia of exile had accustomed them to view themselves as a perennial minority, always vulnerable to the whims of an often hostile majority. Jewish life was by definition "abnormal" compared to that of the Jews' hosts, a perception reinforced by Jewish theologies of chosenness and Christian theologies of supersession. During the century or so before 1881, when mass immigration to America began, movements for Jewish emancipation and integration had proceeded by fits and starts in the various European countries. The process was already well under way in western and central Europe but had only begun in eastern Europe. Yet even in those countries in which emanicipation was well established, in France, for example, Jews often remained a self-conscious minority, indeed, the quintessential minority against whom the status of minority rights was usually defined. Jews came to America with this consciousness of difference firmly ingrained, either as a product of their medieval exclusion or as a result of their newer status as the paradigmatic European minority.

On the other hand, if Jews came to America with a minority mentality, they also viewed America in quasi-messianic terms as a land where they might escape their historic destiny and become part of the majority. The *goldene medina* was not only a state whose streets were paved with gold in the obvious economic sense but it was also a state that seemed to promise political "gold": liberation and equality. Although the mass Jewish immigration to America is often contrasted with the much more ideological Zionist settlement in Palestine in the same decades, both were driven by equally strong material *and* idealistic motives. In their own imaginations, the Jews came to America not as they had wandered from country to country through the centuries of exile but as if they were coming home.

In this regard, then, Jews were not that different from other immigrants, from Europe or elsewhere in the world, all of whom saw in America both an economic and political haven. What made the Jews different was the persistence of the first mentality, that of a minority. Most other immigrant groups were themselves from majority populations, although some, like the Irish and the Poles, were also subjugated by other nations. Yet even these latter groups had more recent historical memories of majority status, while, for the Jews, living as a minority had been an endemic condition for thousands of years. Thus, while Jews almost universally constructed a narrative of liberation to describe their immigration to America, they did so while retaining a strong memory and consciousness of themselves as a minority.

This double consciousness played an important role earlier in this century in prompting various Jewish thinkers to develop new theories of America that might accommodate the Jews. These thinkers continued to view the Jews as the archetypal minority and they attempted to envision an America in which the Jews might be both integrated and still retain their distinctiveness. Thus, much of the discourse about America as a "melting pot" or as a pluralistic nation of cultural minorities was originated by Jews to address the particular situation of Jewish immigrants. Jews therefore not only adapted to America but also played central roles in shaping the definitions of their adopted country. Yet the way contemporary multiculturalists have absorbed this discourse and changed its terms has created profound anxiety among Jews, because of their double consciousness. The question for Jews today is whether they still have something to contribute to the definition of identity in America, as they did earlier in the century.

Israel Zangwill's *The Melting Pot*

A number of key texts in the early Jewish attempt to define America and the Jews' place in it are often taken as paradigmatic statements of fixed positions. Most are actually pregnant with ambiguity and tension, reflecting the very ambiguities of Jewish self-consciousness. I take as my first text Israel Zangwill's play *The Melting Pot,* first produced in Washington, D.C., in 1908.[1] Although Zangwill was an English Jew whose views on assimilation and America were undoubtedly shaped by the context of Edwardian England, the play became a pivotal moment in the American debate about the mass immigration of the early part of the century. Zangwill did not invent the term "melting pot,"[2] but he was instrumental in popularizing its use in American political discourse, thus setting in motion the debate that has raged for most of this century. From Horace Kallen's "cultural pluralism" in 1915 to Nathan Glazer and Daniel Patrick Moynihan's *Beyond the Melting Pot* in 1963 and culminating in the struggles about multiculturalism in the 1980s and 1990s, Zangwill's *Melting Pot* has continued to reverberate in a variety of incarnations and reincarnations.

Opening the script of *The Melting Pot,* one is immediately astonished that such a slender dramatic reed could support a century-long discourse. The play itself is a melodramatic potboiler, full of cardboard caricatures and woodenly sentimental dialogue. Yet Zangwill's timing was evidently exquisite, for the play opened at the height of the pre–World War I immigration wave, as American public opinion oscillated between shock at the Russian pogroms and deep skepticism about the possibility of Americanizing their victims. The opening was attended by Theodore Roosevelt, who applauded the author's sentiments and later agreed to have a revised edition dedicated to him in 1914. The play enjoyed long runs in a number of cities throughout America and even spawned the formation of a "Melting Pot Club" in Boston. Zangwill had clearly touched a nerve.

The most basic tension in *The Melting Pot* lies in the contrast between the play's assimilationist message and its specifically Jewish content. As I hope will become evident, Zangwill's choice of Jews as his immigrant protagonists reflected more than the fact that Zangwill typically wrote primarily about Jews. To put the matter differently, if it was *Jewish* immigration that was emblematic of the problem of Americanization, then Zangwill's "melting pot" conclusion was the inescapable product of a peculiarly *Jewish* discourse. As is often the case, Zangwill's cosmopolitanism turned out to be something like a form of Jewish particularism.

The Melting Pot opens in a living room in a non-Jewish borough of New York (the locale is specified in Zangwill's stage directions). The decor improbably mixes an American flag over the door, pictures of Wagner, Columbus, Lincoln, and "Jews at the Wailing place." "Mouldy" Hebrew tomes contrast with "brightly bound" English books. As Zangwill describes it, "The whole effect is a curious blend of shabbiness, Americanism, Jewishness, and music." The main characters of the drama are David Quixano, a Russian Jew whose whole immediate family was killed in the Kishinev pogrom, and Vera Revendal, a Russian Christian who had been imprisoned by the czarist government for revolutionary activities. David is a composer who has written a symphony entitled "The Crucible" celebrating the idea of America as a melting pot. He and Vera fall in love, but their relationship comes to a stormy halt when David recognizes Vera's father, Baron Revendal, as the officer who had commanded the Russian troops during the Kishinev pogrom. In the end the baron admits his guilt, David's symphony is performed, and he and Vera are reconciled, although the kisses she bestows on him in the final scene are not so much romantic as religious: "as we Russians kiss at Easter—the three kisses of peace."

Zangwill's antipathy to the Jewish religion is manifest throughout the play. Not only are the Hebrew books moldy but each generation of the Quixano family is portrayed as moving successively away from Orthodox practice toward Western culture, represented by music. Even the old Frau Quixano (the mother of David's uncle Mendel), who is the most religious, comes to accept David's violation of the Sabbath in favor of his music.

The figure of David is quite peculiar. He fits the stereotype of the hypersensitive, even feminized male Jew who is easily thrown into hysterical weeping when reminded of Jewish persecutions. Yet the name Quixano turns out to be of Sephardic origin. The Quixanos, we learn, were expelled from Spain in 1492 and went to Poland (historically possible, if improbable). By giving his eastern European hero a Sephardic pedigree, Zangwill implicitly endorsed the well-established trope in nineteenth-century Anglo-Jewish letters in which the Sephardim constitute an assimilable Jewish aristocracy as opposed to the uncouth Ashkenazic *Ostjuden* (eastern European Jews).[3] Thus, through this historically convoluted move, Zangwill covertly turned his neurasthenic Ashkenazic protagonist into an aristocrat like the Russian Vera. So the name Zangwill chose unwittingly signaled the limits of the melting pot. It was as if his American audience might not so easily accept, say, a "Portnoy" as a fitting mate for his Christian heroine.

David articulates Zangwill's primary message in a number of overwrought speeches that are hard to read today as anything but parodies. Europe is the land of persecution and oppression—symbolized by the Kishinev pogrom David has survived—and is rife with ancient hatreds between peoples. America represents redemption through the effacing of all hostile differences:

America is God's Crucible, the great Melting-Pot where all the races of Europe are melting and re-forming! Here you stand, good folk, think I, when I see them at Ellis Island, here you stand in your fifty groups, with your fifty languages and histories and your fifty blood hatred and rivalries. But you won't be long like that, brothers, for these are the fires of God you've come to . . . A fig for your feuds and vendettas! Germans and Frenchmen, Irishmen and Englishmen, Jews and Russians—into the Crucible with you all. God is making the American.[4]

The difference between America and all the other lands that had taken in Jews after the expulsion from Spain (Holland and Turkey, for example) was that "these countries were not in the making. They were old civilisations stamped with the seal of creed. In such countries the Jew may be right to stand out. But here in this new secular Republic we must look forward."[5] Because America is different, Jews will no longer preserve their separate identity but, like all other immigrants, will become something new.

Zangwill's assimilationist vision is based on a recycled version of Gottfried Ephraim Lessing's German Enlightenment drama *Nathan the Wise* in which all religions serve the same God and therefore all Americans are, as Vera puts, "already at one." Yet this Enlightenment ideal contains the seeds of its own subversion. In *Nathan,* the wise Jew's daughter turns out to have really been born a Christian and in the final scene of reunification at the end of the play Nathan is left out of the happy family circle. Everyone is transmuted into an Enlightened Christian except Nathan, who is consequently marginalized.

The ideal of Zangwill's drama is also assimilationist, but, as opposed to Lessing's play, the end product is to turn all true Americans into Jews.[6] The feisty Irish house-servant, Kathleen, who initially denounces the Quixanos' religious practices in virtually anti-Semitic terms, ends up speaking Yiddish and celebrating Purim. Jews, it transpires, are not just any immigrant group but the quintessential Americans, as David announces to the anti-Semite Davenport: "Yes—Jew-immigrant! But a Jew who knows that your Pilgrim Fathers came straight out of his Old Testament and that our Jew-immigrants are a greater factor in the glory of this great commonwealth than some of you sons of the soil."[7] The melting pot might forge a new people out of the immigrant nationalities, but the "American" character of this new people would be cryptically Jewish since the Pilgrim founders were, in fact, spiritual descendants of biblical Jews.

Zangwill even casts aspersions on the marital fidelity of native-born Americans, represented by the philandering Davenport, as opposed to the Jews. In the first version of the play, he has Vera say: "Not being true-born Americans, we hold even our troth eternal." At the insistence of Theodore Roosevelt, no less, Zangwill modified this association of the "true-born Americans" with adultery to an attack on "unemployed millionaires like Mr. Davenport." Zangwill clearly conceived of his play as the celebration of the immigrants as representing both "family values" and the true spirit of America.

Despite Zangwill's prophecy of the disappearance of all prior ethnicities into the crucible, it turns out that "race" is not so easily effaced. In a passionate exchange between Vera and Baroness Revendal (Vera's stepmother), the baroness insists that the Russian pianist Rubinstein was not a Jew since he was baptized shortly after birth. Vera hotly responds by asking: "And did the water outside change the blood within?"[8] Blood remains thicker than water, at least the water of baptism, which raises the question of whether blood is also stronger than the fires of the melting pot.

Zangwill gives some partial and ambiguous answers to such questions in an afterword appended to the 1914 edition of the play. The strange ambiguities of this essay in fact reinforce our reading of the contradictions in the play. One especially peculiar aspect of the afterword is its obsession with the racial theory current at the time. In one place Zangwill argues that Jewish traits are racially "recessive" so that Jews should ultimately disappear as recognizable types in America. This hypothesis of an assimilable Jewish genotype looks suspiciously like a reversal of the anti-Semitic argument that Jewish genes will predominate if Jews are allowed into Western society. Yet Zangwill also claims that the Jew is "the toughest of all the white elements that have been poured into the American crucible, the race having, by its unique experience of several thousand years of exposure to alien majorities, developed a salamandrine power of survival. And this asbestoid fibre is made even more fireproof by the anti-Semitism of American uncivilisation."[9]

This "on the one hand" and "on the other hand" approach characterizes much of the afterword, as indeed it did many of Zangwill's other writings on the Jews: at times extolling the "children of the ghetto," at others calling for assimilation. He preached in favor of intermarriage, much to the outrage of Jewish critics. But he also argued that in light of religious differences intermarriages are generally unwise because they lead to dissension in the home. In any case, he backs off from the miscegenist message of the play by concluding that the "Jew may be Americanised and the American Judaised without any gamic interaction."[10]

Zangwill's treatment of the problem of blacks in America contains similar ambiguities, some of which result in extraordinarily racist conclusions. Against one critic, he protests that he has not ignored the problem of American blacks since he has Baron Revendal defend the persecution of Russian Jews by comparing it to the lynching of African Americans. In this account Jews are the blacks of Russia, a trope later to play a major role in the mythology of the black-Jewish alliance. In a gesture toward racial inclusiveness, David's crucible expressly includes "black and yellow."

Yet Zangwill was skeptical about whether blacks could truly be assimilated. Black traits, he claims, are "dominant" and cannot be easily eliminated from the American genotype. Invoking the language of "scientific" racism of his day, he argued that "the prognathous face is an ugly and undesirable type of countenance [and] it connotes a lower average of intellect and ethics. . . . Melanophobia, or fear of the black, may be pragmatically as valuable a racial defence for the white as the counter-instinct of philoleucosis, or love of the white, is a force of racial uplifting for the black."[11] Intermarriage with African Americans is therefore undesirable on the whole and blacks could "serve their race better by making Liberia a success or building up an American negro State." Zionism may be a good idea for blacks, but not for Jews, although paradoxically Zangwill himself was a collaborator of Theodor Herzl's and also supported a variety of territorial schemes to solve the Jewish problem.

Stripped of its racist language, Zangwill's afterword is to some degree prophetic in terms of the different fates of Jewish and African Americans in the twentieth century. Jews can pass as whites, blacks cannot. Only certain races that share family resemblances are candidates for "melting." Thus, at the very beginning of the debate that Zangwill inaugurated with his play came the grudging admission that Jews and blacks follow very different narrative paths. Moreover, Zangwill's unabashed use of racist language revealed all too clearly why the melting pot had its severe limitations.

Zangwill concedes that even for the Jews the melting pot will work in a much more circuitous and gradual fashion than the play itself suggests. And the process by which assimilation works involves not the disappearance of ethnic traits but rather their recombination into the emerging American genotype. The Jews, in Zangwill's model, will not so much vanish as a separate ethnic group as insinuate much of their own culture into the new America: the American will become "Judaised." Indeed, Zangwill's text itself became part of that process: a Jewish play as the vehicle for an ideology of Americanization.

Beyond *The Melting Pot*

Zangwill's play spawned immediate responses from Jews and others. Within a year of the play's first production, the eloquent New York rabbi Judah L. Magnes preached that "America is not the melting pot. It is not the Moloch demanding the sacrifice of national individuality. The symphony of America must be written by the various nationalities which keep their individual and characteristic note, and which sound this note in harmony with their sister nationalities."[12] In this reference to a symphony, Magnes explicitly stood David Quixano's "crucible" symphony on its head by making the metaphor the antithesis of the melting pot.

As Mitchell Cohen argues elsewhere in this volume, a more sustained response came from the Jewish social thinker Horace Kallen, who published a series of articles in 1915 in *The Nation* entitled "Democracy versus the Melting Pot."[13] Kallen argued that the melting pot could only be achieved by the violation of democratic principles, that is, by coercing the immigrants to accept Americanization and by forbidding expression of their original cultures. Kallen advocated instead what he called "cultural pluralism." Also invoking the metaphor of a symphony, Kallen envisioned the United States as a "democracy of nationalities," united politically, with English as its common language, but in which each nationality would cultivate its own dialect of English under the influence of its native culture. Kallen's essay clearly reflected the cultural reality of the immigrant period, when it was hard to imagine immigrants freely giving up or even inevitably losing their ethnic identities.

Kallen's primary example of an ethnic group with a strong cultural heritage was the Jews. Both the persistence of anti-Semitism and the dynamic character of Jewish culture in America seemed to suggest that Jews would remain an identifiable group: "Of all group-conscious peoples they are the most group-conscious. . . . [O]nce . . . the Jewish immigrant takes his place in American society a free man . . . and an American, he tends to become rather the more a Jew."[14] Kallen's theory of immigration, based largely on his observation of the Jews, argued that after an initial period

of attempting to assimilate, the immigrant group discovers its "permanent group distinctions" and is "thrown back upon . . . [its] ancestry." At
this stage "ethnic and national differences change in status from disad-
vantages to distinctions."[15] It is American democracy that allows this flourishing of ethnic cultures. Toleration of cultural and ethnic differences flows
directly from the federalist principles on which America was founded. For
Kallen, cultural pluralism was much truer to American ideals than the total-
izing ideology of those promoting "Americanization."

Cultural pluralism, in Kallen's account, was based on the involuntary
influence of ethnicity. As he wrote in a much quoted passage: "Men may
change their clothes, their politics, their wives, their religions, their
philosophies, to a greater or less extent; they cannot change their grand-
fathers."[16] Blood, not culture, is the foundation of identity. To force the
immigrants to "Americanize" would be counterproductive since their very
sense of self would be destroyed: a new culture would be grafted onto
them without a new identity.

The intrinsic difficulty with Kallen's position, at least in the 1915 essays,
is that it attributes autonomous power to ethnic or racial origin, as one
of his critics, Isaac Berkson, soon pointed out.[17] For Kallen, culture, as
opposed to ethnicity, is an epiphenomenon that can be changed. But if an
ethnic culture changes so much that it no longer resembles its origins, what
would be the meaning of an identity based solely on ancestry? We might
respond to Kallen by suggesting that identity itself is not a fixed and
autonomous essence but rather an aspect of culture and therefore similarly malleable. Descent may be said to be just as much a matter of cultural construction as other aspects of culture. Kallen himself was later to
recognize the problems in his original position and he took pains to distance himself from a racial definition of identity. Once he recognized the
instability of ethnic identity, he was forced to a more pessimistic evalua-
tion of the future of Jewish culture in America.[18] Starting with a position diametrically opposed to Zangwill's, the author of "cultural pluralism" came to believe that *The Melting Pot* might have been a better
description of the course of American culture than his own prescription.

The concept of malleable ethnic identity is implicit in a famous speech
by John Dewey in 1916, which, as Cohen suggests in his essay "In Defense
of Shaatnez," was generally taken to support Kallen's cultural pluralism:

Such terms as Irish-American or Hebrew-American or German-American are
false terms because they seem to assume something which is already in existence called America, to which the other factor may be externally hitched on.
The fact is, the genuine American, the typical American, is himself a hyphen-

ated character. This does not mean that he is part American and that some foreign ingredient is then added. It means that . . . he is international and interracial in his make-up. He is not American plus Pole or German. But the American is himself Pole-German-English-French-Spanish-Italian-Greek-Irish-Scandinavian-Bohemian-Jew-and so on.[19]

Dewey's notion of American identity was actually closer to what Zangwill meant by the melting pot than to Kallen's original definition of cultural pluralism: not the eradication of difference but the creation of a new identity as the dynamic, constantly changing sum of its parts. It is also striking that Dewey's vision of the hyphenated American, like Kallen's, is based on European immigrants and excludes what are today called "peoples of color."

Beyond the differences between Zangwill's melting pot and Kallen's cultural pluralism lies a certain instructive commonality: in both the Jews are paradigmatic for the future of America. The narrative of Jewish immigration and absorption was believed to hold the key to how the American polity would define itself. If these two complementary, opposing theories anticipated both the terms and the problems of today's multiculturalism debate, they did so as a Jewish discourse. Yet Jews now feel themselves almost totally marginal to the contemporary debate. How, we might ask, have they lost the central position they once held in the struggle over America's identity?

Jews Become White

The answer to this question lies in the fundamental shift in the post–World War II era from ethnicity to race as the paradigmatic problem of America. Race has, of course, never been absent as a defining question for American society, but it was partially submerged during the half-century of mass immigration from Europe starting in the late nineteenth century. Even then, racial stereotypes were commonly used against those who are today considered European whites: Italians, Irish, Poles, and of course Jews. But the racial question in relation to African Americans regained its centrality in the postwar years when immigration was no longer a major issue and as African Americans began to organize what became the civil rights movement. As the vexed relationship of America to its former slaves has come to define race, ethnic groups are now homogenized as either "peoples of color" or "white" (whether they so identify themselves or not). This racial polarization has become even more true as a result of the significant increase in both legal and illegal immigration over the last few decades. Although not all of the more recent immigrants are in fact "peoples of color" (consider, for instance, the Russian Jews), much of the anti-immigrant fever is fueled, as it was earlier in the century, by the racializing of immigrants as "nonwhite."

The theories we have examined from earlier in the century were part of an effort to forge a new American identity open to immigrant ethnicities who were largely European, even though some theorists were cognizant of the existence of Asian immigrants, primarily in the West. While the issue of black Americans was not a secret to any of them, the Jewish writers were preoccupied with European ethnicities. Zangwill's tentative attempts to equate the Jewish with the African American condition came apart in the racist remarks of his afterword. The melting pot had no room for blacks, whose "dominant" genes could not be easily melted. Kallen too was relatively silent on the racial problem of African Americans, a somewhat surprising silence given his initial emphasis on biological descent.

In terms of European immigrant groups, Jews were arguably the most difficult case because they were both ethnically and religiously alien. A theory built around the Jews could be paradigmatic for other immigrant groups since the absorption of Jews appeared at the time to many to be the most problematic. In this respect the early twentieth-century debates about the integration of Jews into America continued a European tradition in which the Jews served as the archetypal minority: how European nations treated their Jews was taken as emblematic of how "enlightened" these nations were. The rise of European racism frequently focused specifically on Jews: in the European context the Jews were the defining opposite of what is now called "white."

When Jews came to America, they assumed both that America was different *and* that their "privileged" status as the emblematic minority would continue. The erection of educational quotas and the rise of a virulent American strain of anti-Semitism in the 1920s and 1930s confirmed the sense of continuities with Europe. The fact that such groups as the Ku Klux Klan targeted Jews together with African Americans reinforced the feeling of a commonality of persecution. But as anti-Semitism and formal discrimination waned in the post–World War II years and as Jews became economically successful, they found themselves for the first time in modern history as doubly marginal: marginal to the majority culture, but also marginal among minorities. They were no longer a minority that defined the central political discourse of the majority culture. In the American histories of victims, Jews were no longer sociologically "the chosen people."

Instead, with the rise of the civil rights movement, a very different narrative focusing on African Americans became dominant. As Cheryl Greenberg shows elsewhere in this book, although it seemed for a period as if Jews might be able to wed their narrative to that of blacks in the rhetoric of the early civil rights movement, it quickly became apparent that the experiences of these two groups were fundamentally different: despite the mythic memory of enslavement in Egypt, the more recent history of the Jews in Europe was not commensurate with the African American experience of slavery. In fact, despite the persecutions and disabilities suffered in Europe, the Jews had still enjoyed a degree of internal autonomy utterly different from that of the African American slaves. Their culture in Europe may well have prepared them better than most immigrant groups for success in America. Thus, not only economic success and social integration but also an intrinsically different history divided the Jews from American blacks. Whether they liked it or not (and usually they did), the Jews in postwar America had become white.[20]

Despite this new reality, the Jewish strategy has often been to continue insisting on minority status. But this strategy is full of ironic contradictions. Consider the success of the American Jewish community in placing the Holocaust on the American political landscape by building a Holocaust museum on the Mall in Washington. It was as if by transferring the *European* genocide to America American Jews might continue their European identity as the chosen minority. Yet the very political influence and economic wherewithal necessary to construct the Holocaust Museum immediately belied this message: only a group securely part of the majority could institutionalize its history in this way. Only the genocide of Europeans by Europeans could find canonical status, while the home-grown mass sufferings of African and Native Americans could not. Almost by definition, the real emblematic minorities are precisely those whose story no one wants to hear.

The Holocaust Museum is an example of how Jews seek to be marked at once as part of the majority culture, by linking their history to the institutions of America, and as different, by insisting on the particularity of their history as a persecuted minority. The desire to connect the negative European Jewish narrative with the positive image of America, as a kind of brief for Jewish integration, has of course a long history in which Zangwill's *Melting Pot* was one early version: we recall that the drama requires the Kishinev pogrom as background and the reconciliation of its transplanted dramatis personae in America. The American melting pot gains its rationale from the brutal history of the Jews in Europe by serving as the site where all the Old World conflicts are resolved. Yet one might argue that the instant success of Zangwill's play, like that of the Holocaust Museum nearly a century later, proves that the Jews may not have been then and certainly are not now the minority whose history was the real stumbling block to a truly egalitarian America.

Jewish Identity and Postethnic America

Echoes of the debate about American identity, in which the Jews played a major role earlier in this century, can be heard in multicultural theory today. There are, however, fundamental differences in both tone and content between the competing theories of the "melting pot" and "cultural pluralism" on the one hand and today's "monoculturalism" and "multiculturalism" on the other. Zangwill was certainly no advocate of Anglo conformism and neither was Kallen a direct precursor of contemporary radical politics of identity. Yet without reclaiming for the Jews a status they no longer have in America, I wish to argue that by recovering something of value from these earlier Jewish theorists, it may be possible to construct an alternative to the increasingly bleak dichotomies that social theory seems to offer today. I believe that it is possible to imagine a Jewish identity that, if not paradigmatic, can at least help to bridge what seems now an unbridgeable chasm between racialized majorities and minorities.

In one place in his epilogue Zangwill makes an interesting argument about the identity of the Britons. Rather than constituting a monolithic ethnicity, he claims that their identity was formed out of a long historical crucible in which virtually every racial type made its way to the British Isles. If the British turn out to be a hybrid people, then perhaps no national identity is actually monolithic or stable. All nations are formed of melting pots. Thus, despite the racial language of the afterword and the ambiguities of the text itself, Zangwill pointed vaguely in the direction of what might be called a postethnic definition of identity.

Only recently emerging as a theoretical construct,[21] postethnic or multiracial theory criticizes multiculturalism's politics of identity as insufficiently radical. The problem with identity politics is that it sees categories like race and ethnicity as static and essential: we are nothing more than who our grandparents were, as Kallen's most extreme formulation had it. Postethnic theory argues that race is not a natural category but rather one that is socially constructed and imposed on groups. Instead of basing identity on these constructs, a new construct would posit that identity can be individually chosen. Identity in such a theory is fluid and often multiple. David Hollinger, for example, poses what he calls "Alex Haley's dilemma."[22] The author of *Roots,* it turns out, was also part Irish American. His dilemma is the question: can Alex Haley choose to march in the St. Patrick's parade? To do so would directly challenge the so-called one drop rule according to which anyone with one drop of black blood is defined as 100 percent black. The "one drop rule," promulgated by antiblack racists over the last century or more, has often been implicitly adopted in a positive sense by multiculturalists in their assumption that identity politics follows racial ancestry. The postethnic theorists wish to overturn this racial discourse by unsettling the very category of monolithic race.

In so doing, the postethnic theorists are responding to a social reality that is increasingly evident in America: there are no longer pure races or ethnicities (if there ever were) but instead multiracial and multiethnic identities. Intermarriage—an inevitability in any open society—has created individuals whose very being subverts any politics of monolithic identity. After nearly a century of counterarguments, Zangwill's melting pot continues to simmer. Moreover, as Zangwill himself held, the result of this melting process is not conformity to a preexistent American identity but the creation of something new to which each of the constituent parts makes its contribution.

Yet postethnic theory suggests something different as well: instead of simply asserting a new amalgam identity, it is possible for a multiracial or multiethnic person to identify at one and the same time as both Irish and Italian, or both black and white, or even Jew and Christian. That is, in place of a new, monolithic identity to take the place of the ethnic or racial identities that make it up, one could imagine multiple identities held simultaneously and chosen as much as inherited. To put it in Horace Kallen's terms, we may not be able to choose our grandparents, but we can choose the extent to which we affirm our connection to this or that grandparent. Freed of its early essentialism, Kallen's cultural pluralism can be resurrected by communities of choice.

Postethnic theory is obviously utopian to a great degree since America continues to be divided along racial grounds: even if race is a figment of our imaginations, it is a figment that has real consequences. While white ethnicities or sexual preferences can be disguised and therefore more easily "chosen," skin color cannot, and as long as prejudice exists individuals will not have the freedom to choose this or that identity marked by what is called race. In addition, the intermarriage argument, relevant for groups like Asian and Hispanic Americans, is far less relevant for African Americans, who are intermarrying with other groups at a far lesser rate (although still at a higher rate than a few decades ago). Despite all these caveats, however, the virtue of postethnic theory is to attempt to change consciousness about categories assumed to be fixed, static, and, above all, "natural." And even if theory cannot totally alter the way Americans think about race, the inexorable forces of the melting pot may ultimately erode these seemingly rock-solid formations of American identity.

How do the Jews fit into this perhaps utopian vision of a postethnic, postracial America? Because they are now seen as white and therefore capable of passing like other whites, I suggest that Jews at the end of the twentieth century are rapidly becoming a good example of just such a community of choice. American Jews constitute a kind of intermediary ethnic group, one of the most quickly and thoroughly acculturated yet, among European immigrant ethnicities, equally one of the most resistant to complete assimilation. Anti-Semites may have conceived of the Jews as a race, but American Jews, with their historical origins in Europe and the Middle East and with an intermarriage rate now at least 30 percent, defy racializing stereotypes even more now than ever. Jews are an ethnic group, but not an ethnic group traditionally conceived. Neither are they characterized by uniform religious practice or belief. The instability and multiplicity of Jewish identity, which has a long history going back to the Bible itself,[23] has become even more true today. In a free society all Jews are "Jews by choice" (a term coined recently for converts).

The indeterminacy of contemporary Jewish identity is often the cause of much communal hand-wringing. But instead of bemoaning these multiple identities, Jews need to begin to analyze what it means to negotiate them and, by so doing, perhaps even learn to embrace them. Reconceiving of Jewish identity along postethnic lines would undoubtedly require a sea change in Jewish self-consciousness, since Jews often continue to define themselves according to the old fixed categories. In particular, the issue of intermarriage, which got Zangwill in so much trouble in *The Melting Pot,* requires radical reevaluation. Far from siphoning off the Jewish gene pool, perhaps intermarriage needs to be seen instead as creating new forms of identity, including multiple identities, that will reshape what it means to be Jewish in ways we can only begin to imagine. For the first time in Jewish history, there are children of mixed marriages who violate the "law of excluded middle" by asserting that they are simultaneously Jewish and Christian or Jewish and Italian. Whether these new forms of identity spell the end of the Jewish people or its continuation in some new guise cannot be easily predicted since there is no true historical precedent for this development: it might be compared to the great sea change that took place with the destruction of the Temple by the Romans in the first century of the Common Era. Such moments of revolutionary transformation are always fraught with peril, but whatever one's view of it, the task for those concerned with the place of Jews in America is not to condemn or condone but rather to respond creatively to what is now an inevitable social process.

Beyond intermarriage, all Jews in the modern period have learned to live with multiple identities: Jew and German, Jew and American, Jew and Israeli. At one time it was fashionable to describe these identities as hyphenated or hybrid, as our discussion of Zangwill and Kallen makes clear. But it is becoming increasingly apparent that multiplicity in the precise sense of the word is more apt a description than hybridity. As opposed to the melting pot in which a new identity emerges or the cultural pluralism model in which only one ethnic identity remains primary, this is the sort of identity in which one might retain at least two different cultural legacies at once. The Jewish Enlightenment slogan "Be a human being on the street and a Jew at home" now comes to fruition in a new guise: one can hold several identities both in the street and at home.

In order to begin this rethinking, Jews will undoubtedly have to give up their sense of themselves as the paradigmatic minority, a sociological version of the older theology of the chosen people. In a postethnic America Jews will no longer be such a minority because the very categories of majority and minority will come into question. Yet perhaps in this respect the Jewish experience does remain relevant, precisely as a subversion of the old polarities. In a sense both Zangwill and Kallen were right about the Jews, for they have simultaneously fulfilled *both* the vision of the melting pot and that of cultural pluralism. At once part of the American majority yet also a self-chosen minority, their very belonging to both of these categories undermines the categories themselves. Between the monoculturalists who wish to erase difference and the multiculturalists who see only difference, the Jews may still have a role to play in the definition of the American future.

Notes

1. The following analysis is based on Israel Zangwill, *The Melting Pot,* rev. ed. (New York, 1926). Zangwill's revision, from 1914, consists primarily of an epilogue. I am particularly indebted to two earlier commentaries on the play by Elsie Bonita Adams, *Israel Zangwill* (New York, 1971), 110–114, and Werner Sollors, *Beyond Ethnicity: Consent and Descent in American Culture* (New York and Oxford, 1986). Steven J. Zipperstein drew my attention to Sollors's very important book. For further information on Zangwill, see Joseph Leftwich, *Israel Zangwill* (New York, 1957).

2. For a history of the use of the term "melting pot" before Zangwill, see Sollors, *Beyond Ethnicity,* 94–101.

3. On this understanding of the Sephardim, see Michael Galchinsky, *The Origin of the Modern Jewish Woman Writer: Romance and Reform in Victorian England* (Detroit, 1996).

4. Zangwill, *The Melting Pot,* 33.

5. Ibid., 96–97.

6. For a similar interpretation of the play which emphasizes the persistence of ethnicity, see Neil Larry Shumsky, "Zangwill's *The Melting Pot:* Ethnic Tensions on Stage," *American Quarterly* 27 (1975): 29–41.

7. Zangwill, *The Melting Pot,* 87.

8. Ibid., 127.

9. Ibid., 204.

10. Ibid., 207.

11. Ibid., 206.

12. Judah L. Magnes, "A Republic of Nationalities," *The Emmanuel Pulpit,* February 13, 1909, p. 5, reprinted in Paul Mendes-Flohr and Jehudah Reinharz, *The Jew in the Modern World* (New York and Oxford, 1980), 392.

13. Reprinted in Horace Kallen, *Culture and Democracy in the United States* (New York, 1924), 67–125.

14. Ibid., 112–113.

15. Ibid., 114–115.

16. Ibid., 122.

17. Isaac B. Berkson, *Theories of Americanization: A Critical Study, with Special Reference to the Jewish Group* (New York, 1920). See also, Milton Gordon, *Assimilation in American Life* (New York, 1964), 149–152.

18. See his "Can Judaism Survive in the United States?" (1925), reprinted in *Judaism at Bay* (New York, 1932), 177–220. On Kallen's change in position, see Gordon, *Assimilation in American Life,* 151.

19. Speech to the National Education Association. Quoted in Gordon, *Assimilation in American Life,* 139. See also the similar argument by Randolph Bourne, "Trans-National America," *The Atlantic Monthly* 118 (July 1916): 95.

20. See Karen Brodkin Sacks, "How Did Jews Become White Folks?" in Steven Gregory and Roger Sanjek, eds., *Race* (Rutgers, N.J., 1994), 78–102.

21. See, for example, Mary C. Waters, *Ethnic Options: Choosing Identities in America* (Berkeley, 1990); Richard D. Alba, *Ethnic Identity: The Transformation of White America* (New Haven, 1990); Paul Spickard, *Mixed Blood: Intermarriage and Ethnic Identity in Twentieth-Century America* (Madison, 1989); and Maria P. P. Root, ed., *Racially Mixed People in America* (Newbury Park, Calif., 1992).

22. David Hollinger, *Postethnic America: Beyond Multiculturalism* (New York, 1995).

23. See my "The Politics of Jewish Identity in Historical Perspective," in Wolfgang Natter, ed., *Disciplining Boundaries* (New York, 1997).

CHAPTER 2

In Defense of Shaatnez

A Politics for Jews in a Multicultural America

Mitchell Cohen

Threads

Here's an argument that is six decades old, yet it remains poignant—as poignant, perhaps, as modernity.[1] In March 1935 Vladimir Jabotinsky, father of the Zionist right wing, wrote to David Ben-Gurion, leader of the Zionist Labor movement, that young Jews would in the future not be drawn to the synthesis of Zionism and socialism which had been articulated by the founders of the Zionist left at the turn of the century. Jabotinsky maintained:

New generations have now arisen who did not know your soul-searching and did not have any part in your quest for truth. The delicate filibrations of logic that helped you weave two threads into one fabric have been forgotten like Stradivarius's secret. There is in general a new trend in the youth today, Jewish and Gentile: not to go into things too deeply. They incline rather to a direct, simple, primal, brutal "yes" or "no." Of the two threads, they see the thicker, or the shinier one. . . . To measure or remeasure the proportions of that merger, they call compromise, cowardice or worse.

With what will you fight this brutality, with what balm? Will you try to teach them your art? I doubt whether this generation is capable of understanding it or wishes to understand it. This generation is exceedingly "monistic." Perhaps this is not a compliment, but it is a fact.[2]

At first Jabotinsky seems to be merely making a practical claim: entwining two ideas in a political program is distracting, dangerously so, when pressing tasks must be done. There is, however, a principled *prise de position* toward the world in Jabotinsky's words. "Monism," for him, was the converse of *shaatnez*, a mixing of wool and linen forbidden by Jewish tradition as an inappropriate bringing together of opposites; an amalgam of Zionism with social democracy was a political equivalent to this transgression. A national struggle had to be unidirectional and unidevotional, drawn forth, one might say, as a single taut thread.

For almost a decade Ben-Gurion had been responding to such contentions with a simple claim: attacking *shaatnez* in politics was a deception, for no national movement was "pure." Any national movement, including that of the Jews, could be good or bad — it all depended on the society it created, the kind of world it envisioned. Jabotinsky's Zionism also exemplified *shaatnez* for it too incorporated "foreign" ideas. Why was capitalism less "foreign" than socialism? Why, Ben-Gurion asked, did right-wingers complain about *shaatnez* when the Labor movement asserted its ideals but declared circumstances to be "neutral" when Labor's foes dominated? "When you war against our '*shaatnez*,' you don't war against '*shaatnez*' in general, but rather against a specific '*shaatnez*' you don't like."[3]

What mattered was not the fact of *shaatnez* but what came together in the mixture and what resulted from it: in Labor's formulation, a universalism (socialism) combined with a particularism (Zionism). Where Jabotinsky's "monism" placed Jews solely within the circle of particularism, Ben-Gurion situated his movement in the overlap of several intersecting circles. "As citizens of Palestine," he had asserted in a November 1932 speech,

we stand in the circle of the Land of Israel; as Jews we stand in the circle of a nation that aspires to its homeland; as workers we stand in the circle of the working class; as sons of our generation, we stand in the circle of modern history; our women comrades stand in the circle of the working women's movement in its struggle for liberation.[4]

Exchanging metaphors — circles for threads — one might say that the validity of *multi-shaatnez* is affirmed here.[5]

One might also say that Ben-Gurion was responding, albeit implicitly since he was a politician and not a philosopher, to basic questions posed by modernity to the Jews: Can a people dwell alone? Should it try to live solely by its "own" ideals, regarding them, moreover, as if they were a singular whole? Ben-Gurion and Jabotinsky clashed, of course, at a time when existence, rather than dwelling, was immediately at stake. Yet the issues underlying their duel remain acute today, both for a Jewish state and for any diaspora that would participate in Western liberal societies and not seek refuge in ghettolike insularity.

Let me present it starkly: *Shaatnez* or monism? This is the great intellectual question of Jewish modernity and no less, if you will, of Jewish "postmodernity." Shall Jews and their culture(s) be entwined with, open to, and engaged by the world or shall they turn inward defensively? An ethnocentric vision, as K. Anthony Appiah observes, always implies "an unimaginative attitude to one's own culture."[6] Appiah, an intellectual of mixed African-English parentage who lives in the United States, has written a penetrating book, *In My Father's House,* examining African cultures and identities. He arrives at some important values that are strikingly akin to those articulated four decades earlier by Hayim Greenberg, the Bessarabian-born American Labor Zionist thinker. The source of commonality is clear: both wrestle with contesting demands made of their identities.

In late 1948 Greenberg published an essay entitled "Patriotism and Plural Loyalties." His aim was to defend the legitimacy of plural loyalties in democratic polities. One source of his meditation surely was anxiety that the recent birth of a Jewish state might provoke accusations that diaspora Jews had "dual allegiances." But his argument extends far beyond these trepidations. Greenberg was a man confident in his Jewish culture—he had no fear of its engagement with the world—and especially in his political commitments, which, democratic socialist and Zionist, were plural. A multiplicity of commitments was legitimate in his view simply because human beings have multiple dimensions. Take, he proposed, an Italian-speaking Swiss citizen. Surely this man is a bundle of conflicting fealties and therefore of prospective betrayals. As the citizen of a state, he owes Switzerland fidelity, but he also will be a patriot of his canton. Though Swiss, he surely has deep cultural ties to Italians in Italy, and if he is Catholic, he has bonds to Catholics around the globe and accepts a certain "sovereignty" of the Vatican.

Now for a "monist" this fellow embodies the worst of all worlds, precisely because he embodies many worlds. How can he be truly Swiss if his Swissness is potentially diluted by or perhaps in conflict with his Italianness or his Catholicism? Greenberg's response was first to argue that the "right to be different" was essential to any democracy; he specified "not only the right to hold different opinions and beliefs than the majority, but to *be* different." And then he insisted that democracy—

a liberal democratic temper, we might add—implied accepting and indeed prizing "pluralistic-social relationships, attachments, sentiments and loyalties."[7]

This stance, of course, requires an imaginative attitude toward one's culture, or rather cultures. We can see this illustrated by Appiah's description of his father, a man of "multiple attachment to his identities." He was an Asante, a Ghanaian, an African, a Christian, a Methodist, and he was able to draw on all of these without "significant conflict." Hence he could be "a model for the possibility of a Pan-Africanism without racism, both in Africa and in its diaspora."[8] The aspiration is much like Greenberg's, that is, to cosmopolitanism and particularism at once: Pan-African, not Afrocentric in one case; Labor Zionist, not ethnochauvinist in the other. Both Appiah and Greenberg are open to the world, to the varied and various threads of human diversity; they are even open to civilizations that oppressed them. "For us to forget Europe," Appiah says to Afrocentrists, "is to suppress the conflicts that have shaped our identity; since it is too late for us [Africans and Europeans] to escape each other, we might instead seek to turn to our advantage the mutual interdependencies history has thrust upon us."[9]

One can easily imagine Greenberg nodding his assent. And while he might recall that Jewry suffered unspeakable savagery, especially in this century, in the lands of Western Christian civilization, he would have nonetheless found it absurd to engage Goethe, for instance, not by his poetic vision but as a dead Christian German. And Greenberg would have had no need, *pace* Jabotinsky, to rediscover Stradivarius's secret in order to assent. He would need only to point out that a single string has limited range, however fine the violin's wood. Try as he might, the monist cannot play a sonata on a solo string; certainly he will be incapable of harmonies or of recognizing disharmonies, whatever and wherever he plays.

Transnationality

Monism always reduces to a "one"; pluralism is its nemesis. Nonetheless, monism is, as Ben-Gurion saw, more of a posture than anything else: there is no social or political world that doesn't mix diverse ingredients in differing measures, sometimes comfortably, often producing tensions. A democrat's concern is these combinations and tensions. What allows citizens and groups of citizens, indeed a society as a whole, to benefit from or simply live with them? Might it be impossible to benefit from or to live with them?

Since America's cultural and ethnic features are being contested nowadays, these are urgent matters of political argument. The central issue is broadly called "multiculturalism," yet only this term is new. How could the subject not have been raised in a country so marked by waves of immigration? Indeed, many of today's debates—and aspects of the atmosphere surrounding them—were rehearsed with acuity shortly before the entry of the United States into World War I. "Racial panic," as one historian calls it, emerged then. It was a time of immigration, economic problems, and the possibility of war. Eugenics was revived as a "scientific" framework for discussing the newcomers to the country and the problems they brought (and, of course, as a "realistic" way to discuss blacks). Statistics were deployed to demonstrate how the "immigration problem" had produced vice and crime. (In 1908 New York's police chief, Theodore A. Bingham, had charged that "perhaps half of the criminals" in the city were Jews.)[10]

Culture warriors clashed. Radical intellectuals chastised American puritanism, feminists advocated birth control, and conservatives railed that this all augured the end of American civilization. Not surprisingly, politicians joined the fray. Theodore Roosevelt blustered on behalf of "unhyphenated Americanism" and insisted on a "simple motto" for Americans, irrespective of origins: "AMERICA FOR AMERICANS." Dual allegiances were akin to "moral treason." (His target was especially "German-Americans.") Woodrow Wilson followed suit in the 1916 presidential campaign, going so far as to abjure publicly the "hyphenate vote."[11] Dominant Anglo-America feared that immigrants retained loyalties based on their European origins and thus jeopardized "Americanism."

Perhaps the most forceful rebuke to this monistic mood was provided by a young, iconoclastic essayist named Randolph Bourne (himself a WASP). Americanization, this radical intellectual proposed, should take place "by the consent of the governed." Americans had to recognize that "America shall be what the immigrant will have a hand in making it, and not what a ruling descendant of those British stocks which were the first permanent immigrants, decides that America shall be."[12] So he proposed that Americanism be embodied in something original, not in a replica of European nationalism but in a democratic "Trans-National America," as he entitled his now celebrated article. Whereas the Anglo establishment growled at the emergence of "hyphenated-Americans"—German-Americans, Jewish-Americans, Irish-Americans, Italian-Americans, and so forth—Bourne reveled in it. "It bespeaks poverty of imagination," he asserted, "not to be thrilled at the incalculable potentialities of so novel a union of men."[13] He drew an obvious conclusion: the old stock ought to be called English-Americans.

A similar summons to American novelty came from John Dewey. He portrayed the American nation as "complex and compound":

Our national motto, "One from Many," cuts deep and extends far. It denotes a fact which doubtless adds to the difficulty of getting a genuine unity. But it also immensely enriches the possibilities of the result to be attained. No matter how loudly one proclaims his Americanism, if he assumes that any one racial strain, only one component culture, no matter how effective it has proved in its own land, is to furnish a pattern to which all other strains and cultures are to conform, he is a traitor to American nationalism. Our unity cannot be a homogenous thing like that of the separate states of Europe from which our population is drawn; it must be a unity created by drawing out and composing into a harmonious whole the best, the most characteristic which each contributing race and people has to offer.[14]

Dewey, like Bourne, had been influenced by Horace Mayer Kallen, a liberal American Jewish philosopher. "Democracy," in Kallen's view, "is anti-assimilationist. It stands for the acknowledgement, the harmony, the organization of group diversities in cooperative expansion of common life, not for assimilation of diversities into sameness."[15] Kallen, anticipating Greenberg's argument on plural loyalties, asserted that hyphenation "permeates all levels of life." One is a spouse, a sibling, a friend, a student, a citizen, a church congregant and a member of a nation all at once— and any of these may outweigh in importance the others at a given moment, leading perhaps to various conflicts. But, he also contended, the hyphen unites as much if not more than it divides.[16] Consequently, America should not be a "melting pot"—the term comes from the title of Israel Zangwill's 1908 play—but a land of "cultural pluralism."

Bourne, Dewey, and Kallen were celebrants of perpetual motion in Americanism. "America" for them was something unfinished, but with democracy, not teleology, working within. In a similar spirit Michael Walzer, who has retrieved Kallen as a precursor of an intelligent multiculturalism, suggests that "America has no singular national destiny—and to be 'American' is, finally, to know that and to be more or less content with it."[17] Another way of saying this is that America will be what Americans make of it; they will be what, through democracy, they make of themselves.

Kallen's metaphor for a culturally plural America was an orchestra. Each instrument has its own sound, timbre, and notes; all play in a larger composition that at the same time links them to one another. Such an "American civilization" would be "an orchestration of humanity," but

with this difference: a musical symphony is written before it is played: in the symphony of civilization the playing is the writing, so that there is nothing so fixed or inevitable about its progressions as in music, so that within the limits set by nature and luck they may vary at will, and the range and the variety of the harmonies may become wider and richer and more beautiful—or the reverse.[18]

Dewey, in a letter to Kallen, expressed agreement "with your orchestra idea," but he was concerned that "we really get a symphony and not a lot of different instruments playing simultaneously."[19] An orchestra, after all, is not simply a collection. Something makes it a whole, and in America, for Kallen, this was to be liberal democracy. Each citizen would be equally a member of the polity and assimilated into it, while cultural particularities, like the differences between a violinist and a clarinetist, would remain. And the symphony depends on the vitality of the hyphens: they link individuals to the whole and to each other, while allowing them—and needing them—to retain their particular characters. "The hyphen works," observes Walzer, "when it is working like a plus sign."[20]

Bourne's "Trans-National America" was similar to Kallen's orchestra, though one senses in Kallen a little more concern to preserve and in Bourne more urge to invent. Still, they both wanted an America whose diverse components, in Bourne's words, "merge but ·. . [do] not fuse." Bourne wanted nothing to do with the "thinly disguised panic which calls itself 'patriotism.'"[21] He asked "What shall we do with our America?" but provided no totalistic—no monistic—answer. Rather, he spoke the language of *shaatnez* (without using the term, of course). The America he envisioned was constituted by a "weaving back and forth with other lands, of many threads of all sizes and colors. Any movement which attempts to thwart this weaving, or to dye the fabric any one color, or disentangle the threads of the strands, is false to this cosmopolitan vision."[22]

Bourne developed these themes further in a lecture to Harvard's Jewish student association in 1916. He went so far as to call "trans-nationalism" a "Jewish idea." (He confessed to stealing the term "from a Jewish college mate of mine who, I suspect, is now a member of your Menorah Society here.")[23] Bourne defined his goal as an "ideal of cooperative Americanism" that allowed the "vigor of cultural self-consciousness without paying the price of terrible likemindedness."[24] But while assimilation was nothing to celebrate, neither was a federation of atavistic groups, "a queer conglomeration of the prejudices of past generations, miraculously preserved here."[25] Transnationalism was a vision of mediation, creating something new and modern. Thus it required innovative political thinking along with cultural vision. Any identification of a state entirely with a single culture or of political with cultural allegiance was to be rejected. The alternative was "a freely mingling society of peoples of very different racial and cultural antecedents with a common political allegiance and common social ends but with free and distinctive cultural allegiances which may be placed anywhere in the world that they like."[26] In other words: political (and, I'd add, social) democracy with multicultural leavening.

Zionism, Bourne proposed, could be an inspired transnationalism. It offered the opportunity to transcend "petrifying outworn expressions" of nationalism by designing "a non-military, a non-chauvinistic state." This "national centre" would serve the religious and cultural needs of Jews and also be a refuge from oppression. It would not pretend to be the political homeland of all Jewry, for this, Bourne reckoned, might jeopardize Jews elsewhere. Instead, "cultural allegiance and political allegiance" needed to be balanced so that "a Jew might remain a complete Jew and at the same time be a complete citizen of any modern state where he happened to live and where his work and interests lay." (Dewey expressed similar sentiments on Zionism.)[27]

The Zionism Bourne lauded, it should be noted, was that of Kallen and Louis Brandeis (the latter was then helping to obtain American backing for the Balfour Declaration). One imagines that Bourne would have especially appreciated Greenberg who, though devoted to the creation of a Jewish state, also warned sternly against "idolaters of the state," those who consider "the state as the object of absolute loyalty, to which all other loyalties must be subordinated at all times and under any circumstances."[28] Of course Bourne knew not Jabotinsky; surely he would have regarded him as a Zionist version of what he wanted to avoid in Americanism.[29] What attracted Bourne to Zionism was the possibility of "a union between the noble old Law and the most enlightened spirit of modern welfare. . . . An ancient spirit of justice and sobriety, expressed with all the technique of modern science and sense of social welfare—what could more perfectly symbolize the nationalism which will keep our old earth rich, sweet and varied?"[30]

Bourne's passion for variation and American multiplicity—for an American *multi-shaatnez*—reflected, he believed, an important trend in the modern world, namely, an increased dispersal and intermixing of peoples. "The age-old problems of Jewish nationalism," he proposed, "have become the burning problems of other dispersed nationalities."[31] Bourne, like Kallen, underestimated the strength of monistic nationalism in the world and indeed of assimilationism in America, which never became quite the federation of nationalities they envisaged. Nonetheless, the issues they raised and, as important, the spirit in which they approached them eight decades ago remain vital at the dawn of the twenty-first century. For we live too in a time of intermixing; thanks to revolutions in technology and communications and the reshaping of national and state boundaries, no people can live alone or afford to try to do so. It is a time in which America and its Jews will have to reinvent themselves yet again. "The political ideas of the future will have to be adjusted to a shifting world-population, to the mobility of labor, to all kinds of new temporary mixings of widely diverse peoples, as well as to their permanent mixings."[32] The point is as fresh as when Bourne penned it (although it is capital that is especially mobile nowadays, to the dramatic disadvantage of labor).

At the same time there is in fact an American melting pot and the fire stoking it remains steady. It is fed as much by America's past self-image as by the desires of many of today's immigrants. In the intellectual world the melting pot has been defended anew and multiculturalism attacked vigorously from a mainstream liberal perspective by one of our most distinguished historians. In *The Disuniting of America* Arthur Schlesinger Jr. is as concerned with what constitutes the "newness" of America as Bourne was in the 1910s. But while Bourne, like Kallen and Dewey, reacted against nativist definitions of "Americanism," Schlesinger reacts against recent scholarship done in the name of multiculturalism and corresponding demands by multiculturalists for a radically pluralist politics. He finds much of the scholarship spurious (with good reason) and he fears (again with reason) that much of the politics could dissolve all cohesion in America's polity.

Schlesinger envisages an America of individual citizens alone, rejecting subnational, that is, group, identities on behalf of an unadulterated Americanism. This type of Americanism, he maintains, perhaps with an echo of Theodore Roosevelt, is what made the United States something new. In this country "a brilliant solution for the inherent fragility of a multiethnic society" was fashioned: "the creation of a brand-new national identity, carried forward by individuals who, in forsaking old loyalties and joining to make new lives, melted away ethnic differences." At the same time Schlesinger insists that we acknowledge that the solvent was Anglo-Saxon, that the ideas underlying the best in American democracy, ranging from individual liberty to cultural freedom, are European in origin. "It may be too bad that dead White European males have played so large a role in shaping our culture," he states, "but that's the way it is." This is just "humdrum historical reality, not conspiratorial teaching."[33]

Schlesinger's view of American novelty is encapsulated in the claim that the melting pot is unique. In fact, this isn't entirely so. Nationalism and national identities are themselves modern phenomena, products of the late eighteenth, nineteenth, and early twentieth centuries. In most cases European nationalists sought a basic cultural and political uniformity—the assimilation of populations into a monistic identity—over a territory. America's incorporation of immigrants may be remarkable and singular in various ways, but it also parallels the efforts by emerging European national states to incorporate diverse regional populations, many with their own vernaculars who were previously distinct and territorially separate. Creating a new national identity out of populations with antecedent loyalties is thus not an American invention. In contrast, it seems to me that a vision of transnational America, of *shaatnez* America, has true originality. Bourne, it should be recalled, conceived it in opposition to European forms of nationalism, whose chief characteristic was precisely the transformation of old, mostly local and religious loyalties into a monistic identity. It is the identity (or identities) and richness that might come of a transnational America that would be a novelty.

There is a parallel problem in Schlesinger's discussion of the European origins of what is best in American democratic culture. The difficulty, of course, is not ideas like individual liberty or the rule of law. Nor is it the fact that such ideas came to America from Europe. They are very good ideas and they did come here with Europeans, though, *pace* some friends and some foes of multiculturalism, how they arrived does not determine their validity. Yet slavery, racial segregation, and the extermination of Native Americans are no less Anglo-American then the political ideas Schlesinger acclaims. And as the late John Plamenatz, a formidable scholar of political thought to whom anti-Western multiculturalist sentiments cannot be ascribed, pointed out long ago, today's vocabulary of freedom may come from Europe, but that doesn't make the idea of freedom "peculiarly, or originally, European." Moreover, liberty of conscience, which, he argued, is of specifically European lineage, came about as a consequence of brutal and bloody religious wars in the sixteenth century.[34]

One cannot define the West's legacy selectively, lauding freedom of religion as central while making, say, the St. Bartholomew's Day Massacre (or the Holocaust) secondary. To inform university students that John Locke provided theoretical justification for expropriating land from the Indians and that among America's founders were men who proclaimed inalienable human liberties while owning other human beings is also not a conspiracy to destroy the West and America. Nor is there a conspiracy when a new generation of historians—they are not all charlatans—seeks to rectify past failures to give proper due in history books to minorities and women.

What Schlesinger does not address adequately in his book—here he is like many foes of multiculturalism—are broader questions concerning the place of cultural tolerance within political democracy and the weight of the protest by Bourne, a dead white American male, against Americanization without consent of the governed. Schlesinger, as a liberal, wants to speak of Unfinished America, and rightly so—but then he reifies what he calls humdrum historical facts. It seems to me that Dewey provided an alterative liberal approach when he wrote that

the American is himself Pole-German-English-French-Spanish-Italian-Greek-Irish-Scandinavian-Bohemian-Jewish and so on. The point is to see to it that the hyphen connects instead of separates. And this means at least that our public schools should teach each factor to respect each other, and shall take pains to enlighten all as to the great past contributions of every strain in our composite make-up. I wish our teaching of American history in the schools would take more account of the great waves of immigration by which our land for over three centuries has been continuously built-up, and make every pupil conscious of the rich breadth of our national make-up.[35]

Supplement Dewey's list with some more recent immigrant groups and some descendants of older inhabitants who did not come to these shores as immigrants, and here is an educational prescription—call it cultural pluralist, multicultural, transnational, or one of *shaatnez*—for an America that appreciates as much as it accepts heterogeneity.

Manichaeans

My argument so far assumes that in general multiculturalism poses the same questions to American Jews as to other Americans: What type of America do you want to live in? How do you understand the evolution of modern American politics? Only by thinking about these broader questions will American Jews be able to address specifically Jewish concerns about multiculturalism. And at first glance one would imagine that American Jewry, as a minority group, would naturally sympathize with advocacy of a plural society.

Yet today's multiculturalism is often expressed in a spirit quite distant from that of Bourne or Kallen or Dewey. And whereas their formulations almost invariably included Jews, multiculturalism is often identified nowadays with a segment of the left that has, to put it bluntly, a Jewish problem. Sometimes this problem is manifested in an obtuse anti-Zionism, other times in insensitivity to Jewish interests and fears, and sometimes in an inability to rebuke anti-Semites without qualification. The Jew, in short, is the problematic Other. The reproduction of this attitude among some advocates of multiculturalism, especially those with third world orientations, threatens to taint multiculturalism in the same way that Communism unfairly tainted the left as a whole.

The problem doesn't necessarily express itself in outright anti-Semitism like that of Leonard Jeffries, former chairman of Afro-American studies at New York's City College, or in the tendency of some people to speak of Israel with a hiss reminiscent of neoconservative pronouncements about the left. Sometimes this tendency is manifested simply as intellectual numbness when it comes to Jews, a numbness multiculturalists quickly protest when it comes to other groups. Moses Maimonides is rarely on the list of authors these multiculturalists aim to incorporate into the canon. Consider, for instance, *Multiculturalism: A Critical Reader,* a recent, weighty collection of some twenty essays. The only references to Jews and Judaism to be found in it are in passing, and Jewish studies, which has flourished across the United States in the past quarter century, does not exist in it at all, even in the essay entitled "Ethnic Studies: Its Evolution in American Colleges and Universities."[36] Marx wrote somewhere that in his vision of the future, the conditions for the liberation of one would be the conditions for the liberation of all. If some American Jewish liberals are wary of some advocates of multiculturalism, the reason is plain: it is not always evident that the multicultural "all" includes Jewish culture.

Multiculturalism is also fiercely attacked by neoconservatives, who are perhaps the most visible and vocal intellectuals within American Jewry.[37] They frequently raise concerns like those I've just outlined. For them, however, criticism of multiculturalism is just one part of a general ideological posture that ought to trouble American Jews—at least as much as issues raised by multiculturalism itself.

In the 1970s and 1980s neoconservatives fought publicly against what they called the "adversary culture." They contended that a liberal, educated "new class"—its ranks ranged from intellectuals, professors, and media figures to city planners and public health doctors—was promoting anti-bourgeois values and thereby subverting America's ethos. The battle against multiculturalism is a follow-up. In fact, the neoconservatives first gained special prominence less as critics of cultural trends than as ferocious anti-Communists. Yet there is a distinct continuity between their earlier incarnation as cold warriors and their anxious campaigns of today. Then, as now, they eagerly obscured distinctions for their own political purposes. Then, the right wanted no sharp differentiation between Communism and the "left" in general; now it wants all types of multiculturalism conflated in the public mind. (Then, as now, part of the left goes along for its own wayward reasons—I will turn to this shortly.)

The cold war is being carried on by other means. Consider, for instance, Irving Kristol's declaration, in *Commentary* in March 1952, that "there is one thing that the American people know about Senator McCarthy; he like them, is unequivocally anticommunist. About the spokesmen for American liberalism they feel they know no such thing." Then ponder what Kristol, now the éminence grise of neoconservatism, announced four decades later—and four years after the fall of the Berlin Wall and Communism:

There is no "after the Cold War" for me. So far from having ended, my cold war has increased in intensity as sector after sector of American life has been ruthlessly corrupted by the liberal ethos. . . . Now that the other "Cold War" is over, the real cold war has begun. We are far less prepared for this cold war, far more vulnerable to our enemy, than was the case with our victorious war against a global communist threat. We are, I sometimes feel, starting from ground zero, and it is a conflict I shall be passing on to my children and grandchildren. But it is a far more interesting cold war—intellectually interesting, spiritually interesting—than the war we have so recently won.[38]

There is a deep consistency in these two statements, and it is to be found in their Manichaeanism. The neoconservative mind-set is curious—conservative in content but rather Bolshevik in style and temper. Its representatives speak as if they were a besieged political minority, a huddled band struggling to proclaim the Truth in the face of evil (such as "liberalism" or "multiculturalism") that has dominated America since the 1960s. Kristol's son William declared in late 1993 that liberals controlled "the commanding heights of American society."[39] Yet in 1995, with Rupert Murdoch's financial backing, he was able to launch a weekly magazine. Reading neoconservatives and their progeny, you would never know that the right dominates political discussion on the radio and a good deal of it on television; that conservative think tanks and intellectual journals are abundantly funded while those of the left are generally starved;

or that Republicans have sat in the White House for all but seven of the last twenty-seven years.

This sense of siege may be genuine or it may be political pretense. Either way, it probably eased the embrace by Jewish neoconservatives of right-wing Christian fundamentalists (one should recall that a Bolshevik mind-set can justify all sorts of alliances). Midge Decter portrays the Christian right as forty million beleaguered souls who only want to thwart power-ful, insidious forces that would deny proper religious instruction to their children. The real problem, she believes, is liberal intolerance of funda-mentalists.[40] Decter is, by her own definition, "engaged in the battle to wrest some saving cultural power from the soiled and grasping hands of the liberal Left."[41] Fundamentalists, it should be obvious, concur with neo-conservatives on many major political issues, none more than the need to war against alleged liberal dominance of American culture. Neoconser-vatives and fundamentalists have targeted the same enemy and find them-selves comfortable together in the same political home. While Decter's figure of forty million may be exaggerated, the organized influence of the Christian Coalition within the Republican party she supports can hardly be minimized.

Yet if there is one thing American Jews know about American liberal-ism, it is that when it has flourished, so have they; about fundamentalists they know no such thing. American Jews long assumed, in contrast to today's neoconservatives, that intensified fundamentalism of any brand enhances intolerance and that growth in fundamentalist political power is cause for concern. History, after all, does not provide copious examples of tolerant fundamentalism, not to mention fundamentalists using political power to pluralist ends. At best fundamentalists—Christian, Jewish, or Moslem—are tolerant when they have no other choice. The Christian Coali-tion is not concerned solely with religious training. It wants to reshape the education of American children, and it supports candidates in school board elections to this end. Is it intolerance that leads liberals to oppose "cre-ationism" in science curricula? And is it tolerance that inspires neoconser-vatives to denounce Afrocentrists one moment only to apologize for fun-damentalists the next? As a former (and non-Jewish) neoconservative journalist wonders aloud, "How can intellectual conservatives credibly attack Afrocentrists for distorting history while passing in silence over efforts to teach American children that the dinosaurs lived with Adam and Eve in the Garden of Eden and drowned in Noah's flood?"[42]

There is, in fact, a credible way to do so. If you believe liberalism and multiculturalism are the major sources of America's woes (rather than, say, dramatic transformations in economic life), and if you believe political conservatism inevitably follows from religious belief, then earnest-sounding calls for religiosity become advantageous means of political struggle, irrespective of the actual quality of religiosity that is thereby promoted. Irving Kristol, when asked if it is appropriate for intellectuals without religious belief to recommend it for others, has answered, "Yes."[43]

Here it is worth recalling that a major influence on the Kristols, *père et fils*, and most Jewish neoconservative intellectuals was Leo Strauss, a political theorist who deemed truth to be accessible solely to an elite properly initiated into philosophy (as he understood it). He believed, moreover, that only such an elite could live in a civilized way with philosophy's truths since they are subversive of myths—like the existence of God— that are needed to bind societies, ensuring that the masses behave reasonably well. Echoing Plato, Strauss writes:

Philosophy or science, the highest activity of man, is the attempt to replace opinion about "all things" by knowledge of "all things"; but opinion is the element of society; philosophy or science is therefore the attempt to dissolve the element in which society breathes and thus it endangers society. Hence philosophy or science must remain the preserve of a small minority and philosophers or scientists must respect the opinions on which society rests. To respect opinions is something entirely different from accepting them as true.[44]

Public culture in general and religion in particular rest on opinion.

Straussianism provides an important clue to the neoconservatives' preoccupation with culture and universities together with their peculiar crusade for intensified religiosity in the United States, a country that is perhaps the most religious in the West. It also suits the neoconservatives' key ambitions for American Jewry: the delegitimation of liberalism as a plausible inference from Jewish culture and consequently a radical realignment of long-standing Jewish voting patterns. Then there could be a neoconservative Jewry in an intensely Christianized, conservative America, with, I suppose, neoconservative intellectuals, those who *know*, as go-betweens, as *shtadlanim* (interceders). The land would be rid of liberalism, secular humanism, and of course multiculturalism. How would tolerance fare? I suppose it wouldn't much need to in this America. In any event, one of the major forms of intolerance as defined by neoconservatives—that of fundamentalists by liberals—would presumably be gone. Stanislas Adotevi, an African philosopher, once remarked of a celebrated black nationalist concept: "Négritude is the *black* way of being white."[45] One wonders: Is neoconservatism a Jewish way of being gentile?

Rooted Cosmopolitanism

If an analogy between the cold war and the culture wars is apt, this is not only because parallel right-wing distemper is found in both cases. There are parallel, profound failures among liberals and in the left as well. Neoconservatives, during the cold war, may have been myopic, but it doesn't follow that perfect vision would have beheld no problem. That right-wingers exploited Stalinism to stain the entire left doesn't make Stalinism any less criminal. Nor does it erase the stain on leftists who effectively joined the right in identifying dictatorship with socialism and who explained that regimes of fantastic brutality embodied "liberation." In fact, some of the finest figures of the American left forcefully opposed such apologetics, but they were too often, it must be admitted, in the minority.

A similar pattern arises in the debate about multiculturalism, as I hinted before. There is, in fact, more than one multiculturalism, even if some shared terminology serves to obscure differences. For instance, multiculturalism can, in the spirit of Bourne, Kallen, and Dewey, advance the idea of a pluralist, egalitarian America that is both cultured and tolerant. Or multiculturalism can be an ersatz politics, an identity politics of resentment, deployed by a left frustrated by the failure of its earlier paradigms, like Marxism. The first multiculturalism advances an inclusive, cosmopolitan America; it integrates "difference" into America. The second reifies "difference," acclaiming it to the exclusion of all else. The first is a multiculturalism that speaks American and can therefore speak to Americans. Adherents of the second resist situating their ideas in a specifically American idiom. Indeed, it is odd that French literary theory seems urgent to them, while the meditations of Bourne, Kallen, and Dewey on American life seem nonexistent. Moreover, if taken to its ultimate conclusion, the second multiculturalism would result in a country that is an agglomeration of ethnic monisms, little more; the "trans" in Bourne's "Trans-National America" is missing.

So just as an earlier generation of liberals and leftists ought to have, regardless of what conservatives contended, dissociated itself from anything called a "democratic dictatorship," anyone committed seriously to a democratic multicultural society today—a truly transnational America, if you will—should, without qualification and regardless of neoconservative crusades, repudiate those who would address Goethe, Racine, and Shakespeare as dead white European males rather than by their poetic visions. This doesn't mean that Goethe, Racine, and Shakespeare should be approached as Esperanto authors or that Prospero and Caliban should provide prototypes for understanding the relation between Western culture and the rest of the world.

A cultured and multicultured America is surely an America that makes distinctions. To recommend that Western students, in addition to Goethe, Racine, and Shakespeare, should also be exposed to, say, Ibn Khaldun, Lu Xun, and Wole Soyinka is not equivalent to professing pseudoscholarship and demanding its acceptance on "multicultural" grounds in the manner, say, of Leonard Jeffries. As the left should not have been reduced to Stalin, so "multiculturalism" ought not to be reduced to a Jeffries. But as the existence of the Soviet dictatorship itself inflicted vast damage to the left everywhere (not to mention to the Soviet population), so counterfeit intellects imperil the idea of cultural pluralism today.

An intelligent multiculturalism would envisage an America whose parts are not subsumed by a whole, yet whose parts nonetheless seek to make up a differentiated whole. Its national conversation would be allergic to Jabotinsky's idiom, to monism, and to any "simple, primal, brutal 'yes' or no'" (which is no less the argot of neoconservatives). This America would have no need of Stradivarius's secret; it would need, in its stead, liberality, democracy, tolerance.

Shaatnez would be celebrated and the legitimacy of plural loyalties—of a root*ed* cosmopolitanism—defended, not just for the enriching possibilities of diversity, as imagined by Bourne or Kallen or Greenberg or Appiah, but also for a contrasting reason: tensions born of overlapping or entwined commitments can educate citizens to tolerance by pressing them to see issues and one another from both cosmopolitan and rooted standpoints, each tempering yet challenging the other. It is true that the value of such tensions may be equal to and perhaps be inseparable from the anguish they cause, especially within minorities. W. E. B. Du Bois, echoing Goethe's Faust in *The Souls of Black Folk,* spoke of his ever present sense of "twoness—an American, a Negro; two souls, two thoughts, two unreconciled strivings" at war, threatening to tear "one dark body" apart. Harold Rosenberg, in "Jewish Identity in a Free Society," expressed a similar strain when he wrote that being "twice identified" is "embarrassingly ambiguous" because of "a modern impulse"—the oft-made demand—to be "one-hundred-percent-something."[46]

But it is better to live with and through modern ambiguities, to wrestle with unreconciled strivings, than to hanker for their easy, one-sided resolution, just as it is better for a society to accept hyphenated citizens rather than impose homogeneity. Moreover, such one-sidedness and homogeneity cannot be achieved in the end. This doesn't mean that variety, which must come with variance, necessarily stands on its own. If I may borrow from (and modulate) Hegel, diversity in civil society needs a countervailing (though not totalistic) unity in the "political moment." The more pluralism within a society, the more vigorous the sense of political citizenship must be, especially within a democracy.[47]

Furthermore, a robust sense of citizenship needs to extend into the social and economic domains. Just as a part of the left uses multiculturalism as ersatz politics, so many on the right have preoccupied themselves with culture wars so as to avoid addressing widespread social pain in this country. This was revealed starkly in the symposium "The National Prospect," published in *Commentary*, the intellectual flagship of Jewish neoconservatism, on its fiftieth anniversary. Here, while warnings abound of cultural decay and its fragmenting consequences, serious treatment of economic malaise, of the fragmenting, devastating consequences of vast and growing inequality between rich and poor, is absent. Gertrude Himmelfarb and Norman Podhoretz retrieve Disraeli's notion of "Two Nations," but where this nineteenth-century British conservative meant to warn of what widespread poverty would bring, for today's neoconservatives the issue is only cultural. Podhoretz contends that "for all the talk about 'increased economic and social stratification,' prosperity is still more widely shared here than anywhere else."[48] Not two economic nations, but two cultural nations are emerging in America, one with and one without the puritan morals and bourgeois manners championed by neoconservatives.

Yet statistics demonstrate overwhelmingly that the United States has the greatest economic inequality of any Western nation, with 1 percent of the population possessing 40 percent of its wealth and the top 20 percent possessing 80 percent. When it comes to incomes ratio, that of the upper 20 percent to the poorest 20 percent is nine to one.[49] One is tempted to compare the neoconservatives to Jabotinsky: he denounced *shaatnez*, they censure multiculturalism, and in so doing they all direct the focus from other matters, especially economic injustice. There is, however, a significant historical difference. The denunciation of *shaatnez* by Jabotinsky was a rhetorical canard since his Zionism was as "impure" as Ben-Gurion's; but multiculturalism is a genuine issue today because of America's pluralism and despite the successes of the melting pot. What is thus needed is some perspective, an ability to recognize when multiculturalism is properly addressed in America, and when it isn't; and also to recognize how urgent it is to address social and economic suffering in this country.

This is to ask, again, of American Jews: In what type of America do you want to live? My answer, as one American Jew, as one rooted cosmopolitan, is that I want to live in an America of democratic citizenship, of social and economic democracy, of liberal tolerance, in a secular state that allows diverse cultures and religions to make of themselves what they will. This America is conceived from a perspective of *shaatnez*; how Judaism fares in it will depend on the cultural life fashioned by American Jews for themselves as a distinct community within the broader society but nonetheless as full participants in it.

Notes

1. An initial version of this essay was presented to the seminar "Comparative History and Historiography of the Jews" at the Ecole des Hautes Etudes en Sciences Sociales in Paris in January 1996. My thanks to Nancy Green, Directeur d'études, for her invitation to address the seminar. I am also indebted to Brian Morton, Michael Walzer, and Steven Zipperstein for their valuable criticisms of early drafts of this essay.

2. Vladimir Jabotinsky to David Ben-Gurion, March 30, 1935, copy in the Jabotinsky Archives and Institute, Tel Aviv.

3. David Ben-Gurion to Vladimir Jabotinsky, April 28, 1935. The letter is reproduced in full in Yaakov Goldstein and Yaakov Shavit, *Lelo psharot: Heskem Ben-Gurion-Jabotinsky vekishlono* (No Compromises: The Ben-Gurion-Jabotinsky Agreement and Its Failure) (Tel Aviv: Yariv/Hadar, 1979), 147–148.

4. David Ben-Gurion, "Ha-Poel ba-tsiyonut"(The Worker in Zionism), in *Mi-maamad le-am* (From a Class to a Nation) (Tel Aviv: Am Oved and Keren ha-Negev, 1974), 249.

5. In ensuing years the development of Ben-Gurion's notion of *mamlakhtiyut* (statism), an assertion of the primacy of the category of state over class, brought his ideas closer to those of Jabotinsky in important ways. Since these changes are not vital to my argument here, I have not pursued the subject. On Ben-Gurion's transformation, see Mitchell Cohen, *Zion and State* (New York: Columbia University Press, 1992), especially Part 3. In my discussion of Ben-Gurion and Jabotinsky in this essay, I draw from chapters 4–10 of this book. In other parts of this essay I have drawn from my "Rooted Cosmopolitanism," *Dissent,* Fall 1992.

6. K. Anthony Appiah, *In My Father's House: Africa in the Philosophy of Culture* (Oxford and New York: Oxford University Press, 1992), 92.

7. Hayim Greenberg, "Patriotism and Plural Loyalties," *The Inner Eye: Selected Essays* (New York: Jewish Frontier Association, 1953), 1:179–180.

8. Appiah, *In My Father's House,* ix.

9. Ibid., 72.

10. I summarize from Henry F. May, *The End of American Innocence* (New York: Columbia University Press, 1992), 346–350. Bingham is quoted in Arthur A. Goren, *New York Jews and the Quest for Community: The Kehillah Experiment, 1908–1922* (New York: Columbia University Press, 1970), 25.

11. On Roosevelt and Wilson I summarize from John Higham, *Strangers in the Land: Patterns of American Nativism, 1860–1925* (New Brunswick, N.J.: Rutgers University Press, 1992), 198–199. Also see Roosevelt's earlier "True Americanism," in Mario R. DiNunzio, ed., *Theodore Roosevelt, An American Mind: Selected Writings* (New York: Penguin Books, 1995), especially 170–171.

12. Randolph Bourne, "Trans-National America," *The Radical Will: Selected Writings, 1911–1918* (New York: Urizen Books, 1977), 249.

13. Ibid., 255.

14. John Dewey, "Nationalizing Education," in *The Middle Works, 1899–1924*, vol. 10: *Essays on Philosophy and Education, 1916–1917* (Carbondale and Edwardsville: Southern Illinois University Press, 1985), 204.

15. Horace Mayer Kallen, "Zionism and Liberalism," in Arthur Hertzberg, ed., *The Zionist Idea* (New York: Atheneum, 1959), 529.

16. Horace Mayer Kallen, "A Meaning of Americanism," in *Culture and Democracy in the United States* (New York: Boni and Liveright, 1924), 62–63.

17. Michael Walzer, "What Does It Mean to Be an American?" in *What It Means to Be an American: Essays on the American Experience* (New York: Marsilio, 1992), 48–49.

18. Horace Mayer Kallen, "Democracy versus the Melting Pot," in *Culture and Democracy in the United States*, 124–125.

19. Dewey's letter is cited in Robert B. Westbrook, *John Dewey and American Democracy* (Ithaca: Cornell University Press, 1991), 213.

20. Walzer, "What Does It Mean. . . ," 44.

21. Bourne, "Trans-National America," 255, 258–260.

22. Ibid., 262–263.

23. Randolph Bourne, "The Jew and Trans-National America," in *War and the Intellectuals: Collected Essays, 1915–1919* (New York and Evanston, Ill.: Harper Torchbooks, 1964), 128. It appeared originally in *Menorah Journal*, December 1916.

24. Ibid., 126.

25. Ibid., 131.

26. Ibid., 130.

27. Ibid., 129–131. Dewey's views are in an article published in 1917 in the same *Menorah Journal* that earlier printed Bourne's lecture. He wrote:

If I do not mistake, the cause of Zionism has great claims upon those who are interested in the future organization of the peaceful intercourse of nations, because it not only guarantees freedom of cultural development in that particular spot in which the new nation is formed, but because it gives leverage for procuring and developing cultural nationality in all the other countries which harbor within themselves large numbers of the Jewish folk. Moreover, the Zionistic state would stand forth to the world as an inspiring symbol of victory against great odds, against seemingly insuperable odds, of the rights of nationality to be itself. From this point of view I feel that the Zionistic movement is one that has a right to appeal to the interest and sympathy of statesmen and of all who care for the future of the world's peaceful organization.

John Dewey, "The Principle of Nationality," in *The Middle Works*, 10:291.

28. Greenberg, "Patriotism and Plural Loyalties," 173.

29. Bourne would surely have had difficulties with the "statism" *(mamlakhtiyut)* advocated by the mature Ben-Gurion as well. See above, this chapter, note 4.

30. Bourne, "The Jew and Trans-National America," 131–132.

31. Ibid., 127.

32. Ibid.

33. Arthur M. Schlesinger Jr., *The Disuniting of America* (New York: Norton, 1992), 13, 122.

34. John Plamenatz, *Man and Society* (London and New York: Longman, 1963), 1:45. Plamenatz's chapter "Liberty of Conscience" provides a trenchant overview of the evolution of this idea.

35. Dewey, "Nationalizing Education," 206.

36. The article on ethnic studies is by Ramon A. Gutierrez. See David Theo Goldberg, ed., *Multiculturalism: A Critical Reader* (Cambridge and Oxford: Basil Blackwell, 1994).

37. "Neoconservative" refers to a group of intellectuals and writers, many of them Jewish, who moved from the left to the right, mostly in the 1960s and 1970s. While I continue to use the term here in order to distinguish them, some of their most prominent figures have declared recently that the prefix "neo" is no longer appropriate as they consider themselves to be absorbed into the broader conservative movement that asserted itself in the Reagan era and thereafter. See Irving Kristol, "An Autobiographical Memoir," in *Neoconservatism: The Autobiography of an Idea, Selected Essays, 1949–1995* (New York: The Free Press, 1995), 40, and Norman Podhoretz, "Neoconservatism: A Eulogy," *Commentary*, March 1996.

38. Irving Kristol, "My Cold War," *The National Interest* 31 (Spring 1993): 144. Midge Decter expresses the same sentiments, speaking of "the domestic cold war . . . in which there is even less possibility of arriving at understandings and settlements than there was in its now-defunct international namesake." Midge Decter, "The National Prospect" (symposium), *Commentary*, November 1995, p. 46.

39. William Kristol, "A Conservative Looks at Liberalism," *Commentary*, September 1993, p.33.

40. Midge Decter, lecture at the Jewish Theological Seminary of America, November 2, 1995.

41. Decter, "The National Prospect," *Commentary*, November 1995, p. 46.

42. Michael Lind, "Why Intellectual Conservatism Died," *Dissent*, Winter 1995, p. 45. Lind was executive editor of *The National Interest*.

43. Irving Kristol quoted in David Frum, *Dead Right* (New York: Basic Books, 1994), 172.

44. Leo Strauss, "On a Forgotten Kind of Writing," in *What Is Political Philosophy? and Other Writings* (Chicago and London: University of Chicago Press, 1959), 221–222. Kristol describes Strauss's enormous influence on him in "An Autobiographical Memoir," 7–9.

45. Quoted in Henry Louis Gates Jr., "African-American Studies in the Twenty-first Century," in *Loose Canons: Notes on the Culture Wars* (Oxford and New York: Oxford University Press, 1992), 126.

46. W. E. B. Du Bois, *The Souls of Black Folk* (New York: Signet, 1982), 45; Harold Rosenberg, "Jewish Identity in a Free Society," *Discovering the Present: Three Decades in Art, Culture, and Politics* (Chicago and London: University of Chicago Press, 1976), 262.

47. On pluralism and citizenship, also see Walzer's "Introduction" in "What It Means to Be an American," 10, and his "Multiculturalism and Individualism," *Dissent*, Spring 1994.

48. Norman Podhoretz, "The National Prospect" (symposium), *Commentary*, November 1995, p. 99. For Gertrude Himmelfarb, see p. 65 in the same issue.

49. *New York Times*, April 17, 1995, and September 3, 1995; *International Herald Tribune*, July 16, 1996.

CHAPTER 3

Pluralism and Its Discontents

The Case of Blacks and Jews

Cheryl Greenberg

Blacks and Jews, once partners in the struggle for civil rights and racial justice, have more recently become estranged. Paralleling the rise and fall of that coalition is the rise and fall of pluralism as an ideal for structuring American social life. It is to those two intertwined narratives that I turn: first to a brief history of the shifting terms of debate, then to an overview of the black-Jewish political partnership, its strengths and its limits. The ideological move away from pluralism occurred alongside the growing polarization of blacks and Jews; an analysis of the connections between these two developments and a critique of the failure of most social relations theories to pay sufficient attention to the "hidden injuries of class" help to illuminate Jews' uncomfortable relationship to multiculturalism.[1]

Multiculturalism, the most recent attempt to address the diversity of America's (and the world's) peoples and histories, challenges traditional historical understandings and redefines the American landscape of racial, ethnic, and religious groups. Rooted in a critique of traditional power relations that favor white male elites and their world view, multiculturalists argue instead for understanding the world as a cacophonous multiplicity of voices and experiences. As David Theo Goldberg explains, "Broadly conceived, multiculturalism is critical of and resistant to the necessarily reductive imperatives of monocultural assimilation."[2] Because multiculturalism received its focus and energy primarily from the later phases of the modern civil rights movement, it has tended to address racial differences. While most definitions of multiculturalism include not only race but also class, gender, and sexuality as fundamental social categories, they nevertheless exclude or finesse other crucial social divisions and (I believe) still enshrine race as first among equals. Positing race as the greatest divide certainly may be valid; my point here is that the most common versions of multiculturalism can therefore all be subject to a similar critique of downplaying other distinctions in favor of racial ones.

But little can be generalized about multiculturalism beyond its commitment to dethroning the white male voice. The term *multiculturalism* itself is contested and is embraced by those with different and sometimes contradictory visions of society, or, as Goldberg puts it, "This critical realignment assumes multiple forms."[3] Some multiculturalism overlaps with the problematic "politics of identity," for example. By denying the multifaceted nature of identity and by reducing human beings to their biology, identity politics distorts by overgeneralizing, insisting on single dimensions of experience, and ignoring the complexities created by the interaction of these different identities within a single individual.

There is yet another version, what I call "fuzzy multiculturalism." Never precisely defined, this popular conception of the word means the teaching about different cultures. Unobjectionable—even desirable—as this form may be, it is not intellectually rigorous enough to be included in this discussion. And even this approach has its dangers and distortions. Often it oversimplifies, thereby trivializing the community under study. The greater danger perhaps lies in its subtlety, for legitimizing and validating diverse cultures implies equality in ways that mask the pernicious effects of noncultural oppressions such as that based on class.

Further complicating the picture, there are several venues in which multiculturalism is played out: in public policy, for example (affirmative action), or in educational policy (diversity programs and the so-called culture wars). In the first, multiculturalism is political—to the multicultural go the spoils. Here, because the definition must be linked with historical disadvantage, it is less inclusive. The second is social—let a hundred cultures bloom. Multiculturalism as redress vies with multiculturalism as celebration. The blurring of these distinctions contributes to the virulence and intransigence of the debate. (There is a growing body of work on "critical multiculturalism" which has begun to address these and other issues; I will return to this topic later.)

Yet despite this apparent indeterminacy, multiculturalism as a sociological concept is grounded in a particular history that gives it much of its contemporary resonance. Since the nation's founding, Americans have debated how to absorb diverse populations, a debate that reached a crescendo with the immigration of eastern and southern Europeans and the migration of southern blacks to urban areas in the north. For traditional Anglo-conformists or "monoculturalists," white Protestant Western European (and male) culture, norms, and values defined the best of America. For them, assimilation to this norm was the only alternative. In the early years of the twentieth century a newly popularized image of America as the melting pot replaced the traditionalist notion with another that posited a new and unique American culture—still a monocultural vision—this time shaped by contributions from many ethnic, national, and religious groups. Alongside this cultural paradigm, others posited pluralism, which called for the recognition of the unique cultures of different groups who were to retain their distinctiveness in private while conforming to the prevailing (monocultural) norm in public.

Cultural pluralism underwent a series of alterations in subsequent decades. While here I describe its most common features—private celebration of cultural difference, public assimilation to putatively American behavioral norms, the presumption of every cultural group's shared commitment to tolerance, democracy, and human equality, the recognition of the unique contributions of various cultural groups to American life and history, and some degree of cultural relativism—pluralists varied tremendously in their definition of what constituted culture and in how they negotiated the boundaries between public and private and between acceptable and unacceptable deviations from the presumed norm. (Judaism was an acceptable deviation, for example, but for most Communism was not.) Regardless of its theoretical variants, the popular understanding of pluralism is perhaps best exemplified by World War II movies like *Bataan*, whose all-American fighting force included Jake Feinberg, Felix Ramirez, F. X. Matowski, Bill Dane, Jesus Katigbay, Wesley Epps, and Yankee Salazar.[4]

Standing against this vision of the ideal society were nationalists: Zionists, followers of black nationalist Marcus Garvey, and others who objected to the assimilative nature of pluralism's public life. Although most of these early groups insisted that their vision of an extranational homeland in which to nurture and sustain their distinctiveness did not contradict their commitment to American values, by the 1960s the separatist Black Power movement and others inspired by it repudiated the integrationist goal altogether. They argued that integration required cultural genocide and in any case was impossible to achieve given the impenetrable barriers of the American racial state. Thus was multiculturalism born. At its most basic level it was pluralism without the element of public conformity and without pluralism's optimism of ultimate inclusion for all.

But multiculturalism was more than a call for diversity. It traced its lineage from a subset of both pluralist and nationalist thought that viewed individuals as inevitable members of their biologically determined group. This essentialist view envisioned what we today call balkanization: a nation of separate entities sharing public power but existing, immutably, as separate and autonomous units.[5]

The notion of essentialism raises the related question of the meaning of "race." A notoriously slippery concept to define, race is no longer considered by virtually any serious scholars as a legitimate biological or genetic category. Technically a race is a population that differs from others in the relative frequency of a certain gene or genes or, put another way, a population sharing a gene pool for whom specific intragroup physical differences are smaller than intergroup differences. Not only has intermixing of populations rendered the concept academic but, as biologists have noted, every physical trait has a unique pattern of distribution, and any of these could plausibly be called on to define the boundaries of "races." A further difficulty in defining race lies in the assumption that individuals have only one race, when many people have ancestors from more than one racial group. The definition of who is black, for example, has changed many times in this country. Nevertheless, "race" has meaning in the United States (and most of the rest of the world) based on the widely divergent historical experiences of populations whose ancestors came from different continents and who enjoyed differential access to power based on that ancestry. In other words, "race" has historical meaning because people acted as if it had meaning. Sociologists Michael Omi and Howard Winant have offered a useful definition: " Race is a concept which signifies and symbolizes social conflicts and interests by referring to different types of human bodies."[6]

Few of the multiculturalists who claim the fixity of race actually argue that it is simply biological. They point out that in American history race has been treated as an inescapable and hereditary social category that determined access to power and privilege and that the experience of racism has shaped nonwhites profoundly and in ways whites can never fully understand. Nevertheless, the claim that race is in any sense fixed suggests a lack of understanding of historical change and the multicultural approach sometimes does drift toward essentialism. The problem is highlighted by considering the views of some Afrocentrists. Afrocentrism, a position on one end of the multiculturalism spectrum, insists any understanding of people of African descent—or indeed of Western civilization—must take Africa and its cultures and values as the point of departure. Many (although certainly not all) Afrocentrists consider race an immutable category, and in defining as black anyone with "one drop" of black ancestry they have ironically endorsed the definition of their racist opponents. At the same time, most Afrocentrists posit a cultural component to blackness, not simply a biological one. As black conservatives have pointed out, such thinking, while not explicitly articulated, nonetheless leads to the ineluctable conclusion that there is a right way (and thus a wrong way) of being black. More to the point for this discussion, the confusion between biology and culture as the basis for "blackness" has left murky its relation to the dialogue on American social relations. It is not clear whether these Afrocentrists and multiculturalists consider integration hopeless or simply undesirable.

Indeed, for black people integration has long been both. As David Biale remarks in chapter 1 above, white ethnics were the sole ingredients for the melting pot; few advocates of this view included Asian or African Americans in their scenarios. Pluralists added these populations into their pantheon of cultures but insisted that members of these groups embrace white Protestant norms in public and acknowledge the Western European tradition as America's unifying cultural heritage. Multiculturalists turn these ideas on their heads, insisting on the primacy of racial cultures in the multicultural marketplace and plumbing American culture to unearth its nonwhite roots. It is no coincidence that the term "people of color" achieved popularity when it did; racial groupings define the central parameters of multiculturalism.

The fact that multiculturalism has been used to promote conflicting political agendas, however, should not prevent critical analysis of the more narrowly and explicitly defined antipluralist theory that emerged as the most recent paradigm of social relations. What is Jews' relationship to it and to previous paradigms? Because they had no place in the Anglo-conformist view, Jews themselves helped create and promote alternative theories that both recognized their differences from mainstream white American culture and valued their unique contributions to society. Thus it was Israel Zangwill who popularized the expression "melting pot," in his 1908 play by that name, and Horace Kallen who pioneered (with others) the concept of cultural pluralism. Both these schemes recognized Jews' continued minority or outsider status, as indeed Jews themselves did. Both also redefined the notion of outsider from unwanted alien to valued societal contributor—part of the multireligious, multiethnic polyglot that shaped America. But multiculturalism, putting race first as it does, removes Jews from the outsider community they had helped to legitimize. Instead Jews have become "Euro-Americans" with their cultures and contributions subsumed under that broad heading (and their victimization by other Europeans thereby effaced). Now outsiders are racial minorities: African Americans, Asian Americans, Native Americans, and Hispanics (that last a problematic category in itself since it does not define a single ancestry group at all, but that discussion is best left for another time). And Jewish social scientists, who had tremendous control over the creation and shaping of pluralism, have far less power over multicultural theory to which they have come later and more hesitantly. Under multiculturalism, then, Jews are as left out as when assimilationists described their version of inside and outside.

Two important caveats here. Some (but not all) feminist multicultural texts include essays by Jewish women as part of the larger narrative of exclusion or oppression. Similarly, more Jewish women than men support affirmative action, one political expression of multiculturalism, since they directly benefit from those programs along with nonwhites. Jewish women, then, have a more ambivalent role in the multicultural community than do Jewish men. Second, during much of the pluralist era Jews were themselves considered a separate race, a notion quashed by the time multiculturalism came of age. Thus one could argue that Jews shifted from outsider to insider because in racial theory they shifted from nonwhite (that is, Jewish race) to white (that is, whites of Jewish background).

Multiculturalism also turns the image of insider on its head. In all three earlier ideologies—Anglo-conformity, the melting pot, and pluralism—"inside" was the ideal, the source of culture and value. It was where everyone, minority and majority, wanted to be. Now to be an insider is to be a cultural imperialist, one who seeks to impose a single set of values, traditions, beliefs, and behaviors on a resistant population of heterogeneous backgrounds and diverse cultures. Thus just as Jews moved from a minority to part of the majority—that is, from outsider to insider status—insider lost its moral legitimacy.

Yet most Jews do not see themselves as privileged, as simply white people, as insiders in American society. Instead, they view themselves as outsiders who belong beneath the multicultural umbrella as an insecure minority with a separate culture and set of beliefs and values. In part the problem here is the use of different standards for comparison. When Jews perceive themselves as vulnerable they compare themselves to the dominant cultural community (that is WASPs), who have excluded them and discriminated against them. When other minority groups look at Jews, however, they compare Jews' status to their own. By that measure, Jews look settled and safe.[7]

To the extent that Jews recognize their own security, they consider it yet another refutation of multiculturalism's insistence on the permanence of barriers to full integration. Jews (I am generalizing here) understand their history in America as the triumph of a racially and ethnically blind meritocracy. Unable—or unwilling—to recognize the limitations of that meritocracy for nonwhites, Jews perceive multiculturalism in its denial of the possibility of race blindness and true equality of opportunity as a dangerous falsehood belied by their experience.

Two factors, then, make the Jewish relation to multiculturalism so problematic: the tension between Jewish self-perception of vulnerability and external perception of Jewish security, and the inability of most Jews to appreciate the radically different historical condition of white ethnics and nonwhites in America. These problems are hardly unexpected. The divergence in perception has been emerging for a long time. And Jewish lack of appreciation for the salience of racial barriers is based on a false but persistent identification of their situation with that of African Americans and a lack of sensitivity to the interrelationship of race and class status. Thus a consideration of the modern history of black-Jewish relations can shed some light on the ambivalence Jews have felt toward multiculturalism as it is currently expressed.[8]

As eastern European immigration picked up momentum at the end of the nineteenth century, xenophobia and anti-Semitism rose with it. In response to a barrage of anti-Jewish exclusionary actions (including quotas in higher education, housing covenants, social restrictions, and employment discrimination) and to widespread caricatures of Jews in books, newspapers, and the new motion picture industry, Jews established civil rights agencies, including the National Council of Jewish Women (NCJW, 1893), the American Jewish Committee (AJC, 1906) made up mostly of long-settled German Jews, and its eastern European Jewish counterpart, the American Jewish Congress (AJCongress, 1917). The Anti-Defamation League (ADL) followed in 1913 and the Jewish Labor Committee in 1934. While different from one another in many respects, these organizations shared an eagerness to prove Jews good Americans. Unlike their Zionist counterpart organizations, which sought Jewish autonomy and separation, most of these groups desired only to help Jews become full participants in American life. (For individual Jews the distinction between Jewish and American nationalisms was less clear, and they saw little contradiction between their commitment to integration and to Zionism.)[9]

Pluralist Jewish agencies challenged restrictions placed on Jews and demanded full access to the bounty of America. They challenged anti-

Jewish stereotypes in the media, fought anti-Semites where they found them, and worked to bring down quotas and restrictions. Yet at the same time they were uneasy at the strong assimilationist measures of those endorsing "100% Americanism" and other nativists who wanted nothing more than to bar immigrants altogether or, where that was impossible, to mold them forcibly into Protestant Anglo-Saxons. Neither subtlety nor compromise were among nativists' strengths; as one New York City teacher put it, newcomers "must be made to realize that in forsaking the land of their birth, they were also forsaking the customs and traditions of that land."[10] Jews resisted, demanding their right to maintain their own culture, language, and religion free from interference by the state or by the outside community. In opposition to the assimilationist vision most Jews embraced pluralism.

Certainly this pluralism had its assimilationist elements. Americanization programs were conducted by Jewish groups as well as by employers and gentile assimilationists. Jewish conceptions of pluralism demanded from every group a shared commitment to democracy and tolerance and stressed unity within difference. Nevertheless, this vision was far broader and more accepting than a strict assimilationist one, and its very assumptions required a breadth of political concern that embraced other outsider groups. Thus, for example, in the 1930s and 1940s the AJC and ADL created "I Am an American" pamphlets and "Lest We Forget" radio programs, reminding listeners of the contributions of Jews, African Americans, Mexican Americans, and others to American life. Obviously there were gaping holes in the broad concern Jews felt for other minorities, the most glaring of which was almost universal Jewish silence during the internment of Japanese Americans.[11] And certainly Jews did not devote equal attention to every other minority group. Black-Jewish cooperation, for example, was far stronger and more frequent than that between Jews and Latino, Catholic, or Asian groups, although these others did occur. Furthermore, Jewish commitment to integration and pluralism rarely extended to friendships or marriage, which remained highly endogamous at least through the 1950s. Nevertheless, Jewish commitment to what I call assimilative pluralism did bring Jews into the broader civil rights struggle.

Jews embraced the cause of black equality also because Jews saw in the black condition echoes of their own. After all, they had been persecuted in Europe, ghettoized, and physically threatened by anti-Jewish mobs. They were Europe's most persistent and vexing minority. Here in America, African Americans faced similar persecution as America's quintessential minority. Furthermore, African American cultural expressions had long reflected an identification with (biblical) Jews, especially Egypt's Israelite slaves. All this offered the illusion of similarity of experience which enhanced mutual expectations that common cause might be made. "We Jews know what restrictions mean. We, too, have had to face handicaps in our efforts to work, to earn, to live. It is, perhaps, because of this common understanding that Jews everywhere show such deep interest in the Negro's problems," wrote ADL's Sidney Hollander in 1947.[12] But this claim of black and Jewish identity in suffering also obfuscated crucial differences between the two communities and set the stage for the frustration and anger of later decades when that mutual support evaporated.

Individual Jews had aided antiracist efforts since the start of the century, including the formation of the National Association for the Advancement of Colored People (NAACP). Jewish newspapers covered stories of African American oppression with a sympathetic eye and frequent reminders of the similarities between lynching and eastern European pogroms. The ADL, founded in reaction to the arrest and anti-Semitic persecution of a Jewish man, Leo Frank (who was lynched by a southern mob two years later), included in its founding platform the commitment to "secure justice and fair treatment to all citizens alike."

At the same time, African American organizations such as the NAACP (1909), National Urban League (NUL, 1911), and National Association of Colored Women (1896) were themselves embracing pluralism (as did the later National Council of Negro Women, 1935). Certainly assimilationists did not consider African Americans full partners in the American experiment. Indeed most of the prominent assimilationists were white supremacists as well. Only pluralism or separatism were viable alternatives and, like Jews, blacks often embraced both views simultaneously. Thousands supported Marcus Garvey, who advocated repatriation to Africa, and other nationalists, yet their long history in this country meant that for most their primary commitment lay in winning equality in the land of their birth. Even Garvey's organization, the Universal Negro Improvement Association, spent considerable time fighting for black equality in the United States.[13]

Given the legal constraints on full participation in American social, economic, and political life, the word black civil rights agencies most often used to describe this goal was integration, which in fact posited pluralism. African Americans should be fully integrated into American institutional life, they argued, because they were full Americans, sharing the same values and aspirations as other citizens. Yet blacks prided themselves on their unique contributions to American society and demanded the right

to celebrate their distinct heritage. Perhaps the clearest articulation of pluralism in the context of race relations came from the National Urban
League's "CREDO":

American citizens of all races who are bound together by their common concern for their common community and by their respect for the rights of their
neighbors have an inescapable responsibility for working to remove social or
economic handicaps from minorities within our population.
The problem faced by these minorities in their everyday living and working situation is not a racial problem, but a problem of American democracy.[14]

Again, the embrace of pluralism brought an awareness of other minority groups. Eager to recruit white allies and recognizing that every victory for an oppressed group furthered their own efforts, most black organizations paid close attention to the struggles of others. Marcus Garvey,
despite his anti-Semitic views, nonetheless positively cited the example
of the Jews when describing his programs. The black Crusader News
Agency covered stories of anti-Jewish atrocities in Europe, and the
NAACP, Brotherhood of Sleeping Car Porters, and NUL spoke out against
anti-Semitism. The National Council of Negro Women and National
Association of Colored Women cosponsored conferences with the
NCJW.[15]

Good talk, however, was seldom followed by organized community
action in the early years of the twentieth century. For a long time, in fact,
blacks and Jews did not see themselves as partners in the civil rights struggle. Although both blacks and Jews recognized their own experience in
the plight of the other, their constituent agencies before World War II
were small, politically weak, and overwhelmed by their own community's problems. And although every poll documented lower levels of
anti-Semitism in the black community than in the white and lower levels of racism among Jews than among white Gentiles, bigotry also con-
spired to keep the two groups politically separate in the early twentieth
century.[16] Their goals were the same—full inclusion in American political and economic life—but their opening salvos in the battle for tolerance were generally fired separately and without coordination.

This reluctance to make common cause changed in the 1930s with the
news of Hitler's rise in Germany. The plight of Jews abroad and the rise
in fascist and anti-Semitic groups in the United States made American
Jews realize that their quiet methods and determination to go it alone
were insufficient to the task. Jewish civil rights organizations formally
reached out to African American groups for the first time to ask their help

in aiding German-Jewish refugees and in antifascist propaganda efforts. African Americans seized the opportunity to raise American consciousness about racism in general,[17] and an institutional dialogue began between the two communities which eventually broadened into a substantial collaboration on a broad range of civil rights issues.

The heyday of black-Jewish political cooperation, the 1940s and 1950s, was an era of pluralism transcendent. Both blacks and Jews (broadly speaking) endorsed a version of pluralism that posited the right of individuals to free choice of employment, housing, and social life, protected against discrimination. Neither group desired assimilation in the sense of loss of separate identity based on religion, history, and a sense of peoplehood, yet both endorsed the assimilationist notion that all groups shared (or should share) the same sense of toleration and acceptance of others. They thus supported an assimilationist form of pluralism (called acculturation by Milton Gordon) that demanded structural equality, or equal public access to all forms of power, but tolerated, even lauded, cultural differences. In private one could choose to be, and celebrate being, a Jew, an African American, but in public one was, and must be treated as, only an American. The element of choice was crucial. One chose one's identity, but one had an equal right not to choose it. The key issue then was freedom— freedom to choose and to celebrate who one was and at the same time freedom to enjoy equal access to all the opportunities others enjoyed without reference to one's background.

Every venture on behalf of integration jointly undertaken by black and Jewish civil rights agencies revealed their shared commitment to assimilative pluralism. Believing that individual equality of opportunity was the goal, along with a protected—but publicly ignored—private and voluntary community life, black and Jewish civil rights agencies collaborated on a host of projects ranging from desegregating hospitals, schools, housing projects, and bowling leagues to barring inquiries by employers or colleges regarding an applicant's race or religion. They worked to challenge restrictive housing covenants, broaden economic opportunity, bar the state from obtaining membership lists of "subversive" groups (since in southern states that included the NAACP), protect civil liberties, and persuade authorities to investigate racially or religiously motivated violence. A joint effort by the NAACP, the AJC, and the ADL convinced the New York state legislature to create a state university system to compensate for racial and religious discrimination at private institutions of higher learning. All the major Jewish organizations filed supporting briefs in *Brown v. Board of Education* while the NAACP fought for higher quotas for European Jewish refugees and in the United Nations argued the case for creating a Jewish state. Together black and Jewish agencies launched programs to promote what they called intergroup relations, stressing tolerance of differences, based on the assumption that more united groups than divided them. All vestiges of formal discrimination were to be rooted out and differences between groups shown to be simply variations on the same moral and patriotic themes. Thus the Institute for American Democracy, a semi-independent organization under the guidance of the ADL, published ads captioned "Let's Tear Out These Weeds!" Hands pulled weeds labeled "class hate," "religious hate," "race hate," prejudice," "nationalist hate," and "group hate." An ADL poster campaign featured Jackie Robinson, Joe DiMaggio, Hank Greenberg, and others with the (factually inaccurate) legend "It doesn't matter what nationality he is; he can pitch." The Association for Tolerance in America, with some of the nation's most prominent African Americans on its board, passed out pamphlets during World War II depicting black men in combat uniforms and insisting that "500,000 of these lads are fighting for you. Let them and theirs share in our democracy."[18] In all these efforts their shared commitments were fully visible: public equality, celebration of private difference, and assurance that such differences masked deeper similarities.

Nevertheless, the roots of blacks' and Jews' current estrangement can readily be identified in this earlier period. Long-standing tensions between the two communities were surmounted only with difficulty, and new conflicts erupted with alarming frequency. While most Jews defined the problem as one of black anti-Semitism, these differences revolved primarily around class. In December of 1935, after discovering "how much sentiment there is among Negroes against certain types of Jews," Walter White of the NAACP investigated anti-Jewish attitudes in black communities. His informal survey of black leaders around the country revealed widespread concern about Jewish business exploitation of African Americans and a certain level of frustration at Jewish unresponsiveness to such problems. Three years later black attorney Charles Houston lamented that he and Walter White were rebuffed each time they had tried to convince Jewish leaders to open a dialogue on relations between the two communities. Finally, in 1939 one of the first such dialogues took place in New York City. The group discussed the relationship between Jewish business practices in black areas and black resentment of Jews.[19] While Jews saw themselves as vulnerable outsiders in America, African Americans who came to the table viewed them as insiders, holders of economic power that they wielded in racist and exploitive ways. These contradictory interpretations of the position of Jews prefigured later disagreement over the efficacy of pluralism because both views were in their own way correct.

Because most Jews had come to this country with skills and urban experience, their stay in the poorest sections of cities was generally short-lived. Since broad social anti-Semitism restricted opportunities for these Jews, they turned to entrepreneurship and later to civil service to improve their class standing. Earning their way out of the slums through shopkeeping, managing or controlling rental properties, or through teaching, social work, and similar pursuits, Jews often kept their neighborhood businesses and jobs long after they had moved away. Less resistant to having black neighbors and clients than were most other poor white communities, Jewish areas all over the country turned slowly to black beginning in the teens and twenties; interactions between blacks and Jews therefore took on a certain hierarchical character.

For Jews, their economic involvement in black neighborhoods affirmed their lack of bigotry and their identification with the struggles of the black community. They saw themselves as fellow strugglers: hardworking, near poor, oppressed by discrimination, managing only by pressing family members into service. Jewish businesses provided affordable—if not high quality—goods and services, and if their prices were higher than some of the downtown stores, so was the risk in a poor area. For African Americans, Jewish store owners' general unwillingness to hire area residents, their high prices and poor quality merchandise, the economic success that enabled them to move out of poor neighborhoods, and their willingness (in the South) to follow segregationist traditions, all marked them as no better than other white people. Indeed even Jewish civil rights agencies recognized the patronizing and occasionally racist behaviors of Jewish store owners and launched programs in New York, Chicago, Miami, Detroit, and several other cities to improve their interaction with the local African American community. Jewish housewives who hired black domestic workers treated them in the same exploitive ways as Christian white women did. Jewish employers were no more likely to hire or promote black workers than were their gentile counterparts and while Jewish-run unions more often accepted black members, their leadership remained firmly Jewish. While not all whites working in black areas were Jewish, a high proportion were, and so black resentment at the pettiness of social workers, the paternalism of teachers, and the greed of landlords and agents redounded upon Jews as well. In fact, given the prevailing attitudes of anti-Semitism which African Americans, as good Christians, often shared and the expectation among many blacks that Jews, fellow victims, ought to treat blacks with more sympathy than other whites did, black resentment and anger against Jews was often more virulent than that directed toward other whites.[20]

The Jewish view of themselves as economically and socially vulnerable and the African American view of Jews as economic insiders both had validity. But because both sides consistently described their differences as arising from racial or religious friction, not in large measure from class distinctions, these tensions were never adequately addressed. Thus they were never resolved and resurfaced again and again, although they did not prevent political cooperation so long as the shared pluralist vision endured. This is not to suggest that racism and anti-Semitism did not play a role in tensions between blacks and Jews. Indeed they did. Rather, the refusal to consider class as an aggravating factor meant that these issues could never be explored to their roots. And because these questions of race, religion, and class were intertwined, disaggregating them yielded a flawed analysis. Jews' race allowed them more mobility up the class ladder, but because they were blind to the structural and institutional components of racism and held racist attitudes of their own, they blamed blacks' failure to rise on black people themselves.[21] Meanwhile Jews' economic power over blacks, however limited when compared to that of white Christians, fanned preexisting anti-Semitism in the black community. Jews, legitimately angry at such bigotry, could not see the class-based resentments that lay beneath.

For a time ideological consensus masked class conflict, and while ordinary blacks and Jews continued to interact primarily in these hierarchical and strained ways, Jewish and black institutions worked more harmoniously on matters of mutual concern. Yet even in these cooperative political activities lay the seeds of future disagreement over the efficacy of the pluralist vision. In the 1940s and 1950s the NAACP, ADL, NUL, AJCongress, and AJC launched joint campaigns in city after city to convince employers not to ask an applicant's religion and race on application forms.[22] Once that was accomplished, Jewish groups concluded that their task was complete. Employers, since they would not know the background of the applicant, would now hire on the basis of merit. And for many Jews, at least those without identifiable Jewish surnames, this was indeed the case. But for African Americans, writing one's race on an application form is usually superfluous. Employers did not need written confirmation of what they could see, and most African Americans continued to be denied employment, housing, loans, and accommodations. The only difference was that the policy was now unofficial. For African

American organizations, unlike Jewish ones, theoretical race blindness was not enough.

This broad political disagreement illuminates one of the deepest cleavages between black and Jewish experience in the United States. Jews, at least those who did not "look" or "sound" Jewish or have Jewish-sounding last names, could pass as members of the mainstream while most black people could not. Indeed, "passing" highlights both elements of the American concept of race: the biologically proper skin color and the socially constructed proper behavior and name. Yet until the 1960s the implications of this deepest of differences were rarely discussed or even recognized by most of the central players.

It was precisely on this issue of white privilege that the black-Jewish collaboration foundered, as Jews held on to a pluralism that worked for them and African Americans began to challenge this approach as ineffective in obtaining civil rights. By the mid-1960s some within the activist civil rights movement had begun raising questions about the role of whites and the efficacy of nonviolent resistance. The primary sticking point for the Student Nonviolent Coordinating Committee's 1964 Freedom Summer project (in which white northern college students came south to work on Freedom Schools, voting rights campaigns, and similar projects) was the issue of whites' place in the movement. Freedom Summer's strategy—bringing in well-connected white people to direct national attention to the problem of racial discrimination—proved the point of its critics and its successes only highlighted the extent of American racism. Reporters and news cameras followed whites, not blacks. Freedom Summer did publicize white racial violence, but largely because white civil rights workers were among the victims. When the FBI dredged rivers in search of black southern civil rights worker Jim Chaney and white (Jewish) northern activists Andrew Goodman and Michael Schwerner, who had disappeared early in the summer, they discovered black bodies, victims of lynchings the police had never investigated. Sharp tensions emerged that summer between northern, generally better-educated whites and veteran southern black activists, and many were disgusted by the overwhelming press attention lavished on the former. And the crowning achievement of that summer, an integrated Mississippi delegation to the Democratic National Convention, was rejected by that allegedly liberal party in favor of the traditional "Dixiecrat" delegation elected in an all-white primary.

These tensions found expression in an increasingly nationalist rhetoric on the part of some members of the Congress of Racial Equality (CORE) and SNCC, fed in part by the charismatic preachings of Malcolm X and the Nation of Islam. Malcolm X had been speaking in the South as well as the North for several years and had an enthusiastic following. Some began to question the whole edifice on which civil rights efforts had been based. They criticized pluralism not only for its inefficacy but also for what they considered its coercive assimilationism. Not only was the media attention given white civil rights workers indicative of the failure to uproot racism by current methods, it was no longer even clear that integration, the stated goal of the movement, was desirable. First, as SNCC's chairman Stokely Carmichael (now Kwame Toure), pointed out, even defining the word was a power struggle. Although for blacks "integration" meant political and economic equality, for whites it meant race mixing, and it was the latter definition that seemed to stick most persistently in white minds. Indeed, as many argued, not only was it a distortion of civil rights goals to focus only on racial intermarriage, that image also underlined a central truth for many blacks: they did not see such intimate assimilation as their goal either. As Chuck McDew, a black (and Jewish) civil rights worker, put it when describing an attack on him while in prison:

A man was hitting me across the face with a rope. He was saying, "You son of a bitch, you son of a bitch, you'll never marry my daughter."

I thought, "These white folks are truly crazy. Here I'm sitting, thinking about dying, and this fool is talking about a daughter I don't know, never met, and . . . he's about to kill me because of some nonsense about my marrying her." I snapped out of my shock and said, "I don't even know your ugly-assed daughter."[23]

Instead, Carmichael insisted, black people must redefine themselves and their goals. Even the struggle for full public integration—fighting to penetrate existing political, economic, and social structures—was undesirable because it was in fact simply covert assimilationism into a value system blacks ought instead to repudiate.

The values of this society support a racist system; we find it incongruous to ask black people to adopt and support most of those values. We also reject the assumption that the basic institutions of this society must be preserved. The goal of black people must *not* be to assimilate into middle-class America for that class—as a whole—is without a viable conscience as regards humanity. . . . The values of the middle class permit the perpetuation of the ravages of the black community. The values of that class are based on material aggrandizement. . . . The values of that class do *not* lead to the creation of an open society. That class *mouths* its preference for a free, competitive society, while at the same time forcefully and even viciously denying to black people as a group the opportunity to compete. . . .

Thus we reject the goal of assimilation into middle-class America because the values of that class are in themselves anti-humanist and because that class as a social force perpetuates racism.[24]

Carmichael's argument for (a racially separatist) socialism, based as much on the fact of blacks' social exclusion as on the moral force of the egalitarian vision, resonated powerfully with many in the movement frustrated with its slow gains. Carmichael stressed the importance of having black people organize themselves separately in order to free themselves from the definitions and limits imposed by whites. For him this was a necessary first step toward the higher goal of overturning capitalism and remaking all of society. It was the first half of that call to action that black nationalists embraced most enthusiastically, and by the late 1960s both SNCC and CORE had redefined themselves as all-black organizations (although not necessarily anticapitalist ones).

For white activists, separatism was a grave insult, and many saw it also as a tactical error.[25] Because many of these activists were Jewish, and because some separatists expounded derogatory views about Jews rooted in a fundamentalist Christian tradition and promoted by the Nation of Islam, many Jews viewed the separatist decision as not only anti-white, but also anti-Semitic. For most Jewish (and many other white) civil rights organizations, separatism confirmed their sense that African Americans were moving away from the pluralist vision they had shared.

Furthermore, if Hasia Diner is correct that Jews considered African Americans a test case for American democracy—if black people can be accepted here, so can Jews—then the shift to a black particularism made Jews uneasy also because it implied that America had failed the test.[26] Jews failed to recognize their own particularism, in the form of support for Israel and Jewish institutions in general, and thus incorrectly concluded that they and African Americans were moving in completely different and incompatible directions.

Most liberal Jewish organizations had long been suspicious of the more militant side of African American protest; they had counseled against CORE's 1947 Journey of Reconciliation,[27] the Montgomery Bus Boycott, mass marches, and sit-ins. In every case Jewish groups reversed themselves in time, but each instance of hesitation reveals Jewish fears that black groups might be more revolutionary than reformist, more confrontational than moderate. Black Power confirmed these fears, as did several occasions of direct black-Jewish confrontation, such as the conflict in Brooklyn's Ocean Hill-Brownsville school district in 1968 which pitted a primarily black community against a primarily Jewish teachers' union. Beginning as a struggle over community control of schools, the tensions escalated with the discovery of anti-Semitic pamphlets and agitators. The United Federation of Teachers (UFT) and the ADL redefined the confrontation from one between a community and the educational establishment to one between blacks and Jews, and they distributed copies of the anti-Semitic handbills widely. On radio station WBAI in New York, Julius Lester invited a black teacher to read his student's anti-Semitic poem on the air. Once again issues of class were clearly present but generally unarticulated. For Jews caught up in the fray, the issue was one of anti-Semitism or anti-white sentiment, with Jews as victim. For community members, Jewish teachers represented the unresponsive and racist power structure: villains or puppets but certainly not victims.[28]

Pluralism emerged as an explicit issue in the debacle. The local black teachers' organization, the African-American Teachers Association, criticized the teaching methods of the white teachers, represented by the UFT. As Jerald Podair, a student of the issue, explained: "The ATA argued that the UFT's pluralist model was far from the cultural empty vessel it purported to be; the very act of embracing race-neutral humanism, of denying important cultural differences between groups, was itself a choice of white-dominated culture."[29] African American residents and Jewish union members screaming at each other across the barricades embodied to many the sharp divergence between the two communities.

The affirmative-action cases of the 1970s confirmed that divergence and made it clear that the schism between the two groups was not marginal or confined to militants. Marco De Funis Jr., a Sephardic Jew, was denied admission to the University of Washington Law School; Allan Bakke was a white Vietnam veteran denied admission to the Medical School of the University of California at Davis. Both sued, arguing that accepting non-whites with lower scores constituted reverse discrimination by the admissions offices. In both cases (*De Funis v. Odegaard*, 1974; *Regents of the University of California v. Bakke*, 1978), black organizations filed amicus curiae briefs on behalf of the university's affirmative-action policies while most Jewish agencies filed briefs in opposition.[30] It was the first time black and Jewish organizations had publicly and formally positioned themselves on opposite sides of a civil rights question.

For Jews the issue was clear. Not only were affirmative-action programs that involved admissions set-asides or quotas reminders of many colleges'

Jewish quotas in the earlier part of the century, they were wrong for the same reason that earlier quotas had been wrong: such programs violated the spirit of the race-blind pluralism Jews still endorsed. They viewed numerically based affirmative-action programs as a retreat from the faith that in the absence of discriminatory rules, all individuals would enjoy full and equal access to the rights and privileges of American life. If university administrators did not view black candidates simply as candidates, without regard to their race, the remedy lay in educating or penalizing the administrators, not setting quotas. In other words, enforcing race blindness should be the response to discrimination. Instead, affirmative-action rules as they existed required that administrators return to an explicit consideration of ancestry, which was as offensive to Jews in this instance as it had been when such considerations had been used to exclude them. (Jewish groups did not oppose affirmative-action programs that sought to broaden applicant pools or otherwise level the playing field. To put it in current terms, they opposed rules that enforced not equality of opportunity but equality of outcome.) Organized Jewry trusted that once rules and incentives were in place, those in power would operate in good faith.

These Jews' stand on affirmative action was entirely consistent with their view of the goal of the civil rights struggle. Committed to the right of black (or any other) candidates to embrace any aspect of their cultural heritage free of persecution, Jewish organizations nonetheless insisted that in any application process heritage could play no role. Thus they continued to file supporting briefs in desegregation and voting rights cases and to promote intercultural understanding through aggressive programming while steadfastly opposing any return to strategies that formally identified race or assigned individuals to fixed legal categories that were not of their own choosing.

Not only was such a race-blind, pluralist stance understandable for a community that had been itself persecuted and excluded on the basis of formal racial categories, it was a political strategy that had proven entirely successful for them. Most members of the Jewish community had moved into the middle and upper classes while maintaining whatever level of religious or cultural distinctiveness they chose.[31] While anti-Semitism remained, barriers to full acceptance were coming down everywhere. In fact even the negative sentiment that remained in some sense verified Jewish success in America. Twenty-one percent of Christian Americans polled in 1990 believed Jews wielded too much power in the United States. While this belief is an old anti-Semitic canard that reinforces Jews' sense of vulnerability, it nonetheless attests to the power and visibility some Jews had in fact achieved.[32] Ironically, some Jews now believe assimilationist pluralism proved too much of a good thing for Jews. As the intermarriage rate continues to rise and synagogue affiliation to drop, as more Jews choose not to live their lives as Jewish in any communal way, many are pressing to bolster Jewish self-identification (Jewish "continuity"), in some sense a separatist or nationalist position, while continuing to demand equal access to the goods of society. But Jews have not budged on their commitment to the other component of pluralism: voluntary or self-chosen identity. If Jews viewed themselves as in any sense a biologically defined group, concern for Jewish continuity would be unnecessary: an intermarried Jew would nonetheless remain a Jew.

African American commitment to affirmative action, by contrast, reflected the growing distrust many felt of assimilationist pluralism or of integration as originally conceived. They could not feel as sanguine about white goodwill. Why would those whites in power, who had historically discriminated against black people, suddenly become race blind because the laws had changed? The slow progress of desegregation and fierce white resistance to it proved their suspicions to be justified; this critique helped build the theoretical structure for multiculturalism. Affirmative action, including set-asides, was crucial to close the gap between the rhetoric of race blindness and the reality of continued discrimination. For African Americans the pluralist or integrationist vision had proven far less effective than it had for Jews, as well as less morally persuasive. For most whites, race continued to act as a relevant and biologically determined category rather than as a private and voluntary identity. Even if blacks wanted to "choose" to ignore or forgo their blackness (whatever that meant), most whites would not allow them to. And so long as the standards for theoretically race-blind admission to social goods were set by whites, it was not clear that those standards were race blind at all. They often required information and skills most whites had greater access to (such as standardized tests that—for a fee—could be coached), and they protected white privilege (in the form, for example, of college admissions preferences for alumni children, homeowner lending rules that protected existing residential patterns, or nepotism in union hall hiring). In other words, the meritocracy that Jews—and others opposed to affirmative action—believe must be reinstated is itself a myth. Here was the structural racism—racism embedded within American institutions themselves—that black activists were challenging. To fully succeed in the existing system blacks had to become, for all intents and purposes, white, something not only undesirable but in any case made impossible by personal and structural racism.

As CORE's national director James Farmer wrote in 1965, "America would become color blind when we gave up our color. The white man, who presumably was no color, would have to give up only his prejudices. We would have to give up our identities."[33] The roots of multiculturalism lay in the limitations of pluralism.

Michael Omi and Howard Winant make a similar point using slightly different terms which links the inadequacy of pluralism with the growing attraction in a portion of the black community for "group rights" (affirmative action is an example of such a program). A political redress for the failure of integration, the concept of group rights moved the emerging theory of multiculturalism still further from pluralism, given the latter's focus on the individual as the locus of struggle. These scholars argue that racial theory in the United States has been based on an ethnic paradigm or immigrant analogy that claims that once discriminatory barriers fall, blacks like white immigrants will be able to rise. These theories ignore or deny the effects of structural racism and therefore rest on the false assumption that individual action is the only significant variable in overcoming disadvantage. As the authors point out, "Many blacks (and later, many Latinos, Indians, and Asian Americans as well) rejected *ethnic* identity in favor of a more *racial* identity which demanded group rights and recognition. Given these developments, ethnicity theory found itself increasingly in opposition to the demands of minority movements." While not necessarily conversant with the theory, Black Power leaders made exactly this argument. Because the notion of an individual meritocracy was so patently false, they insisted, blacks must be compensated as a community, not as a group of disparate individuals.[34]

For these skeptics of pluralism, Jews revealed their true social position as insiders by virtue of their class and their race. Jews might still see themselves as outsiders, but to most on the outside, the Jewish establishment had become cozy with power. They had embraced, knowingly or unknowingly, the attitudes and values of the dominant society, confusing meritocracy with white privilege. These Jews attributed their own success solely to hard work and personal commitment, ignoring the structural constraints race imposed on opportunity. Jewish economic standing had shifted solidly into the middle class and if Jewish voting patterns remained far more liberal than those of their middle-class gentile counterparts (evidence of Jews' continued sense of vulnerability and distrust of Republican social conservatism), they nevertheless began to move rightward, a trend that continues today.[35] Indeed Jewish organizations were, if anything, more liberal on matters of race than their constituents. As a 1960 AJCongress report on black-Jewish tensions warned: "Despite the deep commitment of Jewish community relations agencies and their genuine efforts to reach and teach equality, there is a wide and alarming gap between the leadership and the rank and file in the Jewish community; and in the Negro community too."[36]

Meanwhile, class differences between blacks and Jews widened. The tensions produced by Jews' continued economic and political power over blacks as store owners, employers, and landlords in black communities, as union leaders, social workers and teachers, were exacerbated as Jews continued to rise economically and African Americans did not rise with them. Economic success also brought social success and by the 1960s large numbers of Jews were moving to the suburbs, joining or building country clubs, and enjoying the privileges of their new status. And although they continued to report less racist views than other whites, they nonetheless engaged in the social segregation of blacks that white Christians had made a tradition. As the AJCongress noted in 1960:

Prominent Negroes have been excluded from predominantly Jewish clubs and . . . the best known builder of "whites only" suburban developments is William Levitt. . . .
When Negroes start to move into predominantly Jewish areas, they often encounter resentment. Genuine social acceptance by Jews is at a minimum and, generally, we find the usual fear, panic and flight to the suburbs. In such situations Jews act, in the main, like other whites.[37]

Indeed, some of the explanation for the growing estrangement of blacks and Jews lies in the fact that Jews have in fact been becoming more "white," or in any case, less decidedly "Other"—visible, for example, in the decline in Jewish charitable giving to explicitly Jewish organizations. Thus Jews have moved away from a civil rights agenda in part because it is no longer personally useful. Although self-interest is hardly unusual, the anger of black Americans is particularly acute because Jews never used self-interest as an explanation for their civil rights involvement, preferring a rhetoric of liberalism which insisted that they acted out of morality and altruism. Thus when Jews are revealed to be self-interested, it seems a betrayal, as Jerald Podair argued in the case of Ocean Hill-Brownsville.

In a further indication of the distance between blacks and Jews, if the decline in Jewish giving suggests the declining importance of the concept of diaspora for Jews, its importance has grown for blacks as the civil rights promise has seemed to fail. In other words, as Jews have felt increasingly at home in the United States, many African Americans are coming to the conclusion that they may never feel at home. Yet the black-Jewish split, understandable as it is, is nonetheless a tragedy and bodes ill for progressive political projects. If the civil rights movement was an attempt to build a multiracial, multiethnic democracy, Clayborne Carson has argued, blacks and Jews are central to it because they were the first groups to suggest its possibility. But as the prospects for such a democracy appear increasingly dim, disillusionment spreads, as does resentment of former partners and rejection of any part of the process of coalition.[38]

The conviction that the power structure could not be relied on and that race was the central cleavage in American society reinvigorated black nationalist sentiment. If the more confrontational political programs of the Black Panthers and others had come unraveled, ideological and cultural nationalism gained a strong following as African Americans moved to reclaim their own heritage and to foster greater intragroup cohesion and unity. Always a part of black American thinking, such pride in blackness reclaimed center stage by the 1970s, visible, for example, in such divergent venues as the Black Arts movement and more recently Afrocentrism.

The Black Pride movement of the 1960s and 1970s and the other ethnic and racial pride movements that followed it (including one among Jews) put the final touches on a multicultural theory that would challenge pluralism. Taking the lessons of the civil rights movement to heart, the first and most vocal proponents of multiculturalism posited race as the central division among Americans, argued for a commonality of interests among all nonwhite groups, whom they defined as outsiders, and challenged the prevailing "Eurocentric" view of Western civilization. Multiculturalists stressed the diverse contributive streams that created and shaped American culture and they redrew the lines dividing inside and outside in American life. Now all whites were part of Euro-America: ethnic, regional, and religious divisions subsumed under the racial category that ensured power and privilege. Outsiders were nonwhite groups—black, Asian, Native American, Latino/a. Like "European," these racialized categories also lumped together distinctive cultural groups—Japanese and Koreans, historically antagonists, were homogenized as "Asians," while "African American" ignores distinctions between southern- and northern-born, Protestant, Catholic, Jewish, and Muslim blacks and even includes those (such as West Indians) who trace their heritage from outside the United States.

Multiculturalism celebrates diversity and is an important curative to traditional views of American and Western culture as shaped exclusively by white Europeans. It critiques ethnocentrism and challenges the process of hero formation that whitewashes the bigotry and violence of the American and European past. It insists on the centrality of race and racism as explanatory agents in history and calls attention to the ongoing reality of discrimination and bigotry today. But the ways in which most versions of multiculturalism play down religion, region, class, ethnicity, and similar divisions, thereby narrowing difference to race, and the fact that some multiculturalists posit that difference as a fixed and universal social category trouble many who see a far more complex and fluid picture of what constitutes identity. Indeed, a number of scholars sympathetic to the goals of multiculturalism are beginning to level similar sorts of criticism against the oversimplified and essentialized versions of the theory which have gained such prominence in the public imagination.[39]

For Jews, who can still point to clear instances of anti-Semitic bigotry and discrimination, multiculturalists' insistence that Jews are American insiders is not only false but an insult to a group of people who have been staunch in their defense of outsider groups. On a more personal level, many Jews feel left out by multiculturalism, lumped as they are with those they have long fought to distance themselves from. These perspectives accept the basic assumptions of multiculturalism but argue that it is too narrow. Yet other Jewish critiques deny that multiculturalism is a legitimate world view at all. The insistence of some multiculturalists that racial categories are fixed reminds some outspoken Jewish critics, perhaps unfairly, of Nazi ideology. While some Jews who point to the disquieting reminder of Nazism are sincere in their objections to such essentialism, I believe that others, particularly those who disagree with the idea that racism is implacable and qualitatively different from ethnic discrimination, use such rhetoric in order to inflame the debate. What bringing in the Holocaust as a metaphor or comparison does is return Jews and Jewish experience to the center of the debate and also raises the stakes. Who can support the multiculturalist claim that race has acted as a fixed category in America if such a belief brands one as a Nazi? Nevertheless, there is a real issue here. These Jews are objecting to living in a society that categorizes and essentializes people based on accidents of birth. Jews have had a long history as victims of such categorization and have seen its most horrific consequences played out on members of their own group in this century. In fact, Jewish love for America is based in large measure on its at least legal and rhetorical insistence that rights and privileges accrue to individuals rather than groups. Multiculturalism (and its intellectual if not actual offspring, affirmative action) reverses this. It does so because the United States has in fact always categorized and essentialized — but for Jews, for whom American categories have for the most part been irrelevant or invisible, this feels new, dangerous, and contrary to the spirit of America as they understand it.

This Jewish critique of categorization based on their victim status is certainly a fair one (although their refusal to acknowledge that racial categories predated multiculturalism renders that critique less persuasive). Nevertheless, Jews have not been consistent in their self-portrayal. While they have indeed suffered in the United States, Jews have also stressed the exceptional nature of America, its benign protections and their resulting security, when that has proved most useful. Jews' appeal to victimhood in this case, while honest, has not been the only interpretation of Jewish life in America. It has been employed when it served to justify their position.

For most multiculturalists these objections ring hollow. Every American institution has been shaped by essentializing categorization and racial exclusion; multiculturalism simply calls attention to this and seeks redress. As for Jews' exclusion from the multicultural circle, they argue that religious and ethnic differences have clearly been minimized, if not erased entirely, by the privileges that have accrued to all whites in this country by virtue of their race and by the racism that has continued to shape the lives of all black people (and Latinos, Asians, Native Americans) in similar ways.

There are other problems that stand in the way of resolving the controversy. Both pluralists and multiculturalists fail to integrate class fully into their analysis, and thus they miss a good deal of the story. Religion, ethnicity, race, and the other divisions they recognize play out differently at different class levels both in how they are expressed and how they are viewed by others. For example, the racial violence in Boston after the imposition of busing would not have occurred in wealthier suburbs because whites in those suburbs have enough political clout to prevent a busing decree, because ethnic solidarity and clustering is usually less pronounced in upper-income communities, and because if busing did occur racist whites would have the wherewithal to send their children to private schools.

And class underlies a great deal of the dynamics usually attributed simply to race relations. For example, it is precisely because a serious discussion of class is left out of the analysis that our current political discourse considers "poor" and "African American" virtually synonymous. For blacks and Jews, much of their tension has come from their widely divergent class positions and the different beliefs about access to opportunity one gets from each vantage point, but this difference in perspective is rarely addressed or even acknowledged. Despite the important insights both pluralism and multiculturalism have provided, class remains the dirty little secret of American life.

For both Jews and blacks pluralism provided a useful, if ill-defined approach to American racial and ethnic relations, one that advocated full public integration and celebrated differences that were held voluntarily and did not threaten the essential unanimity over central American beliefs. In pursuit of their goals blacks and Jews worked together as well as separately on broad civil rights and civil liberties issues. Yet beneath their apparent unity lay divisions based on class, race, religion, historical experience, and access to white privilege. These divisions, always problematic, came to a head in the 1960s and 1970s as African American organizations began moving away from their earlier endorsement of pluralism while Jews continued to hold fast to it. Blacks and Jews held their divergent positions for the same reason: the impact of pluralist efforts on their community. Jews had benefited from policies designed to enforce blindness to race and religion, while African Americans enjoyed far more limited success and at greater cost. One reason Jews held onto assimilative pluralism for a longer time than most African Americans may be that the idea of assimilating into the values of the reigning culture was less distasteful to Jews, racist though it may have been. That is, Jews could see anti-Semitism as an aberration in an otherwise inviting social system. For many blacks racism was too deeply implicated in American social structure to see that culture as quite so desirable.

As pluralism gave way to multiculturalism as the dominant paradigm in recent decades, in academic scholarship religion and ethnicity similarly gave way to race as society's most fundamental divide. It would be hard to imagine a book today arguing, as Will Herberg did in 1955, that religion represented the greatest remaining division in America and that the country could be best understood as three melting pots: Protestant, Catholic, and Jewish.[40] Because of their class and their race Jews and blacks have been placed by most multiculturalists on opposite sides of this great racial divide, one that unlike most pluralist conceptions is often depicted as biologically determined and permanently unbridgeable. Liberal Jews, who hold to pluralism because they still view themselves as outsiders or at least vulnerable, consider their placement inside the power structure intolerable. African Americans see Jews' economic and social success and their opposition to affirmative action, the teeth of antidiscrimination, as clear evidence of the Jews' position as insider and so view Jews' sense of vulnerability simply as paranoia. Position is everything in the multicultural debate as it is in race relations—where you are determines what you see.

Or perhaps, as Jerald Podair argues regarding the conflict in Ocean Hill-Brownsville, the issue is the inability to "see" at all.

The teachers failed to see that, to their adversaries . . . "objective standards" and "race-blind merit principles" were canards, designed to perpetuate their disempowerment—America was never "race-blind" and "equality of opportunity" was a myth, a cruel joke. . . . [I]t was not so much the teachers' unwillingness to accept differing black definitions of "equality" that was so tragic, but their inability to "see" their position at all, to suppress the urge to use Jewish reference points to explain a uniquely black experience.[41]

Jews have by and large been unable to see that African Americans desire what Jews already have—the right to embrace difference and yet enjoy access to power. Jews do not recognize the extent to which pluralism, operating within a racialized state, has denied both black identity and black access to political and economic advancement. African Americans remain the Other in the most profound sense. America's ostensible race-blind pluralism, while proving an effective challenge to legal racism, after the 1964 Civil Rights Act could no longer serve as a useful guideline for achieving an egalitarian society because it did not recognize the depth and intractability of America's racial divide. Nor did it acknowledge that racial inequality was in many ways bound up with class inequality. In other words, American pluralism simply has not brought true equality, and it will not, without a complete dismantling of all aspects of race- and class-based hierarchy, from their institutional and overt manifestations to individual and private ones. Until that messianic moment, black people, constrained not because of their individual characters but because of their group membership and place in the socioeconomic structure, will only advance within a system that explicitly recognizes that membership and in some cases provides advances based on it.

To the extent that Jews understand themselves not only as successful navigators of a meritocracy but also as liberals with a vision of a race-blind messianic age, this multiculturalism is a painful and difficult concept to embrace. To the extent that multiculturalism denies them a place and indeed may hinder their continued advancement, Jews' self-interest precludes an endorsement of it. Yet as long as multiculturalism offers the only tenable vision for both black success and black identity in a relentlessly racialized nation, as long as it seeks more equitable access to power, those Jews who care about racial equality will have to continue to argue for it.

Yet multiculturalism must resolve issues of its own. Its reluctance to acknowledge the salience of nonracial forms of oppression, its problematic claim of fixed and single racial identities, and its implicit retreat from the rhetorical ideal of multiracial equality (even if historically honored only in the breach) leave it an imperfect vehicle for progressive politics. Furthermore, the reductive and essentialist form of multiculturalism characterized by the "United Colors of Benetton" trivializes difference as it commodifies it.[42]

These concerns are not merely academic. The many misperceptions and even self-delusions that fuel the multiculturalism debate threaten the stability of the American polity. The fact is that Jews have moved to the inside in a society that still has an outside. Yet many Jews still perceive themselves as at least partly outside. (One needs only to call to mind the Christian Coalition to understand that sense of vulnerability.) Multiculturalism recognizes only the first reality, of Jews as insiders, and Jews feel angry because they recognize only the second, their continued position as outsiders. But it is crucial for both sides to come to understand Jewish vulnerability *and* Jewish security, the simultaneity of Jewish insider and outsider status in America, so they can begin to work together rather than at cross purposes. One reason for cooperation is obvious. Blacks and Jews remain the most reliable liberal voters; the only way to further the political agenda they both share is to shore up their historical political partnership. Or, to cast the argument less parochially, Jews and those marginalized communities identified by multiculturalists have a common interest in promoting political agendas that are inclusive and that protect minority interests.

But there are other reasons it is imperative to try to resolve these differences. The problems symbolized by the "culture wars" go well beyond blacks and Jews or minority groups in general. All Americans must stop viewing race as a fixed category, for it lacks biological validity and poses a danger to our civil society. We must challenge pluralism, since it rests on troubling assimilationist elements and refuses to directly confront the obduracy of racial barriers. Yet multiculturalism, which usefully challenges white ethnocentrism, introduces distortions and exclusions of its own that must be addressed, and, like pluralism, presents a muddy and ill-defined ideology. Finally, we must directly confront the impact of class, without which none of these issues can be fully explicated.

The experience of Jews as simultaneous insiders and outsiders, both victims of and members of a privileged class, can strengthen multicultural theory by reinforcing the multicultural commitment to hybridity and highlighting the complex, shifting, and voluntary nature of identity. At the same time multiculturalism can remind Jews of two crucial points we sometimes act as if we had forgotten: that our own status is liminal and always in flux and, paradoxically, that we have unreflectively enjoyed the privileges of a "Euro-American" whiteness we have denied. Whether we admit it or not, Jews have moved farther to the inside in American society than we have ever been before, and our politics has been affected by that apparent security, as the history of black-Jewish relations makes clear. Before we move too quickly to embrace a monocultural assimilationism that could spell our doom, we need to reflect on the lessons multiculturalism can teach us.

Notes

1. I would like to thank Barbara Sicherman, Jeffrey Melnick, Herbert Hill, Adolph Reed, Michael Galchinsky, David Biale, and the anonymous readers of the book manuscript for their many helpful comments and suggestions. "Hidden injuries of class" is borrowed from Richard Sennett and Jonathan Cobb, *The Hidden Injuries of Class* (New York, 1972).

2. David Theo Goldberg, "Introduction: Multicultural Conditions," in *Multiculturalism: A Critical Reader,* ed. Goldberg (Cambridge, Mass., 1994), 7.

3. Ibid.

4. *Bataan* (1943), directed by Tay Garnett, distributed by MGM. Similarly, *Air Force,* a Warner Bros. production (1943). For an excellent discussion of the history of pluralism as an idea, see Philip Gleason, *Speaking of Diversity: Language and Ethnicity in Twentieth-Century America* (Baltimore, 1992). Also see Werner Sollors, "A Critique of Pure Pluralism," in *Reconstructing American Literary History,* ed. Sacvan Bercovitch (Cambridge, Mass., 1986), 250–279; Michael Omi and Howard Winant, *Racial Formation in the United States from the 1960s to the 1990s,* 2d ed. (New York, 1994). The term "Anglo-conformist" comes from Milton Gordon, *Assimilation in American Life: The Role of Race, Religion, and National Origins* (New York, 1964), 88–114.

5. Horace Kallen's original formulation of pluralism was essentialist; he shifted toward a more voluntary notion of identity by the 1950s: see, for example, Kallen, *Culture and Democracy in the United States* (New York, 1924), 122–123; Kallen, *Cultural Pluralism and the American Idea* (Philadelphia, 1956).

6. On the biology of race see Michael Blakely, "Ideologies of Race and Ethnicity," paper presented at "Race and Ethnicity: Relations between African Americans and Ethnic Groups in American Society," German Historical Institute, Washington, D.C., 22 September 1994. Also see the works of anthropologists and biologists like Stephen Jay Gould. Omi and Winant, *Racial Formation in the U.S.,* 55. Also see F. James Davis, *Who Is Black? One Nation's Definition* (University Park, Penn., 1991).

7. For an interesting discussion of Jews and multiculturalism which criticizes both the political nature of multiculturalism and the failure of Jews to adequately represent themselves and their history in America, see Stephen Whitfield, "Multiculturalism and American Jews," *[American Jewish] Congress Monthly,* September/October 1995, pp. 7–10. Obviously, my discussion necessarily overgeneralizes. I am describing, for the most part, middle-class, white nonimmigrant Jews.

8. Many scholars and writers have considered the question of black-Jewish relations. Only a subset of those are based on careful historical research. These include Peter Rose, "Blacks and Jews: The Strained Alliance," *The Annals* 454 (March 1981): 55–69; Hasia Diner, *In the Almost Promised Land* (Westport, Conn., 1977); Robert Weisbord and Arthur Stein,

Bittersweet Encounter (Westport, Conn., 1970); Jonathan Kaufman, *Broken Alliance: The Turbulent Times between Blacks and Jews in America* (New York, 1988); Joseph Washington Jr., *Jews in Black Perspectives* (Teaneck, N.J., 1984); Murray Friedman, *What Went Wrong? The Creation and Collapse of the Black-Jewish Alliance* (Philadelphia, 1995); Nat Hentoff, ed., *Black Anti-Semitism and Jewish Racism* (New York, 1969); Paul Berman, *Blacks and Jews: Alliances and Arguments* (New York, 1994); David Levering Lewis, "Parallels and Divergences," *Journal of American History* 71 (December 1984): 543–564; Cheryl Greenberg, "Ambivalent Allies," in *Black Resistance Movements in the U.S. and Africa*, ed. Felton Best (New York, 1995), and "Negotiating Coalition," in *Struggles in the Promised Land: Toward a History of Black-Jewish Relations in the United States* ed. Jack Salzman and Cornel West (New York, 1997).

9. Louis Brandeis and Horace Kallen are two examples of men both integrationist and Zionist. For a fuller discussion of Brandeis, see Philippa Strum, *Brandeis: Beyond Progressivism* (Lawrence, Kansas, 1993). For a sample of Brandeis's own writing on such subjects, see Strum, ed., *Brandeis on Democracy* (Lawrence, 1995). On Kallen see Sollors, "A Critique of Pure Pluralism," 265–266.

10. Quoted from Leonard Dinnerstein, Roger Nichols, and David Reimers, *Natives and Strangers,* 2d ed. (New York, 1990), 188.

11. For more detail on these and similar programs see the minutes of the ADL Program Division and National Executive Committee in ADL papers, warehouse box 178, ADL library, New York, New York, and programs of the AJC in the AJC library, New York, New York. On Jews and internment, see Cheryl Greenberg, "Black and Jewish Responses to Japanese Internment," *Journal of American Ethnic History* 14 (Winter 1995): 3–37.

12. Sidney Hollander to David Robinson, 18 December 1947, regarding support of the National Urban League: ADL microfilm "Yellows 1947: Negro Race Problems" (hereafter Y 1947 NRP), ADL library.

13. See, for example, the records of the New York branch of the Universal Negro Improvement Association, at the Schomburg Center for Research in Black Culture (hereafter Schomburg), New York, New York.

14. Lloyd Garrison, "Progress Report of the Committee on Urban League Policy," 22 July 1954, NUL papers, box 11–5, Library of Congress Manuscripts Division, Washington, D.C. Black pluralist organizations, like Jewish ones, also had their assimilationist side. See, for example, E. Franklin Frazier, *The Negro in the United States,* rev. ed. (New York, 1957), 681, and Gunnar Myrdal, *An American Dilemma,* Twentieth Anniversary Edition (New York, 1962), 927–930.

15. Crusader News Agency dispatches are located at the Schomburg. Papers of the NCNW can be found at the Mary McLeod Bethune Museum and Archives, Washington, D.C. Against anti-Semitism: see, for example, A. Philip Randolph, "Our Guest Column," American Press Associates, 23 April 1946, ADL micro Y 1946 NRP; William Pickens, "'Wolfing It' on Our Friends," 8 July 1935, article prepared for the American Negro Press, Pickens papers, micro R996, reel 4, box 8, Schomburg; "Resolutions Adopted at the War-time Conference of the National Association for the Advancement of Colored People," 12–16 July 1944, p. 11, NAACP papers, box II A 28, Library of Congress Manuscripts Division.

16. See, for example, Eleanor Wolf, Vin Loving, and Donald Marsh, *Negro-Jewish Relationships,* pamphlet (Wayne State Studies in Intergroup Conflicts in Detroit #1, 1944), p. 7, AJC Inactive Vertical File: Negro Jewish Relations (hereafter VF: NJR), AJC library, New York, New York; Eleanor Wolf, Vin Loving, and Donald Marsh, "Some Aspects of Negro-Jewish Relationships in Detroit, Michigan," Part I, 1943, ADL Micro Y 1944 NRP; James Robinson, "Some Apprehension, Much Hope," *ADL Bulletin,* December 1957, pp. 4, 6; L. D. Reddick, "Anti-Semitism among Negroes," *Negro Quarterly,* Summer 1942, pp. 113–117; Harry Lyons, "Jewish-Negro Relationships in the Post War Period," n.d., ADL Micro Y 1944 NRP; Elmo Roper, "The Fortune Survey," *Fortune,* November 1942 and October 1947; H. L. Lurie, "Introductory Report on the Study Project of Negro-Jewish Relationships," 9 December 1943, AJC VF: NJR: "AJC 1938–1969," and ADL Micro Y 1943 NRP;

Nathan Edelstein, "Jewish Relationship with the Emerging Negro Community in the North," 23 June 1960, pp. 3, 7, AJC VF: NJR: "AJCongress."

17. See, for example, Roy Wilkins to Walter White, memorandum, 25 March 1938, NAACP I C 208; Walter White to Cordell Hull, telegram, 25 March 1938, NAACP I C 208; George Schuyler, "Abuses of Colored Citizens in U.S," *World-Telegram*, 21 November 1938; NAACP, "NAACP Secretary Denounces Nazi Pogroms; Says All Must Unite to Protect Minority Rights Here and Save Democracy," press release, 18 November 1938[?], NAACP I C 208.

18. ADL ad: Harold Schiff to Frank Trager, 30 October 1947, ADL Y 1947 NRP. Weeds ad: *ADL Bulletin*, February 1946, p. 5. Blacks in combat: Myron Harshaw, Transitads, Inc., to George Schuyler (director of the association), 30 June 1943, Schuyler papers, box 6, Schomburg archives. Other examples of intergroup relations efforts: see the records of the Jewish Labor Committee, Tamiment Library, NYU, New York, New York; AJC's Intercultural Affairs Committee, at the AJC library; NCJW in the Library of Congress Manuscript Division; AJCongress, Commission on Law and Social Action, at the AJCongress library, New York, New York; ADL Intercultural Relations Department in the ADL library. For the specific undertakings described in the text, see, for example, Shad Polier, "Law and Social Action," *Congress Weekly* 17 (27 November 1950): 3; Dan Dodson, "Legislating against College Quotas," *Congress Weekly* 17 (27 November 1950): 7–9; ADL *Bulletin*, February/March 1948, April/May 1949, and May 1950; John Slawson, "AJC Oral Memoirs," 19 June 1969, pp. 34–36, New York Public Library, Jewish Division, New York, New York; Will Maslow to Walter White, 1 December 1947, NAACP II A 360; *New York Times*, 14 March 1948, p. 57; *Brown v. Board of Education* 347 U.S 483 (1954).

19. Walter White to Irvin Mollison, 11 December 1935, NAACP II L 7; Charles Houston to Ovrum Tapper, 5 December 1938, NAACP I C 208; Walter White, "Report of the Secretary to the Board of Directors for the October Meeting of the Board," 5 October 1939, p. 4, NAACP I A 18. Letters from Walter White to black leaders around the country (including Mollison, above) and their replies can all be found in NAACP II L 7.

20. The ADL Micro Y 1941 NRP files, for example, have examples of black anger against Jews from Washington, D.C., Baltimore, New York, Chicago, Miami, and elsewhere. Further instances are in the files for each year of the next decade and a half. Also see AJC VF: "Anti-Semitism" and Inactive VF: NJR; Cheryl Greenberg, "Class Tensions and the Black-Jewish 'Alliance' 1940–1955," Organization of American Historians, Annual Meeting (Atlanta, Georgia, April 1994); Reddick, "Anti-Semitism among Negroes," 116; Wolf, Loving, and Marsh, "Some Aspects"; Kenneth Clark, "A Positive Transition," *ADL Bulletin*, December 1957, p. 6. The problem of apparently racist Jewish behavior was particularly acute in the south, where Jews for the most part did indeed act just like other white people. See, for example, Harry Golden, "The Jews of the South," *[AJ] Congress Weekly* 18 (31 December 1951); Cheryl Greenberg, "Southern Jews and Civil Rights," in *Blacks and Jews in American History*, ed., Nancy Grant and V. P. Franklin (forthcoming, 1998).

21. For a superb discussion of structural racism and the blindness of many white ethnics to it, see Micaela di Leonardo, "White Lies, Black Myths: Rape, Race, and the Black 'Underclass,'" *Village Voice*, 22 September 1992, pp. 29–36.

22. See, for example, H. E. Trevvett to Mr. ___ [sic], 18 February 1942, NAACP II A 360. For joint efforts see, for example, the Bureau on Jewish Employment Problems in Chicago, "Placement Experiences of Applicants to a Private Employment Agency," September 1955, in AJC VF: "Community Files." Also see New York State Commission against Discrimination and Brooklyn's Jewish Community Council's Committee on Community Relations in AJC VF: "Community Files."

23. Chuck McDew, "Thou Shalt Not Resist," in Bud Schultz and Ruth Schultz, *It Did Happen Here: Recollections of Political Repression in America* (Berkeley, 1989), 53. Carmichael, a longtime SNCC activist, became the organization's chairman in 1966, and Honorary Prime Minister for the Black Panther party in 1967.

24. Emphasis in original. Stokely Carmichael and Charles Hamilton, *Black Power: The*

Politics of Liberation in America (New York, 1967), 37 (redefinition), 40–41 (middle-class values).

25. For example, see ADL, "Fact Sheet II: The Negro Revolt," 1 January 1963, p. 1, ADL Micro "Chisub" Reel 12. The expulsion of whites from these organizations was hotly contested by many black members, and in any case it was not simply a reflection of antiwhite sentiment.

26. Diner, *In the Almost Promised Land,* and remarks at meeting of the W. E. B. Du Bois Institute Working Group on Black-Jewish Relations, 8 September 1995, Los Angeles, California.

27. Journey of Reconciliation: black and white CORE volunteers rode through the South together on buses testing the Supreme Court decision of 1946 finding segregated interstate travel unconstitutional. Jewish opposition: Samuel Markle to William Sachs, 28 December 1946; George Harrison to J. Harold Saks, memorandum, 20 March 1947, p. 2; Sol Rabkin to George Houser, 13 November 1947, all ADL Y 1947 NRP. The NAACP also opposed the Journey plan at first: "Negroes Cautioned on Resistance Idea," *New York Times,* 23 November 1946, p. 17.

28. There are many—and conflicting—accounts of the Ocean Hill-Brownsville conflict, including that of Jerald Podair, "Like Strangers: Blacks, Whites, and New York City's Ocean Hill-Brownsville Controversy, 1965–1975," Ph.D. dissertation (in progress), Princeton University; see also Kaufman, *Broken Alliance,* chapter 4; Friedman, *What Went Wrong?* chapter 12; Julius Lester, *Lovesong: Becoming a Jew* (New York, 1988), chapter 6.

29. Jerald Podair, "'White' Values, 'Black' Values: The Ocean Hill-Brownsville Controversy and New York City Culture, 1965–1975," *Radical History Review* 59 (1994): 51.

30. The Union of American Hebrew Congregations and the NCJW filed briefs in support of affirmative action. *De Funis v. Odegaard* 416 U.S. 312 (1974); *Regents of the University of California v. Bakke* 438 U.S. 265 (1978).

31. By any measure of middle-class status—level of education, earnings, proportion in professional and managerial ranks—by the end of the 1960s Jews outperformed most other groups in the United States. See Sidney Goldstein, "American Jewry 1970: A Demographic Profile," in *American Jewish Yearbook,* 1971, ed. Morris Fine and Milton Himmelfarb (New York, 1971); Nathan Glazer, "The American Jew and the Attainment of Middle-Class Rank: Some Trends and Explanations," in *The Jews: Social Patterns of an American Group,* ed. Marshall Sklare (New York, 1958), 138–146; Thomas Sowell, ed., *Essays and Data on American Groups* (Washington, D.C., 1978), 364–365; Thomas Sowell, *Ethnic America: A History* (New York, 1981), 5, 98.

32. Jennifer Golub, *British Attitudes toward Jews and Other Minorities* (New York, 1993), 5, reported in Stephen Whitfield, "Multiculturalism and the Jewish Question," paper presented at American Studies Association, Annual Meeting, 1994, p. 17.

33. James Farmer, *Freedom—When?* (New York, 1965), 87. Farmer, one of the "Big Four" civil rights leaders of the 1960s, was a cofounder of CORE, and became its national director in 1961.

34. Omi and Winant, *Racial Formation in the U.S.,* 20, emphasis in original. On Black Power: Lewis Killian, "Black Power and White Reactions: The Revitalization of Race-Thinking in the United States," *The Annals* 454 (March 1981): 42, 46–49. In the same issue Milton Gordon made similar arguments: "Models of Pluralism: The New American Dilemma," *Annals* 454 (March 1981): 178–188.

35. See, for example, the CBS/New York Times polls for the recent election years. Kathleen Frankovic, Director of Polling, CBS News, provided recent election figures. Sowell, *Ethnic America,* 99, offers earlier data. As more evidence of the rightward shift of some Jews, consider the heavily Jewish makeup of the neoconservative movement.

36. Edelstein, "Jewish Relationship with the Emerging Negro Community in the North," 5.

37. Ibid.

38. Podair, "The Failure to 'See': Jews, Blacks, and the Ocean Hill-Brownsville Controversy, 1968," pamphlet, American Jewish Committee and the Center for American Jewish History, Temple University, 1992, p. 7. Clayborne Carson: Remarks at meeting of the W. E. B. Du Bois Institute Working Group on Black-Jewish Relations, 9 September 1995, Los Angeles, California.

39. See, for example, Goldberg, ed., *Multiculturalism: A Critical Reader*, especially Peter McLaren's "White Terror and Oppositional Agency: Towards a Critical Multiculturalism," 45–74.

40. Will Herberg, *Protestant, Catholic, Jew: An Essay in American Religious Sociology* (New York, 1955).

41. Podair, "The Failure to 'See,'" 6.

42. The Benetton reference is not original to me. See, for example, David Goldberg, "Introduction," in *Multiculturalism,* 8; Chicago Cultural Studies Group, "Critical Multiculturalism," 115, in the same volume.

CHAPTER 4

Multiculturalism and the Politics of Interest

Michael Walzer

Thin Skins

Contemporary multiculturalism is not quite the same thing as the cultural pluralism championed by writers like Horace Kallen and John Dewey earlier in this century.[1] The notions certainly overlap; they probably point toward the same end state: the coexistence of different cultural groups. But multiculturalists are more edgy, nervous, militant than the old pluralists; they express a stronger sense of group oppression, a greater anxiety about cultural loss. Whereas Kallen was confident that the different groups would survive and prosper so long as they were let alone, so long as there was no state program of enforced "Americanization," multiculturalists want the state enlisted on the side of difference. They have a positive political agenda: they are committed to the "outing" of difference — this is their everyday political and intellectual work — and then they seek public recognition for all the previously suppressed and invisible differences.

Many of the groups that constitute multicultural America need governmental support in its most obvious form: tax money. Their most insistent demand, however, is for acknowledgment and respect. In contemporary multiculturalism the politics of interest is replaced or superseded by a politics of identity, where it is not the material condition of a group that is at issue but the value of a culture, history, or way of life. What the collective will is bent on avoiding is not exploitation or even impoverishment so much as insult and degradation, the social experience of "invisibility." Inevitably, rhetoric and gesture take on great importance. These are the double-edged swords of multicultural politics. *We* use them to tell ourselves (and the listening world) how good, strong, proud, and beautiful we are; *the others* use them to convict us of fear, laziness, greed, and violence. Hence the intensity of the debates about "hate speech" and "political correctness," an intensity that survives the ridicule of commentators and critics, since so many of the participants are convinced that words are really helpful or hurtful: the old rhyme about sticks and stones isn't convincing anymore. Hence also the new political emotions (I mean, newly surfaced, publicly expressed): not indignation, which implies a standard of justice, but resentment, offense, mortification, hurt feelings. It is hard to imagine a trade union official telling the representatives of management that their contract proposal has hurt his feelings and should therefore be withdrawn. But hurt feelings are political currency, money in the bank, in the world of multiculturalism.

There is not always enough money, of course, to get what one wants. A year or so ago a group of Jewish students from a nearby university came to me with a complaint: the local black students' organization had invited Louis Farrakhan to campus. The Jewish students were offended; their feelings were hurt. I tried to tell them that Farrakhan on campus would be a political event; they needed to work out an explicitly political response. But perhaps I was wrong. Perhaps Farrakhan had been invited precisely in order to hurt their feelings, in response to similar injuries, real or imagined, on the other side. I was looking for a political struggle, while what was really going on was much more personal. It wasn't a matter of power or interest; what mattered, in fact, were feelings. And so while the response of the Jewish students wasn't persuasive to their black fellows, didn't lead them to withdraw the Farrakhan invitation, it may nonetheless have been the proper response in this sense: that it registered with the blacks, the hurt was somehow acknowledged, it counted toward the next time. But I am still inclined to raise an older question: Was the actual well-being of either group served by this exchange?

In multicultural politics it is an advantage to be injured. Every injury, every act of discrimination or disrespect, every heedless, invidious, or malicious word is a kind of political entitlement, if not to reparation then at least to recognition. So one has to cultivate, as it were, a thin skin; it is important to be sensitive, irritable, touchy. But perhaps there is some deeper utility here. Thin skins are useful precisely because the cultural identities over which they are stretched don't have any very definite or substantive character. People are right to be worried about cultural loss. And because identity is so precarious in modern or postmodern America, because we are often so uncertain about who we are, we may well fail to register expressions of hostility, prejudice, or disfavor. Thin skin is the best protection: it provides the earliest possible signal of insults delivered and threats on the way. Like other early warning systems, of course, it also transmits false signals—and then a lot of time has to be spent in explanation and reassurance. But this too is part of the process of negotiating a difficult coexistence in a world where difference is nervously possessed and therefore often aggressively displayed.

Despite all the misunderstandings generated by the mix of nervous groups and thin-skinned individuals, there is something right about all this. Social peace should not be purchased at the price of fear, deference, passivity, and self-dislike—the feelings that standardly accompanied minority status in the past. The old left wanted to substitute anger at economic injustice for all these, but it is at least understandable that the actual substitute is the resentment of social insult. We want to be able and we ought to be able to live openly in the world, as we are, with dignity and confidence, without being demeaned or degraded in our everyday encounters. It may even be the case that dignity and confidence are preconditions for the fight against injustice.

So it is worth taking offense—I am not sure it is always worth feeling hurt—when demeaning and malicious things are said or done. But a permanent state of suspicion that demeaning and malicious things are about to be said or done is self-defeating. And it is probably also self-defeating to imagine that the long-term goal of recognition and respect is best reached directly, by aiming at and insisting on respect itself. (Indeed, the insistence is comic; Rodney Dangerfield has made a career out of it.) Consider the analogy of happiness, which we don't achieve, despite the Declaration of Independence, by "pursuing" it. We actually aim at goals like satisfying work and good relationships and particular pleasurable experiences, and if we find these, we are happy. Happiness is a by-product. Jon Elster has written extensively about ends of this sort, which can only be achieved indirectly and where focused effort may well be counterproductive, like *trying* to fall asleep.[2] People do not win respect by insisting that they are not respected enough.

What do groups need to do in order to be recognized and respected? (I shall write about individuals only as members of groups.) What should be the direct objects of their pursuit? They need a place in the world: legal standing, an institutional presence, resources. And then they need to coexist with other groups similarly "placed," roughly equal to themselves. The others are necessary, obviously, since they must do the recognizing and respecting, and then they will want to be recognized and respected in turn. The only satisfactory basis for this regime of mutual respect is some kind of equality—not of numbers or even of wealth (though gross inequalities of wealth make multiculturalism very difficult) but of standing and presence. There will still be problems about the politics and also about the etiquette of coexistence, the sharing of public space, access to public funding, and so on. And there will still be group hostility and conflict. But when these are addressed from positions of strength, rhetoric and gesture are likely to be moderated, suspicion reduced. Fights over recognition seem to have an all-or-nothing quality, but the negotiation of difference among groups that already have standing and presence, political and economic resources, invites compromise.

I am obviously assuming that the groups we see around us in America today are capable of achieving standing and presence. My aim is to describe multiculturalism as a workable social system, not to suggest a world more attractive than this, some kind of postmodern, postethnic (postcultural?) utopia in which men and women freely fashion their own identities from the bits and pieces of a pluralist past.[3] The groups such people formed would not be capable of the achievements I mean to describe. Perhaps for that reason, my own sympathies don't lie with postethnicity. In any case, the groups that actually exist, whatever difficulties they encounter, however nervous their members, are not about to be superseded. And so the immediate issue is ethnic (racial, religious) coexistence. If America's diverse communities can manage to live together on reasonable terms, in conditions of rough equality, that will be utopia enough. Now, how can we move toward the necessary forms of standing and presence?

"Meat and Potatoes Multiculturalism"

The experience of American Jews may be of some help here, though their extraordinary economic success requires me to be very cautious about setting them up as a useful example. Certainly, they have been sensitive to insult, as the early founding of the Anti-Defamation League (1913) suggests, and they are still quick to feel insulted and injured in cases like that of the Farrakhan invitation. But they are not today the main protagonists of identity politics and their history suggests an alternative (indirect) political strategy. This strategy is partly revealed in the civil rights movement of the 1960s, where Jews were allies of blacks in the fight against discrimination and inequality.[4] The breakup of this alliance and the drift toward more rhetorical and gestural responses to American racism mark the beginning of identity politics. Jewish participants in the civil rights struggle were applying lessons learned from an earlier experience. Perhaps the lessons were too literally applied—and in conditions where they were bound to lead to frustration (though not always to failure). Nonetheless, it is worth reflecting on them.

What is it that gave the Jews place and standing in American society? First, a strong internal organizational life, communal solidarity reflected in institutions: synagogues, schools, welfare and mutual aid associations, defense leagues, fraternal and sororal societies, a great variety of cultural and political organizations, Yiddishist, Zionist, laborist, and so on.[5] But an intensively organized Jewry can go along, historically has gone along, with isolation and fear vis-à-vis the larger non-Jewish community. It has coexisted with the politics of deference, passivity, and accommodation which is suggested by the image of the "court Jew," an ambassador from the weak to the powerful, who often found himself begging for favors. Something more is needed if Jews are to live with confidence among the "others."

So, second, Jews sought and won legal protection in the form of antidiscrimination laws (the end of restrictive covenants and quota systems) and political protection in the form of friendly politicians and "balanced tickets" and equal access to public funds—which allows, in turn, for the strengthening of Jewish organizational life. Winning these protections required a politics of interest rather than a politics of identity, even though the interests at stake were those of men and women who were similarly identified (rather than similarly situated, say, vis-à-vis the means of production). The leaders of this politics of interest spoke from positions of strength—from a mobilized electoral base and a mobilized socioeconomic base—and their "demands" were highly specific and detailed. Dignity and confidence were achieved not by pursuing them directly but by acting in the world in pursuit of individual rights and collective advance.[6]

The result provides a model of what I will call "meat and potatoes multiculturalism." This Jewish achievement is paralleled by that of other religious groups, Catholics, Lutherans, Methodists, and Baptists among others (who mostly didn't need to win the same kind of political battles). Thus far, only religious groups have been able to deliver the meat and potatoes, although these groups often have ethnic subsets: Irish Catholics, German Lutherans, black Baptists. These are the chief protagonists of a concrete multiculturalism. Purely ethnic and racial groups, by contrast, though some of their representatives are leading defenders of the multicultural idea, have had greater difficulty putting it into practice—or at least into the specific kind of practice that I now want to describe. They don't have organizational histories comparable to those of the mainstream religions.

Culture requires social space, institutional settings, for its enactment and reproduction. Among the Jews (and other religious groups too), this space is provided by the full organizational gamut that I have already described, greatly expanded now so that it forms a (partially) publicly funded sector of the American welfare state. The crucial institutions cover the life cycle: day-care centers, nursery schools, day schools and after-school schools, synagogues, museums and historical societies, family services, hospitals, old-age homes, and cemeteries. These are not only places where highly specific services are provided; they are also places where Jews meet, socialize, help one another, observe the dietary laws, perform religious rituals, teach and learn, lecture about Jewish history or literature, organize dramatic productions, sing the traditional songs, celebrate the holidays, comfort the sick, mourn the dead. All this is what I mean by cultural meat and potatoes. Cultures don't survive in people's heads; they need bounded spaces and organized activities of this kind. Multiculturalism without multiple institutional networks is a fake.

But even the Jews, who have 2,000 years of experience in taxing themselves—most of that time without the political power to tax—cannot provide these spaces and activities on their own, at least, not as they would have to be provided today for millions of people dispersed across a modern mass society. The semiautonomous communities of medieval Jewry, the *kehillot,* had something close to the taxing power, and even without it they could mobilize social pressure against recalcitrant individuals. The communities were very small and very precarious, and their members mostly had no place to go.[7] But American multiculturalism is constituted on a largely voluntary basis. The different groups consist of a central core of believers and activists and a spreading periphery of partially committed or entirely uncommitted individuals. It is easy to fade away into the peripheral distances—easy too to reappear on some special occasion (the birth of a child, the illness or death of a parent) and expect that communal services will be available. The activists at the center want to be welcoming on such occasions. Still, the services won't be available, not on the necessary scale, unless tax money can be spent to maintain them.

The extent to which tax money is being spent by organizations based in the various religious communities may surprise people committed to the "separation of church and state." Except with regard to schools, however, this expenditure has never been a controversial feature of American welfarism. And even with regard to religious schools, tax money has sometimes been allowed to filter across the divide—for "secular" uses like transportation, public health, care for disabled children, textbooks in nonreligious courses, and so on. These expenditures have been contested in the courts,[8] but funding for other welfare services has been a purely political matter, with religious organizations lobbying for public funds like any other interest groups. In theory, the welfare state could be run entirely by government officials. But in fact it isn't, and the constituent communities of American multiculturalism are able to hold their members only insofar as they can run some piece of it themselves.

That is why communal organization must be seconded by political power if multiculturalism is to work and if it is to provide people with the social basis of respect and self-respect. To adapt a presidential metaphor: the "points of light" in American civil society depend on a publicly run electricity grid. How does this work? It is time to talk *tachlis*—to pay attention, in the more current phrase, to the bottom line. Political theories about civil society and voluntary association are too often distanced and abstract.

Consider a Jewish nursing home near a major metropolitan center. Its financial structure will have roughly this form: about one-fifth of the necessary money, perhaps a little less, will come from fees paid by those residents who are able to pay; another third, perhaps a little less, will come from philanthropic funds raised in the Jewish community (through the United Jewish Appeal or more directly by the nursing home and its local support group); more than two-fifths will come from federal and state tax money, mostly in entitlements carried by individuals but also in other forms, including, of course, tax deductions for philanthropic gifts.[9] (The state of New Jersey pays for kitchen inspections in Jewish nursing homes not only to guarantee cleanliness but also to guarantee *kashrut* (observance of the dietary laws)—what friendly politician arranged this breach in the wall between synagogue and state?)

But money is only part of the story. A considerable investment of volunteered time and energy is necessary to raise philanthropic funds, and volunteers also work in the nursing home itself, providing auxiliary services, most important, perhaps, visiting with lonely or sick residents, but also organizing talks, games, concerts, birthday celebrations, and so on. These kinds of activities make the home a better place than a state-run or for-profit institution is likely to be. And the Jews (or Catholics or Lutherans) earn respect in the larger community because they run and partly pay for institutions of this sort, which are open, at least in principle, and often in fact, to the wider public. These institutions also provide the community as a whole, and perhaps its individual members too, with a thicker skin, so that some of the nervousness and nastiness of multiculturalism-without-meat-and-potatoes can be avoided.

Politics

The strength of multiculturalism depends on the capacity of all its groups to deliver the cultural goods. It doesn't depend on anything else. But this capacity is by no means equally distributed in American society today. Institutional density, communal resources, and political power are in fact unevenly possessed by the different groups. And the weakest or most deprived groups in these three areas are also the ones most committed to identity politics and most insistent on the importance of its rhetoric and gestures. Some of their critics, including internal ones, call on the members of these groups to turn inward, mobilize their own people, build their base, take responsibility for expanding the social spaces and activities that already exist. That this call sometimes takes a hostile, xenophobic, separatist form, as in the case of the Nation of Islam, does not make it any less plausible. No doubt, communal inwardness is a good thing. Multiculturalism won't work unless people attend to their own culture and its necessary institutions. I have already argued that it isn't helpful to face outward and demand respect: there must be an inner world that *commands* respect.

But under conditions of great and growing economic inequality, these inner worlds can't be built and sustained without significant outside help. I mean *built up,* for obviously cultural life can be and commonly is sustained — it can even thrive — in the absence of governmental recognition and tax money: this absence of support may actually be a requirement for the growth of oppositional cultures. But institutions that engage and protect ordinary men and women and that provide opportunities for cultural expression at every stage of the life cycle will not grow or thrive, will not even exist for many people, unless there is some serious public investment in them.

And that investment, if it is to contribute to the achievement of recognition and respect, has to be fought for; it has to be defended in the democratic arena; it has to be earned politically. An inward turning that is also a turn away from citizenship and democratic politics is therefore a very bad idea. But building a community from the inside and fighting on the outside for a larger role in American politics—these activities in fact go together and reinforce each other. That is the Jewish experience, and in this case it seems clearly transferable to other groups. Only a cohesive community capable not only of voting in a disciplined way but also of providing money and/or workers to selected campaigns and movements can have a visible political impact.

American Jews contribute large sums of money to political campaigns.[10] These contributions reflect the affluence of the community as well as, I suspect, a very old exilic practice: the collection and distribution of protection money to gentile officials and political leaders. While this practice has now taken on a democratic form, it still expresses a characteristically Jewish sense of vulnerability. Other communities in multicultural America are in fact more vulnerable; they are also, however, less affluent and without a tradition that demands of their wealthy members that they buy protection for everyone else. But these groups do have votes and their ordinary members have talent, time, and energy, and these too can be traded in the democratic marketplace.

I have purposely described such transactions in the crassest way, in keeping with my commitment to meat and potatoes. But all such transactions have, in a democratic setting, another aspect. Democratic politics is not only a materially enabling but also a morally ennobling practice. When a democracy is working well, it gives its citizens a sense of efficacy, which is a source of pride, and it makes them actually effective, which is a source of respect. In a decent multicultural society, the members of the different cultural communities will also be citizens, equal to all the other citizens. They will have a double identity (some of them, the children, say, of intermarried couples, may have a more complicated identity), the two sides of which will strengthen one another.

This last point about complex identity brings the argument back to the old pluralists, who believed firmly in a common citizenship alongside and in support of a great diversity of ethnic and religious cultures. For pluralists, citizenship supported diversity by holding the different groups together: participation in democratic politics (and therefore in coalitions of different sorts) was the functional alternative to cultural Americanization. If America was to be a "nation of nationalities" rather than simply a nation, democratic commitment would have to be its unifying creed and democracy itself its practical unity. This is, of course, an argument against public funding for any parochial or separatist schools that don't make a serious commitment to the education of citizens. Such schools might foster sectarian survival, but they wouldn't provide the cultural or intellectual support necessary to sustain a large, dispersed community of "hyphenated" Americans.

The pluralists did not envision significant state funding for the different cultures. But they lived in a smaller country, where politics, the economy, the communications media, and social life in general were far more decentralized than they are today and where the various ethnic and religious (and, though the pluralists had less to say about this, the various racial) groups were more segregated and so more capable of maintaining themselves by themselves. Even so, John Dewey argued that the state should not be "only an umpire to avert and remedy trespasses of one group upon another." Political power has, he thought, a larger function: "It renders the desirable association solider and more coherent . . . it gives the individual members . . . greater liberty and security; it relieves them of hampering conditions."[11]

That is the argument I have tried to revive and elaborate in this essay, with an account of what it means, on the ground of everyday life, to make associations solid and coherent. The conclusion is easy to summarize: in modern society *no group can make it on its own*. It is a maxim of the socialist left that "the liberation of the working class must be the work of the working class itself." In fact, however, political coalitions and state support have everywhere been necessary features of labor movement success. The success of cultural groups can only come in a similar way. And that means that all the multicultural citizens have to work politically to create a state committed to sustaining its own pluralism: to distribute resources in a roughly egalitarian way to all the constitutent groups so as to help them help themselves.

The necessary combination of political integration and cultural diversity won't be advanced very much by controlling hate speech. That's not a bad thing to do, if it is done sensibly; it may well ease the tensions of everyday life. But it won't strengthen identity or communal loyalty, for it has no serious connection to the hard work of creating communities capable of accumulating resources and engaging their members. Nor will it make for a democratic campaign against Dewey's "hampering conditions," the actually existing patterns of discrimination and inequality. The material success of multiculturalism therefore depends on an older, premulticulturalist politics of interest.

Notes

1. Horace Kallen, *Culture and Democracy in the United States* (New York: Boni and Liveright, 1924); John Dewey, *The Public and Its Problems* (1927; Athens, Ohio: Swallow Press, 1985).

2. Jon Elster, *Ulysses and the Sirens: Studies in Rationality and Irrationality* (Cambridge: Cambridge University Press, 1979).

3. For a more sympathetic account of postethnicity, see the essay in this volume by David Biale, "The Melting Pot and Beyond," and also David A. Hollinger, *Postethnic America: Beyond Multiculturalism* (New York: Basic Books, 1995).

4. For an account of this alliance of blacks and Jews which pays attention to its internal tensions, see Robert Weisbord and Arthur Stein, *Bittersweet Encounter: The Afro-American and the American Jew* (New York: Schocken, 1970), especially chapter 7.

5. For a brief account and a useful list of organizations, see Daniel J. Elazar, "The Jewish Community as a Polity," in Marshall Sklare, ed., *Understanding American Jewry* (New Brunswick: Transaction Books, 1982), 186–216.

6. On Jewish politics in the United States, see Lawrence Fuchs, *The Political Behavior of American Jews* (Glencoe, Ill.: The Free Press, 1956).

7. See Salo Wittmayer Baron, *The Jewish Community* (Philadelphia: Jewish Publication Society, 1942); David Biale, *Power and Powerlessness in Jewish History* (New York: Schocken, 1986), especially chapter 3.

8. For an account of court challenges to expenditure of tax money for religious schools, see Frank J. Sorauf, *The Wall of Separation: The Constitutional Politics of Church and State* (Princeton: Princeton University Press, 1976).

9. For a more general account of the uses of tax money, see Dean M. Kelley, *Public Funding of Social Services Related to Religious Bodies* (Institute of Human Relations, the American Jewish Committee Task Force on Sectarian Social Services and Public Funding, 1990); for recent numbers, see "Charities Aiding Poor Fear Loss of Government Subsidies," *New York Times,* February 5, 1996, p. B8.

10. For a sharp critique of American Jewish political engagement, see Benjamin Ginsberg, *The Fatal Embrace: Jews and the State* (Chicago: University of Chicago Press, 1993).

11. Dewey, *The Public and Its Problems,* 71–72.

PART TWO

Canons
and Counterhistories

CHAPTER 5

Jewish Studies
as Counterhistory

Susannah Heschel

The recent rise of multiculturalism has become an impor-
tant moment for the academic field of Jewish studies to reconceive itself.
During its early years in nineteenth-century Europe, Jewish studies was
stimulated by a radical impulse to question or even overthrow the standard portrayal of Western history. The study of Judaism was not simply
to be added to history books; rather, assumptions about the course of the
Christian West were deliberately undermined by looking at its development from the perspective of Jewish experience. Today's muticulturalism
is attempting something similar: not only adding a multitude of different
peoples' experiences to the presentation of history but changing the
configurations that mark the nature of that history—the values that govern it, the powers that shape it, the judgment of its significance.

The initial radical impulse of Jewish history began to diminish by the
turn of the century and was lost with the transfer of Jewish studies to the
American university. Taking another look at the origins of Jewish studies and its own effort to challenge European historiography brings to light
the alliance that can be achieved between the study of Jewish experience
and the theoretical frameworks offered by multicultural theory. The question is how multicultural theory, particularly postcolonialism, can be useful in illuminating aspects of Jewish experience. Postcolonial literary interpretations examine the political role of European colonization in the
creation of literature as well as the resistances to political domination that
are expressed literarily. Although the Jews did not constitute a territorial
colony of Europe, they formed an internal colony within Europe, under

the domination of Christian powers. How does Judaism, the subaltern voice of Europe, speak back, so as to resist and disrupt the hegemony of the Christian West? Judaism's voice, I will argue, began its resistance and disruption with the rise of Jewish studies in the nineteenth century, as it not only presented its own history but reconfigured the history and significance of Christianity by undermining its central claims.

The most widespread depiction of nineteenth-century German Jews portrays them as struggling to assimilate fully into German society, even at the cost of abandoning their sense of identity as Jews. Their synagogues were transformed into Jewish versions of Christian churches, and in their personal identity they have been described as inverted Marranos, Jewish on the outside, Christian on the inside.[1] In the early generations of the nineteenth century Jewish men, who began to flock to German universities during the 1830s (sixty years before Jewish women were admitted), were forced to confront the Christianity-centered studies that prevailed.[2] The history of the West was the history of Christians, just as the philosophy and theology that were taught were exclusively Christian. As the discipline of Jewish studies began to emerge, its scholarship was not simply a presentation of Jewish history but a counterhistory of the prevailing Christian scholarship. Judaism, they argued, was not a degenerate religion that had outlived its significance with the dawn of Christianity, nor were Jews a fossil of history, as the Christian construction of "Judaism" claimed. Rather, the Wissenschaft des Judentums presented Judaism as standing at the center of Western civilization, having given birth to both Christianity and Islam. Neither of those religions was original or unique because both derived their central ideas and religious practices from Jewish texts and traditions. Islam was Jewish monotheism for the Arabs, Christianity a paganized version of Judaism which betrayed the message of its Jewish founder. Several prominent nineteenth-century German Jewish historians, including Heinrich Graetz and Abraham Geiger, argued that the intellectual narrow-mindedness and intolerance of the Middle Ages were the genuine products of Christianity, whereas modernity's open-mindedness stemmed from Judaism's teachings concerning tolerance and acceptance of others. They criticized Christian interpretations, particularly of Jewish texts, as biased or distorted, seeking to deliberately misrepresent the religious insights of Judaism.

Through such criticisms the first practitioners of Jewish studies saw the study of Judaism as not simply an addition to the general curriculum but as a revision of that curriculum, an effort to resist and even overthrow the standard portrayal of Western history. In this version, at the heart of the West would stand the Hebrew Bible and rabbinic literature, not classical Greek civilization or the New Testament, and the history of Christian thought would be presented as a derivatory offshoot of Jewish ideas. Even modernity, with its claims to secularized scientific forms of knowing and its insistence on tolerance and diversity, was to be understood as the product of Judaism, not of Christianity.

The privilege granted the Christian West also prevailed at American universities through the middle of the twentieth century, where knowledge was viewed as a means to protect Christianity's privileges, as scholars of the humanities saw themselves as preservers of Christian moral values and aesthetics.[3] A Jew could hardly be permitted to teach English literature, and that discipline did not open to Jews until mid-century. As much as the academy was a male domain, the pen a metaphor for the penis, it was also a Christian domain, and the hegemony of the Christian West over academic knowledge suggested that the very act of acquiring knowledge, interpreting, and transmitting it was a Christian act, on behalf of Christian society. Even the architecture of many American colleges, with a Christian chapel as its focal point, lent physical confirmation to the intellectual message.

Unfortunately, the original radical political thrust of Jewish studies was lost when the field was transferred to the United States. Although the United States has always been a multiethnic country, built on the federalism of multiple groups, it is here that Jewish studies became transformed into a conservative field whose goal was the incorporation of Jewish history into the larger framework of Western civilization. The study of Judaism was presented as an effort not to undermine Christianity but to contribute to its understanding and reinforce its hegemony. American Jewish scholars trying to overcome the exclusion of Jewish studies generally presented Judaism as part of the established curriculum, an ally of the canon of Western Christian civilization, not a challenge to it. Jewish studies, its proponents argued, deserved a seat at the banquet because of its contributions to the West, not because it unsettled any established understandings of the West. Maimonides, for example, was to be studied in order to better understand Aquinas, without implying any challenge to the preeminence of medieval Christian scholasticism. Consequently, current attempts to establish multiculturalism within the academy have been eyed warily by Jewish studies scholars. The multicultural agenda, with its assault on the canon of Western civilization, seems to many to be antithetical to the interests of Jewish studies by identifying Jews and Judaism with the curriculum of dead white European males. As a result, Jewish studies and multiculturalism frequently have come to view each other as enemies.

The question today is whether Jewish studies as a field can revitalize the radicalism that inspired its early development in the nineteenth century. The recovery of its radicalism would enable Jewish studies to enter the multicultural academy, disrupt antagonistic claims about Jews and Judaism, and eventually develop a multiculturalism within the study of Judaism. Through multiculturalism, Jewish studies might be restored to its more interesting position as challenger of the established definitions of the Western canon. The study of Judaism might itself be transformed, from the religion of white Western European Jewish males into a multivocal Jewish history that includes the geographic, gender, and class distribution of Jewish experience. Simultaneously, the example of Jewish experience contradicts multiculturalism's tendency to view Jews as white European oppressors. Finally, theoretical developments within multiculturalism, such as gender theory and postcolonialism, could be applied to illuminate the situation of Jews as a marginal minority group within a broader Christian or Muslim society.

Recognizing the intimate relation between knowledge and power stands at the heart of multicultural assertions.[4] As Simon During has noted, since the 1970s culture has been analyzed through the spectrum of Antonio Gramsci's understanding of hegemony as relations of domination which are not visible as such.[5] Illuminating those relations has become a contemporary preoccupation within the academy. The intimacy shared by knowledge and power has been most influentially illustrated by Edward Said's 1978 study, *Orientalism*, which describes the modern European academy's construction of "Orientalism" as a field of study put to use by European colonizers.[6] While the book abounds in problematic assertions and has been subjected to widespread attack for misunderstanding the field of Islam and the course of modern European history as well as for overlooking "the potential contradiction between [Foucauldian] discourse theory and Gramscian hegemony,"[7] it has nonetheless become a banner for multicultural studies concerned with the politics of scholarship.

From the perspective of the history of Jewish studies, the enormous acclaim given to Said's book seems odd; comparable criticisms of the academy's construction of "Judaism" and the political uses to which it was put is nothing new. Jewish scholars have investigated and criticized that construction and its politics for over a century. Indeed, the intimacy between knowledge and power may be better known to Jewish historians than anyone else. Surely the control of the university throughout most of its history by Christians, the censorship of anti-Christian statements from Jewish texts, and the powerfully influential denigrating definitions of Judaism by Christian scholars are just some examples of the subordination and distortion of Jewish knowledge at the hands of Christian powers.[8] Indeed, the New Testament's negative depiction of Pharisaic Judaism stands as a model of how distorted knowledge can become a regime of "truth" via the strength of the politically powerful. Going further, we can see that definitions of early Christianity in opposition to early Judaism incorporate the latter of necessity into the Christian hegemonic framework; the control and delimitation of the Jewish becomes necessary to define the Christian. Almost every study of Christian origins includes a contrasting description of a degenerate first-century Judaism, as if an affirmation of Christian teachings by itself were insufficient to establish its legitimacy. Yet by defining Christianity as the "not-Jewish," Judaism is made the signifier of Christianity. "Can the subaltern speak?" Gayatri Spivak, one of the leading postcolonial theorists, asks;[9] how does Judaism speak to the master narrative of Western history, which is rooted in traditions of Christian religious supremacy?

Spivak concludes that the very construction of the subaltern carries the seeds of its undoing. In the particular case of the Christian repression of Judaism through its construction of "Judaism," the subaltern Jewish voice begins by insinuating itself as necessary to Christian, even while claiming that the Christian is not necessary to the Jewish. It is not the Jew who desires Christianity, but the Christian who requires a myth of Jewish desire in order to legitimate Christianity. Had the Jews not been in a desperate religious state in the first century, there would have been no reason for Jesus to initiate the reform of Judaism that turned itself into Christianity.

Modern European scholars' construction of "Orientalism" took place in the absence of Arabs or Muslims, but "Judaism" was constructed by Christian scholars in the presence of Jews, who were able to talk back. The German Jewish scholars who shaped the first generation of the Wissenschaft des Judentums condemned the exclusive control of Jewish knowledge by Christians. Judaism was being portrayed in a "hateful light" by Christian theologians, asserted Immanuel Wolf, who published the first manifesto of Jewish studies in 1823.[10] Leopold Zunz, one of the towering figures of Jewish scholarship in nineteenth-century Germany, complained of the tendentious view of Jews in academic writings. Jews, according to Zunz, were depicted either as witnesses or opponents of a victorious Christianity, but always as representatives of disputed principles, never as subjects of their own self-defined historical narratives.[11] Whatever the case, Zunz suggested that Christian scholars took on a "demonic nature" when studying Judaism.[12] The alternative was the emergence of a coterie of Jewish scholars of rabbinics who became gatekeepers, guarding a scholarly treasure of rabbinic literature that, they insisted, would transform historical arguments. Even though they called for training scholars in Hebrew and rabbinics within faculties of Protestant and Catholic theology, the goal was to establish faculties of Jewish theology at German universities, just as feminist scholars called for the establishment of women's studies programs at universities even as the study of women was integrated into the general curriculum.

Multiculturalism, however, is concerned not only with giving voice to neglected groups within history; it is also concerned to develop new analytic tools to better understand the position of the socially marginal and to expose the exercise of power within the mainstream academy. Stephen Greenblatt's analyses of the roles of racism, misogyny, and anti-Semitism in Shakespeare's writings have provoked outrage among opponents of multicuturalism, who view the approach as an intrusion of the political into literature.[13] Opponents of multiculturalism term his exposure of the political agenda at work in Shakespeare an irresponsible exercise of left-wing politics, a politicization of the academy. Underlying such polemics is the myth of apolitical knowledge, as if multiculturalists do not represent one among many competing political viewpoints but are the only ones with a political agenda.

The myth is not new, nor is the challenge to it. Rather, the contemporary debate over multiculturalism recapitulates much of the debate that took place between Christians and Jews during the nineteenth century, as each group created conflicting scholarly approaches to its canonical texts and histories. Whereas the multicultural debate in contemporary America focuses on a range of topics, in the last century the debates were between Jews and Christians and they were most often carried out over the question of the historical figure of Jesus and his relationship to Judaism.

Like Jewish studies of the nineteenth century, contemporary multiculturalism is concerned with destabilizing the hegemonic claims of the academy. African American studies and women's studies are two examples of efforts to include a multiplicity of voices in the presentation of history and literature. Whose history and whose literature should be studied? When the story of male, white, Christian Western civilization is related, should not its cultural glories be tempered with the evidence of its racism and misogyny? That kind of question headed the agenda of the Wissenschaft des Judentums as well; Heinrich Graetz opened nearly every section of his eleven-volume *History of the Jews* with a description of the cruel persecutions perpetrated by Christians against Jews.[14] The history of the Christian West, for Graetz, is coterminus with the history of anti-Semitism. Indeed, when Graetz turns to explaining the rise of Christianity, his formulation comes as a kind of Jewish theodicy, trying to account for the origins of Jewish suffering by analyzing Jesus and Paul. So too with contemporary feminist analyses of the history of philosophy; for instance, the study of Aristotle concerns not simply the origins of Western philosophy but also reveals the origins of the profound gender biases that have infiltrated Western thought.[15]

In its day the Jewish perspective on Western history was perceived by Christian scholars as radical, even a potential threat. The Christian West had been used to looking at Judaism, dissecting its flaws and defining its nature. Now, for the first time, Jews were looking at Christianity and that shift in gaze was not accepted easily; on the contrary, as Jewish scholars began their exploration of Christianity, they aroused an intense acrimony among Christian theologians which far exceeded the conventional bounds of scholarly discourse. For example, Graetz's claims about Christianity led Heinrich von Treitschke to accuse him of holding an anti-Christian bias that was shared by all German Jews and that served, for Treischke, as grounds for denying Jews German citizenship.[16]

Thus, Jewish studies emerged not as a politically neutral field concerned with describing the history of the Jews but as a politically charged effort to reconceive Christian history as well. The central focus of discussion was the first century, the era that saw the rise of both rabbinic Judaism and early Christianity as well as the destruction of Jewish political autonomy. The historical description of that era, which concerned both Jewish and Christian scholars, was crucial for determining the nature of the two religions and quickly became a debate over the merits of each. That debate centered, for Jewish and Christian historians, on the figure of Jesus and his relation to first-century Judaism.

One of the most influential figures among nineteenth-century Jewish historians was Abraham Geiger, who wrote extensively on the historical background of Jesus in early Judaism and whose arguments can be taken as an early example of multicultural challenge.[17] In his survey of Jewish history, published during the 1860s, Geiger argued that Jesus was not only a Jewish religious leader but specifically a Pharisee whose goal was nothing more than that of the Pharisees: the democratization and liberalization of Judaism. Nothing in Jesus' teachings was new or unexpected: he interpreted the commandments, encouraged greater piety, and engaged in the sort of rabbinic disputes that were typical of Pharisaism. The later dogma of Christian theology concerning Jesus—the virgin birth, the Incarnation, the Resurrection—were later theological inventions that resulted from pagan philosophical influences. Geiger's arguments not only sought to counter the widespread image of Judaism as a degenerate religion, which was current in the Christian scholarship of his day, but went further, insisting that Judaism was the original, true religion from which Christianity—and Islam, according to his book on the Koran—was a deviant derivative.[18]

The implications of Geiger's argument for Christians were highly problematic, and Protestant theologians responded to him with anger.[19] According to them, Jesus was the first Christian, not just one among the rabbis of his day. Indeed, Jesus was presented by nearly all Christian theologians as standing in sharp contrast to the Judaism of his day, which they depicted as a degenerate, immoral legalism, hardly a religion at all.[20] By insisting that Jesus was a Pharisee, Geiger implied that those Christians who sought to follow the faith of Jesus, rather than the dogma about Christ, would have to convert to Judaism. If Jesus was simply a Jew, what defined the originality and uniqueness of his message, and what was the difference between Christianity and Judaism?

The nature of Geiger's arguments about Jesus or Graetz's claims about Christian persecution of Jews is best understood as a form of counterhistory, a genre that has been operative since antiquity but that was identified in its relation to Jewish studies by David Biale in his study of Gershom Scholem.[21] Counterhistory is a genre of interpretation which characterizes the methods frequently employed by today's multiculturalism, in which the sources of one's adversary are exploited and turned "against the grain," in Walter Benjamin's phrase.[22] Counterhistory also characterizes traditional Christian theological histories of the Jews, which (mis)read the Hebrew Bible as anticipating the coming of Christ (theological promises) or as explanations for the rise of Christianity (the degenerate state of postexilic Judaism). As counterhistory, these Christian revisions of Judaism, whether intentional or not, "deprive the adversary of his positive identity, of his self-image, and substitute it with a pejorative counter-image."[23]

At the same time, Geiger's arguments also have to be acknowledged as betraying a large degree of Jewish triumphalism. Amos Funkenstein is correct in observing that the "forger of a counteridentity of the other renders his own identity to depend on it."[24] That was Hegel's argument, presented as the master-slave dialectic, that the master's identity as a master depended on its recognition by the slave. The master narrative of Christianity may not realize its dependence on a subjugated Judaism, but once the subaltern Jewish voice began to speak, its potential to undermine Christian claims began to be clear. Yet the subaltern voice of Geiger's counterhistory of Christianity also poses a threat to Jewish identity. Making Judaism's significance to Western civilization so intimately linked to the figure of the Jewish Jesus forges a dependence that relies on the Christian theological realm rather than resting independently on Jewish identity.

Now it is well worth asking why Jewish historians, including Geiger, gave so much attention to the history of Christian origins and the figure of Jesus, especially given their concern with anti-Semitism and Christian anti-Judaism. After all, the Jesus story has been responsible for inordinate Christian violence and Jewish suffering. Why not dismiss or refute or ignore Jesus and the Gospels? Multicultural theory, which concerns itself with understanding the efforts of socially marginal groups to overcome prejudice against them, can illuminate underlying motivations of Jewish historiography and demonstrate the politics at work in their allegedly objective scholarship and that of their opponents.

Telling the story of Christian origins from a Jewish perspective was an act of Jewish self-empowerment. The position of Jews entering the world of Christian theology is not unlike the position of women novelists entering the nineteenth-century literary world. In their landmark study of women novelists in Britain, Sandra Gilbert and Susan Gubar argued that women were required to "kill the angel in the house," the aesthetic ideal of the female promoted in male literature, before they could generate their own literature.[25] Similarly, Jewish theologians initiated an effort to destroy the image of Judaism in Christian theology as part of their project of self-definition. Nina Auerbach has observed in connection with women writers in Victorian England who appropriated male-authored misogynous myths that the power of mythologies lies both in their ability to oppress and in their ability to endow strength.[26] To deny a myth or try to sidestep it will neither destroy its power nor subvert its meaning. The nineteenth century witnessed the rise of women's efforts to cope with the misogynist myths of literature by retelling the conventional narrative but subverting its plot. In a similar pattern, modern Jewish thought has been formed not simply by creating a Jewish historical narrative but by attempting a rebirth of the Christian mythic potential under Jewish auspices. What is particularly interesting in Geiger's work is not so much his denial of individual Christian anti-Jewish myths but the second look he takes at those myths and the power he reclaims from them. Like women characters in the English novel, the Jewish victim of Christian persecutions—slain, dismembered, powerless—is revived, made whole, and empowered through a Jewish retelling of the Christian story. In this theological construction, Jews are thereby enabled to become the self-restoring hero who tries, in Auerbach's words, to merge "imperceptibly with the lives of those who believe in [the myth] and thereby into the history they make."[27] Seen in this light, the modern Jewish retelling of Christian origins is not merely a matter of Jews wishing to "set the record straight." Rather, it demonstrates a Jewish desire to enter the Christian myth, become its hero, and claim the power inherent in it. Reform Jews in particular concentrated so much attention on early Christianity in part to uncover a model for their own acts of revisioning Judaism, since they saw Christianity itself as beginning in a strong misreading of Judaism.

From the Christian perspective, the widespread research on the Jewish background to the New Testament became so prevalent during the nineteenth century not simply to gain information about Jewish history. Rather, it was a necessary element in constructing the hegemony of Christian scholarship. Studies of first-century Judaism provided information about the historical background of the New Testament, but, more important, they established the preferred Christian interpretation under the pretense of an objective, scholarly gaze. The creation of a devalued Judaism as "Other" to Christianity made the Christian theological gaze seem to be a transcendent, rational subject able to undertake analysis without being affected by subjective factors or personal biases.[28]

Christian scholarly investigation of Jewish history established a radical dichotomy between Christianity and Judaism which was required to maintain Christian theological order. Presenting the historical relationships between the two religions was simultaneously a construction of contemporary social relations and of relations of power within the realm of scholarship. The Christian made himself the transcendent subject of theological Wissenschaft, necessitating a radical dichotomy with an Other in order to maintain order. The gaze of historical theology was Christian; the ordering of history, the questions raised, the evidence examined, all revolved around the central issue, explaining the rise of Christianity. Other religions, other peoples' histories, other texts, were viewed from the Christian perspective, weighed and evaluated with reference to the Christian standard of measurement. Edward Said has noted the function of the Orient in the imagination of Christian Europe: "European culture gained in strength and identity by setting itself off against the Orient as a sort of surrogate and even underground self."[29] The role of the "Jewish" in the

European Christian imagination is very similar, even in the parallel
metaphors that establish both the Jewish and the Oriental as feminine.

Geiger's reinterpretation of Christian origins is more complex than simply the story of the powerless demanding that the powerful relinquish
their power. Rather, his engagement with Christian history remakes both
Jewish and Christian theology; he is like Paul, whose work is "a struggle
over interpretations of power, conflicts over authority and truth."[30] The
impact of Geiger's view of Christianity is comparable to the impact
achieved by the gaze of the nude woman in Edouard Manet's famous paint-
ing *Olympia*, first displayed in Paris in 1863, the same year Geiger delivered his lectures on Jesus in Frankfurt. By reversing the position of the
observer, from Christians writing about Judaism to a Jew writing about
Christianity, Geiger reversed the power relations of the viewer and the
viewed. Until now, the gaze of scholarship had been a Christian gaze and
Judaism appeared occasionally as the object viewed. In Geiger's writings,
the gaze is Jewish, and Christianity is transformed into a semiotic representation within Judaism. The first Jew to be so thoroughly versed in New
Testament scholarship and to be armed with an array of rabbinic textual
evidence unknown to his Christian counterparts, Geiger did not simply
refute Christian claims but entered the Christian story. Telling the story
of the life of Jesus became Geiger's appropriation of the Jesus myth.
Through his retelling, Geiger the Jew became the hero, claiming the power
that inheres in the story for himself and his community. Yet as much as
Geiger railed against Christian anti-Judaism, his own anti-Christian attitudes remained equally tenacious. The theological gaze was indeed
reversed, but its ferocity was not diminished. Geiger defied the scholarly
gaze as Christian theology had defined it; in his work Judaism is no longer
merely the object of representation but the subject gazing at Christianity, which is transformed into an object of Jewish representation. Geiger's
gaze is defiant, disruptive, and subversive. Christian reactions to his writings frequently intensified the negative depiction of Judaism, particularly
of the Pharisees, and insisted on the opposition between Jesus and
Judaism. Perhaps the rage Geiger's interpretation evoked among Christian historians demonstrates just how powerful his gaze was.

By presenting an example of the ideology underlying Jewish studies
as it developed during the nineteenth century I do not intend to suggest
a continuation of the particular arguments developed by Geiger, nor do
I urge a focus on Jewish-Christian relations or a return to the figure of
Jesus as the site of multicultural debate. Rather, I intend to describe the
methodology of counterhistory and its usefulness in formulating a radi-

cal challenge to hegemonic forms of knowledge. Both the examples of the Jews and of Jewish studies as a field can make a theoretical contribution to the development of the multicultural academy.

Contemporary multiculturalism, if it is to be effective, should not concern itself exclusively, or even primarily, with providing a rainbow of data concerning the experiences of diverse cultures. Rather, its goal ought to be the establishment of a variety of gazes that will unsettle and throw into question the complacency of academic categories and analyses. Feminist theory, for example, has been most effective in pointing out the narrow-mindedness of identifying the "human" with the male. One of the most prominent examples is Carol Gilligan's challenge of the stages of children's moral development, which had been established by Lawrence Kohlberg solely on empirical evidence drawn from boys.[31] Gilligan argued that the moral development of girls occurs along a wholly different spectrum and that morality, when viewed from a female perspective, would have to be entirely redefined. Although feminist educators have criticized Gilligan's work for not taking into account variations in girls' experiences based on social, economic, and racial background,[32] her fundamental challenge still holds true: that male experience cannot be equated with human experience and that categories of morality based solely on male behavior and judgment are at best partial and at worst immoral. Women's studies, in other words, is not simply about the inclusion of women's experiences but about reconsidering the very categories of definition and analysis used in the academy, a kind of counterhistory illustrated by the example of nineteenth-century Jewish studies.

Ultimately, even multiculturalism itself might be subjected to a kind of counterhistorical analysis. The simplistic distinctions between oppressor and victim which too frequently operate in multicultural discourse relegate Jews to the side of white Europeans. Awareness of Jewish history, however, would reveal a more complex identity not only of Jews but also of Europeans. As much as Jews in the modern era began to participate actively in the construction of European society, they became its greatest victims. Jewish identity stands in many ways as a challenge by insisting on the complexity of white European identity. As much as Jews are inside the Christian world, they are also outsiders; they occupy a position of ambivalence and ambiguity that functions as a kind of counterhistory to the multicultural account of the West: not all white Europeans are Christians. The danger lies in the tendency of multiculturalism to construct a counterpart to Europe's "Orientalism" in the form of a distorted myth of European hegemony.

In Jewish studies multiculturalism points out the problematic nature of retaining a unified construct of "Jew." The multiplicity of Jewish experience begins, most fundamentally, in radical distinctions between the historical experiences of men and women. To speak of the entry of "Jews" into German universities in the early nineteenth century, for example, is to presume an identity between Jews and men, since Jewish women did not gain entry until all women, Jewish or not, were admitted in the late nineteenth century. Aspects of the social emancipation of "Jews," then, take on greater complexity, since Jewish women can be said to have attained societal integration in some respects not as Jews but as women. Yet that assertion in itself presupposes the equation of "Jewish" with "male" experience. Who is the Jew as woman and how is her difference to be taken into account when speaking of the "Jew"? With that question begins the entry of multiculturalism into Jewish historical experience.

However much some Jews may rail against multiculturalism, and multiculturalists themselves may reject Jews from their intellectual community, multicultural theory itself lies at the heart of modern Jewish experience. The struggle over multiculturalism so intensely characterizes the Jewish adventure because it expresses both the relationship between the Jew and non-Jewish society and also the relationship between the Jew (female) and Jewish society. In many ways, women's experience within Judaism reproduces Jewish experience within the larger society: enduring a sense of exile within one's own social and linguistic world; finding oneself an immigrant within one's own society or community; calling for acceptance and equality from hostile or ambivalent compatriots; striving for an identity against the tide of definitions that diminish one's sense of self. Over and over in the encounters with Judaism, the Jew as woman asks: What of the Jewish expressions of politics, morality, or faith applies to me as a woman? What can be created to give voice to the tenuous balance of identity as Jew and woman? These are the questions of multiculturalism, questions about identity and meaning, knowledge and power, experience and definition. They are the central questions asked by Jews and of Jews.

Notes

1. Abraham J. Heschel, "The Meaning of Repentance," in *Moral Grandeur and Spiritual Audacity,* ed. Susannah Heschel (New York: Farrar, Straus, and Giroux, 1996), 68–70.
2. Monika Richarz, *Der Eintritt der Juden in die akademischen Berufe: Jüdische Studenten und Akademiker in Deutschland 1678–1848* (Tübingen: JCB Mohr, 1974).
3. Susanne Klingenstein, *Jews in the American Academy, 1900–1940* (New Haven: Yale University Press, 1991).

4. See, for example, the highly influential work by Michel Foucault, *The Archeology of Knowledge,* trans. A. M. Sheridan Smith (London: Tavistock Publications, 1972).

5. Simon During, "Introduction," *Cultural Studies* (New York: Routledge, 1993).

6. Edward Said, *Orientalism* (New York: Vintage Books, 1979).

7. Dennis Porter, "Orientalism and Its Problems," in *Colonial Discourse and Post-Colonial Theory: A Reader,* ed. Patrick Williams and Laura Chrisman (New York: Columbia University Press, 1994), 150–161, 160.

8. See Frank E. Manuel, *The Broken Staff: Judaism through Christian Eyes* (Cambridge: Harvard University Press, 1992).

9. Gayatri Chakravorty Spivak, "Can the Subaltern Speak?" in *Colonial Discourse and Post-Colonial Theory: A Reader,* ed. Patrick Williams and Laura Chrisman (New York: Columbia University Press, 1994), 66–111.

10. Immanuel Wolf, "Über den Begriff einer Wissenschaft des Judenthums," *Zeitschrift für die Wissenschaft des Judenthums* 1 (1823): 1–24.

11. Leopold Zunz, *Zur Geschichte und Literatur,* 2d ed. (Berlin: Louis Lamm, 1919).

12. Cited by Altmann, "Jewish Studies," 84.

13. Stephen Jay Greenblatt, *Shakespearean Negotiations: The Circulation of Social Energy in Renaissance England* (Berkeley: University of California Press, 1988).

14. Heinrich Graetz, *Geschichte der Juden von den ältesten Zeiten bis auf die Gegenwart,* volumes 3–11 (Breslau, 1853–1870).

15. Susan Moller Okin, *Women in Western Political Thought* (London: Virago, 1980); Elizabeth V. Spelman, *Inessential Woman: The Problem of Exclusion in Feminist Thought* (Boston: Beacon Press, 1988).

16. Heinrich von Treitschke, *A Word about Our Jewry,* trans. Helen Lederer (Cincinnati: Hebrew Union College-Jewish Institute of Religion, 1958); Walter Böhlich, *Der Berliner Antisemitismusstreit* (Frankfurt am Main: Insel Verlag, 1965).

17. Abraham Geiger, *Das Judentum und seine Geschichte,* 3 vols. (Breslau, 1865–1871); English translation, *Judaism and Its History,* trans. Charles Newburgh (New York, 1911).

18. Abraham Geiger, *Was hat Mohammed aus dem Judenthume aufgenommen? Eine von der Königl. Preussischen Rheinuniversität gekrönte Preisschrift* (Bonn, 1833; 2d ed., Leipzig: M. W. Kaufmann, 1902). Translated as *Judaism and Islam* by F. M. Young (Madras, 1898; 2d ed., New York: Ktav, 1970).

19. For a review of the reception of Geiger's work, see my *Abraham Geiger and the Jewish Jesus* (forthcoming), chapter 7.

20. Emil Schürer, *Lehrbuch der neutestamentlichen Zeitgeschichte* (Leipzig: J. C. Hinrichs'sche Buchhandlung, 1874); second edition published as *Geschichte des jüdischen Volkes im Zeitalter Jesu Christi* (Leipzig: J. C. Hinrichs'sche Buchhandlung, 1886–1887; 3d ed., 1898); Joseph Langen, *Das Judenthum in Palaestina zur Zeit Christi* (Freiburg im Breisgau: Herder Verlag, 1866); Julius Wellhausen, *Die Pharisäer und die Sadducäer: Eine Untersuchung zu inneren jüdischen Geschichte* (Greifswald: Bamberg, 1874; Hannover: Orient-Buchhandlung H. Lafaire, 1924; Göttingen: Vandenhoeck und Ruprecht, 1967).

21. The motif of counterhistory is developed by David Biale, *Kabbalah and Counter-History* (Cambridge: Harvard University Press, 1979); see also Amos Funkenstein, *Perceptions of Jewish History* (Berkeley: University of California Press, 1993), 36 f.

22. Walter Benjamin, *Illuminations,* trans. Hannah Arendt (New York: Schocken Books, 1969), 257; cited by Funkenstein, *Perceptions of Jewish History,* 36.

23. Funkenstein, *Perceptions of Jewish History,* 48.

24. Funkenstein, *Perceptions of Jewish History,* 48.

25. Sandra M. Gilbert and Susan Gubar, *The Madwoman in the Attic* (New Haven and London: Yale University Press, 1979).

26. Nina Auerbach, *Woman and the Demon: The Life of a Victorian Myth* (Cambridge: Harvard University Press, 1982), 12.

27. Auerbach, *Woman and the Demon,* 15.

28. The effort was similar to the establishment of the transcendental rational subject outside of time and space as a necessary part of the nineteenth-century colonialist enterprise. See Nancy Hartsock, "Foucault on Power," in *Feminism/Postmodernism,* ed. Linda J. Nicholson (New York: Routledge, 1990), 160.

29. Edward Said, *Orientalism* (New York: Vintage Books, 1979), 3–8.

30. Elizabeth Castelli, *Imitating Paul: A Discourse of Power* (Louisville: Westminster/John Knox Press, 1991), 44.

31. Carol Gilligan, *In a Different Voice: Psychological Theory and Women's Development* (Cambridge: Harvard University Press, 1982).

32. Critical reviews of Gilligan's work include Judy Auerback, Linda Blum, Vicki Smith, and Christine Williams, "Commentary on Gilligan's *In a Different Voice,*" *Feminist Studies* 11 (Spring 1985): 149–161.

CHAPTER 6

The Paradox of Jewish Studies in the New Academy

Sara R. Horowitz

Motive: The Personal as Political

Conceived in Harlem, New York, my father nonetheless landed in Ellis Island in the 1910s at the age of two months. My grandmother, after sampling life in the United States and finding it not to her liking, told my grandfather he could seek her and their four children back in Warsaw. Then she packed up and left him to face the vagaries of the New World alone. Several months later, realizing she was pregnant with my father, she felt it unseemly to remain without her husband. She waited out the months and once again made the journey, this time for good.

My father's early chronology had important consequences. Had he been born a few months earlier or later, he would have been a native son rather than a naturalized citizen.

Educated in New York public schools, first in Harlem and then in the Bronx, he graduated from City College in the 1930s along with many other children of immigrants. For my father, the Convent Avenue campus held out the lofty promise of his family's American dream. The serendipity of being born to an Orthodox Jewish family—and even his choice to remain an observant Jew—would prove no barrier to his entry into the pubic arena, the common culture. His intellect, his hard work, would be the means by which he would claim his place. So he thought.

Soon after graduation my father applied for certification to teach. Brilliant and bookish, he met all requirements for a teaching license. But the climate for Jews in America was less sunny than my father had been led to expect in his classes on Convent Avenue. His naturalized status—his early months in eastern Europe—was the peg on which was hung the denial of his teaching license. The accented English presumably spoken by Jewish immigrants (even those, like my father, whose native tongue was a flawless American English) rendered them unfit to educate American youth. Decades later, when Nazi atrocity had made blatant anti-Semitism unseemly in America, my father received the coveted license from the state of New York. All traces of the putative accent had apparently vanished. In the meantime, however, he worked as a cutter in New York's garment district.

At City College my father had believed, as Allan Bloom would later put it, that "[a] Jew in America . . . is as American as anyone."[1] Peering into the universalist mirror held up at the university, my father thought he could discern his own features. But outside the walls of Convent Avenue he realized he had been staring at nothing.

Many years later his daughter squints into that same mirror on Convent Avenue. Peering back, an image only vaguely like herself. Already she sees that the magic mirror does not reflect back woman, does not reflect back Jew.

Context: The Political as Personal

The undergraduate multicultural course requirement where I teach stipulates that every student enroll in at least one of a roster of courses designated as bearing significant "multicultural, ethnic, or gender-related content." This recently instituted requirement reflects a growing interest in non-Western cultures and in the mosaic of subcultures of our own country. It emerges from a desire that the university curriculum reflect national and global cultures, systems, beliefs, and traditions, particularly of those groups commonly shut out of academic discourse. For the dominant culture, these courses are to promote sensitivity to culture-based issues and to oppression. From the point of view of the previously excluded or marginalized groups, the courses offer a corrective to the distorted glass through which they have seen themselves—if they have seen themselves at all—in the academy.

The proliferation of multicultural courses across the country forms a vital part of what has come to be termed the "new academy." By both broadening the range of texts taught and radically altering the theoretical prism that refracts what we currently teach, its advocates hope to enact, through teaching, an active cultural oppositionism. As director of a newly constituted Jewish studies program at my own institution, I looked toward existing programs—women's studies, minority studies, black studies (what many of us have come to refer to informally as departments of the Other)—to serve as models and as allies. Much to my surprise, what seems intuitively correct to me seemed intuitively off base to many of my colleagues: that Jewish studies has a natural and important place in the exchange of ideas and methodologies of the new academy, that it properly belongs to the complicated and often problematic alliance that includes gender studies, African American studies, minority studies, literary theory, film studies, and other multidisciplinary (or antidisciplinary) forces in the university. For when the inevitable borderlines were drawn, Jewish studies lay outside my university's rubric of multicultural studies, just as it lay outside the boundaries of many professional dialogues on multicultural theories and practices. At an overwhelming number of universities, too, the place of Jewish studies in multicultural discourse has been strongly contested.[2]

On a national level, as the profession adopts a more progressive stance toward the multicultural agenda, it has largely come to ignore the presence of Jewish studies, except as presented in radicalized contexts, already preconfigured to the radicalized multiculture. The Modern Language Association, for example, has consistently denied petitions to create a national Division of Jewish American Literature, or of Jewish Literary and Cultural Studies, despite the creation in the last fifteen years of Divisions of Black American Literature and Culture, American Indian Literatures, Women's Studies in Language and Literature, Ethnic Studies in Language and Literature, and Gay Studies in Language and Literature. At stake, of course, is not only recognition for the academic legitimacy of Jewish studies within the multiculture but also organizational resources, professional visibility, access to journals for one's work, the creation of new positions at member universities, collective stature, and personal prestige.

Ironically, the expansion of multicultural programs on campuses makes a place for Jewish studies, facilitating the establishment of such Jewish studies programs.[3] Our growing sense of the diversity and fragmentation of Western culture, in light of postmodernism and postcolonialism, allows for Jewish fragments too. Yet insofar as I speak out of Jewish studies and not, more broadly out of literary or cultural studies, my natural allies do not always seek dialogue with me. Increasingly I and a growing number of progressive critics and scholars in Jewish studies notice that we are talking almost exclusively to each other.

The Paradox: Jewish Studies
in the New Academy

The basis of the new multiculturalist academy is a radical interrogation of the foundations of our disciplines and our ways of knowing, a challenge prompted, shaped, and reshaped by literary studies, psychoanalysis, philosophy, political theory, linguistics. In different and sometimes colliding ways, the new academy seeks to uncover, acknowledge, and ultimately subvert the hegemonic vision of culture and society. We speak repeatedly—and correctly—of the hegemony of gender, class, race, ethnicity—assumptions that the dominant culture makes about people with reference to those categories which may not be true or representative. Yet the hegemony of religion has slipped somehow from consciousness: Christianity as shaping and underlying Western cultural constructs, ways of thinking, ways of knowing, ways of being; Christianity as colonial force and motive for nearly two millennia.

Jewish studies—the study of the texts, histories, and cultures of the Jewish people—developed alongside and within Western and non-Western civilizations. Uniquely Jewish intellectual, philosophical, literary, theological, and social traditions developed from the biblical period onward, distinct from but in steady interaction with the traditions of countries in which Jewish life flourished. During the last 3,000 years Jewish communities have existed throughout the world, contributing to and absorbing from the cultures they touched. The geographic and intellectual history of Jews in the world addresses the way the outsider coexists and often struggles with the insider in order to maintain both physical and cultural survival. As an academic discipline, or nexus of disciplines, Jewish studies concentrates on its own inner continuities as well as on the ways it has affected and been affected by its host cultures. Not contained within a single discipline, Jewish studies draws on the multiple methodologies that have evolved in the academy. At the same time, it subverts the ways of knowing which have consistently ignored, effaced, or distorted its presence both in the academy and in culture.

In the context of the Western academic tradition, Jewish studies explores the continued presence of the outsider within, a people both a part of and apart from Western culture. Consistently, the Jewish voice—or, more appropriately, Jewish voices—have been silenced, except insofar as they mimic or reproduce the voice of normative culture and modulate themselves in timbres pleasing and nonthreatening to the larger society. Consistently, these voices have been domesticated, distorted, misread, unread.

Jewish studies is the study of Jews in their (or our) own terms. It recognizes that Jewish culture has been subordinate in Western culture, marginalized, translated, and appropriated. While Western thought has been notably occupied with the figure of "the Jew" and with the "Jewish question," the internal perspectives of Jews have been largely invisible. With rare exception the university has systematically effaced the study of Jews and Judaism except under the hyphenated misnomer "Judeo-Christian," or from the unstated but implied point of view of Christianity. Strangely enough, although the independent presence of Jewish studies is new on campus, to many it somehow seems as though we've been here all along. But the study of Jewish texts in the academy—whether biblical or contemporary—traditionally occurs only to the extent that these texts have been already colonized by or absorbed into Western (Christian) literature. Thus the "Old Testament" is seen presaging or paving the way for the New, which then supersedes it as Christianity is seen as superseding Judaism. Just as the dominant culture has presumed that the male voice tells the story for the female or that the white narrative incorporates black experience, the Jewish voice is presumed to be included in the story of Western civilization and "Judeo-Christian" culture.

Ironically, critics all along the political spectrum have relegated Jewish studies to their opponents' camp. The right recognizes and resists the counterhistories and counterreadings inherent to Jewish studies perspectives. The left views Jewish studies as inherently conservative, serving reactionary rather than progressive forces. Defenders of the universalist ideals of the Enlightenment have seen Jews and Jewish texts as matter to assimilate (that is, efface) into a universalized (that is, homogenized) vision, while radical critics see traditional Jewish liberalism as opposing a genuine multiculture. Judaism and Jewishness are made to stand for (and be accountable for) patriarchy. Or rendered invisible, elided into "white" or "Anglo" culture (despite the fact that many Jews are neither). One senses hostility toward things Jewish in an unreflective anti-Israel stance; an inclination to overlook, minimize, or trivialize racism when aimed against Jews; a denigration of Jewish traditions, communities, habits, cultural markings, learning. Thus, peculiarly, what historically has been consistently and aggressively excluded from Western culture is seen as part of Western hegemony.

Why? Although Jewish studies is by no means limited to the study of traditional texts, these texts are indeed an important way in which Jewish culture comes to know and distinguish itself and to assert or maintain historical opposition. The association of Jews with the canon—that is, the Torah or Hebrew Bible or "Old" Testament—in a context that questions the special position of canonical or culturally privileged texts—links Jewish studies with the old guard. In addition, Jewish studies has garnered support from the right of late. Against the perceived threat of liberal relativism and radicalized politics, new allies see Jewish studies as bringing back to campus "that old-time religion," with its ideal of absolute knowledge and truth (keeping students safe from drugs, sex, moral relativism, "deviant" sexuality). Furthermore, Jewish studies programs often have real but complicated relationships with an off-campus Jewish community that may look to the programs to validate faith claims or solidify group identity or facilitate pluralistic tolerance. Sometimes conflicting and sometimes coalescing, the pulls of scholarly rigor on the one hand and community activism on the other challenge Jewish studies, much as they do gender, minority, and ethnic studies.

In feminist writing, Jews—or at least the Jewish tradition—frequently represent patriarchy. Susannah Heschel has pointed to the unacknowledged presence of anti-Judaic biases in Christian feminist theological writing. As Heschel observes, this writing holds the Jewish tradition and the Jewish Bible accountable for the invention and persistence of patriarchy in Western culture. In the assessment of many Christian feminist theologians, then, Christianity has presumably managed to overcome the Judaic food prohibitions and ban on iconography but has not yet jettisoned its supposed misogyny. According to Heschel, this attitude toward Judaism pervades nontheological feminist writing as well.[4]

Why this intersection of feminism and anti-Judaism in certain writers?[5] Because, as black feminist writers insist when writing of their quarrel with white feminists, one may be situated in marginality and privilege at the same time. By ascribing the source of patriarchy to the "Judeo roots" of the "Judeo-Christian tradition," the critique of Jewish patriarchy put forth by Christian feminists simultaneously deconstructs the dominant culture (patriarchy) and protects the dominant culture (Christianity). Moreover, while contemporary feminist thinking acknowledges the special oppression and exclusion experienced by women of color in a way that distinguishes them from "white women," the special oppression and exclusion of Jewish women are not validated. The complicated issues of composite identities of Jewish women becomes homogenized even in contexts that elaborate the ethnopoetics of the *mestiza,* the culturally mixed woman,[6] a concept that bears importantly on questions of identity and community for Jewish American women. Much feminist writing across racial lines elides Jewish women into white women, ignoring not only experiential differences but also the history of anti-Semitic practices. For example, Gloria Anzaldúa, in her introduction to *Making Face, Making Soul*, describes a university colloquium in which "most of the white Jewishwomen in the class did not want to identify as white. . . . Some declared they 'belonged' more to the women-of-color group than they did to the white group." But according to Anzaldúa, "Whitewomen and white Jewish women . . . could not get it into their heads that this was a space and class on and about women-of-color,"[7] a place where Jewish feelings of isolation, exclusion, and oppression had no voice. Although encompassing women whose actual communities often find themselves in conflict or competition, the *mestiza* did not encompass the Jewish woman. Women of color are viewed in relation to men of color, to white women, and to white culture in general, while Jewish women are seen simply as "white women," only more so.

Moreover, there is a mistaken apprehension that a Judeo-Christian culture is a shared culture, a hybrid product. Seen as part of a Judeo-Christian culture that has aggressively conquered and colonized other cultures, Judaic culture appears to bear responsibility for historical wrongs. This view masks the ways in which Judaism itself has been colonized or cannibalized by a more powerful culture that has absorbed but also reinterpreted its textual and cultural resources. The "New" Testament retroactively interprets and rewrites the "Old," first by renaming, then by renarrativizing. It effectively negates rather than retains the Hebrew (Jewish) Bible, effacing its Jewish meanings in a competing hermeneutic, or system of interpretation, that claims absolute and singular truth. The calendar notation currently in use in the West—B.C. and A.D.— imposes Christian teleological assumptions on all events it describes. For this reason, many Jewish scholars prefer to use B.C.E. and C.E.—"before the common era" and "common era"—although even that seeming neutrality speaks for Christian rather than Jewish time constructs. Jewish culture and history easily dismiss the apocalyptic worries (and hopes) precipitated by the approaching millennium; the year 2000 (A.D.) is by Jewish reckoning the year 5760.

Finally, the multicultural agenda fails to see Jewish studies as representative of a marginalized culture because the generous presence of Jews in the academy contrasts with the underrepresentation of women and other racial and ethnic minorities. Real and imagined Jewish economic successes in America contribute to the perception of Jews as a privileged rather than an oppressed minority, not only "white" but "elite." Like Asian Americans, Jews are victimized by their own positive stereotypes, which mask the gender, class, ideological, and ethnic differences that distinguish them from one another, and fragment them from within. The invisibility of Jewish studies as an academic field, moreover, is hidden behind the presence of Jews as scholars in all fields. Historically speaking, the hospitality of the academy to Jews is a relatively new phenomenon. And if Jewish professors have been present in recent decades, Jewish texts, cultures, and concerns have not. It seems to me that Jews often enter the professions (in the United States and elsewhere) at the price of visible Jewish affiliation.[8] Irving Howe recalls, for example, the allure of "the spacious arena of American culture, which was decidedly gentile in origins and tone" when measured against the "narrow habits of response" of a "parochial" Jewish culture. With ambivalence, he reflects many years later on his own complicity with the "universal" culture whose constructed image of "the Jew"—even the "free-thinking Jew"—demanded his own silence, especially about anti-Semitism. "It was we," Howe recalls, ". . . toward whom [T.S.] Eliot could not indulge 'an excess of tolerance.'"[9] As in postemancipation (and pre-Hitlerian) Germany, a Jew remains a Jew at home, a mensch outside. Or, as with Howe and others, "Jewishness" defers to a cosmopolitan, universal humanism.

Where does Jewish studies fit into the new academy? What can its perspectives contribute to a rethinking and reshaping of cultural studies? The difficulty we may observe in getting the people who see themselves as "doing Jewish studies" to agree on just what constitutes Jewish studies is a promising place to start. What is its scope? The traditional (sacred) Jewish texts: Torah, Talmud, Midrash? Any literature written in Jewish languages (Hebrew, Yiddish, Ladino, Aramaic, and others), even when explicitly anti-Jewish or simply non-Jewish in content and concern? A medieval love poem, for example, written in Judeo-Espagnol or a homoerotic poem in Spanish by a poet who also wrote liturgical poetry in Hebrew? A novel by an American Jew, even one like Saul Bellow who eschews the category "Jewish American writer"? Any novel written by an Israeli Jew or Arab or only one written in Hebrew? By a Palestinian? Anything concerning the study of the state of Israel? Demographic studies on Jewish populations anywhere in the world? A study of unemployment among middle-aged male Jews in Buenos Aires? In Cairo? In Tel Aviv?

Even more fundamentally, what is meant by the adjective "Jewish"? A nationality? A system of beliefs? Race? Ethnicity? None of these terms suffices, suggesting that the categories we use to sort knowledge may be off the mark, not only for things Jewish, but in general. Susan Handelman's suggestion that Jewish studies encompasses anything Jews do, say, think, and write seems appropriately inclusive but begs the question of definition.[10] That very insufficiency, however, that very lack of closure, implies a complex view of cultures, a breakdown of categories and of certain kinds of thinking, crystallizing complicated questions regarding culture formation, exchange, and interaction.

While Jewish studies exemplifies, either implicitly or explicitly, the struggles of an oppressed group against the dominant culture, "Jews" as such do not fit neatly into the categories evoked most frequently in contemporary academic discussions of oppression: gender, class, race, ethnicity. Jews are viewed as no different from other immigrant groups which come to a host country, experience hard times, and finally adapt and assimilate into the dominant culture. By contrast, the marginalization of blacks, Chicano/as, and Latino/as in America is seen as enduring. In this view, all white ethnic groups soon meld with white America, merging into the white European culture to which they always belonged.[11] The distinguishing marks of immigrant outsiders—that they come from another place, speak another tongue, eat other foods—soon blur into a residual nostalgia that displaces a sense of difference. Jews—like Irish, Italians, Poles—are then seen as sharing in collective white complicity with racism against people of color, while their own instances of oppression and marks of difference recede and vanish.

The conflation of Jews into white European culture ignores—indeed, falsifies—the historical marginalization and systematic oppression of Jews in and by European culture, both before and after the Enlightenment. An unintended, ahistorical (or antihistorical) irony becomes visible when one considers, for example, the connection between the imperialism underlying the "discovery" of the Americas and the inquisitory practices of what would become Spain. Both the Age of Discovery and the Spanish Inquisition are emblemized by the year 1492, when Columbus set sail for the Americas and when the Inquisition culminated in the murder of crypto-Jews and the expulsion of professing Jews from Granada, the last of the provinces incorporated into Spain where Jews (and Moslems) still remained.

In addition, current thinking in cultural studies considers Jews as a kind of ethnicity and defines this ethnicity as "people from another place." Unlike other ethnic groups (like Italian Americans, Irish Americans), however, Jews are not defined by where they come from but in spite of (or against) where they come from—and because of what they carry with them or what others assign to them (the idea that they are Jewish). So while individual Jews may assimilate, Jewishness does not always fade away.

Like being "of color," being "Jewish" is also enduring. Certainly in the discourse of the far right, Jewishness has been viewed as "race"—by neo-Nazis, by the KKK, by white supremist (Christian) groups. The racialist discourse places Jews outside the dominant culture[12] and figures Jews as people of color. Actual Jewish skin color then is seen by these groups as misleading, posing a heightened threat of "racial impurity" through miscegenation. Unlike other people of color, the race ("blackness") of Jews may not be immediately discernible to the "pure" (that is, "Christian") whites, who may mistakenly misbreed.

Thus, in the discourse of the left Jews are elided with "European-descended whites," while in the discourse of the far right Jews are another kind of "black." This dichotomy suggests both that Jewishness (ethnos) washes away and that Jewishness (race) is indelibly marked. Each of these mutually exclusive models is partly true but insufficient. Unlike other ethnic groups defined by place of origin, Jews, whether immigrant or native-born, may be said to have never left their origins, which are defined not by geography but by collective historical memory. Unlike other people of color, Jews define themselves other than racially. Moreover, many Jews in America today have the sense of having chosen to perpetuate their "Jewishness" (whether defined culturally, religiously, historically); they inscribe rather than are inscribed by "Jewishness." The inadequacy here of the categories "ethnos" and "race" and "religion" unravel the constructed nature of these terms.

The history of Jewish traditional texts and the evolution of interpretive strategies and methodologies illustrate ways that readers make, subvert, and remake meanings in response to changing historical and political forces. As such, Jewish studies offers a means to recover oppositional practices which may serve as resources for postcolonialist readings. Some Jewish texts, considered esoteric by most Westerners until recently, have lately become part of the contemporary discourse. Midrash, for example, fascinates contemporary readers, in part because it exemplifies and privileges the development of interpretive practices.[13] A type of interpretive narrative, rather than pure analysis or free-standing imaginative narrative,

Midrash offers an extensive and fragmentary commentary or gloss on Torah. Midrash responds to textual gaps, intertextual inconsistencies, and philosophical problems within biblical narrative as well as to extratextual sociopolitical issues. Midrashic writers generate multiple and contradictory—and sometimes transgressive—alternative narratives, often in opposition to dominant readings. Contemporary literary theory has seized on these interpretive practices while simultaneously opening up new ways of viewing them; however, it also sometimes obliterates the radical otherness of the texts and of the hermeneutical traditions from which they emerge.[14] For example, because Midrash deconstructs Torah, it has been appropriated by contemporary critics in a way that domesticates and depoliticizes it.

Traditional Jewish modes of study offer a surprisingly less hierarchical paradigm for learning than the traditional organization of university education. Yeshiva learning, for example, both product and producer of a radically decentralized religious institution, is based on an aggressively interactive relationship to inherited wisdom and texts. Traditional "learners," working in pairs (exclusively male until recently), interrogate layers of text and one another. The "learners" generate alternative readings to received texts and pull out potential interpretations, sometimes generating new texts. This potentially transgressive practice, as well as the texts it reads, writes, and rewrites, reflects an epistemology different from that of the Western academy, an epistemology built on argumentation and multiple interpretations that do not result in a totalized system and that resist closure.

Philosophers left outside the boundaries of the Western philosophical tradition and narratives (historical, legal, fictional, interpretive) left outside the history of Western narrativity offer ways of exploring historical and cultural development from oppositional perspectives, distinct from (yet connected with) Western traditions and geopolitics. The study of Jewish history, for example, as distinct from "World History" or "World Civ," taught me at an early age to read with a critical and suspicious eye.[15] I particularly remember studying the Crusades from two distinct (and incompatible) vantage points. In World History I learned to call the Crusades "the most successful failure." This phrase from my fifth-grade textbook described a holy mission that, while falling far short of its goals, nonetheless opened up valuable trade routes to the "East," thus advancing the forces of "progress." Simultaneously, in Jewish History, I recoiled at the brutal massacres inflicted by hordes of hooligan soldiers as they came upon peaceful, civilian Jewish communities in Europe and the Holy

Land. Those uncontrollable, illiterate, marauding armies murdered Jewish families and laid waste to valuable centers of Jewish learning. By fifth grade, then, through the "vision of the vanquished" I saw that one defines "progress" according to one's own system values and that conflicting systems vie for the right to interpret historical events.

The narratives absented from Western discourse reveal the impact of Westernization on Jewish experience—a form of inner colonization, because the colonized people live amongst the colonizers rather than in some other place. The seven-book memoir of seventeenth-century Gluckel of Hameln, for example, narrates the life and times of a German Jewish woman engaged in international trade.[16] The journal of Pauline Wengeroff explores the implications of modernity for traditional Jewish women at the turn of our century, as her husband's eagerness for assimilation deprives her both of her religious practice and her active role in business.[17] As both of these memoirs indicate, Westernization (and particularly the Enlightenment) introduced oppressive practices with regard to Jewish women. To make these texts available in the academy subverts the unreflective identification of Judaism with patriarchy and recovers historical oppositional practices.

In addition, the events of the Holocaust radically challenge the structures of society and culture which foster racial thinking and racism and culminate in genocide. The Holocaust puts in question—and ultimately holds accountable—systems of meaning (including religious institutions, theological beliefs, humanism, high culture, education, romanticism, populism) which have ordered Western thought.

Thus, Jewish studies provides a counterhistory to the historical clichés of Western culture even as it posits and debunks historical clichés of its own. Jewish collective history competes with, coexists with, and displaces the collective memory of Western history (and other collective histories if we speak, for example, of the Jews in Islamic countries or in the Far East). At the same time, versions of history compete within Jewish studies. I refer not only to religious disputations among Orthodox, hasidic, conservative, Reform, and reconstructionist institutions but also to ideological and political conflicts shaped by Jewish and non-Jewish contexts (such as Jewish Bundists, Zionists, communists, liberals, conservatives).

Even at its most conservative, the presence of Jewish studies in the university forces Western tradition to confront the limitations of its epistemological and interpretive approaches and offers competing sets of meanings. Jewish studies reveals the existence of a counteracademy— or, more properly, counteracademies—each with its own competing canonical and ideological stance: the Yeshiva, the maskilic center, the secular academy.

Because the Jew has been the historical outsider in the West (and elsewhere), Jewish studies offers for examination a continued record of racism, persecution, exclusion, and survival. To examine the construction of the Jew as Other and the Jews as a race challenges the idea of Other and of race as construct. Jewish studies looks at the feminized image of the Jew in Western texts (for example, in Nazi propaganda), the continued prevalence of anti-Semitism even in places where Jews no longer reside, the development of Judaism in Christianity and in Islam. It examines the concept of dual and composite identities (what it means to be a German Jew, a Jewish American woman), bi- and multilingualism, and the problems of participation in two parallel discourses where one negates the other (as in my example of the Crusades).[18] Jewish studies offers a systematic, formidable, and substantial documentation and interpretation of history from the point of view and in the voice of the exile, the outcast, the forcibly converted, the expelled, the cordoned off. Against myriad projections and constructions of the Jew stand the texts of Jews in their own (often discordant) voices.

The recent transformations of the academy in terms of postmodernism and postcolonialism in principle (if not in practice) invite the voice of Jewish studies, alongside black, gender, and Chicano/a studies. At the same time, these transformations fragment the thoroughgoing Enlightenment version of Jewish studies itself. The methodologies and perspectives of the new academy offer ways of critiquing Enlightenment Jewish studies and providing new resources for reenvisioning Jewish studies. They offer new strategies for reading old texts and they bring into purview new kinds of material. In light of postmodernism, postcolonialism, gender theory, and other theoretical approaches, traditional texts (including the Torah, Talmud, and rabbinic responsa) offer traces of the lives of women and the daily concerns of ordinary people (not only the intelligentsia), reveal sets of political tensions that shaped intellectual and religious development, and chart encounters with other cultures. Feminist and radical theologies reshape even the religious discourse. In addition, film, folklore, feuilletons, comics, jokes, memoirs, and other material expand Jewish studies' sense of itself.

But there needs also to be an internal resistance to the new academy, lest it turn into the "old academy" and erase Jewish texts and voices. Jewish studies must resist utterly reshaping itself and reinventing its texts to fit into the new academic climate. Without its cultural specificity, Jewish studies fades into the "universal" and out of existence. There exists, thus, a tension between two important but different aspects of Jewish studies: subverting and reinventing traditional Jewish texts and retaining those texts insofar as they serve as countertexts to the Western (Christian) culture that has systematically silenced them and rendered their presence invisible.

Who reads Jewish texts these days anyway? Who understands Jewish languages? Who has heard of the thinkers (other than Maimonides) central to the Jewish philosophical tradition? Aside from Bellow, Roth, and Malamud—the trinity of postwar Jewish American writers, literature students rarely encounter Jewish authors, especially contemporary writers who take Jewishness as their context, such as Anne Roiphe, Tova Reich, Daphne Merkin, E. M. Broner. These texts, the ancient and the modern, constitute our record and map—our packable, portable culture—our tracks across time and space, through cultures, histories, and languages. In reading them, in reading ourselves in them and against them, we enact the multicultural.

Notes

1. Allan Bloom, *The Closing of the American Mind* (New York: Simon and Schuster, 1987), 33.

2. See, for example, Edward Alexander's discussion of the multicultural task force at the University of Washington in Seattle, in "Multiculturalism's Jewish Problem," *Congress Monthly* 58, no. 7 (November/December 1991): 7–10.

3. Arnold Eisen has made this point before me in a discussion of the debate surrounding the core curriculum at Stanford, in "Jews, Jewish Studies, and the American Humanities," *Tikkun* 45 (1989): 23–29.

4. Susannah Heschel, "Anti-Judaism in Christian Feminist Theology," *Tikkun* 5, no. 3 (1990): 25 ff.

5. Anti-Judaism and anti-Semitism are not identical, and the presence of the first does not necessary imply the presence of the second. The former targets the Jewish religion but not necessarily Jews.

6. See, for example, Gloria Anzaldúa, *Making Face, Making Soul = Haciendo Caras: Creative and Critical Perspectives by Women of Color* (San Francisco: Aunt Lute Foundation, 1990), and Cherrie Moraga and Gloria Anzaldúa, eds., *This Bridge Called My Back* (Watertown, Mass.: Persephone Press, 1981).

7. Anzaldúa, *Making Face, Making Soul,* xx.

8. The relegation of Jewishness to the private rather than the public realm is continuous, of course, with the double bind of the Enlightenment for Jews, as elaborated in the introduction to this volume.

9. Irving Howe, "An Exercise in Memory," *New Republic,* 11 March 1991, pp. 29–32.

10. Susan Handelman, "The State of Contemporary Literary Criticism and Jewish Studies," *Association for Jewish Studies Newsletter* 1, no. 37 (1988): 3 ff.

11. See Edward Alexander's account (in note 2 above, this chapter) of the debate on whether to include the study of Italian Americans, Irish Americans, and Jews in the ethnic studies requirement.

12. As Anna Quindlen correctly discerns, in the discourse of the far right the "authentic American is white and Christian . . . his ethnic origins lost in the mists of some amorphous past, not discernible in accent, appearance or allegiance." "Making the Mosaic," *New York Times,* 20 November 1991, p. A27.

13. See, for example, Susan Handelman, *The Slayers of Moses: The Emergence of Rabbinic Interpretation in Modern Literary Theory* (Albany: SUNY Press, 1982), and *Midrash and Literature,* ed. Geoffrey H. Hartman and Sanford Budick (New Haven: Yale University Press, 1986).

14. See, for example, David Stern's comments in "Midrash and Indeterminacy," *Critical Inquiry* 15 (Autumn 1988): 133–161.

15. Post-colonial cultural theory refers to this way of reading, questioning, and interpreting history as hermeneutics of suspicion.

16. *The Memoirs of Gluckel of Hameln,* trans. M. Lowenthal (New York: Harper, 1932)

17. Shulamit Magnus, "Pauline Wengeroff and the Voice of Jewish Modernity," *Gender and Judaism: The Transformation of Tradition,* ed. T.M. Rudavsky (New York: New York University Press, 1995), 181–190. See also Paula E. Hyman, *Gender and Assimilation in Modern Jewish History: The Roles and Representation of Women* (Seattle: University of Washington Press, 1995).

18. Jean-François Lyotard's concept of *le différend* is useful in this connection: see *The Differend: Phrases in Dispute* (Minneapolis: University of Minnesota Press, 1988).

CHAPTER 7

The Double Canonicity
of the Hebrew Bible

Robert Alter

One might reasonably assume that the Bible provides contemporary cultural criticism the very paradigm for the idea of a canon.
Indeed, as late as 1955, the Oxford English Dictionary, while never applying the term *canon* to works of secular literature, offers as its only entry
relevant to current usage this thoroughly unambiguous definition: "the
list of books of the Bible accepted by the Christian Church as genuine
and inspired." The Christian character of the canon taken for granted in
this definition is worth noting, for, as I shall try to show in detail, the
canonicity of the Bible for Jews from late antiquity to the modern era has
in part meant something quite analogous but also something quite
different. The authoritative certitude fixed in the canon according to this
dictionary definition vividly illustrates the tendentiousness in the recent
widespread adoption of the term for secular literary works, fostering as
it does a tacit notion of a kind of synod of cultural authorities who have
dictated a list of "genuine and inspired" writers, excluding proponents
of the wrong ideological or aesthetic bent or the wrong ethnicity. In fact,
the reasons why certain works become popular beyond their own times
and are anthologized, reprinted, cherished by readers, even included in
curricula, are more complicated, more fluid, and more multifarious than
the ecclesiastical model of a canon suggests. But the canonicity of the
Hebrew Bible itself proves to be, on closer consideration, more ambigu-

ous and also more overdetermined than is allowed by this idea of a list of genuine and inspired works.

We have only an imperfect, highly inferential notion of how the can-onization of Hebrew Scriptures actually took place—apparently, by stages—among Jews sometime around the turn of the Christian era. The conventional construal of the talmudic account as a kind of parliamen-tary vote on a list of canonical works by the Sanhedrin on a single day in Yavneh in 90 C.E. has been questioned by recent scholars, and such a notion is surely a schematization of a more complicated historical process.[1] The Torah was evidently accepted as canonical by the time of Ezra the Scribe (later sixth century B.C.E.), for he could not have prescribed its reading as a public ritual without assuming, or at any rate effectively imposing, such acceptance (though we have no way of being sure that the Torah he decreed for reading was textually identical with that of later tradition). The Prophets, including the narrative books designated the Former Prophets, appear to have become canonical over the next four centuries, as evidence from the Dead Sea Scrolls and elsewhere suggests. So far so good, a proponent of the idea of canon as a list of genuine and inspired books might say. The Torah, after all, gives us an account of the origins of the world, the formation of the people of Israel, and its divine elec-tion and redemption from slavery, together with the body of laws—moral, civil, and cultic—to govern it. The Former Prophets continue the story of God's covenanted people to the end of the First Commonwealth. The Latter Prophets explicitly represent themselves as carriers of God's mes-sage to Israel (the so-called messenger formula, "thus saith the Lord," is often invoked in their writings), articulating in a new way the moral impli-cations of the Covenant and making a set of assertions about the future course of history.

The third large unit, however, of what became the Hebrew Bible, the miscellaneous Writings (Ketuvim), raises questions about any clear-cut ideological or theological criteria for the constitution of the canon. The Writings include, after all: a kind of carnivalesque political fairy tale in which God's name is never mentioned (Esther); a profound challenge to traditional notions of divine justice and reward and punishment which concludes with a radical revision of the anthropocentric vision of Cre-ation in Genesis (Job); an exuberantly sensual celebration of the pleasures of young—and evidently unmarried—love, again with no mention of God (the Song of Songs); a brooding series of poetic-philosophic reflections on the futility of all human endeavor and desire and the leveling prospect of cyclical recurrence in all things (Ecclesiastes). How did such wayward or nearly heretical texts come to be part of the Hebrew Bible? A provisional answer may help us understand more clearly the role played in the cultural life of later Jews not only by these "problematic" books but by the entire Hebrew Bible and may give us a clearer notion of how canons in general are made.

Let me begin by observing a rudimentary fact that has had more far-reaching consequences than is generally realized: the Jews, from late antiquity to relatively recent times, read the Bible, unlike all other peoples, in the original Hebrew. There are some limited exceptions to this rule. The Hellenized Jewish community of Alexandria in the last centuries of the pre-Christian era seems to have been dependent on the Greek translation of the Bible. The wide dissemination of the Aramaic Targums in the early Christian era is a clear indication that large numbers of Jews, in a time and place when Aramaic had displaced Hebrew as the vernacular, needed a translation, at least as a pony for understanding the original. It would be extravagant, moreover, to imagine that the educational system at any time or place in the history of the Diaspora produced universal literate comprehension of Hebrew among Jewish males. It is likely that quite typically an ordinary person would end up only with a dependable ability to sound out the Hebrew letters on the page and identify the meanings of some primary items of vocabulary. Nevertheless, anyone who could be considered truly educated in traditional Jewish society would have been intimately familiar with the Bible in its original language; and, indeed, despite the fact that after the first few years of schooling the curriculum centered on the Talmud, not the Bible, there is considerable literary evidence that a nearly verbatim recall of the entire Hebrew Bible was by no means an unusual accomplishment. The group that achieved Hebrew literacy may have been an elite but it was by no means a tiny one. My guess is that the proportion of the Jewish population in eleventh-century Andalusia or eighteenth-century Lithuania which could read Genesis and Job in the original was at the very least comparable to the proportion of people in eighteenth-century English society who read Virgil in the original, at a time when English poetry was modeled on Augustan verse.

It is obvious that a great work of literature can have a profound effect on readers in translation, as the enormous impact of Homer, Dante, and Shakespeare in many languages demonstrates. But it is equally obvious that the tonalities, the associations, the order of imaginative authority, shift, usually with some palpable diminution, when a work manifesting great verbal mastery is transferred from one language to another. Such shifts are particularly drastic in the case of the Hebrew Bible because most of the languages into which it has been translated are so different from Hebrew in structure, idiom, sound, and semantic coloration. The effect of reading the Bible in its original language is, I suspect, paramount in the inclusion in the canon of the four books I have mentioned which ended up in the miscellaneous Writings. Apart from any considerations of ideology, if the Jews of late antiquity had read these texts in Greek or Aramaic, I think it is quite unlikely that they would have felt impelled to put them in the Bible.

The continuing possibility of an unmediated engagement with the details of the Hebrew text led to a relation to the Bible among Jews through the centuries which was strikingly different from the characteristic Christian relation to Scripture. The Jews never had a centralized authority that could confidently claim to be the arbiter of biblical interpretation. Hebrew exegesis would remain more a free-for-all than an ecclesiastical chorus. In the printed Hebrew Bibles with medieval and Renaissance commentaries studied by traditional Jews, the biblical text is a small island of type surrounded by a sea of vigorously competing interpretive voices—rationalist, philological, mystical, homiletic, literary. In this polyphonous interpretive tradition, the very notion of the authoritative character of the canon—instructively, a term not used by Jews—is in effect unsettled, for different readers detect different orders of authority in the text.

But to return to the question of the original shaping of the canon, why would a book that either rejects doctrinal consensus or pays no attention to doctrine be taken into the supposedly doctrinal canon? The two most plausible explanations, literary power and sheer popularity, in part overlap, in part complement each other. Both Esther and the Song of Songs are self-evidently popular works. Esther would have had wide appeal because it provided the rationale for a new festive holiday, Purim, while playing on feelings of national pride and solidarity in an inventive satiric narrative. Neither of these considerations is related to the language in which the story is written. The liveliness of the tale, however, is strikingly enhanced by the Hebrew in which it is conveyed, with its playfulness, its puns, its descriptive vividness so different from earlier Hebrew prose, with its colorful borrowings from the Persian. (Such considerations at first carried little weight in pietistic circles: the absence of any fragment of Esther from Qumran—Esther is the only biblical book not represented in the library of the Dead Sea sectarians—suggests that as late as the first or second century B.C.E. there were groups that rejected its canonicity.) The popular character of the Song of Songs is attested by the objection in the Tosefta (Sanhedrin 12:10) to a common practice of singing it, with plainly erotic intention, in places of public revelry. But the popular attraction of the Song surely derives not merely from its subject—the wasteland of the extracanonical through the ages is littered with erotica—but from its extraordinary poetic vehicle, which in the lushness of its imagery, its subtle musicality, its sense of drama, its fusion of delicate sensuality and verbal wit turns biblical Hebrew into an instrument of enchantment.

The other two problem books, Job and Ecclesiastes, raise the question of ideology and canon more directly because both are philosophic challenges to views generally accepted in the dominant body of beliefs of ancient Israel. It is not unreasonable to surmise that the very profundity of the challenges—a profundity that would have spoken to an intellectual elite more than to a popular audience—arrested the attention of certain Hebrew readers and drove them to argue for the inclusion of these texts in the canon. If that was in fact the case, it would indicate that ideological consensus among the makers of the Jewish canon was less a matter of party-line agreement than one might imagine, that the canon makers were willing to tolerate a certain spectrum of outlooks, or perhaps felt that it was salutary for the consecrated literature to incorporate some dialectic elements of autocritique. But an equally important aspect of the appeal of both these books is their unique power as instances of literary Hebrew, a power that manifestly focuses the boldness of the philosophic critique they articulate. The metaphoric vigor of the poetry of Job, its stunning ability to inscribe pain and outrage and cosmic vision in taut, muscular language, give it an awesome intensity of a kind attained by only a few other works—the *Inferno, King Lear,* perhaps a few poems of Paul Celan's— in the whole Western poetic tradition. Ecclesiastes, moving back and forth between highly rhythmic prose and passages of poetry, is a haunting evocation of the hazy insubstantiality of ambition and hope which has a mesmerizing effect in the Hebrew because of its echoing cadences, verse after verse registering in sound the writer's underlying sense that all things are wearingly repeated in an endless cycle of futility.

I don't mean to propose that ultimately what the Hebrew Bible represents is the twenty-four best-selling books of ancient Hebrew literature. The limits of the canon were, after all, defined by a system of belief, even if it was in a few respects surprisingly flexible, and there may well have been works composed in Hebrew in the biblical period which had no chance of admission to the canon because they stood outside the system or addressed concerns entirely irrelevant to it, even by way of challenge. (We have no way of knowing what was the nature of the lost books mentioned in the Bible: the Book of Yashar, the Book of the Battles of YHWH, the Chronicles of the Kings of Judea, and the Chronicles of the Kings of Israel. Perhaps the first two were deemed too mythical in character for retention even in the precanonical stage of anthologizing the national literature, and the last two may have expressed too limited a dynastic view of historical events.) Nevertheless, the stylistic and imaginative authority of the works that became canonical must have played a role in the desire to preserve them in the national legacy; and, conversely, it seems plausible that there were Hebrew texts excluded from the canon not for doctrinal reasons but because they were inferior as works of literature. The soaring and searing poetry of Job, the lovely lyricism of the Song of Songs, were so keenly appreciated by the ancient audience that it was unwilling to have them lost to posterity, for all the theological radicalism of the former and the sensual secularity of the latter.

The case, moreover, was not fundamentally different for ancient Hebrew texts that posed no challenge to doctrine. Genesis might be thought of as a perfectly "orthodox" work, authoritatively defining the hierarchy of Creation and the election of Israel, but it is also one of the supreme achievements of narrative art in all of ancient literature, on the level of style, story, dialogue, and the complex representation of character and theme. The Hebrew audience in the Second Commonwealth period no doubt readily assented to the canonical status of the redacted text we call Genesis because it consciously viewed the book as a veracious report of Creation and national origins, but it is hard to imagine that the ancient audience did not also respond with deep approbation to the brilliant literary artistry of the book (which surely was not exercised by the authors and editors merely for their own amusement, in disregard of any audience). This double responsiveness to Scripture read in the richness of its original language has continued to manifest itself in the Jewish relation to the Bible through the ages. The nearly ubiquitous presence of allusions to the Bible in postbiblical Hebrew literature is a major index of this binocular vision of the Bible: the allusions occur because the Bible provides later Hebrew writers a thick concordance of phrases, motifs, and symbols that encode a set of theological, historical, and national values (a canon in the strict sense of the OED); and the allusions occur, as I shall try to show, because the Bible in Hebrew speaks resonantly, even to the most pious readers, as a collection of great works of literature.

The persistent power of this second, literary canonicity for readers of the Hebrew Bible, including those in ages dominated by doctrine, helps explain one of the great enigmas of Jewish cultural history, the dramatic rebirth of a secular literature in Hebrew, twice: first in late tenth-century

Spain, initiating a rich tradition that would continue down to eighteenth-century Italy, and then in central and eastern Europe, beginning falteringly in Enlightenment Prussia and reaching artistic maturity in Russia toward the end of the nineteenth century. A necessary condition of the first of these rebirths was a conscious return of the Andalusian Hebrew poets to the language of the Bible, in competitive imitation of the Arabic poets who vaunted the purity of Koranic style of their verse. Literary historians often represent this biblicizing impulse of the Andalusian poets as chiefly a linguistic undertaking: with a clarity of understanding derived from the new Semitic philology of the era, the poets could cut away the grammatical and morphological excrescences of antecedent liturgical poetry, go back to the precision of biblical usages, and mine the Bible for vocabulary and idiom. Although all this is true, what is equally impressive is the way they evince in poem after poem a subtle responsiveness to the literary artistry and the imaginative worlds of the biblical writers. The celebration of nature, the expression of physical passion, the articulation of loneliness and personal loss, the broodings on mortality and the ephemerality of all things in this extraordinary body of secular poetry would be inconceivable without the poets' profound imaginative experience of Psalms, the Song of Songs, Job, Ecclesiastes, Proverbs, and other biblical texts as works of literature.

What I want to stress is that this sort of imaginative experience of Scripture did not suddenly begin in tenth- and eleventh-century Cordoba and Granada and Barcelona because members of the Jewish cultural elite there picked up from the surrounding high Arab culture a newfangled notion of secular literary expression. Even in periods when Jews had no option at all of secular cultural activity, the evidence of what they composed in Hebrew argues that they never ceased to respond to the literary dimension of the Bible, however fervently they saw it in doctrinal or theological terms. The double canonicity of the Song of Songs is a particularly instructive instance of this general phenomenon. As is well known, the Song's reveling in the pleasures of love was elevated to canonical acceptability through allegorical interpretation—in the Jewish treatment, by reading the lover as the Holy One and the beloved as His bride, the Community of Israel. Imaginative energy was lavished on this allegory through the centuries and, far from being an arid scheme, it became deeply moving for countless Jews, as liturgical, mystical, and homiletic texts bear witness (the classical kabbalah would have been immeasurably diminished without it). Judah Halevi (1075?– ca. 1141), perhaps the greatest poet of the Spanish period, could use the allegory quite poignantly in some of his liturgical poems by boldly reviving the frank eroticism of the Song in his representation of Israel's relationship with God. But Hebrew readers, however piously they accepted the allegorical interpretation, could scarcely forget that the Song of Songs was a collection of love poems; and so even in the period before the Andalusian renascence, one finds pointed allusions to the Song in Hebrew epithalamia, poems composed to celebrate the unions of flesh-and-blood brides and grooms. Even the liturgical chanting of the Song had a double justification. The synagogal recitation was fixed for the Sabbath of Passover. Since Passover celebrates the Exodus from Egypt, the doctrinal warrant for the linking of the Song with this holiday would be the wilderness phase of the nation's history, which in the allegorical scheme corresponds to the period of honeymoon intimacy between God and Israel His bride (compare the bridal metaphor in Jeremiah 2:2). But Passover is also a spring festival, and the evocation of the beauty of the vernal landscape in the Song of Songs was surely not lost on the framers of the liturgy, even if they were often inclined to obscure the connection between spring and the delights of young love in these poems.

Here are the first five lines of an anonymous alphabetic acrostic composed in Palestine sometime in the Byzantine period and intended for use in the Passover liturgy. The repeated farewell that is bid to the rain is not only a mark of the end of the rainy season in Palestine during the month of April but a formal prelude to the prayer for dew, invoked in the alternating refrain, that is inserted in the Passover service.

> Let me utter song as the songbird's season comes,
>   and I shall call out in song: go in peace, O rain.
> On the deeds of my Rock let me look, they are sweet in their season,
>   and sweetly shall I speak: come in peace, O dew.
> The rain has gone, the winter's past,
>   and all is new-minted in beauty: go in peace, O rain.
> Mandrakes give off their scent in the lovers' garden,
>   and cares are gone: come in peace, O dew.
> The earth is crowned with grain and wine,
>   every creature shouts: go in peace, O rain.[2]

Here, at the heart of the holiday liturgy, the poetry of nature and love of the Song of Songs comes to life again in the evocative play of allusions of the *paytan*, the anonymous liturgical poet. In this setting of public worship, he duly praises "the deeds of my Rock," which are not invoked in the biblical Song, but God's wondrous acts are manifested in these lines in the vernal freshness of nature, the passing of the rainy season, the lovers' garden—in the Song it is both a metaphor for the woman's body and the couple's trysting place. The language of the *paytan* is a supple interweave of his own formulations with phrases from the Song of Songs, liberated from the vehicle of allegory—"the songbird's season comes," "The rain has gone, the winter's past," "Mandrakes give off their scent." A small but instructive measure of the poet's relation to his biblical source is his deployment of sound-play in the fourth line. In the acrostic scheme, the line begins with *dalet*, the fourth letter of the Hebrew alphabet; the poet highlights the prominence of the initial consonant by reproducing a lovely pun from the Song and then trumping it. The Hebrew for "mandrakes" is *duda'im*, a supposedly aphrodisiac fruit matched in sound and meaning with *dodim*, "lovers" (the plural form of this noun also means "lovemaking"). To this biblical pun the poet adds, in the next part of the line, the vanishing of "cares," *deva'im*. This last little move is not one he would have made had he not been reading the Song with a careful eye to its poetic craft. A Hebrew poet himself, he observes with great nicety the harmonious orchestration of delicate poetic effects in the Song, and he gives evidence of having in effect asked himself: How can I use this beautiful material, make it part of my own idiom, even go it one better? None of this calls into question the liturgical poet's acceptance of the Song of Songs as a "genuine and inspired book," in all likelihood with the sublimation of human love into theological allegory as the proof of its inspired status. But it was also canonical for him in the same way that Shakespeare was canonical for Keats or Blake for Yeats—as one of the luminous poetic achievements in his language which could both kindle his imagination of the world and suggest to him a set of technical resources.

When secular Hebrew poetry experiences its astounding rebirth in Spain a few centuries later, the range of allusive relation to the biblical texts becomes much broader, with specific instances of allusion often proving to be remarkably subtle, inventive, and sometimes quite surprising. Some of the more broad-gauge invocations of biblical models are of a sort familiar in other literatures. Just as the blind Milton could associate his plight, cast among the new Philistines of the Restoration, with that of the blind Samson, Solomon ibn Gabirol (1021–1050s), shunned by many of his fellow Jews for his mystical beliefs and suffering from tuberculosis of the skin, repeatedly identified his painful destiny with that of Job. A writer may read Scripture as a purely doctrinal canon and yet allow himself such personal identifications. Indeed, he may want to give a large theological-historical resonance to his own experience precisely through this sort of identification, as did Samuel Hanagid (993–1056), who as vizier of Granada

and commander of its army saw himself as a second David and after leading his forces in military triumph, composed two striking victory poems,
each with 150 lines, the number of psalms in the canonical collection.

But literature, as every good writer knows, exists in the details, and it
is particularly in the Spanish Hebrew poets' imaginative response to the
minute details of the Hebrew text of the Bible that they register their fine
understanding of its literary and not just its religious canonicity. Here is
the opening line of a poem by Hanagid which is part of a cycle of poems
on the death of his brother Isaac (a cycle that is one of the great peaks of
personal poetry in all medieval literature). The poet has returned to visit
his brother's grave the day after the burial: "Alas, I've come back in my
spirit's strait, / God be gracious to you, my brother."[3] The second
hemistich, as unexceptional as it may seem in translation, is an extraordinary condensation of meaning through allusion to the Bible. Even as
it perfectly fits a metrical scheme that allows no variations ($^{u}{-}{-}{-}{^u}{-}{-}{-}$), it
is a verbatim quotation of Genesis 43:29, with a single term of familial
relation altered. When Benjamin, Joseph's only full brother, is brought
down to the Egyptian court by the sons of Leah and the concubines, the
man who is vizier of Egypt greets him by saying, "God be gracious to
you, my son." Hanagid's substitution of *aḥi*, "my brother," for *beni*, "my
son," shows, among other things, how shrewdly he has read Genesis 43
as a great story. Joseph in Egypt beholds the only person in the world he
can call "my brother" without emotional or legal reservation, but, still
preserving appearances as an Egyptian nobleman, he is careful to address
the younger man as "my son." The moment when he will "fall on the neck
of Benjamin his brother and weep" (Gen. 45:14) is not yet ripe. Hanagid
understands that "my son" is a mask for "my brother," which Joseph longs
to pronounce but cannot yet permit himself to utter. The medieval poet's
predicament is painfully the reverse of the biblical figure's quandary (his
identification with the Hebrew lad who became vice-regent of Egypt
would surely have been encouraged by the similarity to Hanagid's own
political career): Joseph says "my son" just before he will be reunited with
his brother after two decades of separation; Hanagid says "my brother"
in the wrenching knowledge that he is now separated from him forever.
In the next five lines he implores his brother to respond to his greeting
and then cannot keep himself from imagining the body already beginning to moulder in the grave. Hanagid was, of course, a believing Jew
who accepted the inspired status of Scripture (he was also a recognized
authority on rabbinic law), but at moments like this, which abound in his
poetry and in that of his contemporaries, he speaks as a person wrestling

with his individual human fate who reads in the Bible not law or doctrine but the profound representation of human relationships and of people struggling with the burden of their individual destinies.

The language and imagery of the Bible provided the medieval poets a vehicle for imagining the world, for seeing its beauty, its depth of meaning, sometimes its contradictions and ironies. In many instances, like the one from Hanagid that we have just considered, the relation between the medieval poem and the biblical intertext proves to be one of dialectical complexity. Often, the relation between the two texts is richly consonant, as in the allusion to the Creation story near the end of *Hatirdof na'arut*, Judah Halevi's exquisite poem about an imagined sea voyage. After an awesome night storm that almost destroys the ship, the sky clears and the surface of the water gradually returns to tranquillity: "and the stars are bewildered in the heart of the sea / like exiles banished from their home, // and in their likeness, by their image, they make light / in the heart of the sea, like flames and fires."[4] The lovely paradox of the stars reflected in the still undulating water as bewildered exiles banished from their true home sets off a whole train of associations. The stars recall "the heavens . . . and all their array" of Genesis 2:1. By implication, the storm that has just passed is identified with the primordial "welter and waste" (Gen. 1:2) that preceded the first act of Creation. The starlight reflected in the water thus intimates a renewal of Creation. (In the three remaining lines of the poem after the two I have quoted, the poet will play with the opposition in Genesis between the waters above and the waters below, divided by a "vault," *raqi'a*, with a linking and mirroring between above and below stressed instead of the biblical theme of separation.) The stars in the sky which seem to reproduce themselves in the depths of the sea replicate the act of the Creator who made the "human in our image, by our likeness, to hold sway over the fish of the sea and the fowl of the heavens" (Gen. 1:26).[5] After the storm, the world is knit together again in beautiful harmony, as it was in the first creation. Halevi's use of the allusion demonstrates that reading the two canonicities of the Bible can be entirely simultaneous for the Hebrew poet. To think of Creation as it is represented in the first two chapters of Genesis is, necessarily, to think of divine creation, and though this poem is intensely personal and in its vividness is also a descriptive nature poem, it begins by referring to the poet's obligations to God, and it would be thoroughly misleading to call it a secular poem. And yet the poet has clearly read Genesis both as the inspired account of how the world came into being and as a complex of suggestive images, virtually a model for the poet's craft. In this way, there is a seamless continuity of poetic artifice between the ornate trope for the night's beauty borrowed from the Arabic tradition which appears in the line before the two we are considering—"the night . . . is like a Negress adorned with golden spangles"—and the image of the stars "in their likeness, by their image" making small flames in the heart of the sea.

There is another, more radical manifestation of intertextuality in medieval and Renaissance poetry in which the words of the biblical texts are willfully wrenched from their original setting and flaunted by the poet in a context that is disparate from or even antithetical to the biblical one. There is a dizzying variety of such radical intertextuality through eight centuries of secular Hebrew poetry and rhyming prose. I will cite one brief example, a two-line poem by Judah Halevi, before reflecting on what so bold a use of Scripture might imply about the relation of the poet to the canonical text. The Arabic superscription in the Halevi *diwan* introduces the poem as follows: "and he spoke [it] in the genre of love poems when he saw one of his friends asleep."

> Arise, O my friend, from your slumber, / sate me when awake with
>   your image.
> Should you behold someone kissing your lips in a dream, / it is I who
>   will solve your dreams.

The biblical idiom "solver of dreams" (*poter halomot*) is associated with Joseph, but in this playfully erotic context, solving the riddle of the dream is not an act of interpretation but a kiss given by the speaker to his friend, a fulfillment, that is, of the "prophecy" of the dream. The "slumber" and "image" at the end of the first and second hemistichs are the same word transformed by metathesis (*tenumatekha* turned into *temunatekha*) and a small indication of how Halevi's virtuosity defies translation. But the second hemistich is also a verbatim quotation of the last three Hebrew words of Psalm 17 (only one syllable modified for the sake of the meter). When the Psalmist says, "Sate me [literally, "Let me be sated"] when awake with your image," he is of course addressing God. The poetic parallelism in the first half of this verse reads, "I in righteousness shall behold Your face." Halevi is recalling the whole biblical line when he chooses the verb "behold" (*tehezeh*) for the friend's erotic dream-vision. The intertext from Psalm 17 may also suggest that the speaker is unable to see his friend's face because of the position in which he is sleeping, which would be a further motive for urging him to awake. In sum, "when awake," a phrase of rhetorical emphasis with approximately the force of "actually" in Psalms, is entirely literalized in the poem, while the physical matrix of the verb "to be sated" (*'esb'a*) is actualized here by the appetitive narrative context of the hoped-for kiss.

What does it say about the Hebrew poet's relation to Scripture that he should feel free to make such audacious and frankly erotic use of a devotional text from the Bible? Let me stress that the radical freedom of allusive play with the Bible manifested in this little poem of Halevi's is thoroughly characteristic of countless love poems, whether homosexual or heterosexual, in the Spanish period, as it is of the bawdy passages of Emmanuel of Rome in the fourteenth century and of a whole spectrum of Hebrew poets of the Italian Renaissance—and not only in instances of erotic verse. There are no grounds to question the fact that Judah Halevi and nearly all the participants in the great medieval and Renaissance tradition of Hebrew literature were religious Jews—not only in their formal commitment to the laws and institutions of rabbinic Judaism but also, in his case and that of a good many others, in possessing a deep sense of piety. Halevi surely must have believed that the Book of Psalms, with the rest of Scripture, was the inspired word of God. What allowed him, then, to take this verse from Psalm 17 and flagrantly turn it around from God to man, from epiphany to a kiss? If the canonicity of the Bible were strictly a matter of doctrinal truth (or, as contemporary critics applying "canon" to secular works would say, of ideological conformity), such radical redirecting of biblical language would be unimaginable. But for Halevi, as for hundreds of other Hebrew poets—and many thousands of Hebrew readers—in the tradition he helped to define, the canonicity of the Bible also inheres in its being the literary repository of the language of the culture. By "language" I mean first, in the fundamental sense, the words and idioms through which it becomes possible to say anything at all. (One must keep constantly in mind that Jews never ceased producing literature in Hebrew, even through the many centuries when it had no vernacular base, and if they also wrote in other languages, Hebrew remained the privileged vehicle of national literature.) In this basic lexical sense, the Bible does not generate allusion in any strict application of the term but rather enables expression. The Bible is also, however, the great compendium of cultural references for its Hebrew readers, who are presumed to have a word-by-word familiarity with it: images, motifs, narrative situations are there to be called up by a writer with the flick of a phrase, and just as in the case of shared cultural references in a purely secular setting, the writer feels free to ride with the semantic sweep of the original text or to swim against it with athletic vigor, recontextualizing the biblical materials, wittily turning them on their head, even sometimes deconstructing them.

The sort of operation T. S. Eliot performs in *The Hollow Men* on a nursery rhyme ("Here We Go Round the Mulberry Bush") in making it, rather startlingly, the expression of a kind of vapid apocalypse ("This is the way the world ends, / This is the way the world ends . . .") is not different in kind from what the Hebrew poets do again and again with the Bible: one could even say that in Jewish societies in which the nursery rhymes were, after all, sung in Judeo-Arabic, Ladino, and Yiddish, the Bible was the Hebrew text everybody educated would immediately know, like a nursery rhyme. As a pious Jew, Halevi no doubt heard in Psalm 17 an authentic anguished cry of the believer for God to rescue him from the arrogant and grant him a glimpse of the divine presence. As a lively member of a living Hebrew literary culture, Halevi seizes the concluding verse of the psalm with manifest delight as matter for inventive transformation: the "beholding" of God's face becomes the friend's beholding of a kiss in his dream, and the longing to be sated with God's image turns into a longing for the image of the friend. From a doctrinal point of view, this is double blasphemy, substituting man for God in the biblical text and man for woman in the expression of passion, but the poet does it without noticeable compunction, for in his sense of the *literary* canonicity of the Bible, considerations of doctrine are suspended.

Such acts of free play with Scripture, it must be said, are carried out in this tradition within a delimited arena. At least some of the poetic genres of the Spanish period, like the love poem, might in fact be thought of precisely as an arena of this sort, a safe space—roughly analogous to the social institution of carnival—in which anything goes with the Bible. The basic difference, I think, between this whole movement of secular Hebrew literature and the one that is launched in central and eastern Europe in the wake of the Enlightenment and then romanticism is that in the more recent movement the second canonicity of the Bible becomes the matrix for the conscious creation of a secular Hebrew culture. In the medieval and Renaissance tradition, any transvaluing of biblical texts is played out locally, hedged in by the limits of poetic genre. In the formative European phase of modern Hebrew literature (schematically, 1751 to 1917), the transvaluation is global in a double sense: it involves, for increasing numbers of the writers with the passage of time, an impulse to displace entirely the doctrinal canonicity of the Bible with its literary canonicity, and it is sometimes manifested not merely in playful transformation of biblical texts (this still abounds) but in ideological polemic with biblical values.

Both in poetry and in prose, the age-old sense of the Hebrew Bible as a literary canon, not only a religious one, was what initially made it possible for the new Hebraists to find their way, however awkwardly, into the realm of European literature. The centrally influential poem of the German period of the Haskalah (Hebrew Enlightenment) is Naphtali Hertz Weisel's *Shirei tiferet* (Songs of Glory), published in segments between 1789 and 1811, a didactic epic on the life of Moses loosely imitative of the German Enlightenment poet Friedrich Gottlieb Klopstock. This turgid rhetorical performance is almost unreadable today, but it excited Hebrew imaginations throughout the nineteenth century because it was felt to demonstrate how the literary grandeur of the Hebrew Bible might be the source for new works that could take their place in the high epic tradition of European literature. Two generations later, in Russia, the first Hebrew novel, Avraham Mapu's *Ahavat Tsiyon* (Love of Zion, 1853), which is set in the time of Isaiah, in a style that is a florid pastiche of biblical phrases, reflects an analogous aspiration to build on the aesthetic resonances of the Bible and make of them a new edifice of secular culture in Hebrew. This early step in prose fiction was only a little less stumbling than the ones in epic poetry, but what concerns us here is not the level of artistic success—that would come with a remarkable group of Russian Hebrew writers around the turn of the twentieth century—but rather the nature of the cultural enterprise, the creation of a secular literature enabled by the literary perception of the biblical canon.

Still more instructive in regard to the two orders of authority exerted by the Bible on its Hebrew readers are the polemic engagements with Scripture in a variety of modern Hebrew texts, for they vividly demonstrate how the imaginative power of biblical literature could energize a writer in the very act of his rejecting its ideological values. The two commanding poets of the great efflorescence of Hebrew literature which began in Odessa in the 1890s, Hayyim Nahman Bialik (1873–1934) and Saul Tchernikhovsky (1875–1943), express this polemic impulse in strikingly different ways. Bialik, the more deeply rooted of the two in traditional Jewish culture, was inclined, as Tchernikhovsky was not, to see his role as Hebrew poet in light of the vocation of the biblical prophet, reading the dedication of the prophet in Isaiah 6 back through Pushkin's recasting of it as a trope for the calling of the poet. But both historical circumstances and the nature of his audience led Bialik more and more to despair of his supposedly prophetic vocation and thus to transform it radically in a series of daunting poems in which the poet-prophet brings a vision of death or nihilistic hopelessness to his audience. In several ways the most extreme transformation of the prophetic calling is Bialik's awesome long poem on the Kishinev pogrom of 1903, *Be'ir haharegah* (In the City of Slaughter). Rhetorically, the poet draws on all the prophetic books but in particular on Ezekiel: the poet-prophet is addressed as "son of man," Ezekiel's idiom, by the voice, presumably God's, that speaks the poem, and he is enjoined to "go forth into the city of slaughter" and witness, corpse by mangled corpse, the mayhem perpetrated there. But this God is one who has "declared bankruptcy" (*yaradti minekhasai*) in allowing such horrors to happen, and the poem is informed by a corrosive rage against both God and the Jews who cravenly submitted to their attackers. If biblical prophecy is the vehicle for conveying divine wrath to a wayward Israel so that the people can change its course, thus implying the urgent engagement of prophet with people, this poem ends with God's commanding the prophet to flee to the rocky wilderness, where he is to "tear [his] soul to ten pieces" and "let [his] heart be consumed by impotent rage." The poetic power of biblical prophecy thunders through this great poem, but in the baleful historical light of the horrors witnessed by the poet, the prophetic idea of divine reward and punishment in history and the biblical prospect of national redemption are scathingly rejected.

In Bialik there is often antagonistic tension with the biblical vehicle he uses because his ideological agenda, prompted by his mentor, Ahad Ha'am, is the perpetuation of classical Jewish values in the modern secular context, a project that in his most probing poetic perceptions sometimes seemed a maddeningly desperate contradiction. Tchernikhovsky, altogether a less "Judaic" poet, is associated with the turn-of-the-century Nietzschean trend in Hebrew writing that aspired to a radical transvaluation of Jewish values. Instead of Bialik's sharp confrontation with biblical assumptions, Tchernikhovsky uses the magic of the Bible's poetic language—which is predominant in many of his strophic poems, in contradistinction to his hexameter idylls—to conjure up what amounts to a counterbiblical world. The implicit theology of Tchernikhovsky's poetry is vitalistic pantheism. His typical move is to inscribe in vivid biblical language at the center of his poems what is proscribed in the Bible: the sun god, Tammuz, Baal, Ashtoreth, fertility rites, the exultation of sacred ecstatic dance. (In invoking this ancient Near Eastern polytheism, he was the precursor of the so-called Canaanite Movement that became prominent in Hebrew literature in Palestine in the early 1940s.) Here is the sestet of "My Ashtoreth," a sonnet written in Russia just after the First World War. The speaker, a young woman, is marveling over a statuette of the fertility goddess Ashtoreth which she imagines may have been brought from Phoenicia in the north by a camel caravan making its way past Danite—that is, Israelite—marauders:

> Wondrous to me, O wondrous, your emerald eyes,
>   all ivory-wrought, the whole your limbs comprise,
> And none shall betray how I got you—none.
>
>   A basket of dates for you—I've scooped up fine flour,
> A *log* of olive oil—to you, in prayer's hour:
>   "Lead him, a shining lad, to me bring him soon."[6]

In the Hebrew the only word in these six lines that is not biblical is "emerald"—but even that postbiblical term is assimilated to a biblical idiomatic pattern, *ʿeynayikh ʾismaragdim* recalling the Song of Song's *ʿeynayikh yonim* ("your eyes are doves"). There is also a kind of reminiscence of the Song of Songs, not quite an allusion, in "all ivory-wrought" (literally: "all of you they have made from ivory"), as "all of you" (*kulakh*) in the Song punctuates the ecstatic descriptions of the beloved, and the lover's loins are said to be fashioned from ivory. But in contrast to the playful little love poem by Judah Halevi, the poem does not turn on any pointed allusion. Tchernikhovsky's sonnet could not have come into being without his deep experience of the imaginative power of the Bible in Hebrew, but he is not ultimately concerned with the Bible as a system of meanings with which to wrestle, verse by verse. What the Bible presents to him is not doctrinal authority—the first of its two canonicities scarcely exists for him—but a living world bodied forth in language, like the world of Homer (whom Tchernikhovsky translated) or the world of *War and Peace*. The purpose of the poem is to tease out of the shadowy margins of the biblical world into the sunlight of poetic attention what biblical doctrine opposed and suppressed: the fresh pagan (or perhaps syncretistic) faith of a nubile young woman offering sacrifice and imploring the goddess to send her a lover. The celebration of the aesthetic and of the beauty of the body in the sonnet and in Tchernikhovsky's poetry as a whole expresses a countervalue to the dominant value system of the Bible, though this very celebration takes off, instructively, from a whole set of biblical cues. Some of this imaginative re-creation of paganism reflects reading the Bible against itself, as when the poet draws items from the sacrificial lists in Leviticus and uses them for the offering to a fertility goddess. But the intrinsic heterogeneity of the biblical canon is also vital to the poet's undertaking. The fragmentary hints the Bible incorporates of an epic background that was of little interest to the monotheistic writers come to life in the compact vision of a large and exciting Near Eastern horizon evoked in the octave of the sonnet. The celebration of the lovely statuette is predicated on the celebratory love poetry of the Song of Songs, a biblical text that, as we have seen, is exceptional and in a way heterodox. Most pervasively, the implicit feeling of so many of the biblical writers in different genres and books for the expressive loveliness of their Hebrew medium makes possible Tchernikhovsky's own aestheticizing of the biblical world.

Tchernikhovsky's poetic enterprise is, I think, one of those instances of the extreme case that illuminates an underlying dynamic of the typical. His brave attempt to help forge a secular or at any rate nonmonotheistic cultural identity in Hebrew has encountered serious challenges in the half-century since his death. This is not the place to speculate as to whether Jewish secularism or Jewish cultural nationalism still has a future. What is pertinent to our concerns here is the sheer power of the Bible's second canonicity that created the possibility of the cultural alternative articulated in Tchernikhovsky's poetry. If the formation of the biblical canon two millennia ago reflected the crystallization of a religious ideology, there were also, as is patently true in secular canons, impulses that transcended ideology, or even subverted it, which went into the making of the canon. For Hebrew readers through the ages, these impulses were not merely archeological traces of vanished literary aims but palpable presences in the texts. Through them creative imaginations have been repeatedly sparked, and some of the most surprising cultural blossoms have sprung from the rich old soil of the Bible. If the canon, in this supposedly exemplary case, turns out to be more dynamic and multifaceted than its doctrinal function would require, we should not be surprised to discover that secular canons similarly prove to be bustling junctions of contradictory aims and values and not, as many of the new critics of the canon claim, chiefly vehicles for the enforcement of ideological conformity.

Notes

1. See Sid Z. Leiman, *The Canonization of Hebrew Scripture: The Talmudic and Midrashic Evidence,* 2d ed. (New Haven, 1991).

2. The translation is mine, the Hebrew text is taken from T. Carmi, *The Penguin Book of Hebrew Verse* (New York, 1981), 203. I have made somewhat related observations on this poem in my book *Hebrew and Modernity* (Bloomington, 1994), though there I used Carmi's translation.

3. My translation; the Hebrew text is taken from H. Schirmann, *Hashirah ha'ivrit beSefarad ubeProvence* (Hebrew Poetry in Spain and Province) (Jerusalem, 1954), 1:107.

4. Schirmann, *Hebrew Poetry,* 1:496.

5. All translations of Genesis are from my own version (New York, 1996).

6. My translation is from the Hebrew text in Saul Tchernikhovsky, *Shirim* (Poems) (Jerusalem and Tel Aviv, 1957), 290.

CHAPTER 8

The Idea of Judaism
in Feminism and Afrocentrism

Amy Newman

One of the most controversial trends to emerge from the American experiment with multicultural education is the proliferation of narratives that purport to reconstruct the origins and histories of social groups marginalized in traditional Eurocentric discourse. Since standard accounts of the history of Western civilization reflect almost exclusively the interests of European males, some feminists, for example, have attempted to reconstruct history from the standpoint of women, and some scholars of African descent have attempted to reconstruct history with the African continent at the center. A difficulty that has plagued these efforts to create alternative cultural narratives, however, is their tendency to reproduce many of the logical, rhetorical, and structural conventions of Eurocentric discourse. The nature of this difficulty may be clarified by considering two methods of social criticism employed frequently in the texts of American and European feminists and Afrocentrists, namely, the Marxian method of reversal and the Nietzschean method of transvaluation.[1] While these nineteenth-century strategies are viewed by many contemporary academics as still the most effective modes of radical social criticism, other scholars have begun to question their potential in this respect. For example, Ghanaian philosopher Kwame Anthony Appiah of Harvard University asserts that in the logic of reversal "the terms of resistance are already given us, and our contestation entrapped within the Western cultural conjuncture we affect to dispute. The pose of repudiation actually presupposes the cultural institutions of the West and the ideological matrix in which they, in turn, are imbricated."[2] Thus, Appiah maintains, those who employ these methods of criticism against Eurocentrism "are of its party without knowing it."[3]

Perhaps the most disturbing possibility raised by Appiah's critique is that those who employ some version of the method of reversal in their social criticism may actually be perpetuating certain forms of cultural domination *without knowing it*. The question of the nature of this "forgetting" has recently been addressed by cultural critics Homi Bhabha and V. Y. Mudimbe. In *The Location of Culture* Bhabha analyzes what he terms, following Derrida, "anti-ethnocentrism thinking itself as ethnocentrism."[4] One characteristic trait of colonized discourse, Bhabha thinks, is the simultaneous expression of contradictory attitudes, a phenomenon that he sees as a reflection of the cultural "double bind" in which the colonized often find themselves. It is this double bind, he asserts, that produces the logic of reversal.[5] Examples that Bhabha gives of this logic at work are "Montesquieu's Turkish Despot, Barthes's Japan, Kristeva's China, Derrida's Nambikwara Indians, [and] Lyotard's Cashinahua pagans."[6] All of these constructions, Bhabha maintains, function as "strategies of containment" within the confines of which exotic subjects are "cited, quoted, framed, illuminated, encased in the shot/reverse-shot strategy of a serial enlightenment." But never are these subjects permitted "to signify, to negate, to initiate . . . historical desire, to establish [their] own institutional and oppositional desire." They exist, rather, only as abstractions, premises in arguments, illustrations of favorite theories.

The phenomenon of "forgetting" is linked also to the experience of "double consciousness" often reported by those whose traditional culture has been displaced, suppressed, or restructured from without. In *The Idea of Africa* Zairean theorist Mudimbe perceives this phenomenon lurking behind the way in which the concept "Africa" is sometimes employed in contemporary cultural studies. "Africa," he suggests, is a concept that has been "conceived and conveyed through conflicting systems of knowledge."[7] At the end of the nineteenth century, Mudimbe explains, the European colonization of Africa "cohesively binds the diverse, often antagonistic, collective memories of many African cultures."[8] A profound erasure of memory was one result, the consequence of the superimposition of the traditional history and memory of European Christian culture upon African memory.[9] The hybrid "memory" thus constructed is neither entirely African nor entirely European; and over a period of time, for subsequent generations, these categories become mixed and intermingled and at many junctures indistinguishable.

The logic of reversal is often touted as an effective method of recovering repressed traditional memories. This was in fact the way that Nietz-sche himself conceived of his "transvaluation of all values": that is, as a reversal of the values of European Christian society which would effect a return to what he imagined to be the mode of consciousness enjoyed by humanity prior to the "slave revolt in morality" that originated, he thought, in the Jewish religion and had been translated into a "universal world religion" by Christianity.[10] But Nietzsche's fantasy of an originary amoral state of human nature turns out to be entirely defined by the struc-ture of the contemporary morality of which it is a conceptual reversal, and his radical agenda turns out to be substantively ineffectual, a revolu-tion in theory only which was as amenable to appropriation by National Socialists as by poststructuralists.

The growing realization among scholars in the field of cultural stud-ies that reversal and transvaluation tend to covertly reproduce the struc-ture of domination raises new questions not only concerning how these strategies manipulate and distort the reality of the oppressed but also how the concept of the "oppressor" is constructed. On the other side of the reification and romanticization of oppression and otherness that often accompanies these methodologies, for example, is a rather predictable understanding of the structure of domination that also serves the inter-ests of the status quo. A particularly striking example of this is found in the idea of Judaism that appears in some feminist and Afrocentric texts.

What is most ironic about this idea of Judaism is that, despite the expressed intent of the authors of these texts to invert, subvert, and oth-erwise undermine the discourse of European ethnocentrism, the "Judaism" in these texts is strikingly similar to the highly stereotyped image of Judaism found in the conventional Christian Eurocentric narrative. In effect, the methods of reversal and transvaluation themselves are curiously suspended when it comes to Judaism and instead a distinctively European Christian image of Judaism is proffered; most often this image seems to have been lifted whole cloth from early twentieth-century German social theory. This image of Judaism is not only ahistorical and nonempirical but is derived from a system of thought that was explicitly anti-Semitic.

Judaism in Recent Feminist and Afrocentric Texts

In *Yurugu: An African-centered Critique of European Cul-tural Thought and Behavior,* Afrocentric scholar Marimba Ani employs the concept *"Asili"*—which she translates as "cultural seed"—to explain European culture as a whole. She asserts that using this concept, European culture can be understood in its totality, because everything in a given culture is an expression of the "seed," or ideological core, lying at the heart of that culture. The ideological core of European culture, according to Ani, is Hebrew theology, which contains "the germ of 'universalism', the critical ingredient of European cultural imperialism." Hebrew theology, she asserts, is "incipient European cultural chauvinism." That is, one finds in the religion of the ancient Hebrews "an accurate statement of the European self-image."[11]

Ani cites a variety of European and American scholars to support this interpretation of the Jewish tradition, among them the late historian of religion Mircea Eliade and Christian feminist theologian Rosemary Radford Ruether. Ruether's analysis of the origins of "male monotheism" describes the ancient "nomadic peoples" who embraced this form of religion as "characterized by exclusivism and an aggressive, hostile relationship to the agricultural people of the land and their religion."[12] Eliade, in *A History of Religious Ideas,* maintains that while most ancient people believed that "the divine is incarnated, or manifests itself in cosmic objects and rhythms," this belief was "denounced by the adherents of Yahweh as the worst possible idolatry." It was the Hebrew prophets, Eliade maintains, who "finally succeeded in emptying nature of any divine presence."[13] Ani takes up this theme, asserting that European *Asili* "is lacking in spirituality and therefore seeks power over others as a substitute."[14]

Ani further elaborates on Ruether's and Eliade's claims by asserting that in the ancient world there existed "two divergent world-views." On the one hand, there was the worldview of the ancient Africans and other nature-worshiping cultures, which was holistic and emphasized such principles as "the harmonious interaction of the complementary Divine Feminine and Masculine" and "the eternal cycle of life that offers the possibility of transcendence, of harmonious interrelationship, of wholeness, integration, and authentic organicity."[15] On the other hand was the worldview of the ancient Hebrews. "How profoundly different was the Hebrew conception of meaning from the Kemetic and other 'non-European' conceptions," Ani declares.[16] It is from Hebrew theology, Ani asserts, that Europeans derived the ideas that "being can be mechanically, technically 'created'" and that "it is only as laws become alienated from the human spirit that conformity to them requires that they be put on paper."[17] The "Judaic statement," she alleges further, laid the groundwork for the "desacralization of nature," and this "attack on nature," in turn, "went

hand in hand with the Hebrew submergence of the power of women."
While she admits that ancient Hebrew society was "distant in time from
the [modern technological] colossus that we now experience," she insists
that "the view of reality on which this colossus was constructed" was "put
in place" in the Hebrew Bible.[18]

Using the strategy of transvaluation, Ani sets a highly idealized portrait of ancient African culture against a starkly devalued Hebraism. The
ancient Hebrew religion, in her system, represents the exact antithesis of
all things African. Furthermore, she postulates a logical cause-and-effect
relationship between the religion of the ancient Hebrews and modern
European cultural values, so far removed from each other in time and space:
the *reason* that modern Europeans became cultural imperialists is *because*
they adopted the values of the ancient Hebrews, and this adoption, she
thinks, is the key to understanding the history of European chauvinism.

Similar portrayals of the culture of the ancient Hebrews are found in
recent texts by Stanford professor Nel Noddings and feminist historian
Gerda Lerner. In *Women and Evil* Noddings argues, like Ani, and following
Mary Daly, that the Hebrew Bible "undergirds destructive patterns in the
fabric of our culture."[19] In her view the Hebrew Bible is the primal source
of patriarchal values and thus of sexism. According to Noddings, the biblical accounts of conflicts between the ancient Hebrews and contemporaneous cultures, particularly Canaanite culture, depict "violent attempts
to overthrow feminine deities and to subjugate women." The purpose of
the conquest of Canaan, according to Noddings, was "to gain political
and religious domination over an area in which the goddess was still worshipped." The Israelites "competed for land and resources with people
who worshipped 'pagan idols,'" which is to say, in her opinion, that they
worshiped "the Great Goddess known by such names as Ashtoreth,
Inanna, Asherah, Ishtar, and Hathor," who represented these other cultures' reverence of "sexual pleasure, reproduction, prophecy, serpents, and
fig trees."[20]

In addition, Noddings treats the aggressive behavior of the ancient
Hebrews as unique both in kind and intensity. She cites Martin Gardner's assertion, in regard to the level of violence described in the Hebrew
Bible, that "it is hard to find its equal in any other sacred book."[21] She
lists as evidence of this the "killings of Nadab and Abihu for a mistake in
the mixing of incense, the stoning of a young man for blasphemy, the
swallowing up of rebels against Moses and Aaron, the plague that murdered 14,700 people because some complained about their god's cruelty,
[and] the fiery serpents sent to bite and kill when people objected to the

taste of manna." She concludes that "it is hard to deny the wickedness of Yahweh as he is portrayed in the Old Testament," where he is revealed to be "jealous, vengeful, and small-minded."[22]

In *The Creation of Patriarchy* Gerda Lerner also argues that the religion of the ancient Hebrews was primarily "an attack on the widespread cults of the various fertility goddesses."[23] Like Noddings, Lerner conceives of the ancient world in terms of a vast cultural divide with the God of the ancient Hebrews on one side and the "Great Goddess" on the other. She provides a detailed description of the Goddess's "consistently recurring symbolic attributes" with which Lerner believes her to be associated wherever she was found in the ancient world:

The Goddess is shown amidst pillars or trees, accompanied by goats, snakes, birds. Eggs and symbols of vegetation are associated with her. These symbols indicate that she was worshiped as a source of fertility for vegetation, animals, and humans. . . . She was venerated in Sumer as Ninhursag and Inanna; in Babylon as Kubab and Ishtar; in Phoenicia as Astarte; in Canaan as Anath; in Greece as Hekate-Artemis. Her frequent association with the moon symbolized her mystical powers over nature and the seasons. The belief system manifested in Great Goddess worship was monistic and animistic. There was unity among earth and the stars, humans and nature, birth and death, all of which were embodied in the Great Goddess.[24]

The formation of the ancient Hebrew religion, symbolized by the Mosaic covenant, represents, according to Lerner, "the *historic moment* of the death of the Mother-Goddess."[25]

Employing this dichotomizing structure is rhetorically convenient, for once it is set into place, the values represented by the opposing poles are firmly established, while the terms that may be used to represent these values are entirely arbitrary. Afrocentric scholar Yosef A. A. ben-Jochannan, for example, sees the story of the conquest of Canaan not as an effort to wipe out goddess worship but rather as an attempt to wipe out black people, terming the "extermination" of the Canaanites "one of the earliest acts of genocide in man's history . . . the very first recorded 'holocaust.'"[26] The Senegalese scholar Cheikh Anta Diop, similarly, suggests in *The African Origin of Civilization* that white racism is of Hebrew origin, that is, it originated with the story of Noah's curse on his son Ham in the Hebrew Bible.[27] While Diop allows that this is a misinterpretation of the Hamitic myth, other Afrocentric scholars assert that Jews are responsible for this misreading itself. According to Tony Martin, professor of African American studies at Wellesley College, although Christians have often been blamed for interpreting this myth in a racist way, this interpretation itself was "invented by Jewish talmudic scholars."[28] Martin, following the now familiar pattern, portrays the Jewish and African world-views as polar opposites. The Jewish perspective, according to him, is "the antithesis of Afrocentrism" and "considers Afrocentrism its natural enemy."[29] John Henrik Clarke, who some view as the founder of American Afrocentrism, likewise asserts that there is "a world-wide Black-White conflict which is part of the broader conflict between European and non-European people," and in this conflict "African people are on one side of that conflict and the people we refer to as Jews are on the other side."[30]

Another important theme found in some recent feminist and Afrocentric texts is the idea that these interpretations of the history of the ancient Hebrew religion can be transposed into explanatory theses in regard to modernity. In effect, it is sometimes maintained that the displacement of ancient woman-centered and African-centered cultures by the religion of the ancient Hebrews was recapitulated in the fifteenth and sixteenth centuries in Europe by the arrival of Jews expelled from Spain and Portugal. Tony Martin, for example, maintains that the Hamitic myth provided "a major rationalization for the enslavement of Africans" and served as "the moral pretext upon which the entire [slave] trade grew and flourished." He concludes that Jews are therefore responsible for the deaths of "many millions more than all the anti-Jewish pogroms and holocausts in Europe."[31]

In *The Secret Relationship between Blacks and Jews* (1991), a controversial text published by the Nation of Islam, the authors also present an account of the institution of slavery in which the slave trade is a distinctively "Jewish" occupation, being predominantly financed by rich Sephardic Jews. This text also attempts to demonstrate that Jews were not only disproportionately represented among those who profited from the slave trade but also made up the majority of actual slave traders and those who owned slaves in North and South America and the Caribbean.[32] The authors maintain that after the Jews were expelled from Spain and Portugal at the end of the fifteenth century, they migrated to Amsterdam and Dutch colonies in the Americas, where they became deeply involved in the slave trade. The Dutch West India Company welcomed the participation of Jews in their endeavors, according to this account, because Jews were thought to be experts when it came to unethical financial dealings.[33]

Notably, Gerda Lerner also traces the origin of slavery to the Jews. The practice of slavery, she says, followed logically from the ancient Hebrews' domination of women. Patriarchal dominance, in other words, demonstrated that one could establish "dominance and hierarchy over other people," and, according to Lerner, this planted the idea in the ancient mind that such relations could extend beyond gender dominance: "As subordination of women by men provided the conceptual model for the creation of slavery as an institution, so the patriarchal family provided the structural model."[34]

Carolyn Merchant, in *The Death of Nature*, also follows this approach, explaining that many of the characteristic features of modernity were of Hebrew origin, and she understands the religion of the ancient Hebrews as a uniquely oppressive institution. According to Merchant, a feminist historian of science, until the sixteenth century nature was conceived as female in European society and "organic concepts of the cosmos" dominated. This worldview was displaced in the early modern era by a view of nature as a "disorderly and chaotic realm to be subdued and controlled." This latter view, Merchant explains, originated in the Hebrew tradition, within which the natural world was viewed as something "to be overcome and subdued," and this is the understanding of the relationship between humanity and nature that came to predominate in the early modern period.[35]

Similar motifs appear in recent texts by French and German feminists. Of special note in this respect is Bulgarian-French psychoanalytic theorist Julia Kristeva's treatment of Judaism in *Powers of Horror*. Kristeva's expressed purpose in this text is to offer a feminist analysis of the concept of "abjection," an analysis to which she deems a discussion of the history of religions essential.[36] The evolution of the Jewish religion plays an important role in Kristeva's narrative because in her view traditional Jewish observance is rooted in the male fantasy of separation from "the phantasmatic power of the mother."[37] Jewish law, she explains, involves the transfer of the "impurity and defilement" attached to "food that did not conform to the taxonomy of sacred Law" to "the mother and to women in general." This "inscribes the logic of dietary abominations within that of a limit, a boundary, a border between the sexes, a separation between feminine and masculine as foundation for the organization that is 'clean and proper', 'individual', and, one thing leading to another, signifiable, legislatable, subject to law and morality."[38]

In this text Kristeva follows faithfully the standard strategy of portraying "Christianity" and "Judaism" as conceptual opposites. Jesus, she thinks, introduced a "new logic" into the world, a logic best illustrated by his relationship with the Pharisees. "After having noted that the Pharisee's faith is completely centered in appearances (too strongly tied to orality?) — 'This people honoureth me with their lips, but their heart is far from me'

(Mark 7:6) — Jesus affirms, 'Not that which goeth into the mouth defileth a man; but that which cometh out of the mouth, this defileth a man' (Matthew 15:11)." What this means, according to Kristeva, is that "the threat comes no longer from outside but from within." In Christianity morality no longer depends on observance of "the Law" but rests on "a concrete, genetic, and social authority — *a natural one*," which in her view constitutes an "invitation to mend the initial filial relationship."[39]

Kristeva finds this same message in the story of Jesus and the woman who "stood at his feet behind him weeping, and began to wash his feet with tears, and did wipe them with the hairs of her head, and kissed his feet, and anointed them with the ointment" (Luke 7:38).

Contrary to the prophet who, according to the Pharisee, would have recognized impurity in this woman and withdrawn from her, Christ gives himself up to it, deluged with a kind of overflowing — of sin or love? It is, at any rate, the overflow of an interior flux and its ambiguity [that] bursts forth in that scene. Sin, turned upside down into love, attains, on account of the ambivalence, the beauty that Hegel tells us is displayed right here for the one and only time in the Gospels.[40]

Kristeva's mention of Hegel is not insignificant, because the understanding of the relationship between Judaism and Christianity that she is articulating here is explicitly Hegelian. Especially her view of the moral significance of the "Gospel" is straight from Hegel. In his lectures on the philosophy of history Hegel offers the following description of the "general principle" lying at the heart of all "oriental" religions, of which, in his system, Judaism was a variety: "Moral distinctions and requirements are expressed as Laws . . . so that the subjective will is governed by these Laws as by an external force. Nothing subjective in the shape of Disposition, Conscience, formal Freedom, is recognized. Justice is administered only on the basis of external morality, and Government exists only as the prerogative of compulsion."[41] Christianity, in contrast, is for Hegel, as for Kristeva, the religion of freedom, where "purity of heart" rather than conformance to the law is primary.

This "New Testament" understanding of "Jewish law" appears frequently in contemporary feminist texts. It is found, interestingly enough, even in Judith Butler's *Gender Trouble*, where Butler, in an uncharacteristically reductionistic discussion of "paternal law," criticizes Lacan's notion of the law as "bearing the mark of a monotheistic singularity," which she elaborates on in an explanatory note, declaring that this "singular structuralist notion of 'the Law' clearly resonates with the prohibitive law of the Old Testament."[42] Butler goes on to credit Nietzsche with initiating poststructuralist criticism of this "Old Testament" concept, asserting that Nietzsche "faults the Judeo-Christian 'slave-morality' for conceiving the law in both singular and prohibitive terms." Nietzsche's concept of the will to power, according to Butler, reveals "both the productive and multiple possibilities of the law, effectively exposing the notion of 'the Law' in its singularity as a fictive and repressive notion."

Butler's opposition of Nietzsche's concept of the will to power to "Old Testament law" reveals a telling flaw in her interpretation. That is, she "forgets" that Nietzsche himself used the "God of the Old Testament" to illustrate the will to power in its purest form. This God, Nietzsche contends in *The Anti-Christ*, represents "everything . . . thirsting for power in the soul of a people," and it is on the basis of this view that he issued his famous defense of the Hebrew Bible in *Beyond Good and Evil*.[43] Nor did Nietzsche make Butler's reductionistic mistake of erasing several millennia of Jewish history by recourse to the mythical entity popularly known as "Judeo-Christianity," on the one hand, or the anachronistic error of collapsing the entirety of the Hebrew tradition into the Christian caricature of the "law of the Old Testament," on the other. While Nietzsche's treatment of Judaism is by no means unproblematic, he at least expresses an awareness of the existence of different strands of Jewish tradition—of a difference, for instance, between ancient Judaism and rabbinic Judaism.

An even stronger condemnation of "Jewish law" is articulated by Kristeva in *Powers of Horror*. The beauty of Christianity, Kristeva thinks, lies in its ability to have "gathered in a single move perversion and beauty as the lining and the cloth *of one and the same economy*."[44] The central significance of this principle in Kristeva's thought becomes most evident in the theory of fascism that she articulates in the last few chapters of *Powers of Horror*. Hebrew law, she maintains, "sets in motion a *persecuting machine*" that becomes the mechanism behind such social movements as fascism and anti-Semitism, for such persecutory belief systems are always founded on a "fierce belief in the Absolute of Jewish Religion as religion of the Father and of the Law."[45] The anti-Semite, as much as the observant Jew, is bound to this concept of "the Absolute" as "its possessed servant, its demon, its 'dibbuk.'" In fact, Kristeva maintains, anti-Semitism is merely a "symptom" of "monotheistic power," an expression of "the traumatic *topoi*" of the Jewish religion. Says Kristeva: "*The anti-Semite is not mistaken*. Jewish monotheism is . . . *the most rigorous* application of Unicity of the Law and the Symbolic." And: "Do not all attempts, in our own cultural sphere at least, at escaping from the Judeo-Christian compound by means of a unilateral call to return to what it has repressed (rhythm, drive, the feminine, etc.), converge on the same . . . anti-Semitic fantasy?" And are not "Nazi excesses . . . cathartic upon the whole"?[46]

In her astute analysis of *Powers of Horror* in *Saints and Postmodernism,* Edith Wyschogrod observes that while Kristeva writes "with an abhorrence of Fascism," it is at the same time for her "a lure, a . . . seductive power."[47] This ambivalence in Kristeva's text comes most clearly into focus in her study of French novelist Louis-Ferdinand Céline. Kristeva spends four chapters psychoanalyzing Céline's Jew-hatred, as expressed in texts composed between 1933 and 1945. Kristeva concludes that the figure of the Jew represented for Céline "a conjunction of waste and object of desire, of corpse and life, fecality and pleasure, murderous aggressivity and the most neutralizing power."[48] In effect, Céline the anti-Semite is portrayed by Kristeva as the living embodiment of the "Christian" principle that "perversion and beauty [are] the lining and the cloth of one and the same economy." The "Jew" that Céline despises turns out to be, in her analysis, not a "real" Jew at all, but rather the figurative "Jew" inside Céline himself. Thus Kristeva produces a masterful demonstration, using the techniques of reversal and transvaluation, that the prototypical fascist is really a "Jew," the oppressed are in reality the oppressors, and the persecutor himself the persecuted.

Kristeva's dissociation of Céline's anti-Semitism from the policies of extermination that were in effect in Europe during the period in question and her reduction of anti-Semitism to a psychological quirk amounts to a massive erasure of memory. This move is required to achieve the desired result, which is a dissolution of the distinction between Nazi and Jew. And as Susannah Heschel has recently shown, this approach to the problem of anti-Semitism is not unique to Kristeva but occurs with some regularity in the theories of German feminists also, where "patriarchy's responsibility for Nazism and Judaism's responsibility for patriarchy" is a not uncommon theme.[49]

The Standard "History of Judaism"

While it is evident that the idea of Judaism that emerges in these texts is an ideological construct, the frequency with which one encounters versions of this idea in contemporary academic discourse indicates that it continues to be seen by many scholars not as ideology but as historical fact, illustrating Appiah's observation that "ideologies succeed to the extent that they are invisible, in the moment that their fretwork of assumptions passes beneath consciousness."[50]

The standard, formulaic account of the "history of civilization," from which this idea of Judaism derives, is so widely accepted among American and European scholars that rarely is it questioned in academic disciplines outside the fields of Jewish and Near Eastern studies. This narrative was developed within the European Christian tradition and originated in an effort to formulate an entirely Christocentric interpretation of the Hebrew Bible for apologetic purposes, that is, to demonstrate the superiority of Christian faith in relation to Jewish observance. This narrative goes as follows: In the beginning humanity existed in a state of blissful harmony with the world of nature. The sudden emergence of the religion of the ancient Hebrews brought this idyllic state of affairs to an abrupt and violent end. The worldview of the ancient Hebrews was one that posited a sharp dichotomy between humanity and nature, between males and females, and between the Hebrews and all other people. The ancient Hebrews were unusually xenophobic and aggressive and they brutally eradicated the indigenous nature- and goddess-worshiping religions of the Levant, replacing them with a monotheistic religion requiring the worship of a singularly wrathful deity. The worship of this god, Yahweh, was enforced through the installation of the Mosaic code, a rigid, inflexible, authoritarian system of law. Christianity was born of opposition to this legalistic tradition and thus took shape as the antithesis of Judaism. The Christian worldview, the narrative continues, predominated in Europe until the late Middle Ages. During the early Middle Ages European Christians enjoyed a "self-world unity" reminiscent of that which existed in the ancient world prior to the birth of Hebrew monotheism. This holistic, participatory state of existence was disrupted by the reemergence of the Jewish impulse in European society following the migration of thousands of Jews to western Europe in the fifteenth and sixteenth centuries.

Four significant stages in the development of this narrative are identifiable in the early modern era. First of all, its transformation by the Protestant reformers, by Martin Luther in particular, into an account of radical social changes taking place in Europe in the fifteenth and sixteenth centuries; second, the elaboration of Luther's revolutionary social agenda into a formal system of logic by Hegel in the early nineteenth century; third, the transformation of this logic into a tool of radical secular social criticism in the Marxist tradition; and fourth, the efforts of the early twentieth-century German cultural philosophers—especially Wilhelm Dilthey,

Max Weber, and Werner Sombart—to historicize this narrative, that is, to demythologize and empirically verify it.

Dilthey, the founder of contemporary cultural studies, outlined an evolutionary theory of world history which in its overall structure is very close to that of Hegel and is thus an expression of a specifically European Protestant worldview. In his *Introduction to the Human Sciences* Dilthey deftly weaves a Christian apologetic into his theory of culture, identifying Paul the Apostle and Martin Luther as pivotal figures in the evolution of modern historical consciousness, understood by Dilthey as the most highly developed mode of human cognition. "When Jewish law, pagan consciousness of the world, and Christian faith clashed with one another in Saint Paul's struggles of conscience," Dilthey explains, "when in his experience faith in the Law and faith in Christ were juxtaposed," then Paul experienced "an interior transition by which the total consciousness of a historical development of the entire life of the soul awakened in him."[51] Christianity "victoriously superseded" Judaism, according to Dilthey, because it "bore within it a powerful historical reality, a reality which made contact in the life of the soul with the innermost core of every reality which had existed historically before it."[52] "And so," he concludes on this basis, "historical consciousness, taking the expression in its highest sense, first came into being."

Martin Luther's contribution to this process of consciousness evolution was twofold, according to Dilthey: first, with his radical reinterpretation of the Christian doctrine of "justification by faith alone," he introduced the principle of "the independence of experiences of the will," and second, he "separated personal faith from all metaphysics."[53] The effect, Dilthey asserts, was that Luther moved Protestant Germany beyond "everything people willed, or felt, or thought earlier." The Protestant Reformation was therefore "decisive for the rise and the justification of modern scientific consciousness" and in fact marked "the appearance of modern man." In Germany in particular, Dilthey maintains further, the Reformation initiated a "new constitution of the inner structure of culture," which represented "a higher step in developing the new generation of European peoples."[54]

Weber and Sombart

Two of Dilthey's contemporaries who were significantly influenced by his philosophy of culture and who have been influential in perpetuating Dilthey's theory of Judaism among contemporary students of German cultural studies were Max Weber and Werner Sombart. Both Weber and Sombart held to the view characteristic of European scholarship that, as Weber puts it in the famous first paragraph of *The Protestant Ethic and the Spirit of Capitalism,* "in Western civilization, and in Western civilization only, cultural phenomena have appeared which . . . lie in a line of development having universal significance and value."[55] The proof of this, for Weber as for Dilthey, was the intellectual culture of modern Europe.[56] In his *Sociology of Religion* Weber in effect attempts to demonstrate empirically (that is, historically and comparatively) the validity of popular Christian caricatures of the Jewish religion. For example, he maintains that the ancient Hebrews were the first group in history to dedicate themselves to the worship of a deity whose primary qualities were negative ones like wrathfulness and jealousy. In doing so, the Hebrews set themselves apart from every other culture in the world. This concept of deity and the separatist mentality that accompanied it became the model in turn for the Jews' relationships with both other human beings and the world of nature.

"In no other religion in the world," Weber maintains, "do we find a universal deity possessing the unparalleled desire for vengeance manifested by Yahweh."[57] According to Weber, the Jewish religion is "a religion of retribution" through and through, not only in the distant past but also in contemporary society.

In the mind of the pious Jew the moralism of the law was inevitably combined with the aforementioned hope for revenge, which suffused practically all the exilic and postexilic sacred scriptures. Moreover, through two and a half millenniums this hope appeared in virtually every divine service of the Jewish people, characterized by a firm grip upon two indestructible claims—religiously sanctified segregation from the other peoples of the world, and divine promises relating to this world. . . . When one compares Judaism with other salvation religions, one finds that in Judaism the doctrine of religious resentment has an idiosyncratic quality and plays a unique role not found among the disprivileged classes of any other religion.[58]

This form of religious observance spawned a distinctive kind of intellectual organization among those who practiced it, leading to the development among the Hebrews of a mode of cognition characterized by distance and objectivity—"instrumental rationality."

Prior to the emergence of instrumental rationality among the ancient Hebrews, according to Weber's narrative, human cognitive and affective experiences were of a participatory nature, so that people had a profound sense of unity with the natural world. The emergence of nonparticipating consciousness in the form of the ancient Hebrew religion was the beginning of what Weber termed *die Entzauberung der Welt,* the "disenchantment of the world." Morris Berman offers a vivid description, based on Weber's theory, of what he thinks life was like prior to this process of disenchantment:

The view of nature which predominated in the West down to the eve of the Scientific Revolution was that of an enchanted world. Rocks, trees, rivers, and clouds were all seen as wondrous, alive, and human beings felt at home in this environment. The cosmos, in short, was a place of *belonging.* A member of this cosmos was not an alienated observer of it but a direct participant in its drama. . . . This type of consciousness [may be termed] "participating consciousness" [and] involves merger, or identification, with one's surroundings.[59]

The dissolution of this blissful state of unity with Mother Nature began during the fifteenth and sixteenth centuries when a "rationalization process" gained momentum in Europe, producing "that state of mind in which one knows phenomena precisely in the act of distancing oneself from them," which instigated, in turn, the disenchantment of nature.[60] In Berman's account this mentality was distinctively "Jewish" because it was the ancient Hebrews who introduced humanity to the idea that "participating consciousness" was sinful. The Hebrew Bible, according to him, is "the story of the triumph of monotheism over Astarte, Baal, the golden calf, and the nature gods of neighboring 'pagan' peoples."

Here we see the first glimmerings of what I have called nonparticipating consciousness: knowledge is acquired by recognizing the *distance* between ourselves and nature. Ecstatic merger with nature is judged not merely as ignorance, but as idolatry. . . . The rejection of participating consciousness . . . was the crux of the covenant between the Jews and Yahweh. It was precisely this contract that made the Jews "chosen" and gave them their unique historical mission.[61]

The mentality of the ancient Hebrews, Weber maintains further, was also characterized by "ethical indifference." The origins of this trait, he suggests, are to be found in interpretations of Hebrew law which allowed Jews to engage in unethical business dealings with non-Jews while at the same time perceiving themselves to be strictly observant, a practice Weber thought to be illustrated by the Jews' maintenance of a double standard in their dealings with Jews and non-Jews. Thus, Weber explains, "the acquisitive drive" among Jews was "directed primarily to trade with strangers," because strangers, like all non-Jews, were considered "enemies." Thus business dealings with them did not have to conform to the ethical

requirements that applied to relations with other Jews; this dehumanizing tendency within Judaism, in Weber's opinion, conditioned the economic behavior of most Jews in his day.

Werner Sombart, a friend and colleague of Weber's, also made a
significant contribution to German social theory at the turn of the century, constructing a synthesis of Marx's socioeconomic critique of society and Weber's sociology of religion. Like Marx, he finds the "Jewish
spirit" at the heart of the modernization process, and like Weber, he asserts
a correspondence between the fundamental tenets of the Jewish religion
and this Jewish spirit. Sombart, though not as well known as Weber
among contemporary scholars, was "far more representative of the intellectuals of his generation than was Weber" and his books enjoyed great
popularity in Germany during the first decades of the present century.[62]
He went on to become an active supporter of National Socialism during the Hitler era.

Of most interest in the present context is Sombart's *The Jews and Modern Capitalism* (1911), a critique and reformulation of the ideas in Weber's
The Protestant Ethic and the Spirit of Capitalism. In this text Sombart maintains, *contra* Weber, that at the heart of the capitalist spirit is not Puritanism, but Judaism. In fact, Sombart asserts, "Puritanism *is* Judaism."[63]
Whereas Weber himself had insisted unequivocally that "Jews were relatively or altogether absent from the new and distinctive forms of modern capitalism" and that "neither that which is new in the modern economic system nor that which is distinctive of the modern economic temper
is specifically Jewish in origin," Sombart holds that both rationalism and
capitalism are distinctively Jewish impulses.[64]

Sombart anticipates the views of many contemporary social theorists
when he maintains that Jews began to play a disproportionate role in European economic and political affairs in the fifteenth century, after being
expelled from Spain and Portugal. Says Sombart of the Jewish migration
to Europe and the Americas: "Scarcely were the doors of the New World
opened to Europeans, than crowds of Jews came swarming in." Beginning in the fifteenth century, "European Jewry was like an ant-heap into
which a stick had been thrust."[65] Sombart maintains that Jews had played
a particularly prominent role in American society, explaining that "the first
European to set foot on American soil was a Jew" and that Columbus himself might have been Jewish—"the oldest portraits show him to have had
a Jewish face."[66] Not only this but, Sombart adds, "the first traders in the
New World were Jewish" and the "first industrial establishments in America were those of Jews." Sombart goes on to claim that North America

"owes its existence" to Jewish merchants and in fact "what we call Americanism is nothing else, if we may say so, than the Jewish spirit distilled."[67]

Ironically, one of Sombart's primary sources for these claims concerning Jewish influence in America was the *Jewish Encyclopedia*, the first volume of which appeared during the time that he was writing *The Jews and Modern Capitalism*. The *Encyclopedia* was a project of the American Reform community, conceived in response to the anti-Semitism that had become rampant in Europe at the turn of the twentieth century. The editors of the *Jewish Encyclopedia* sought to demonstrate the positive—if not indispensable—role that Jews had played in world history in order to counter accusations, typical of European anti-Semites, of Jewish parasitism and cultural inferiority. Thus, as Shuly Rubin Schwartz puts it, "the *Jewish Encyclopedia* unabashedly sings the praises of Jews and Judaism in America."[68] Queen Isabella, according to the *Encyclopedia*, was "under the influence" of Jewish associates when she decided to finance the voyage of Columbus; Jews were "instrumental in securing the funds for the first and second voyages"; Jews invented the navigational instruments employed by Columbus on his journey; a Jew was "the first European to tread the soil of America," "the first to discover the use of tobacco," and "the first to receive a detailed statement of the voyage and discoveries of Columbus."

Sombart's implementation of this material demonstrates the dangers inherent in the logic of reversal. Sombart concludes on the basis of these exaggerated claims that "Jewish money called into existence all the grand undertakings of the seventeenth century and financed them" and that it was Jewish migration into Europe during the fifteenth and sixteenth centuries that produced the rationalization of the modern world described by Weber. The Jewish presence in Europe and America was thus determinative for both the external form of modern capitalism and "its inward spirit." This "Jewish spirit" was a product of the Jewish religion, which was "mechanically and artfully wrought, destined to destroy and conquer Nature's realm and to reign itself in her stead." The "characteristic trait of Judaism as of Capitalism," Sombart concludes, is rationalism, which is the enemy of "that creative power which draws its artistic inspiration from the passion world of the senses."[69]

Judaism in the Singular

So completely is modern biblical scholarship the grateful recipient of the gifts of the German historiographic tradition that the general tenets of that tradition are immediately assumed to be one and the same with what any right-minded student of the religion of Israel would do almost intu- itively. But perhaps a caution should be penned: "Beware of Germans bear- ing historiographic gifts"![70]

One of the most questionable gifts bestowed on European scholar- ship by German historiography is the idea of Judaism as a monolithic, univocal tradition embodying beliefs and values that are inherently and fundamentally oppositional to the best interests of humanity, universally speaking. What contemporary scholars who take up this idea of Judaism fail to realize, however, is that this understanding of Judaism represents an ideology that is not only morally offensive but logically and empiri- cally indefensible. During the past three decades, as Jacob Neusner points out, a "glacial shift in paradigm" has occurred in the academic study of Judaism.[71] At the heart of this paradigm shift lies the relatively recent real- ization among scholars in the field that the term "Judaism," as conven- tionally used in both popular and academic discourse, has no external ref- erent. "When people use the word 'Judaism,'" Neusner explains, "they use it only in the singular, and they assume that the word refers to a single religion, or religious tradition, extending (if not from Creation) from Sinai to the present."[72]

People until just now have employed categories and classifications that served to foster the association of diverse sorts of evidence, so to produce aggre- gates and conglomerates, in all, to harmonize cacophonies and yield uniform constructs. The principal category, which had taken form early in the nine- teenth century and served without challenge from that time, was, of course, "Judaism." That "Judaism" was variously defined, of course. But "Judaism" invariably observed as the "thing out there," to which all documents . . . attested in some way or other.[73]

But, he continues, "when we treat as uniform and harmonious—as tes- timony to a single 'Judaism'—the entire extant corpus of documentary evidence for Judaism in its formative centuries, we misunderstand what we have in hand."

Neusner extends this principle, for example, to the ubiquitous assump- tion among American and European scholars of the accuracy of popular, stereotyped conceptions of "Jewish law," contending that "no single sys- tem of law governed all Jews everywhere" and therefore one cannot describe Jewish law as "one encompassing system."[74]

The Scripture's several codes of course made their impact on the diverse sys- tems of law that governed various groups of Jews, or Jewish communities in various places. But that impact never proved uniform. In consequence, in no way may we speak of "Jewish law," meaning a single legal code or even a common set of encompassing rules everywhere held authoritative by Jewry. The relationship between the legal system of one distinct group of Jews to that governing some other proves various.[75]

David Aaron has recently made a similar observation in regard to both popular and scholarly accounts of the origins of the so-called Hamitic myth, noting that it is still common to encounter the assumption that midrashic and talmudic interpretations of this myth constitute "one homogenous corpus, uniform in thought and . . . representative of 'Jewish' thought."[76] Aaron points out that this assumption fails to take into account, for example, that the rabbinic literature in question was "fundamentally incomprehensible to other than the specialist" and that "even among specialists, there is considerable controversy as to how it should be read."[77] Aaron maintains further that despite the current popularity of the notion that racist interpretations of the Hamitic myth are Jewish in origin, the widespread acceptance—or even the existence—of a racist version of this myth within Judaism has not been verified. European Christians, he points out, were hardly "in need of midrashic parables . . . to find a theological justification for slavery."[78]

The diversity that characterized Judaism from the earliest period of its existence contradicts many common assumptions concerning "Jewish" ideas and values. Jonathan Z. Smith, like Neusner, asserts that it is no longer possible to "sustain the construct of a normative Judaism."[79] Smith maintains that from ancient times forward there have existed "a variety of early Judaisms, clustered in varying configurations." This diversity within Judaism goes beyond the standard division of Jewish history into biblical, prophetic, and rabbinic periods, beyond recognition of the independent development of the Ashkenazi, Sephardic, and Falasha traditions, and beyond even the contemporary differentiation of Judaism into multiple branches in the American context. Efraim Shmueli has identified seven different cultural systems that have existed in Jewish history: the biblical, talmudic, poetic-philosophic, mystical, and rabbinic as well as the Emancipation and national Israeli cultures.[80] Shmueli emphasizes the significant differences among these cultures by listing ten items "out of many more" on which these cultures sharply disagree; he notes that these points of disagreement "do not lie in valuations of minor or trifling points" but rather involve "decisive and momentous issues." What this indicates, he concludes, is that these cultures are not properly understood if they are seen as simply variations on one monolithic worldview, but rather each must be seen as "anchored in its own sense of reality."[81]

Not only is the idea of Judaism contained in many contemporary texts structurally inadequate but it also betrays a lack of familiarity with the most basic conclusions of the last several decades of research in the field of Near Eastern studies. Recent research concerning ancient goddess worship, for instance, does not support the notion that the various goddesses worshiped in ancient cultures were just different representations of the same archetypal "Great Goddess" or that geographically distant civilizations shared a common belief system involving reverence for nature and for stereotypically feminine traits such as sensuality and fertility.

Nor does the evidence support the idea that religions in which goddesses were worshiped represented a system of values that was diametrically opposed to that of the ancient Hebrews.[82] There are numerous biblical fragments as well as an abundance of extrabiblical evidence, indicating that not only did Yahweh worship *not* involve an organized campaign to wipe out goddess worship but that "Asherah worship was so accepted by the people that she was worshiped right along with Yahweh in the Temple."[83] A primary piece of evidence for this survival is found in the Hebrew Bible itself, where the "Asherah pole" that was set up in the temple next to the altar is described (Deuteronomy 16:21). "This is the pinnacle of syncretism, the joining of religions at the very highest level, the official Temple cult. It is almost startling to realize that the Hebrews, who saw their living God present in the Temple, believed that a living Asherah was equally present at their worship."[84] And as Saul Olyan observes: "It is important to note that we are not speaking only of popular religion here; the asherahs of Samaria, Bethel and Jerusalem were a constituent part of state Yahwism."[85]

Feminist theorists who set up a radical dichotomy between the religion of the ancient Hebrews and that of goddess-worshiping cultures are working with a biased image of both Israelite and non-Israelite religions, as Jo Ann Hackett has pointed out. Hackett suggests that this bias originates in an overdependence on secondary literature written by European Christian scholars holding very conventional views of gender roles.

This secondary literature sets up a dichotomy between Israelite religion and the "fertility" religion of the surrounding peoples and then often rejects these "fertility" deities and "fertility" religions in favor of Israel's official religion. . . . Many [feminists accept] the dichotomy between Yahwism and "fertility religion" that is set up in the secondary literature, but rather than rejecting the "fertility religion," as the secondary literature clearly expects us to do, they often look for models in the goddess- and nature-centered worship that is what they understand to be the ancient alternative to worship of the male Yahweh, the god of Israel. They are defying the bias against nature and goddesses, and celebrating the other half of the dichotomy, celebrating the "fertility goddesses" and "fertility cults" of ancient Canaan and Mesopotamia. By embracing rather than rejecting the "fertility religion" that is presented as the rival of the official religion of Israel, they think that they are defying the male-centered religion of Israel and of the scholars who write the secondary literature.

Rather than being an act of defiance, however, the view of goddess worship expressed in these recent feminist texts is merely a reiteration, as Hackett puts it, of "the fears and fantasies of modern Western scholars." That is, Western feminists often derive their views of the Israelite religion from a transvaluation of conventional, familiar interpretations of the Hebrew Bible rather than on "independent scholarly accounts of the Israelite religion." What such independent scholarly accounts show, Hackett asserts, is that "fertility" religion is "everywhere" in the ancient world. "It is all over the Bible, it was part of Canaanite and Mesopotamian religion, and it is part of modern Western religion, too."[86]

One scholar whose work was especially influential in popularizing the idea that non-Israelite religions were orgiastic "fertility cults" was James G. Frazer. As Neal Walls explains:

The central importance of Frazer to the study of Ugaritic myth . . . rests in the continuing influence of his thought to the present day. In particular, his views on the fertility function of primitive religion, his implicit theories of myth and ritual, and his concept of the dying-rising vegetation god haunt Ugaritic interpretation long after these ideas have been abandoned by historians of religion as essentially groundless. This fact contributes greatly to the *outdated quality* of much contemporary Ugaritic myth interpretation.[87]

Available evidence concerning the goddess figures who populate non-Hebrew ancient Near Eastern religions reveals that in some cases these goddesses make Yahweh seem rather anemic by comparison. Many of these female deities are portrayed as delighting in carnage and gore.[88] Canaanite, Phoenician, and Carthaginian goddesses were believed by their worshipers to demand ritual human sacrifice. Carthaginian and Phoenician sacrificial stelae record the regular incineration of infants and children, sometimes "by the hundreds."[89] "The actual burning of the child took place, according to literary sources, while music was played to drown out any lamentation by the parents. Children, probably already drugged or dead, were incinerated one by one. . . . Their remains were carefully collected, placed in cinerary urns along with small trinkets or pottery provided by the parents."[90] Child sacrifice continued well into the Common Era among the Carthaginians and among other groups (for example, the Aztecs) until the early modern period.

Current knowledge concerning cultures contemporaneous with that of the ancient Hebrews also discredits the idea that the ancient Hebrews were unusually violent and aggressive. Conquest narratives similar to the biblical account of the conquest of Canaan were common in the region, and most such narratives conform to a formula similar to that found in Hebrew literature, such as reporting that "casualties within one's own army are rare" while claiming "the total annihilation of the enemy."[91] Not only the ancient Israelites but also the Assyrians, Hittites, and Egyptians composed heroic accounts of their military exploits, and although there are significant differences between these different traditions, there are also many similarities, including the "view of the enemy, calculated terror, the high use of hyperbole, a jural aspect, and the use of stereotyped syntagms to transmit the high-redundance message of the ideology."[92] In ancient Egyptian sources, for instance, one finds not only the vision of cosmic harmony posited by some Afrocentric scholars but also "a binary and imperialistic system in which the enemy was viewed as vile, wretched, and evil."[93]

The feminist and Afrocentric scholars I have surveyed seem unaware that few experts in the field of Jewish or Near Eastern studies take the biblical account of the "conquest of Canaan" as a record of actual historical events. Archeological research indicates that some of the political configurations and cities that were supposed to have been destroyed by the Israelites did not even exist at the time the conquest was supposed to have taken place and others had been abandoned long before.

The site of Jericho was occupied only briefly in the fourteenth century B.C., or about 1325 B.C.; the site of Ai was unoccupied. When Ai was reoccupied as a village about 1200 B.C., there was nothing at Jericho. If we accept the most popular date for the conquest, about 1250 B.C., which is held by both American and Israeli scholars based on destruction levels at other major sites, there was nothing at either Jericho or Ai at the time. And at no time during this period between 1400 B.C. and 1200 B.C. was there any settlement at both sites.[94]

And while some sites were destroyed during the right time period, the evidence points not to the ancient Israelites as the conquerors but rather to a group referred to in ancient texts as the "Sea Peoples," who also plundered the Egyptian coast.[95]

Although Egypt controlled Canaan during the thirteenth century B.C.E., there is no mention in Egyptian records of an Israelite conquest of the region. Considering the long history of Egyptian interest in the area and the nature and extent of Egyptian record keeping, it is hard to explain why the kind of massive devastation reported in the Hebrew Bible would have gone completely without mention.

Niels Peter Lemche, professor of biblical studies at the University of Copenhagen, proposes that there is an absence of evidence supporting the biblical account of the conquest of Canaan because this account is not a historical record of events that occurred during the Late Bronze Age, as traditionally assumed, but rather served within the early cultus of Israel as "a kind of ideological prototype." The biblical passages containing the most detailed descriptions of the conquest were written much later than the events described — between the fifth and seventh centuries B.C.E. — and this leads Lemche to conclude that the description of the Canaanites in this account "has little or nothing to do with the ancient pre-Israelite inhabitants of Palestine."[96] In Lemche's opinion, the story of the conquest of Canaan is not the story of an actual military campaign and may even depict political conditions existing not in the thirteenth century but rather in the *fifth* century B.C.E. The story may in fact be a symbolic representation of "religious and political disagreements . . . between the Jews living in the Egyptian diaspora and the Jews of Jerusalem."[97] In other words, both the ancient Israelite religion portrayed in the biblical literature and the Canaanite opposition might be metaphorical representations of postexilic Jewish communities.[98]

In fact, the idea of Judaism reproduced in the feminist and Afrocentric texts I have examined has long been abandoned by all but the most literal-minded religious fundamentalists. Virtually the only statement that may be made with some degree of certainty concerning the ancient Hebrews is that their religious beliefs and practices were mainly of Canaanite origin, with an admixture of Mesopotamian, Egyptian, and Babylonian influences.[99] As Mark S. Smith explains, "Despite the long regnant model that the Canaanites and Israelites were people of fundamentally different cultures, archaeological data now cast doubt on this view." In fact, he maintains, "Israelite culture cannot be separated easily from the culture of Canaan" during the dates traditionally given for the conquest of Canaan, nor can one maintain "a radical cultural separation between Canaanites and Israelites for the Iron I period" (ca. 1200–1000

B.C.E.).[100] For example, the idea of an Israelite culture and religion separate and distinct from the Canaanite during this period can be substantiated on the basis of neither epigraphical nor linguistic evidence: rather, the Canaanite and Hebrew languages "so closely overlap that the ability to distinguish them is premised more on historical information than linguistic criteria."[101] Nor can the material cultures of the Israelites and Canaanites be clearly differentiated from one another on the basis of such evidence as pottery design, burial practices, or architecture.[102] What evidence is available points rather to a definition of Israelite culture as "a subset of Canaanite culture."[103]

Nor do most scholars consider viable the popular concept of "Hebrew monotheism" as a uniquely Israelite invention that appeared suddenly and involved the worship of Yahweh as the one true God. The watershed in this regard was the discovery in 1929 of the Ugaritic texts at Ras Shamra in Syria; scholars for the first time had an extrabiblical source providing information about Canaanite religion. In light of this and subsequent discoveries, many scholars began to take a new look at passages in the Hebrew Bible containing references to Canaanite deities, such as the aforementioned reference to the "asherah pole" in the Temple. Long-held assumptions about the character of Hebrew monotheism came into question, and it soon became clear that much of what European scholarship had taken for granted about Israelite religion for centuries constituted a substantial misinterpretation of the historical record. The earliest Israelite religion, it now appears, included worship not only of Yahweh but also of El, Asherah, and Baal. Yahweh, rather than being an original, singular, Hebrew deity, is most often taken to represent a conceptual "coalescence" of an assortment of ancient Canaanite deities.[104]

The religious practices linked with Yahwism seem to be of Canaanite origin as well. Frank Cross, following Albrecht Alt, explains: "The early cultic establishment of Yahweh and its appurtenances—the Tabernacle, its structure of *qerasim,* its curtains embroidered with cherubim and its cherubim throne, and its proportions according to the pattern (*tabnit*) of the cosmic shrine—all reflect Canaanite models, and specifically the Tent of 'El and his cherubim throne."[105] What this evidence indicates, among other things, is that there are *no* aspects of *contemporary* Judaism that can be shown conclusively to be uniquely Hebrew in origin.

Considering that both the monothetic view of Judaism derived from a literal interpretation of the Hebrew Bible and the antagonistic view of Judaism based on New Testament theology have long been discredited by the available evidence, it is curious that these ideas still find wide acceptance among contemporary scholars. And most curious of all is the frequency with which one encounters such outmoded constructions embedded in social and political theories that are conceived, by both their advocates and their opponents, as being of a radical or revolutionary nature. What the use of a negative idea of Judaism as a mode of social criticism reveals is that anti-Jewish assumptions originating in the European Christian tradition remain deeply entrenched in the rhetorical and discursive conventions that many scholars continue to depend on in order to maintain the structural integrity of their thought.

The specific content of these negative images of Judaism, however, is remarkably malleable. During the eighteenth century, when European scholars were infatuated with pure reason, Judaism was criticized as an irrational faith. Now that rationalist ideology has come to be viewed with suspicion, however, Judaism is more often conceived as the source of sterile rationality. When the hallmark of rational religion was its universalism, Judaism was criticized for its particularism; now that universalism has given way to an emphasis on difference, some assert that Judaism is the original source of universalistic thinking. In nineteenth-century German revolutionary thought, scientific method was viewed as a good thing and the Jewish tradition was accordingly conceived as hostile to a modern scientific worldview. In contemporary social criticism, scientific method has come under suspicion, and now we learn that the desire to dominate the natural world often equated with the scientific worldview originated in the Hebrew tradition. In modern German theories of race, Jews were often categorized as "black" because their ancestors had intermingled with Africans; in some recent Afrocentric scholarship, Jews are portrayed as the original "white" racists.[106]

This same interpretive flexibility becomes evident when theories of contemporary feminists are compared with those of Afrocentrists. Whereas American and European feminists classify monotheism as an oppressive development invented by the ancient Hebrews, many Afrocentrists continue to take the traditional view of monotheism as an important advance in the evolution of civilization and maintain that it was invented by Africans (and co-opted by the ancient Israelites during their sojourn in Egypt). Feminists often claim that the religion of the ancient Hebrews is the original source of the cultural practices leading to the "desacralization of nature" in the European tradition, whereas Afrocentric scholars, interested in portraying the ancient Africans as systematic thinkers, more often assert that it was in Africa that forms of social organization first emerged the purpose of which was "to challenge nature."[107] And whereas many feminists assume that the ancient Hebrews invented instrumental rationality, many Afrocentric scholars insist—with good reason—that the ancient Africans were the first to engage in practical, technological, and scientific thinking.

Some Afrocentric scholars also assert that it was in ancient Africa, not among the ancient Hebrews, that the first hierarchical forms of social organization were invented. In *Civilization or Barbarism* Cheikh Anta Diop points out that during the Eighteenth Dynasty the Egyptians colonized the entire "known" world and imposed their own system of order on the occupied territories. This system, he thinks, is the same as that later adopted by Alexander the Great, Charlemagne, and Napoleon.[108] In Diop's view, the ancient Egyptians established "the first world empire" and introduced universalistic thinking into the ancient world. And whereas feminist scholars often assert that the displacement of matriarchy by patriarchy in the Mediterranean region was initiated by the Hebrew priesthood, according to Diop it was from Africa that hierarchical and patriarchal forms of social organization were "exported almost everywhere in the world." Diop treats matriarchy as an immature stage of social organization that *should* disappear with the emergence of more advanced—patriarchal—political structures.[109] In Diop's account, it was the evolution of patriarchal forms of government that made possible the ancient Egyptians' conquest of neighboring cultures and introduction of technological developments that served to bring these other cultures, in his words, "into the historical cycle of humanity."[110]

While some Afrocentric scholars view European cultural values as immoral and corrupt and trace the origin of these values to the Jews, others assert that European beliefs and values are themselves African in origin. Donald Matthews, for example, argues that "African/Egyptian thought played a crucial and central role in the development of the most cherished values of Western civilization" and criticizes the habit among American and European scholars of teaching their students that Western values derive from "Jewish moral law." The values that people of European Christian descent think of as "Jewish," Matthews asserts, are in fact derived from the ethical system contained in ancient African texts such as the *Book of Coming Forth by Day*.[111] Likewise, Molefi Kete Asante asserts that Africans invented most of the cultural practices usually attributed to Greek and Hebrew sources, including "medicine, science, the concept of monarchies and divine kingships, and [the concept of] an Almighty God."[112] Asante contends that it is also in Africa that "the origin of European philosophy" is to be found.[113] In fact, in his view, accounts of the birth of "Western civilization" that ignore "the origin of civilization in the highlands of East Africa" are nothing but "malicious racism."[114]

When one juxtaposes the feminist historical reconstructions that I have examined with these Afrocentric accounts, it is evident that from an African-centered point of view, the exclusive focus of some feminist scholars on the Mesopotamian origins of Western civilization may be seen as blatantly racist. By the same token, many of the ideas embraced in these Afrocentric texts seem patently misogynist from a feminist standpoint.

This conflict of interpretations creates a dilemma for feminists who wish to construct antiracist narratives and for Afrocentrists who wish to avoid misogynistic assumptions. It would severely disrupt the internal logic of the feminist theories I have examined if an effort were made to introduce into these theories an acknowledgment of the extent of the influence of African thought on European cultural values, since this internal logic assumes that whatever culture first invented monotheism and hierarchical forms of social organization is responsible for the subsequent oppression of women throughout the history of civilization. In such theories, since monotheistic religion is assumed to be the original source of the oppression of women, and the oppression of women is thought to provide the conceptual model for the practice of slavery, then, if the invention of monotheism is credited to ancient Africans, people of African descent end up bearing historical responsibility for the institution of slavery.

Such logical absurdities expose not only the logic of reversal at the heart of the theoretical model borrowed by contemporary scholars from early twentieth-century German social theory but also the way in which this logic absorbs and diverts effective social criticism by its incessant transposition of the roles of oppressor and oppressed. One of the reasons this logic is so difficult to analyze effectively is that its terms never remain the same, but are constantly shifting and changing, which serves to obscure the process by means of which this structural model progressively transforms meaning and value into their opposites. In the case of Judaism, specifically *which* beliefs and values are identified as "Jewish" in this logic vary from decade to decade, from theorist to theorist, and from cultural location to cultural location, following popular trends in social criticism. What remains constant, however, is the systematic use of a negative concept of Judaism to legitimate criticism of *whatever* ideas and practices are viewed as most corrupt and oppressive.

Notes

Many thanks to the editors and the anonymous reviewers. Thanks also to Jo Ann Hackett for her many helpful suggestions and to those who took the time to discuss this material with me, especially C. Dale Gadsden, Arifah Shaheed, and Waldo B. Phillips.

1. Marx explained in the preface to the 1873 German edition of *Capital* that the German philosophical tradition, epitomized by Hegel's system, seemed to him to be "standing on its head" and he contended that "it must be inverted, in order to discover the rational kernal within the mystical shell" (Karl Marx, *Capital: A Critique of Political Economy,* trans. Ben Fowkes [New York: Random House, 1977], 103). Friedrich Nietzsche applied this same model of criticism to Christianity, asserting that in the Christian tradition "*value judgement* is stood on its head, the concepts 'true' and 'false' are . . . reversed" (Friedrich Nietzsche, *The Anti-Christ,* trans. R. J. Hollingdale [New York: Penguin Books, 1968], 120). The church, Nietzsche maintains, is nothing but an "ecumenical synagogue," the vehicle by means of which Jewish values were universalized (Friedrich Nietzsche, *On the Genealogy of Morals,* ed. Walter Kaufmann [New York: Vintage Books, 1989], 34–35).

2. Kwame Anthony Appiah, *In My Father's House: Africa in the Philosophy of Culture* (New York: Oxford University Press, 1992), 59.

3. Ibid.

4. Homi K. Bhabha, *The Location of Culture* (New York: Routledge, 1994), 127.

5. Ibid., 132, 137.

6. Ibid., 31.

7. V. Y. Mudimbe, *The Idea of Africa* (Bloomington: Indiana University Press, 1994), xi.

8. Ibid., 129.

9. Ibid., 130.

10. Friedrich Nietzsche, *The Genealogy of Morals* (New York: Vintage, 1967), 34–35.

11. Marimba Ani, *Yurugu: An African-centered Critique of European Cultural Thought and Behavior* (Trenton: Africa World Press, 1994), 120.

12. Ibid., 173; Rosemary Radford Ruether, *Sexism and God-Talk: Toward a Feminist Theology* (Boston: Beacon Press, 1983), 53.

13. Mircea Eliade, *A History of Religious Ideas,* trans. Willard R. Trask (Chicago: University of Chicago Press, 1978), 1:354. Cited in Ani, *Yurugu,* 188.

14. Ani, *Yurugu,* 67, 174.

15. Ibid.

16. Ibid., 119.

17. Ibid.

18. Ibid., 189.

19. Nel Noddings, *Women and Evil* (Berkeley, Los Angeles, London: University of California Press, 1989), 39, 52–53. Noddings's sources are Mary Daly, *Beyond God the Father* (Boston: Beacon Press, 1974), and Merlin Stone, *When God Was a Woman* (New York: Dial Press, 1976).

20. Noddings, *Women and Evil,* 53.

21. Ibid., 12; Martin Gardner, *The Whys of a Philosophical Scrivener* (New York: Quill, 1983), 249.

22. Ibid.

23. Gerda Lerner, *The Creation of Patriarchy* (New York: Oxford University Press, 1986), 9.

24. Ibid., 148.

25. Ibid., 198. Emphasis mine.

26. Yosef A. A. ben-Jochannan, *We the Black Jews* (Baltimore: Black Classic Press, 1993), xxix. Ben-Jochannan also follows the pattern among some Afrocentric scholars of taking

an extremely negative view of Islam and Arabic culture. While he asserts the African origins of all three major Western religions, he views them as having been corrupted by foreign influences: thus Islam is "no better than Judaism and Christianity" as far as people of African descent are concerned, since it was Arab Muslims who introduced chattel slavery in the African context. The visions of the Holy Prophet, he says, mark "the beginning of an era which witnessed the ravaging of [Africa's] peoples and territories as she had never experienced before." On this basis he lambastes African Americans who convert to Islam as having "denied their own origin from Alkebu-lan (Africa)" (*African Origins of the Major "Western Religions"* [Baltimore: Black Classic Press, 1970], 197, 213, 254). Similarly, Molefi Kete Asante remarks at one point that "Islam is as contradictory to . . . Afrocentricity as Christianity" and that "Arabic culture" is "anathema to Afrocentrism and like Christianity makes us submit to a strange God" (*Afrocentricity* [Trenton: Africa World Press, 1988], 3). For a critique of anti-Islamic and anti-Arabic sentiment among American Afrocentrists, see Ameen Yasir Mohammed, *Afrocentricity, Minus Al-Islam, Cheats* (Los Angeles: Dawahvision, 1993).

27. Cheikh Anta Diop, *The African Origin of Civilization: Myth or Reality,* trans. Mercer Cook (Chicago: Lawrence Hill Books, 1974), 7, 107.

28. Tony Martin, *The Jewish Onslaught* (Dover, Mass.: The Majority Press, 1993,), 33.

29. Ibid., 4, 51, 54.

30. John Henrik Clarke, "'Black Demagogues and Pseudo Scholars': A Dissenting View," *Black Books Bulletin: WordsWork* 16 (Winter 1993–1994): 10. See also Martin's article in this same issue of *Black Books Bulletin,* "The (No Longer) Secret Relationship between Blacks and Jews," 22–25.

31. Martin, *Jewish Onslaught,* 35.

32. *The Secret Relationship between Blacks and Jews* (Chicago: The Nation of Islam, 1991), 10.

33. Ibid., 24.

34. Lerner, *Creation of Patriarchy,* 77, 198, 89.

35. Carolyn Merchant, *The Death of Nature: Women, Ecology, and the Scientific Revolution* (San Francisco: Harper and Row, 1983), 127, 131. See also Sandra Harding, *The Science Question in Feminism* (Ithaca: Cornell University Press, 1986), 207, 113 ff.

36. Julia Kristeva, *Powers of Horror: An Essay on Abjection,* trans. Leon S. Roudiez (New York: Columbia University Press, 1982), 31.

37. Ibid., 100.

38. Ibid.

39. Ibid., 114–115. Emphasis mine.

40. Ibid., 122–123.

41. G. W. F. Hegel, *The Philosophy of History* (New York: Dover, 1956), 326.

42. Judith Butler, *Gender Trouble: Feminism and the Subversion of Identity* (New York: Routledge, 1990), 29, 156n.

43. Friedrich Nietzsche, *The Anti-Christ,* trans. R. J. Hollingdale (New York: Penguin, 1968), section 17; *Beyond Good and Evil,* trans. R. J. Hollingdale (New York: Penguin, 1972), section 52.

44. Kristeva, *Powers of Horror,* 125. Emphasis mine. See Edith Wyschogrod, *Saints and Postmodernism* (Chicago: University of Chicago Press, 1990), 246 ff.

45. Kristeva, *Powers of Horror,* 112.

46. Ibid., 180, 184–186. Emphasis mine.

47. Wyschogrod, *Saints and Postmodernism,* 251.

48. Kristeva, *Powers of Horror,* 184–185.

49. Susannah Heschel, "Configurations of Patriarchy, Judaism, and Nazism in German Feminist Thought," in *Gender and Judaism,* ed. T. M. Rudavsky (New York: New York University Press, 1995), 149.

50. Appiah, *In My Father's House,* 60.

51. Wilhelm Dilthey, *Introduction to the Human Sciences: An Attempt to Lay a Foundation for the Study of Society and History,* trans. Ramon J. Bentanzos (Detroit: Wayne State University Press, 1988), 230.

52. Ibid., 231.

53. Ibid., 271.

54. Ibid., 287–289.

55. Max Weber, *The Protestant Ethic and the Spirit of Capitalism* (New York: Routledge, 1992), 13.

56. Weber, like Dilthey, believed that his judgment that European Christian culture was the only civilization of universal significance and value was not a value judgment but a statement of fact. As he assures the reader in the introduction to *The Protestant Ethic:* "The question of the relative value of the cultures which are compared here will not receive a single word." Ibid., 30.

57. Max Weber, *The Sociology of Religion* (Boston: Beacon Press, 1993), 112.

58. Ibid., 113.

59. Morris Berman, *The Reenchantment of the World* (Ithaca: Cornell University Press, 1981), 16; Berman derives his views from Owen Barfield's *Saving the Appearances* (New York: Harcourt, Brace and World, 1965).

60. Berman, *Reenchantment of the World,* 39.

61. Ibid., 70–71, 73; Barfield, *Saving the Appearances,* chapter 16.

62. Arthur Mitzman, "Personal Conflict and Ideological Options in Sombart and Weber," in *Max Weber and His Contemporaries,* ed. Wolfgang J. Mommsen and J. Osterhammel (London: Allen and Unwin, 1987), 99. Sombart's first major work, *Sozialismus und soziale Bewegung im 19. Jahrhundert* (Socialism and the Social Movement in the Nineteenth Century), went through ten editions between 1896 and 1929 and was translated into twenty-four languages.

63. Werner Sombart, *The Jews and Modern Capitalism,* trans. M. Epstein (Glencoe, Ill.: Free Press, 1951), 236.

64. Weber, *Sociology of Religion,* 248–250.

65. Ibid., 31–32.

66. Ibid.

67. Ibid., 37, 44. Cf. Karl Marx, "On the Jewish Question," in *The Marx-Engels Reader,* ed. Robert C. Tucker (New York: W. W. Norton, 1958), 49.

68. Shuly Rubin Schwartz, *The Emergence of Jewish Scholarship in America: The Publication of the* Jewish Encyclopedia (Cincinnati: Hebrew Union College, 1991), 119.

69. Sombart, *Jews and Modern Capitalism,* 206–207. Sombart's understanding of "the Jewish spirit" as "contrary to nature" also led him to attribute to Judaism a singularly negative attitude toward the body, sexuality, and women. "All earlier religions saw something divine in the expression of sex," according to Sombart. "None of them condemned what is sensuous, or looked upon women as a source of sin," as Judaism did. Notably, Sombart's understanding of Judaism in this respect was another point of contention between him and Weber. Sombart insisted that Puritan asceticism in particular was "Jewish" in origins: "The dominating ideas of Puritanism," Sombart maintains, "were more perfectly developed in Judaism . . . [and at] a much earlier date." By contrast, Weber had contended that the main difference between Judaism and Puritanism lay "in the relative . . . absence of systematic asceticism" in the former tradition. According to Weber, Christian asceticism "did not derive from Judaism, but emerged primarily in the heathen Christian communities of the Pauline mission." Compared to Christianity, in Weber's view, Judaism was "not in the least ascetic, but rather highly naturalistic." See Sombart, *Jews and Modern Capitalism,* 231, 248; Weber, *Sociology of Religion,* 246.

70. K. Lawson Younger Jr., *Ancient Conquest Accounts: A Study in Ancient Near Eastern and Biblical History Writing* (Sheffield: Sheffield Academic Press, 1990), 26.

71. Jacob Neusner, *The Formation of Judaism: In Retrospect and Prospect* (Atlanta: Scholars Press, 1990), 5.

72. Jacob Neusner, *Judaism and Its Social Metaphors* (New York: Cambridge University Press, 1989), 2.

73. Jacob Neusner, *Formative Judaism: Religious, Historical, and Literary Studies* (Chico, Calif.: Scholars Press, 1983), 1.

74. Jacob Neusner, *The Formation of Judaism*, 62.

75. Ibid.

76. David Aaron, "Early Rabbinic Exegesis on Noah's Son Ham and the So-Called 'Hamitic Myth,'" in *Journal of the American Academy of Religion* 63, no. 4 (Winter 1995): 724.

77. Ibid., 751.

78. Ibid., 752.

79. Jonathan Z. Smith, *Imagining Religion* (Chicago: University of Chicago Press, 1982), 14.

80. Efraim Shmueli, *Seven Jewish Cultures: A Reinterpretation of Jewish History and Thought*, trans. Gila Shmueli (New York: Cambridge University Press, 1990), 15.

81. Ibid., 14–15.

82. See Saul Olyan, *Asherah and the Cult of Yahweh in Israel*, Society of Biblical Literature Monograph Series, no. 34 (Atlanta: Scholars Press, 1988); Steve A. Wiggins, *A Reassessment of 'Asherah': A Study According to the Textual Sources of the First Two Millennia B.C.E.* (Neukirchen-Vluyn: Verlag Butzon and Bercker Kevelaer, 1993); and Jo Ann Hackett, "Can a Sexist Model Liberate Us? Ancient Near Eastern 'Fertility' Goddesses," *Journal of Feminist Studies in Religion* 5, no. 1(Spring 1989).

83. Richard J. Pettey, *Asherah: Goddess of Israel?* (New York: Peter Lang, 1990), 206.

84. Ibid.

85. Olyan, *Asherah and the Cult of Yahweh in Israel*, 34. Johannes C. De Moor provides a concise summary of the evidence supporting this thesis in *The Rise of Yahwism: The Roots of Israelite Monotheism* (Leuven: Leuven University Press, 1990), 10–13.

86. Hackett, "Can a Sexist Model Liberate Us?" 68.

87. Neal H. Walls, *The Goddess Anat in Ugaritic Myth* (Atlanta: Scholars Press, 1992), 4. Emphasis mine.

88. Hackett, "Can a Sexist Model Liberate Us?" 69; cf. Walls, *The Goddess Anat*, 26.

89. Shelby Brown, *Late Carthaginian Child Sacrifice and Sacrificial Monuments in Their Mediterranean Context* (Sheffield: Sheffield Academic Press, 1991), 22, 29.

90. Hackett, "Can a Sexist Model Liberate Us?" 172.

91. Younger, *Ancient Conquest Accounts*, 261.

92. Ibid., 233–235.

93. Ibid., 194.

94. Joseph Callaway, "The Settlement in Canaan: The Period of the Judges," in *Ancient Israel: A Short History from Abraham to the Roman Destruction of the Temple*, ed. Herschel Shanks (Englewood Cliffs: Prentice-Hall, 1986), 55.

95. For a detailed and comprehensive survey of the evidence concerning the Sea People, see Donald B. Redford, *Egypt, Canaan, and Israel in Ancient Times* (Princeton: Princeton University Press, 1992).

96. Niels Peter Lemche, *The Canaanites and Their Land: The Tradition of the Canaanites*, in *Journal for the Study of the Old Testament, supplement series* 110 (1991): 164–165.

97. Ibid., 165.

98. Ibid., 20–21, 171.

99. Ibid., 22, 171.

100. Mark S. Smith, *The Early History of God: Yahweh and the Other Deities in Ancient Israel* (San Francisco: Harper and Row, 1990), xxii, 1.

101. Ibid.

102. Ibid.

103. Ibid., 3. See also Redford, *Egypt, Canaan, and Israel in Ancient Times*, 266, 268; Callaway, "The Settlement in Canaan," 78.

104. Smith, *The Early History of God*, xxiii.

105. Frank Moore Cross, *Canaanite Myth and Hebrew Epic: Essays in the History and the Religion of Israel* (Cambridge: Harvard University Press, 1973), 72. Cf. Albrecht Alt, *Essays on Old Testament History and Religion*, trans. R. A. Wilson (Garden City, N.Y.: Doubleday, 1967).

106. Cf. Sander Gilman's *On Blackness without Blacks: Essays on the Image of the Black in Germany* (Boston: G. K. Hall, 1982), and *Blacks and German Culture*, ed. Reinhold Grimm and Jost Hermand (Madison: University of Wisconsin Press, 1986).

107. Cheikh Anta Diop, *Civilization or Barbarism: An Authentic Anthropology*, trans. Yaa-Lengi Meema Ngemi (Brooklyn, N.Y.: Lawrence Hill, 1991), 111, 151.

108. Ibid., 102.

109. Ibid., 112, 167, 313.

110. Ibid., 151.

111. Donald Matthews, "Proposal for an Afro-Centric Curriculum," *Journal of the American Academy of Religion* 62, no. 3 (Fall 1994): 885, 888.

112. Molefi Kete Asante, *Afrocentricity* (Trenton: Africa World Press, 1988), 39.

113. Ibid., 89.

114. Ibid., 38.

PART THREE

Diaspora Negotiations

CHAPTER 9

Scattered Seeds
A Dialogue of Diasporas

Michael Galchinsky

American Jewish intellectuals have tended to assert that their diaspora is "exceptional." The prevailing view has been that because of the relatively scarce amount of anti-Semitism American Jews experience and the wide range of cultural and economic opportunities available to them, they function outside the traditional narratives of diaspora through which, for two thousand years, European Jews have interpreted their existence. This deeply held conviction is, however, only partially accurate. While the American Jewish diaspora is indeed exceptional in Jewish history, its exceptionalism is not merely a result of economic opportunity and freedom from anti-Semitism but is primarily a result of the historically and structurally unique relationship of the American diaspora to the land of Israel.

Moreover, its exceptionalism in Jewish history by no means implies that the American Jewish diaspora is exceptional in world history. By regarding their diaspora as unique and therefore incomparable, American Jews have neglected to participate in cross-cultural conversations to which they might make valuable contributions. They have enhanced their reputation among other diasporic groups as inward-looking and isolationist. They have alienated themselves from Jewish history as well as from potentially crucial resources, information, and support. And they have hampered their efforts to forge a constructive relationship with the state of Israel.

Perhaps the most significant cross-cultural conversation from which American Jews' ideology of exceptionalism has deprived them is that which is now taking place among cultural critics who call themselves "postcolonial theorists," that is, theorists of the massive population shifts that have resulted from the dismantling of the various colonial powers. Until recently the proposition that Jews might engage in dialogue with post-colonial theorists might have seemed absurd to all but the most naive American Jews. After all, such theorists have generally understood "Jews" as members of the white power structure in the United States, "Zionism" as an expression of Western imperialism, and "Israel" (especially after the Six-Day War) as an American imperial proxy and colonialist entity. Rejecting each of these assertions as limited or distorted, Jews have considered themselves outsiders to postcolonial models, just as postcolonial theorists have considered Jews outsiders to their theories.

But recent postcolonial theorists have begun to reevaluate and diverge from this initial analysis, offering American Jews a potentially constructive new direction. First, these theorists have begun to recognize that the entities to be resisted are not monolithically comprised of "people of color" hegemonically dominated by "whites" (although no doubt this is primarily the case). Postcolonialism's studies of "white" communities like the Irish or Australians suggest that whiteness is complicated and needs to be analyzed rather than merely asserted.[1] A desire to subvert forms of identity politics like nationalism and imperialism has led these theorists to reject the simplistic identity politics often favored by other strands of multiculturalism. They realize that the global phenomena they seek to interpret cannot be explained according to any theories of racial "essences."

Second, while earlier theorists saw Jews at best as pawns or victims of the nation-state and at worst as among its most heinous exploiters, the recent theorists have begun to understand Jews' history and theories of diaspora as crucial to postcolonialism's attempts to subvert identity politics of all kinds, especially nationalism and imperialism. The postcolonial adaptations of the concept "diaspora" emphasize the transnational, hybrid, and fluid communities created by both forced and voluntary migratory flows and suggest that in the era of decolonization these diasporic communities can be subversive of the brutally homogenizing ideologies and practices of nations and empires. They argue that the multiplying number of diasporas whose members pour information, funds, and affection back and forth across national boundary lines works to unsettle nations' ongoing attempts at "imagining communities" that are self-contained and nonporous.[2]

Although recent postcolonial theories have much to recommend them, they need to be criticized for unduly minimizing the suffering that is the frequent companion of diaspora, making unconvincing claims for the privileged visionary potential of diaspora intellectuals, and decontextualizing the ideology of nationalism. Moreover, as a comparison with the traditional Jewish narrative of diaspora articulated in Deuteronomy and subsequent prophetic and rabbinic literature will suggest, the postcolonial theorists have overstated the potential of the "diasporas" to subvert nationalism and imperialism and they have understated its potential to subvert the diasporans themselves.

Nevertheless, the theories of postcolonialists may serve a crucial function for American Jews in enabling them to articulate a new and necessary kind of self-understanding. By engaging in systematic comparisons of their condition with the analogous conditions of postcolonial diasporas, American Jews may be able both to learn from and to contribute to dialogues of inordinate importance in a time of global population shifts and the thrilling but frightening restructuring of nations.

Postcolonialism's Discourse of Diaspora

Since a dialogue can only be established after all the participants have heard and understood one another's positions, I will begin by attempting to ascertain the shape of the postcolonial discourse of diaspora, both in its general outlines and with particular attention to its potential benefits and limitations for an American Jewish audience.

The news that the term *diaspora* has become an important analytical tool for those engaged in describing various postcolonial situations has permeated many levels of public discourse, academic and otherwise. In the spring of 1991 Khachig Tölölyan of the Zoryan Institute for Armenian Studies in Cambridge, Massachusetts, edited the first edition of a new interdisciplinary journal entitled *Diaspora: A Journal of Transnational Studies*. A short list of groups to whom various writers in the journal have since applied the term *diaspora* includes Irish, Native Americans, Cubans, Eritreans, Kurds, Palestinians, Sikhs, Tibetans, Lithuanians, Turks, Nigerians, Indians, Pakistanis, Egyptians, Sri Lankans, Filipinos, Iranians, Franco-Maghrebians, Mexicans, and under certain conditions women.[3] The term has even metaphorically been applied to "the novel" as a literary form.[4] The beautifully designed coffee-table book *The Penguin Atlas of Diasporas* by French Marxist historians Gérard Chaliand and Jean-Pierre Rageau appeared in French in 1991 and in English in 1995 and presents a similarly diverse list.[5] Other journals, such as *Callaloo*, *Public Culture*, and *Contemporary Sociology* have since begun paying attention to "diaspora" and "diasporic groups."[6] Theorists as diverse as Edward Said, Paul Gilroy, Daniel Boyarin, Arjun Appadurai, Gloria Anzaldúa, and Benedict Anderson have put the concept in play.[7] The October 1995 edition of the *MLA Job Information List* advertised for the first time a number of positions in various areas of "diaspora studies."

Although postcolonial theorists have increasingly employed the concept "diaspora," they have disagreed with one another about what the term actually means and how it is to be employed. "There is no ambiguity about the term *diaspora*," Chaliand and Rageau claim, "when it is used in relation to the Jewish people" (a problematic statement, as we shall see below). But they admit that once the term is "applied" to other groups, "it becomes immediately apparent how difficult it is in many cases to find a definition that makes a clear distinction between a migration and a diaspora, or between a minority and a diaspora."[8] While social scientists like Chaliand and Rageau attempt to use *diaspora* as a descriptive term to identify the populations to be studied, other theorists have not been interested in the term merely for its descriptive capacities.

Rather, as John Lie points out in his review of the journal *Diaspora* in *Contemporary Sociology*, for most theorists the term has been a central concept in their prescriptive attempt to recast certain traditional sociological narratives for polemical purposes. In particular, the theorists Lie considers are attempting to revise the narrative of "international migration" and replace it with a narrative of "transnational diaspora." The traditional narrative imagined migration as immigration, that is, as a unidirectional move from one well-defined national territory to another. This type of move "entails a radical, and in many cases a singular, break from the old country to the new nation." Migrants are "uprooted" and "shorn of premigration networks, cultures, and belongings." The "melting pot" assimilates them by permanently removing what is unique to them. While they may retain a sentimental attachment to the old world, eventually they construct new networks in the new world and cease to consider return a serious possibility.

But theorists in the journal *Diaspora* and elsewhere have been attempting to describe a different trajectory than unidirectional international immigration: a trajectory of multidirectional transnational migratory flows. A transnational community maintains its networks in the old world and continues to exchange information, political support, contractual obligations, funding, and perhaps above all affection with members of its ethnic or

religious group in the old world. In Lie's words, "Multiple, circular, and
return migrations, rather than a singular great journey from one seden-
tary space to another, occur across transnational spaces."[9] The technolo-
gies of the fax, overnight express, email, and other outgrowths of the information age have made it increasingly possible for migrants to maintain
living and not merely nostalgic connections with those they've left
behind.[10] The "homeland" is not understood to be a unified field but, as
Purnima Mankeker suggests in her attempt to "subvert the binaries of
homeland and diaspora," a place that is not "a comfortable, stable, inherited, and familiar space, but instead . . . an imaginative, politically charged
space where the familiarity and sense of affection and commitment lay in
shared collective analysis of social injustice, as well as a vision of radical
transformation." According to many of the writers in *Diaspora*, this new
narrative entails an altered attitude toward both the old world and the
new. The new diasporans' mobility and the fact that they occupy experiential "border zones" engender in them multiple allegiances and resistance
to the homogenizing impulses and seemingly impermeable boundaries
of the nation-state.[11]

Perhaps the desire to transgress boundaries is nowhere more apparent
than in the writing of the editor of *Diaspora* himself. Recognizing from
the outset that "the term [diaspora] once described Jewish, Greek, and
Armenian dispersion," Tölölyan argues in the journal's opening article,
"The Nation-State and Its Others: In Lieu of a Preface," that the term
now "shares meanings with a larger semantic domain that includes words
like immigrant, expatriate, refugee, guest-worker, exile community, over-
seas community, ethnic community. This is the vocabulary of transna-
tionalisms." (Note the slipperiness between "migration" and "diaspora"
that worried Rageau and Chaliand.) In this enlarged conceptual domain,
"diasporas are the exemplary communities of the transnational moment"
because "they embody the question of borders, which is at the heart of
any adequate definition of the Others of the nation-state. The latter always
imagines and represents itself as a land, a territory, a place that functions
as the site of homogeneity, equilibrium, integration." But this imagined
homogeneity is disrupted by the existence of diasporas. According to
Tölölyan, in fact, the increased visibility of diasporas is the ground condition for an entirely new vision: "The vision of a homogeneous nation
is now being replaced by a vision of the world as a 'space' continually
reshaped by forces . . . whose varying intersections in real estate constitute every 'place' as a heterogeneous and disequilibriated site of . . .
negotiated identity and affect."[12] As a social formation that forces nation-

states to recognize the limitations of their harmonious and unitary self-perception, diaspora is potentially subversive.

Diaspora's insertion of "disequilibrium" into the nation-state might not be possible except that diaspora forces an awareness of "hybridity" and "impurity" into the public discourse. Many postcolonial theorists seem to share a vision of diaspora as a state of hybridity and impurity (although not every theorist uses the terms to mean the same things) as against an empire or nation-state that is ideologically concerned to promote homogeneity and purity. The Columbia University author of *Culture and Imperialism,* Edward Said, argues that "American identity is too varied to be a unitary and homogenous thing; indeed the battle within it is between advocates of a unitary identity and those who see the whole as a complex but not reductively unifed one. This opposition implies two different perspectives, two historiographies, one linear and subsuming, the other contrapuntal and often nomadic." The burden of his favored "nomadic" criticism is to demonstrate that "cultural forms are hybrid, mixed, impure." As a literary critic, he argues that even literary artifacts presumed free from relations to hegemonic power are complicit in articulating imperialist ideology and pivot on the relation of the nation-state with its colonial others. His conclusion is that because of their "hybridity"—their inclusion of both domestic and colonial elements—these works "irradiate and interfere with apparently stable and impermeable categories founded on genre, periodization, nationality, or style, those categories presuming that the West and its culture are largely independent of other cultures, and of the worldly pursuits of power." They are "far from being fixed and pure."[13]

In this view, because diasporans do not share the homogenizing impulse of the nation, they (or at least some of them) are able to attain a powerful critical perspective. When Said analyzes works by writers like Cesaire, Fanon, Rushdie, and Yeats who have themselves experienced colonialism, he suggests that they resist imperialism by making visible the hybridity that the nationalist or imperialist rhetorics seek to efface. Their strategy for promoting this alternative vision is "to live as migrants do," for

liberation as an intellectual mission, born in the resistance . . . to the . . . ravages of imperialism, has now shifted from the settled, established, and domesticated dynamics of culture to its unhoused, decentered, and exilic energies, energies whose incarnation today is the migrant, and whose consciousness is that of the intellectual and artist in exile, the political figure between domains, between forms, between homes, and between languages.[14]

Said recognizes that this vision of the intellectual nomad, the diasporic critic, minimizes the misery of refugees in order to call attention to what he sees as their privileged critical position. Yet he insists that only by so conceiving of themselves can politically engaged postcolonial theorists "distill and articulate the predicaments that disfigure modernity—mass deportation, imprisonment, population transfer, collective dispossession, and forced immigrations." For Said, as for many postcolonial theorists, the "hybrid counter-energies" that can resist imperialist hegemony may only be annexed by an "exilic" or diasporic consciousness.[15]

Claims for the subversive hybridity of diaspora and the critical potential of disaporans are also made by Paul Gilroy, an Anglo-African scholar at the University of London, in *The Black Atlantic: Modernity and Double Consciousness*. Focusing on a trans-Atlantic black social and intellectual formation that he calls the "black Atlantic," he demonstrates the hybridity and creative impurity of the thought and art that results from the encounter of African American, Afro-Caribbean, and Anglo-African cultures both with each other's artistic and intellectual heritage and with the nonblack European and American artistic and intellectual traditions. He does so in order to argue that a fluid black diaspora culture traverses back and forth across the Atlantic Ocean. For Gilroy, *diaspora* is valuable as a concept "lodged between the local and the global" that offers "an alternative to the nationalist focus which dominates cultural criticism." For, like Said, he believes that nationalist ideology is injuriously monolithic, and that since the concept of diaspora by definition cannot be co-opted by a single nationalism, it can function as a crucial part of a subversive cultural criticism and politics.[16]

Gilroy is aware (as some other postcolonial theorists are not) of the "dangers of idealism and pastoralisation associated with this concept," aware that the condition of diaspora is often misery. But he asserts that even the suffering of diasporans "has a special redemptive power, not for themselves alone but for humanity as a whole." By making visible the terror at the heart of modern rationality and modern social formations like the institution of slavery, the suffering of diasporans can force nations to acknowledge and repent of their brutality. Like Said, Gilroy believes that "what was initially felt to be a curse—the curse of homelessness or the curse of enforced exile—gets repossessed. It becomes affirmed and is reconstructed as the basis of a privileged standpoint from which certain useful and critical perceptions about the modern world become more likely."[17] These privileged perceptions do not, however, seem available to every diasporan but only to exilic intellectuals. Like Said, then, Gilroy sees "diaspora" as a privileged and clear-sighted "position" from which engaged intellectuals might mount effective resistance against imperial power.

There is room here for criticism of the developing postcolonial model.

Undoubtedly, postcolonial theorists' conception of the exiled intellectual as harbinger of liberation has its attractions, but these critics seem at times to claim more for themselves than responsible comparative analysis might legitimately permit. Any theory that tries to take account of phenomena (like colonialism and imperialism) that have been dispersed throughout the globe and across many centuries must articulate explicitly the conditions under which comparative analysis might legitimately take place as well as the limits beyond which such analysis cannot go. But Said's and Gilroy's almost generic understanding of the exile as visionary sometimes prevents them from acknowledging the boundaries on whatever vision the exile might produce. Ironically, such vision without boundaries is precisely the nationalist and imperialist dream that postcolonialists reject: they are in danger here of "using the master's tools to dismantle the master's house," a procedure that can only succeed by reproducing the forms of oppression it seeks to subvert.[18]

Moreover, as Benedict Anderson points out in his 1994 essay "Exodus," diaspora is not always subversive of nationalism. In fact, the condition of diaspora may inspire nationalist sentiment. He agrees with the other theorists that "nomadism" has the potential for subversion of nationalism, and he sees the Jonathan Pollard trial as a case in point, arguing that "the resentful spy was understood [by Jewish Americans] as representing a transnational ethnicity." He asks appreciatively, "What else could so subversively blur American and Israeli citizenship?" Yet Anderson is not as sanguine about the necessity of the nomad's subversive character as other postcolonial theorists. On the contrary, he suggests that "the rise of nationalist movements and their variable culminations in successful nation-states" can be accounted for as "a project for coming home from exile, for the resolution of hybridity, for a positive printed from a negative in the darkroom of political struggle." Nationalism is not necessarily expunged during periods of exile; indeed, it can be inspired by the experience. He quotes John Dalberg-Acton who writes that "exile is the nursery of nationality."[19] Exile can be described as the progenitor of the violence of nationalism and colonialism as well as the motive for subverting the nation or empire. Anderson's corrective is necessary so that the idealization of diaspora does not obscure the ambiguity of its relations with state power.

Even Anderson's corrective, however, might itself need a corrective before it can be useful to American Jews. For like the other theorists, Anderson continues to privilege diaspora over nation-statehood almost reflexively, as if diaspora communities were a priori more ethical than other types of "imagined communities," in particular, the nation-state. If this decontextualized interpretation of the relative ethics of diaspora and nation-statehood were applied uncritically to Jewish history, then diaspora would appear to have been Jewish history's grandest contribution to world history, while the formation and continuing existence of Israel as a nation-state would seem to be, at best, a highly unethical moment in Jewish history, a moment that obviously needs to be subverted. This decontextualized understanding of the emergence of Israel as a nation-state is not a view that many American Jews will accept, although the critique of Israeli nationalism voiced by Daniel Boyarin and Jonathan Boyarin in a recent essay (to be discussed below) is an exception.[20]

Still, despite its somewhat incoherent efforts to find a generalizable definition for "diaspora," its overly sanguine conception of the exiled intellectual's vision, its insufficient appreciation for diasporans' suffering, and its rather ossified ethical compass, the postcolonial discourse of diaspora may have much to offer Jews. For one thing, postcolonialism may serve as a catalyst for alliance building between Jews and groups from whom they have been estranged. Gilroy, in particular, acknowledges black intellectuals' debt to Jewish history, and he extends an invitation to Jews and blacks to engage in specific comparative analyses of their respective diasporas. He hopes that the links that would be revealed by such analyses "might contribute to a better political relationship between Jews and blacks at some future distant point." In fact, he initiates such a comparative analysis himself by tracing the influence of modern political Zionism in the nineteenth century on such black liberation projects as the establishment of Liberia and by tracing the consequences for black/Jewish relations of the movement within black thought from gospel singers' identification with the slaves in the Exodus narrative to pan-Africanists' identification with the Egyptian pharaohs. Beyond making specific comparisons of moments in black and Jewish history, he measures the two communities' respective theories of diaspora, recognizing that they are not completely commensurate. He argues that while they share "the notion of a return to the point of origin" and "the condition of exile, [or] forced separation from the homeland," they also diverge in terms of the attitudes toward diaspora they prescribe for their respective exiled communities. Specifically, unlike Jewish culture, black Atlantic culture has developed strategies for relating to a diaspora that is a permanent condition and something other than a curse.[21] Without engaging in comparative analysis of the kind for which Gilroy and other postcolonial theorists appeal, there is no way to gauge whether any of the strategies developed by other groups might be useful for American Jews.[22]

Traditional Jews' Narrative of Diaspora

Perhaps there is no need to look outside of Jewish history and intellectual tradition for theories of diaspora. Perhaps postcolonial theory has only repeated what Jews already know from their own experience. By investigating the traditional Jewish narratives of diaspora—biblical, prophetic, and rabbinic—I will show that postcolonialism is actually proposing quite a different way of understanding diaspora than that embedded in traditional Jewish narratives. Perhaps the traditional narrative and the postcolonial discourse can each make visible what is missing in the other's approach.

In justifying their invocation of the concept "diaspora," a number of postcolonial commentators have noted that the term was first used in the Septuagint, the Egyptian Jews' translation of the Hebrew Bible into Greek around 250 B.C.E. The literal English translation of *diaspora,* "to be scattered" (like seeds), shows that the translators were filial to the original Hebrew term from Deuteronomy 28:64, *v'hefitz'cha* ("you will be scattered"). But this is as far as most postcolonial commentators' interest in philology takes them. [23] Satisfied that the term originates in Jewish literature, many then abstract it from its original context as well as its subsequent history in Jewish literature and philosophy. In doing so, they alter its meaning substantially, without explicitly recording their adaptations.

Note, to begin with, that the language of the term *diaspora,* Greek, is an indicator of the very condition the term describes. The translation of the Hebrew Bible into Greek would not have been necessary had Jews not already been scattered throughout the Greek (and subsequently Roman) empires—that is, had they not already been "colonials," exiles forced to live within imperial domains. Was their exile the vital and subversive existence predicted by postcolonial theory? Before we can fully appreciate the answer, we must be aware that there was already another predictive theory—or better, predictive *narrative*—in whose light the Hellenized Jews themselves must have understood their existence. This narrative was first articulated in the very Deuteronomic text from which the term *diaspora* was derived. For in Jewish history, the Diaspora is not a theoretical concept in a "discourse" but a historical condition that can only be understood as part of a narrative containing a particular and cyclical sequence of events.

"Diaspora" is first introduced in the Deuteronomic narrative when Moses, nearing his own death, recounts the history of the people of Israel to a new generation. All those who had been liberated from Egypt with

him, save two, are dead. In an attempt to inspire this new free-born generation of Israelites, Moses describes the manifold blessings that will accrue
to the people if they uphold the Covenant—pledged at Sinai by their
parents—after they have crossed the Jordan and taken the land of Canaan
by military force. These blessings will benefit the people if they "obey the
Lord your God to observe faithfully all His [*sic*] commandments" (Deut.
28:1). But if they are forgetful, neglectful, or rebellious, and do not "obey
the Lord your God to observe faithfully all His commandments and laws"
(Deut. 28:15), they will be cursed—the most extreme of the curses being
"diaspora." Thus, diaspora makes its first appearance as the divine punishment for breach of contract.

Such a breach proves to have devastating consequences. For the text
predicts that "the Lord will scatter you [*v'hefitz'cha*] among all the peoples from one end of the earth to the other, and there you shall serve other
gods, wood and stone, whom neither you nor your ancestors have experienced" (Deut. 28:64). In diaspora Jews shall be made to commit the
Bible's ultimate transgression, idolatory, and Deuteronomy goes on to
foretell the profound political and spiritual degradation that scattered Jews
will experience:

Yet even among those nations you shall find no peace, nor shall your foot
find a place to rest. The Lord will give you an anguished heart and eyes that
pine and a despondent spirit. The life you face shall be precarious; you shall
be in terror, night and day, with no assurance of survival. In the morning you
shall say, "If only it were evening!" and in the evening you shall say, "If only
it were morning!"—because of what your heart shall dread and your eyes shall
see. The Lord will send you back to Egypt in galleys, by a route which I told
you you should not see again. There you shall offer yourselves for sale to your
enemies as male and female slaves, but none will buy. (Deut. 28:65-68)

Moses' curse is the first of many elaborations in biblical, prophetic, and
rabbinic literature of the narrative of Israel's transgression against God
and subsequent exile from blessing. While the term *diaspora* seems to have
a potentially positive connotation—the notion that, like seeds, those once
scattered can take root and continue to thrive amid foreign flora—this
meaning is increasingly foreclosed in prophetic literature by the replacement of the term *t'futsoth* (scatterings, "diaspora") with the more strongly
negative term *galut* (exile). As the above passage suggests and Arnold Eisen
has shown in detail, the Deuteronomist conceives the condition of diaspora to have both political and metaphysical dimensions. On a political
level, diaspora reminds Jews that property and security are gifts from God

that can be taken away. On a metaphysical level, diaspora represents expulsion from nurturance, alienation from nature, and estrangement from God, others, even oneself—from all potential sources of blessing. The Deuteronomist depicts the time of diaspora as Jews' bleakest hour: they are trapped in a condition of political and spiritual homelessness, in the aftermath of a glorious past, in a present full of danger and discontent, with only dread for a future. [24] Thus the attitude envisioned by the first use of the term *diaspora* is alienation from home and hopelessness in the present host land.

While the vision of alienation in this text is profound, there is a promise hidden in the Deuteronomic narrative that is exploited by subsequent prophetic and rabbinic tradition: Jews might be able to seek redemption from diaspora, if they atone for their many transgressions against God.[25] If they pass their time of trial through acts of atonement, Jews can expect a "return" to and fulfillment of the Deuteronomic blessings. In contrast to Gilroy's understanding of the automatic redemption brought about by diasporic suffering, the traditional Jewish narrative understands diasporic suffering as only *potentially* redemptive. It may be redemptive only if Jews respond to it with the proper action, known as *teshuvah*, often translated as "repentance" or "return." Appropriate *teshuvah* has been interpreted variously in Jewish history as prayer, social justice work, mysticism, national liberation struggle, or most frequently the multitude of daily acts defined in the halakhah, the Jewish code of daily ritual observance. The mere fact of suffering, without an appropriate active response, does not guarantee redemption. This appears to be a difference between traditional Jewish thought and that emanating from the black diaspora, the latter of which has been influenced by Christian interpretations of suffering and redemption.

According to the prophets, if Jews do respond appropriately, the "scattered seeds" will be "ingathered," the Jews restored to their homeland in Zion, and peace and prosperity will reign once more. The metaphysical and political alienations will cease. As Anderson suspected, the pain of diaspora does generate an intense longing to return to the "homeland" (although not necessarily a homeland defined in "nationalist" terms). For the prophets, however, the homeland is understood not merely as a geographic source, nor merely as a source and origin of cultural integrity and authenticity, but as a *sacred* source that represents the promise and proof of God's continuous care over the obedient covenanted community.

The cyclical narrative of Jewish history in which the concept "diaspora" is embedded might be schematized, then, as follows: Prosperity-Transgression-Diaspora-Repentance-Redemption. From this vantage point, the term seems to have little in common with its homonym in post-colonial discourse. The premodern rabbis would have been able to make little sense of the postcolonial theorists' idealistic vision of diaspora as a "border zone" or "mestiza" consciousness redolent of vital impurities.[26] In the Mishnah and Gemara, they repeatedly sought to demarcate the "pure" from the "polluted," through systems of halakhic regulations such as *kashrut,* or the family purity laws. They did so in order to create what Eisen calls "an order of Torah" outside of the Land through which it would be possible to ensure Jewish cultural survival in the midst of pressures to convert and assimilate. Indeed, the halakhic system gained such central-ity that medieval diasporic Jews, unlike the prophets, only infrequently expressed political aspirations to return to the homeland: for centuries the desire to return to the homeland meant primarily a metaphysical desire for wholeness. In this way the Land remained a "center of aspiration" but was on the "periphery [of] actual existence."[27] This is one of the rea-sons that for 1,800 years nationalist ideology was generally *not* a product of exile.[28]

Nor does the traditional narrative conceive of the condition of dias-pora as inherently subversive of the systems of power in the midst of which the scattered must survive. If anything, the rabbis' interpretation of dias-pora as a punishment made them rule warily when questions of obedi-ence to the imperial Greco-Roman, Christian, or Ottoman rulers arose, to avoid bringing further harm to their vulnerable communities. While they succeeded in re-creating Jewish time outside of the Land, they were not always able to fend off threats to their security—the Jews were per-haps "subverted" more often than their hosts. This evidence of the limi-tations of diaspora's subversive potential may not be welcome to post-colonial theorists, but for medieval Jews (or later for Soviet or Ethiopian Jews), for whom "migrant consciousness" was not merely an intellectual exercise, the curse of exile remained potent.

It is perhaps instructive, however, that neither the postcolonial discourse nor the traditional Jewish narrative proves fully accurate, at least when applied to the Hellenized Jews. While the existence of the Greek term *diaspora* indicates that the Deuteronomic curse did to some degree come true—Jews had to read even their sacred text in the language of the dom-inant power—the fact that a translation of the Hebrew Bible came into being at all suggests that living in "diaspora" was not quite as alienating as the Deuteronomic curse predicted. Life within the Greek and Roman empires must have been precarious for Jews: tributes were exacted from them and they were prohibited at various times from sacrificing at the

Temple (while it still stood) or from praying in their synagogues after the Romans destroyed the Temple in 70 C.E. Some were forced into slavery, others displaced from their homes. Still others, like the Maccabees, the zealots at Masada, and Bar Kokhba, lost their lives in resistance. But that at least some Jews were able to read their sacred text (if only in translation) meant that at least some of them were not being made to "serve other gods, wood and stone." A community that could produce such a translation was probably not as powerless as the Deuteronomic narrative had foretold.[29] But neither was it as powerfully subversive as the postcolonial theory would imply. Ultimately, it would take a proliferating imperialistic ideology with aspirations for global domination—post-Pauline Christianity—to "subvert" (convert) the Roman Empire.

American Jews' Exceptional Diaspora

While the traditional Jewish narrative may be useful in calling attention to an excess of idealism in postcolonial discourse, postcolonial discourse may in turn be useful in calling attention to an excess of exceptionalism in American Jews' attitude toward diaspora. Here, therefore, we must attempt to engage three parties in dialogue at once.

Twentieth-century American Jewish intellectuals have generally resisted many of the elements of the traditional Jewish narrative. In particular, they have rejected the equation of the United States with *galut* (exile) and the state of Israel with Zion. These intellectuals, for the most part not traditionalists, have been unwilling to see their diaspora as a divine punishment for their transgressions. Moreover, while they have conceded that Israel is the Jewish cultural center in the second half of the twentieth century, they have resisted the notion that Israel is the spiritual center. They have not seen Israel as the "homeland" in the metaphysical sense, rejecting the notion that the Land is a sacred source of wholeness.

The conclusion Arnold Eisen reaches on completing his survey of twentieth-century American Jewish thought is that a rather Kaplanian consensus has been reached: "America is not home, yet neither is Israel. The latter *is* the Center and is certainly not exile, but neither can the former be compared to any previous diaspora. 'America is different.' Nor should its rich Jewish resources be underestimated. The two communities [are] interdependent."[30] I hope to show that this ideological consensus is, however, only partially accurate and has some quite negative consequences.

As a result of their exceptionalism, American Jews are isolated from other cultural groups in the United States and alienated from all but a sentimentalized Jewish history. How has this model come into being? And how can it be overcome?

America's "difference" is usually justified by pointing to the relative absence of systematic persecution and concomitantly to the many freedoms American Jews enjoy. Since the colonial period, American Jewish intellectuals have maintained that this New Jerusalem (as the Puritans called it) was a place of promise—a Promised Land—unlike any other. The Jews' embrace of the basic benignity of the Bill of Rights has perhaps most recently been exemplified in Lynne Sharon Schwartz's short story "The Opiate of the People," in which David the Russian Jewish immigrant memorizes the Constitution in order to be more American than Americans themselves.[31] An attitude toward their condition that includes trust in the United States, trust that the United States is not *galut* but a hothouse nurturing self-expression and experimentation, pervades American Jewish theology and literature.

In the United States experimental theologies have come into being ranging from reform to reconstructionism to Heschelian awe to renewal to feminism. These theologies have consistently deemphasized the role of the land of Israel as "center" and have interpreted terms such as *land* and *aliyah* (ascent to the land of Israel) in ways that divest them of any literal implication. Early advocates of reform called for the decentralization of Judaism: they called their prayer sites "temples," the lower-case *t* signifying that genuine Jewish spirituality could occur outside the land in which the Temple had been located. Mordecai Kaplan's reconstructionist vision of Judaism as a religious civilization emphasized the mutual interdependence of the state of Israel and the American diaspora. The state of Israel would "provide an essential source of inspiration" for Jews in the diaspora. For its part, the American diaspora, free of the moral hypocrisies engendered by the state's attempt to balance democracy and Jewish power, free of the state's stark polarization between secular and devout Jews, would be able to maintain a vital spirituality that would in turn be a crucial resource for Israelis.[32] While Abraham Joshua Heschel's *Israel: An Echo of Eternity* saw the formation of the state of Israel as a crucial moment in Jewish history, he tended to invoke "Israel" as a holy state of being to which one aspires rather than a territory to which one returns. Similarly, he tended to speak of *aliyah* as the ascent to the holiness of "Israel," wherever one may happen to be living.[33] Arthur Waskow's vision of Jewish renewal is focused on revivifying the holiday cycle and gaining an environmental appreciation for land—any land—rather than on geographical *aliyah*.[34] Judith Plaskow's feminist Judaism defines the term "Israel" not as a geographical place but metaphorically as "the nature of Jewish community and the Jewish people" and she calls on Judaism to realize an "Israel" that fully includes women.[35] While Israeli Zionists have consistently negated the function of the diaspora in the aftermath of the formation of the state, American Jewish theologians have just as consistently maintained the importance of the continuing existence of Jewish communities outside Ha-aretz (the Land), communities understood not as cursed but as blessed with opportunities for spiritual creativity. There is no need to look abroad for Zion when Zion is right here—or more accurately, when Zion is right *now*, a time rather than a place, an experience rather than a territory, to be reached through the practice of a particular kind of attention, or *kavanah*.

In contrast to this vision of America as *heimisch*—familiar, secure, and creative—the state of Israel has seemed to many American Jews what Freud would have called *unheimliche*, unfamiliar.[36] While the traditional narrative of diaspora functioned to unite scattered Jews from diverse locations in a common dream of return, the realization of that dream by the ingathering of Israel's hundred diasporas has had the ironic effect of producing an awareness of Jews' heterogeneity. For many American Jews, for whom Jews appear fairly homogeneous—Ashkenazic, white—the hundred diasporas call attention to Israel's diversity and unfamiliarity. For many American Jews, then, this heterogeneity is another indication (alongside Israel's continuing national insecurity and economic deprivation) that Israel is not Zion, that Israeli nationhood is not the fulfillment of a sacred promise but the partial, haphazard, sometimes elating and sometimes distorting realization of generations of Jewish dreams and nightmares.

Even the familiar Western aspects of the modern Israeli state, like its parliamentary structure and principle of majority rule, can produce an awareness of Israel's distance from the traditional vision of Zion, for if the state is comprised in part of political and cultural institutions transplanted to the Land from *galut*, then the center begins to seem less distinct from the periphery after all. These "impurities" attendant on Israel's realization must conflict with the prophetic promise of a return to wholeness and the rabbinic vision of spiritual purity. When Philip Roth's Portnoy makes his brief and catastrophic sojourn to the Land, the state appears exotic, dangerous, even emasculating.[37] American Jews may still "sing the songs of Zion in a strange land," but they do so with the consciousness that the land in which they sing is not so strange and the land of which they sing is not so familiar.

If American Jewish writers have longed to return to any Zion, it is not to Jerusalem but to Bialystok. For many the Old World is the American Jewish homeland. To be sure, it is an imaginary homeland, not remembered in its particularities, a homeland sentimentalized as a quaint and timeless place of Jewish wholeness, a seamless *Yiddishkeit*. The important differences between German and Russian Jewish immigrants—and between Jews from Galicia and Warsaw, for that matter—have been replaced by a pan-Ashkenazi "American" Jewish identity. American Jews are alienated from the reality of this homeland more even than from the Israeli nation-state, separated by a distance of anguish that cannot even be imagined, much less traversed. The desire to return to the Old World has gained a certain tragic pathos in the work of writers like I. B. Singer, Jacob Glatstein, Cynthia Ozick, and Art Spiegelman, whose writing tries to bridge the gap between a New World we inhabit and an Old World to which, because of the Holocaust, we cannot return.[38] Short story writer Steve Stern has taken this desire to make contact with the Old World in a more nostalgic direction in his collection *Lazar Malkin Enters Heaven.* He creates a shtetl in Memphis, Tennessee, a shtetl in which no pogroms ever occur and all the Jews are Americans. He brings the sentimentalized version of the Old World to us.[39]

Alienated from both "homelands," American Jews have felt they had no choice but to create an existence unlike any their forebears ever knew. Because of their ideology of exceptionalism, they have not, for the most part, looked to other eras of stability and promise in diaspora Jewish history for aid in understanding their situation. In consequence they suffer an emotional and intellectual distance from Israel, the Old World, and the rest of Jewish history. For this reason, American Jews' commitment to the promise of America simultaneously affirms the solidity and the fragility of their freedom. The triumphalism that since 1948 has seemed endemic to certain kinds of American Jewish thinking about the relation of the "periphery" to the "center" hides what might be called an anxiety of the lack of influence.[40] In less defensive moments, what American Jews celebrate as their freedom from the dictates of tradition, they also lament as the loss of their continuity with the past.

What makes American Jews since 1948 truly exceptional is not in any case the absence of anti-Semitism or the economic or cultural opportunity provided by the Golden Land. The "lachrymose" view of Jewish history to the contrary, there have been many such eras. Rather, American Jews' exceptionalism rests on two startlingly new facts of Jewish history: that they are among the first Jews in two thousand years to have had the option to literalize the notion of "return" and that for the most part they

have chosen not to be "gathered in." Along with other poststatehood diasporic Jews, American Jews are faced with two questions that their ancestors never had to confront: What sort of attitude is appropriate toward
a "Zion" that has been realized as a nation-state? and What does it mean
to desire to continue living outside of that "Zion"?

The range and limitations of recent American Jewish attempts to answer
these questions can be seen in a comparison of an essay by Daniel Boyarin
and Jonathan Boyarin, "Diaspora: Generation and the Ground of Jewish Identity," with Philip Roth's "confession," *Operation Shylock*, both from
1993. The Boyarins' essay takes the triumphalism in certain versions of
American Jewish thought and postcolonialism to an extreme. The Boyarins
idealize the condition of diaspora and seem to oppose the formation and
continuing existence of Israel as a nation-state. In a rather too certain fashion their essay elevates wilderness over Canaan, wandering over settlement, diaspora over statehood, and genealogy (that is, biologically determined "kinship" or "race") over geographical territory. The Boyarins want
to "propose a privileging of Diaspora" and to argue that "Diaspora, not
monotheism, may be the most important contribution that Judaism has
to make to the world." They identify with what they describe (wrongly,
in my view) as "a prophetic discourse of preference for 'exile' over root-
edness in the Land."[41] They seem to support a race-based—or, as they
say, "ethnocentric"—definition of Jewish community, as long as that community does not "seek domination over others." And they describe this
ethnocentricity as a proposal endorsed by "the Rabbis," that is, by ancient
diasporic Jewish teachers.

How to ensure that one's ethnocentricity does not devolve into dominance over others? Simply by acting like the members of the Neturei Karta,
an ultra-Orthodox sect that in its mission statement denies "any desire to
exploit the local population in order to attain statehood." Like the Neturei
Karta, other Jews need to divest themselves of any attachment to land
and power. In the Boyarins' assessment, Jews who divest are in the position to be perpetual exiles, subversive of all state power formations because
they always call attention to hybridity in power's midst. They are in the
position to be morally pure.

But the Boyarins' call to divestment is curiously contradictory. On the
one hand, their theory seems determined to idealize the diasporic condition and to minimize the tragic suffering the Rabbis (and all the other
diasporic Jews) also experienced and recorded. On the other hand, while
downplaying Jewish suffering, the Boyarins' theory places supreme importance on Palestinians' suffering, without recognizing any of the Zion-

ists' claims as legitimate. The Boyarins claim that only by living in the "wilderness"—in perpetual exile—can Jews maintain moral purity. But the Boyarins also position themselves as postcolonial theorists interested in impurity and hybridity. On the one hand, they want to "privilege Diaspora," but on the other they want to privilege a sect for whom Diaspora is nothing less than a punishment for sin. As their mission statement says, the members of Neturei Karta "repeat constantly in our prayers, 'since we sinned, we were therefore exiled from our land.'" How can diaspora be plausibly construed as both a positive position and a curse at the same time? (And is it really a greater "privilege" to be in a state of sin than in a Jewish state?) Finally, the Boyarins appear to position themselves as politically engaged critics, but they champion a form of political behavior that can only be seen as utopian in the most unconstructive sense. They apparently wish to restrict Jews to the role of Cain or Ahasuerus, the legendary wandering Jews. Their call to divestment is not a solution to the challenges of Jewish power—it is an evasion of the question.

A more satisfactory and more nuanced—although still incomplete—attempt to articulate an American Jewish relationship to the nation-state is Philip Roth's doppelgänger novel, *Operation Shylock*. Yet even Roth's more complex vision cannot dispense with the negative consequences of American Jews' exceptionalism. Roth conjures up a second Philip Roth, a fraud pretending to be him in order to gain support for a theory called "Diasporism." The theory is that Zionism is dead, that the state of Israel will either be the physical or moral death of the Jews, and that the Ashkenazim who once fled Europe for Israel need now to return to Europe and resettle there. In Israel, according to a Palestinian nationalist with whom the fraud sympathizes, Jews have merely built themselves "a Jewish Belgium, without even a Brussels to show for it." [42] It was only in diaspora that Jews could thrive morally. True, anti-Semitism was a distinct problem for European Jews, but much has changed in Europe since the Holocaust, and residual anti-Semitism may be dealt with through the creation of a twelve-step group with chapters in every European city to be called Anti-Semites Anonymous (A-S.A.).

The "real" Philip Roth distances himself from this prankster's theory, sometimes calling it absurd and monomaniacal, other times merely pointing to its "exaggerations." In the fiction of this confession, he sets out to defeat the other Philip Roth—whom he renames Moishe Pipik ("Moses Bellybutton" in Yiddish) so as to satirize the trivializing impulse behind this imaginary reverse Exodus. (As Roth says, Pipikism is "the antitragic force that inconsequentializes everything—farcicalizes everything, trivializes everything, superficializes everything—our suffering as Jews not excluded.") [43] As part of his attempt to defeat Pipik, Roth goes to work for the Mossad, posing as an agent of Palestinian nationalism in order to identify "other" Jewish anti-Zionists. By working on behalf of Israel's national security, Roth gives evidence for the Mossad agent Smiles-burger's contention that "Diaspora Jews constitute a pool of foreign nationals such as no other intelligence agency in the world can call on for loyal service"—shades of Pollard! At one level, then, the "real" Philip Roth seems to suggest that Pipik's Diasporism is nonsense, that Jews' suffering in diaspora (especially during the Holocaust) and the continued existence of anti-Semitism in Europe justifies the necessity of the Jewish state, and that American Jews like himself should organize their life choices around the state's needs. Israel is the center.

But this is only one of many levels of analysis in a novel that takes Paul Gilroy's notion of "double consciousness" to new extremes. Ironically, the most ruthlessly honest figure in the book is the character who is paid to distribute disinformation, the Mossad agent, Smilesburger. He admits that the occupation and in some sense even the foundation of the state itself have been the occasions for Jews' moral degeneration. As he says:

What we have done to the Palestinians is wicked. We have displaced them and we have oppressed them. We have expelled them, beaten them, tortured them, and murdered them. The Jewish state, from the day of its inception, has been dedicated to eliminating a Palestinian presence in historical Palestine and expro-priating the land of an indigenous people. The Palestinians have been driven out, dispersed, and conquered by the Jews. To make a Jewish state we have betrayed our history—we have done unto the Palestinians what the Christians have done unto us: systematically transformed them into the despised and sub-jugated Other, thereby depriving them of their human status.

Statehood has thus not only been a grievous violation of the "indigenous people" but a violation of Jews' own vision of themselves. The center can-not hold. Perhaps then the periphery may have more to recommend it after all. But lest we draw that conclusion, Smilesburger goes on to assure Roth that even diaspora Jews have been morally defiled by the existence of the state, for self-righteous and sanctimonious American Jews have impugned the memory of the Holocaust by invoking it to justify the "imperialist, colo-nialist theft that *was* the state of Israel." They have also supported Israel's oppression of Palestinians through their monetary donations and their exer-tion of political pressure on Israel's behalf. Between diaspora and the state, it seems there is no right. Smilesburger's honest justification for his own actions on behalf of the state is "I did what I did to you because I did what

I did to you"—in other words, European Jews could not have done any-thing else if they were to survive. Yet this necessity does not absolve them of responsibility for their oppression of Palestinians.[44]

While Roth undermines the attempt of his anti-Moses to lead a reverse Exodus to Europe and complicates any easy identification with the state of Israel, he never really questions the legitimacy of the American Jewish diaspora. Instead, toward the end of the novel it begins to appear that he has introduced such an absurd version of "Diasporism" in the plot about Moishe Pipik so that by comparison his own version of diasporism will seem more palatable. Not that he recommends a reverse Exodus to Amer-ica, but he nevertheless does make a claim for the ongoing validity of Amer-ican Jewish settlement and cultural expression. True, American Jews are still hypocrites for invoking the Holocaust to support an oppressive state. But they cannot be accused of living with the false consciousness imputed to all diaspora Jews by Israeli Zionism. America *is* different from Europe, and its relative lack of anti-Semitism lends diasporism a more solid credibility than Moishe Pipik's version. No need for an A-S.A. in the U.S.A. While Roth avoids suggesting a Pipikist moral triumphalism for American Jews, he also avoids advocating a mass transfer of American Jews to Israel.

For himself, having had his Israeli adventure (and having milked Demjanjuk's trial, Leon Klinghoffer's death, and the intifada for a novel), Philip Roth returns to New York. The final chapter of *Operation Shylock* takes place in a New York delicatessen that becomes a metonym for the American Jewish diaspora. In a novel whose parodic structure eschews realism, the detailed and nostalgic description of this restaurant and the memories and reflections it inspires are remarkable:

[The store] served breakfast and lunch on a dozen formica-topped tables in a room adjacent to the bagel and bialy counter and that looked as though, years back, when someone got the bright idea to "modernize," the attempt at redecoration had been sensibly curtailed halfway through. . . . In Newark, back in the forties, we used to buy . . . silky slices of precious lox . . . at a family-run store around the corner that looked and smelled pretty much as this one did— . . . wafting up from behind the showcase . . . the bitter fragrance of vinegar, of onions, of whitefish and red herring, of everything pickled, pep-pered, salted, smoked, soaked, stewed, marinated, and dried, smells with a lineage that, like these stores themselves, more than likely led straight back through the shtetl to the medieval ghetto and the nutrients of those who lived frugally and could not afford to dine à la mode, the diet of sailors and com-mon folk, for whom the flavor of the ancient preservatives was life.[45]

Here Roth expresses a nostalgic secular vision of the American diaspora at its creative best, insisting that this diaspora is "more than likely" the true descendant of the culture of the "common folk," whose "ancient" preservative arts hold the secret of Jewish self-preservation. He revels in the material reality—the lavishly imagined smells, flavors, and textures, almost, one could say, the *heimisch* quality—of this evidence of continuing links between the American Jewish culture and Jewish cultures past. After all, this "humble" store is only half modernized—the other half still belongs to the medieval Jewish world. Roth seems to suggest that American Jews are the ancestral standard-bearers of an expressive tradition that reaches back at least a thousand years. He seems to relate the American Jewish diaspora to eastern European Jewish history. Has he abandoned exceptionalism?

Surely not, for Roth represents Yiddish folk culture in the timeless, quaint, homogeneous, and sentimental vein. His delicatessen epiphany may appear to relate American Jews to history, but it is in fact antihistorical since it represents Jews in an unchanging (and inaccurate) still-life portrait. He replaces history with nostalgia. In this way, he enables American Jews to see themselves both as filial to their ancestors and as utterly unique. He satisfies their felt need for at least the illusion of historical continuity while maintaining their exceptionalism.

But this criticism needs to be tempered with one important qualification: while Roth insists that *Yiddishkeit* in America is *heimisch*, he is equally insistent that America itself is not home. Rather, Roth goes on to say that these stores with their "satisfying folk cuisine" bear "the stamp of provisional homeliness."[46] Roth may appear to suggest that gefilte fish is the only homeland, but even that great expression of Jewish continuity and culinary art can only ever aspire to a rough approximation of "homeliness." For, like the four-letter name of God, home itself is a food whose flavor Jews have definitively forgotten and for which they nevertheless are destined to continue to yearn forever—even in America. American Jews may not be "strangers" in their land in quite the same sense as their European forebears were strangers in theirs, but they are still singing the songs of longing for the wholeness and purity of Zion. And even if they rename the desired wholeness "hybridity" and the desired purity "impurity," their yearning will remain—only partially satisfied, forever deferred. America is *not* the Promised Land, Roth implies, because no land ever will be.

But because the United States supports the material marks of Jews' "provisional homeliness," Roth believes it is a valid social location for Jewish dwelling and indwelling. The United States serves more easily as provisional homeland for Roth than Israel, precisely because it has enabled the expression of the preservative folkish values of the Old World. Just as Roth is committed to his friend the Israeli novelist and Holocaust survivor Aharon Appelfeld, he is committed to the necessity of Jewish statehood—but he is not anxious about his own cultural or moral inferiority to Israelis, for he belongs to a venerable and proudly nonelite lineage.

Roth's claim for the ancient, secular, and folkish legitimacy of the American Jewish diaspora depends on his abandonment of the traditional categories through which Jews have understood the term *diaspora*—clearly the old narrative that interprets diaspora as a curse and Israel as sacred and whole will not suffice. But Roth cannot make any general claims for the validity of his alternative vision. Instead, he must construct his narrative as a "confession," a highly personal account of the shenanigans of an exceptional man. He is acutely aware that there is no Sanhedrin or Babylonian Academy or Beit Din that might validate his confession for all American Jews. This atomized individual, with his alienation from any but a sentimentalized antihistory and his isolation from contemporary non-Jewish communities, seems to exemplify the negative consequences of American Jewish exceptionalism, even at its best.

A Dialogic Framework for the American Jewish Diaspora

Perhaps it is precisely on this question of American Jews' exceptionalism, however, that postcolonial theory has something of value to contribute. If, rather than gauging their experience relative to the traditional Jewish narrative of diaspora (and its traditional procedures of adjudication), American Jews began to see their experience within the framework of transnational migrations, they might discover that they are not so exceptional after all. They might find analogs for their vision in other diasporic communities.

For it appears that in the late twentieth century diaspora is a condition for which Jews have not been uniquely chosen. Mexican Americans in California, Cuban Americans in Miami, and Irish Americans in Boston are having analogous, if not precisely similar, experiences. While postcolonial theorists have overstated the subversive character of these social formations, these critics have been able to articulate a different vision of diaspora from that expressed in the traditional Jewish narrative. Given the American Jews' unprecedented attempt to remain in existence side by side with an existing Jewish state, elements of this alternative vision may be of more use to them at present than the traditional narrative. For post-colonialism has described a diasporic consciousness not based on a hierarchical distinction between center and periphery, nor on a coding of the homeland as whole and sacred as against the cursed and fragmented diaspora. The diaspora's relationship to the homeland is not imagined as a sinful community's repentant desire for a prior sacred place but as a living and ongoing exchange of information, financial and political support, contractual obligations, and above all affection. These communities do not regard violation of the relationship as a sin against the sacred but as a transgression against kinship, friendship, and contract. The ideal form of the relationship they work toward is interdependence, mutual support, and respect. The homeland (like the diaspora itself) is recognized as "impure," a site of hybridity and struggle, and it is not held up to the unforgiving standard of moral exemplarity. But the diasporans do have the right and the responsibility, as engaged yet distant participant-observers, to criticize the homeland if it participates in oppression and to pressure it to cease.

American Jews stand to gain much by adapting this vision to their peculiar needs. By carrying out comparative analyses, Jews may discover practical strategies for supporting Israel as well as models for emotional attitudes toward it appropriate to the statehood era, which is exceptional in Jewish history. Arnold Eisen, for one, rejects the possibility that Jews might learn from the experience of others, for he says that "the attempt to come home . . . —not merely to achieve liberation from a colonialist oppressor, not merely to regain lands conquered by a neighboring state, but to come home, in a sense defined by three thousand years of reflection—precludes essential likeness to other developing nations."[47] But Eisen's conclusion is too hastily drawn, for he makes this rather sweeping, inward-looking, and isolationist statement without attempting any comparative analyses in his book. He forgets one of the most important insights to have emerged from postcolonialism—that wisdom has the character of a great diaspora, its seeds scattered throughout all the nations, and it is our task to search for its fruits in all the niches where they grow.

Not only will American Jews be able to draw from the ongoing dialogues, they will also be able to enrich these dialogues with information and ideas emerging from their own histories and experiences. Even this brief survey of American Jewish writers has added further evidence to support Benedict Anderson's contention that diasporans do not necessarily desire to subvert nationalisms: while these writers have qualified their support for American and Israeli forms of nationalism with awareness of the

brutal potentials of nations, they have in the main taken stances of support toward nations that enable the development and flourishing of Jewish cultures. In the case of Israel in particular, the writers' qualified support poses an implicit challenge to many postcolonialists' assumption that
to desire "subversion" in every case is necessarily the only ethically defen-
sible stance.

What further contributions American Jews might make to these discussions remain to be seen. I have tried to show that by ceasing to regard
their condition as exceptional and by taking up the challenge to engage
in comparative analysis Jews (and other groups for whom thriving in diaspora is a central preoccupation) will make significant gains in information exchange and cross-cultural understanding. If the American Jewish
community is to thrive in what has been called "the time of nations"—
which is necessarily also the time of diasporas—its members will need to
draw from and confront their own histories and traditions as well as the
histories and traditions of their partners in dialogue.

Notes

1. Arjun Appadurai, "The Heart of Whiteness," *Callaloo* 16 (Fall 1993): 796–807 (special issue on postcolonial discourse). Multiculturalists who have begun to analyze whiteness include Ronald Takaki, *A Different Mirror: A History of Multicultural America* (Boston:
Little, Brown, 1993), who includes chapters on Irish and Jews; Peter McLaren, "White Terror and Oppositional Agency: Towards a Critical Multiculturalism," in David Theo Goldberg, ed., *Multiculturalism: A Critical Reader* (London: Basil Blackwell, 1994), 45–75; and
Ruth Frankenburg, *The Social Construction of Whiteness: White Women, Race Matters* (Minneapolis: University of Minnesota Press, 1993).

2. Benedict Anderson, *Imagined Communities: Reflections on the Origin and Spread of
Nationalism* (London: Verso, 1991).

3. Cf. Susan Koshy, "The Geography of Female Subjectivity: Ethnicity, Gender, and
Diaspora," *Diaspora* 3 (Spring 1994): 69–84; and Daniel Boyarin and Jonathan Boyarin,
"Diaspora: Generation and the Ground of Jewish Identity," *Critical Inquiry* 19 (Summer
1993): 693–725. Although highly esteemed, *Diaspora* was discontinued in 1996 by Oxford
University Press and Tölölyan is now searching for a new press for his journal. See Rick
Perlstein, "On the Road," *Lingua Franca* 6 (March/April 1996): 27.

4. Artemis Leontis, "The Diaspora of the Novel," *Diaspora* 2 (Spring 1992): 131–147.

5. Gérard Chaliand and Jean-Pierre Rageau, *The Penguin Atlas of Diasporas*, trans. A. M.
Berrett (New York: Viking Penguin, 1995).

6. John Lie, "From International Migration to Transnational Diaspora," *Contemporary
Sociology: A Journal of Reviews* 24 (July 1995): 303–306.

7. Edward Said, *Culture and Imperialism* (New York: Vintage, 1993); Paul Gilroy, *The
Black Atlantic: Modernity and Double Consciousness* (Cambridge: Harvard University Press,
1993); Arjun Appadurai, "The Heart of Whiteness"; Gloria Anzaldúa, *Borderlands/La Frontera* (San Francisco: Aunt Lute Books, 1987); Benedict Anderson, "Exodus," *Critical Inquiry*

20 (Winter 1994): 314–327; also cf. Werner Sollors, "Introduction: The Invention of Ethnicity" in Sollors, ed., *The Invention of Ethnicity* (Oxford: Oxford University Press, 1989).

8. Chaliand and Rageau, *Atlas,* xiii.

9. Lie, "From International Migration to Transnational Diaspora," 304.

10. Benedict Anderson, "Exodus," *Critical Inquiry* 20 (Winter 1994): 314–327.

11. Purnima Mankeker, "Reflections on Diasporic Identities: A Prolegomenon to an Analysis of Political Bifocality," *Diaspora* 3 (Winter 1994): 349–371 (quote on p. 364).

12. Khachig Tölölyan, "The Nation-State and Its Others: In Lieu of a Preface," *Diaspora: A Journal of Transnational Studies* 1 (Spring 1991): 4, 5, 6. See also his "Note from the Editor" in *Diaspora* 3 (Winter 1994).

13. Said, *Culture and Imperialism,* xxv, 14, 111–112.

14. Ibid., 331–332.

15. Ibid., 332–333, 335.

16. Paul Gilroy, *Black Atlantic,* 6.

17. Ibid., 81, 208, 111.

18. Audre Lorde, "The Master's Tools Will Never Dismantle the Master's House," in *This Bridge Called My Back: Writings by Radical Women of Color,* ed. Cherrie Moraga and Gloria Anzaldúa (New York: Kitchen Table, 1983), 98–101.

19. Anderson, "Exodus," 325, 319, 315.

20. Daniel Boyarin and Jonathan Boyarin, "Diaspora."

21. Gilroy, *Black Atlantic,* 206, 205–212, 208. See also William Safran, "Diasporas in Modern Societies: Myths of Homeland and Return," *Diaspora* 1 (Spring 1991): 83–99.

22. For an interesting case of cross-cultural dialogue between Jews and Tibetan culture, see Rodger Kamenetz, *The Jew in the Lotus: A Poet's Rediscovery of Jewish Identity in Buddhist India* (San Francisco: Harper San Francisco, 1994).

23. Cf. Stefan Helmreich, "Kinship, Nation, and Paul Gilroy's Concept of Diaspora," *Diaspora* 2 (Fall 1992): 243–249. All biblical translations are taken from *Tanakh* (Philadelphia: Jewish Publication Society, 1990).

24. Arnold M. Eisen, *Galut: Modern Jewish Reflection on Homelessness and Homecoming* (Bloomington: Indiana University Press, 1986). Also see Eisen's article "Exile" in *Contemporary Jewish Religious Thought,* ed. Arthur A. Cohen and Paul Mendes-Flohr (New York: The Free Press, 1987), 219–225.

25. Eisen, *Galut,* 33.

26. The term *mestiza* has been put most prominently to use in Anzaldúa, *Borderlands/La Frontera.*

27. Eisen, *Galut,* 51.

28. Another reason for arguing that nationalist ideology was not a product of exile is that in complex ways such an ideology is historically tied to the rise of capitalism. See Anderson, *Imagined Communities.*

29. I do not go as far as Louis A. Ruprecht Jr., "On Being Jewish and Greek in the Modern Moment," *Diaspora* 3 (Fall 1994): 199–220, who traces the impact of Jews on Hellenism and reverses the standard view that Hellenism triumphed over Hebraism. See also David Biale, *Power and Powerlessness in Jewish History* (New York: Schocken Books, 1987).

30. Eisen, *Galut,* 156–180.

31. Lynne Sharon Schwartz, "The Opiate of the People," in Joyce Antler, ed., *America and I: Short Stories by American Jewish Women Writers* (Boston: Beacon Press, 1990), 233–251.

32. Jack J. Cohen, "Reflections on Kaplan's Zionism," in Emanuel S. Goldsmith, Mel Scult, and Robert M. Seltzer, eds., *The American Judaism of Modecai Kaplan,* 401–414 (New York: New York University Press, 1990). In the same volume, see also Mel Scult, "Kaplan's Reinterpretation of the Bible," 312–313. See also Eisen, *Galut,* 159.

33. Abraham Joshua Heschel, *Israel: An Echo of Eternity* (New York: Farrar, Straus, and Giroux, 1969). See also Eisen, *Galut,* 169–172.

34. Arthur Waskow, *Seasons of Our Joy: A Celebration of Modern Jewish Renewal* (Boston: Beacon Press, 1982).

35. Judith Plaskow, *Standing Again at Sinai: Judaism from a Feminist Perspective* (New York: HarperCollins, 1990), 75. Eisen, *Galut,* 159, 172.

36. Sigmund Freud, *Das Unheimliche: Aufsätze zur Literatur,* ed. Hrsg. von Klaus Wagenbach (Frankfurt am Main: Fischer, 1963).

37. Philip Roth, *Portnoy's Complaint* (New York: Random House, 1969).

38. Cf. I. B. Singer, *Enemies: A Love Story* (New York: Farrar, Straus, and Giroux, 1972); Jacob Glatstein, *Selected Poems of Yankev Glatshteyn,* trans. and ed. Richard J. Fein (Philadelphia: Jewish Publication Society, 1987); Cynthia Ozick, *The Shawl* (New York: Vintage Books, 1983); Art Spiegelman, *Maus I* (New York: Pantheon Books, 1986), and *Maus II* (New York: Pantheon Books, 1991).

39. Steve Stern, *Lazar Malkin Enters Heaven* (New York: Penguin Books, 1986).

40. Harold Bloom, *The Anxiety of Influence: A Theory of Poetry* (Oxford: Oxford University Press, 1973). See Biale, *Power and Powerlessness,* 203–205, for a counterexample.

41. Daniel Boyarin and Jonathan Boyarin, "Diaspora: Generation and the Ground of Jewish Identity," *Critical Inquiry* 19 (Summer 1993): 693–725. A preference for exile could be found later in rabbinic literature but rarely in the prophetic literature. Cf. Jer. 15:7, Ezek. 22:15–16 and Hos. 9:17, in each of which exile is seen as a punishment for Israel's transgression against God.

42. Philip Roth, *Operation Shylock* (New York: Random House, 1993), 126.

43. Ibid., 389.

44. Ibid., 349–350, 351.

45. Ibid., 378–379.

46. Ibid., 379.

47. Eisen, *Galut,* 143–144.

CHAPTER IO

Language as Homeland
in Jewish-American Literature

Hana Wirth-Nesher

The first official statement made by the president of the United States after Yitzhak Rabin's assassination ended with two words in Hebrew, "Shalom Haver," delivered with a southern drawl. At the state funeral several days later Bill Clinton repeated those words along with the last few lines of the Kaddish—"v'hoo ya'asah shalom aleinu v'al kol Yisrael v'imroo amen"—the foreign sounds produced with effort and in sharp contrast to the ease with which the emotions were expressed. As many journalists have noted, Bill Clinton is the first American president completely at ease among Jews, a man who studied among them at Yale and at Oxford, who relies on them as advisers and trusted friends. But more relevant for the topic of Jewish-American identity is the fact that vast numbers of liberal Jews, particularly in his generation and into the next, are comfortable with him. At the same time that the rainbow coalition and the multiculturalism that it expresses has posed problems for Jewish communal identity, Clinton has made significant numbers of Jews feel at home in America as never before. When he uttered those two familiar Hebrew words, he was addressing this Jewish-American community as much if not more than he was addressing Israelis. The WASP president from Arkansas was speaking *their* language. A Jewish speechwriter had undoubtedly transliterated those lines of the Kaddish into phonetic English so that the president could read them. Every Jew who had even minimal Hebrew school training or exposure to Jewish ritual would have understood them. In this respect, American Jews are part of a long tradition of bilingualism and even multilingualism.

Knowledge of languages other than the one in which the Jewish community lived has always characterized Jewish civilization, and the Hebrew alphabet has always been a central feature of Jewish life, as it forms the Hebrew language itself, Aramaic, Yiddish, and Ladino. In *Bilingualism in the History of Jewish Literature* published in America in 1941 (in Yiddish), Shmuel Niger made the case for bilingualism as a continuous feature of Jewish civilization from biblical times, "Take an old Jewish book—take the Bible, the most famous of all books—and you will see that one language has never been enough for the Jewish people."[1] Baal-Makhshoves had already made this argument in eastern Europe at the turn of the century.[2] But today this multilingual tradition has taken on new meaning, as American multiculturalists require recognizable signs of difference other than that of religion to qualify a group for membership. As neither race nor country of origin are viable options for American Jews, they have turned increasingly toward language, toward the foreignness of the Hebrew alphabet to underscore their difference. What part does language play in the self-definition of Jews in multicultural America? In a discussion of this subject, two factors play critical roles: the status of the author in terms of immigration and the date of the publication, more specifically whether a work was written before or after the Holocaust and the establishment of the state of Israel and before or after the near annihilation of Yiddish and the revitalization of Hebrew.

English: The New Promised Land

From the turn of the twentieth century until the Second World War, the bulk of Jewish-American literature was written by immigrants or the children of immigrants for whom Yiddish was the mother tongue and English an acquired language as well as their passport to acculturation in America. In works by authors such as Abraham Cahan, Mary Antin, Anzia Yezierska, and Henry Roth, the writer would often weave Yiddish or Hebrew words into the novel accompanied by a variety of strategies for translating the phrases into English for non-Jewish readers. As the drive to assimilate was paramount, writers withheld nothing from their American audiences, translating not only the words but also the rituals and customs into equivalences that their gentile readers could immediately grasp. Unlike the highlighting of foreignness and difference that characterizes some contemporary works, accessibility was crucial for immigrant writers, who sought poetic strategies to make the Old World accessible to the New. For this reason, it is startling to occasionally come across a reference where the author stubbornly refuses to translate in order not to jeopardize his or her full acceptance into American society. In Mary Antin's reminiscences about her various names and nicknames as a girl in the Pale, she wrote in *The Promised Land:* "A variety of nicknames, mostly suggested by my physical peculiarities, were bestowed on me from time to time by my fond or foolish relatives. My uncle Berl, for example, gave me the name of 'Zukrochene Flum,' which I am not going to translate because it is not complimentary." (The translation is "a slovenly prune," although "flum" could also refer to a "flame" and thus be a further embarrassment to the writer's modesty.)[3] Antin affectionately reconstructs the multilingual Old World, including her Hebrew lessons: "What I thought I do not remember; I only know that I loved the sound of the words, the full, dense, solid sound of them."[4] As for her other languages, she recalls, "I have no words to describe the pride with which my sister and I crossed the threshold of Isaiah the scribe . . . who could teach Yiddish and Russian and, some said, even German."[5] But her paean to English is most representative of assimilationist yearnings in 1912 when the melting pot still dominated American thought:

I shall never have a better opportunity to make public declaration of my love for the English language. . . . It seems to me that in any other language happiness is not so sweet, logic is not so clear. I am not sure that I could believe in my neighbors as I do if I thought about them in un-English words. I could almost say that my conviction of immortality is bound up with the English of its promise.[6]

Not all immigrant writers were as ardent about the displacement of Yiddish by English, but for many there was almost an erotic attachment to the latter as it embodied their desires to be made over by their new country. In Cahan's novel *The Rise of David Levinsky,* published in 1917, Levinsky's affair with Dora is characterized by her passion for English refinement and their mutual striving for linguistic perfection. "Sometimes, when I mispronounced an English word with which she happened to be familiar, or uttered an English phrase in my Talmudic singsong, she would mock me gloatingly. On one such occasion I felt the sting of her triumph so keenly that I hastened to lower her crest by pointing out that she had said 'nice' where 'nicely' was in order."[7] Dora is the nurturing Jewish mother in every respect but one: her merciless exploitation of her daughter as English tutor for herself. When the child Lucy pleads to be relieved of her reading lesson, her mother's obsession takes over. Dora commands "Read!" and then Dora "went on, with grim composure, hitting her on the shoulder. 'I don't want to! I want to go downstairs,' Lucy sobbed, defiantly. 'Read!' And once more she hit her."[8]

Even in a novel as conflicted about Americanization as Anzia Yezierska's *Bread Givers,* in which the college-educated heroine eventually marries the boy next door from the Old World and their home is overshadowed by her patriarchal father's chants in Hebrew, the courtship scene intertwines desire for English and sexual desire as the body is roused to produce consonants without debasing traces of other languages. At the very moment that the Yiddish-speaking immigrant girl-turned-English-teacher shamefully slips back into the vernacular in the classroom—"The birds sing-gg"—Prince Charming and future husband enters in the form of Hugo Seelig, principal and landsman, in time to rescue the damsel in distress. "The next moment he was close beside me, the tips of his cool fingers on my throat. 'Keep those muscles still until you have stopped. Now say it again,' he commanded, and I turned pupil myself and pronounced the word correctly."[9]

The passion for assimilation that characterized the literature of immigrants earlier in the century contrasts sharply with the recognition in later generations that translation entails loss. Compare Mary Antin's unequivocal embrace of English in 1912 with Cynthia Ozick's resigned embrace of 1976.

They are English words. I have no other language. Since my slave-ancestors left off building the Pyramids to wander in the wilderness of Sinai, they have spoken a handful of generally obscure languages—Hebrew, Aramaic, twelfth-century French perhaps, Yiddish for a thousand years. Since the coming forth from Egypt five millennia ago, mine is the first generation to think and speak and write wholly in English. To say that I have been thoroughly assimilated into English would of course be the grossest understatement—what is the English language (and its poetry) if not my passion, my blood, my life? . . . Still, though English is my everything, now and then I feel cramped by it. I have come to it with notions it is too parochial to recognize. . . . English is a Christian language. When I write English, I live in Christendom.[10]

Henry Roth had already reached this conclusion in *Call It Sleep* in 1934 where his child protagonist David Shearl journeys from Yiddish to English and thus from Hebrew to Christian symbology and hermeneutics. Although David thinks of himself as the kid in the Passover liturgy and although he seeks the God of the book of Isaiah in Jewish scriptures, he is perceived by America's masses as a Christ figure. At the end of the novel, in his semiconscious state, the English language speaks through him and it kills the kid who is reborn as Christ.[11] The Judaic liturgical references, when translated into their English equivalents, are infused with Christian theology. Ozick's Yiddish writer Edelstein makes this point forcefully in "Envy—or, Yiddish in America": "Please remember that when a goy from Columbus, Ohio, says 'Elijah the Prophet' he's not talking about *Eliohu hanovi*. Eliohu is one of us, a *folkmensch*, running around in second-hand clothes. Theirs is God knows what. The same biblical figure, with exactly the same history, once he puts on a name from King James, COMES OUT A DIFFERENT PERSON."[12]

Translating into America

As these writers have observed, translation has the effect of Christianizing both Yiddish and Hebrew or of transforming a *folkmensch*, a character rooted in a civilization that does not compartmentalize religion within the totality of its way of life, into only a religious persona. Whereas Jewish-American immigrant writers chronicled the shift from old language to new, the children of immigrants translated and reinvented Jewish literature to accommodate it to American culture. An extraordinary moment in this transition to American English occurs in Saul Bellow's translation in 1953 of Isaac Bashevis Singer's story "Gimpel Tam" into "Gimpel the Fool," a literary occasion involving the only two Jewish-American Nobel laureates. In the Yiddish story an outcast in his village is repeatedly tricked and ridiculed by his neighbors, a fate to which he is resigned. The rational, empirical world has no hold on Gimpel, whose gullibility makes him a saintly fool and whose love for his children overrides his pride at being the town's much taunted failure. Hence the aptness of the word *tam* which in Yiddish (and Hebrew) may mean "innocent" or "simpleton" as well as "fool." Finally, Gimpel's wife's deathbed confession that she has deceived him all along and that his children are not his drives him to the devil, who incites him to do evil. In a godless universe that is only a "thick mire," Satan urges him to take revenge on the town by defiling the loaves of bread in the bakery so that his deceivers eat filth. But Gimpel chooses to believe, nevertheless, for "the longer I lived the more I understood that there were really no lies" and that what may appear to be outside of human possibility "before a year had elapsed I heard that it actually had come to pass somewhere."[13]

In translating this story originally written for an audience well versed in Jewish tradition but now aimed for a *Partisan Review* readership removed from Judaic texts and sources, Bellow retained only seven Yiddish words in his translation: *golem*, *mezzuzah*, *chalah*, *kreplach*, *schnorrer*, *dybbuk*, and *Tishe B'av*. With the exception of the last term, Tishe B'av, a fast day commemorating the destruction of the Second Temple and the beginning of a two-thousand-year exile, the other terms had already seeped into the American Jewish lexicon, in part through familiarity with literary works about dybbuks and golems and in part through popular culture, culinary and otherwise. Retaining words such as *chalah* underscored the quaint ethnic character of the story while also providing a few "authentic" markers of the lost culture. Actual liturgical references, however, no matter how common, were converted into American equivalents. And this is where the cross-cultural plot thickens. For in the English translation of "Gimpel" Bellow translated the well-known Hebrew prayer for the dead, "El molei rachamim," into the Christian "God 'a Mercy," a shift that transformed Gimpel's eastern European setting into Southern Baptist terrain.

In the case of Bellow's translation of "Gimpel," not only did he transform Hebrew liturgy into Christian parlance, he also omitted any phrase that either parodied the Jewish religion or, more to the point, ridiculed Christianity. In defense of Gimpel's gullibility in the face of persistent mockery from the townspeople, particularly when he refuses to doubt his paternity of the child born to Elka seventeen weeks after their as yet unconsummated marriage, Gimpel appeals to the *mass* gullibility of Christians: "ver veyst? ot zogt men dokh as s'yoyzl hot in gantsn keyn tatn nisht gehat" (Who knows? They say that Jesus'l didn't have any father at all). This somewhat coarse and demeaning reference to Jesus (the diminutive "yoysl") could be offensive to Christians, and although, according to Bellow, it was the volume's editor Eliezer Greenberg who deleted it when he read the story aloud to him, neither Singer nor Bellow had it reinstated in reprintings of the text.[14] Even in the decade of the timid emergence of Jewish-American literature in the shadow of the Holocaust, this was a risk that neither Singer, nor Greenberg, nor Bellow wanted to take.

In Bellow's novella *Seize the Day,* published only three years later (also in *Partisan Review*), there is only one non-English rupture, and it is *precisely* that *same* prayer for the dead as recalled by Tommy Wilhelm in connection with his visit to his mother's gravesite. "At the cemetery Wilhelm had paid a man to say a prayer for her. He was among the tombs and he wanted to be tipped for the *El molei rachamin* [sp. *sic*]. 'Thou God of

Mercy,' Wilhelm thought that meant. *B'gan Aden*—in Paradise. Singing, they drew it out. *B'gan Ay-den*."[15] In other words, what was erased in the English translation of the Yiddish story reappears in Bellow's American story set in New York, the tale of another man who is a failure in his community, who is gullible, tricked, and repeatedly deceived. This is not simply a matter of influence, of Singer's story bearing down on Bellow's; it is an intertextual referent that places Bellow's work in relation to both Hebrew and Yiddish as purveyors of a lost civilization, the Jewish world annihilated in the Holocaust. It is apt that the only non-English in Bellow's text is a prayer for the dead.[16]

In the translation from "Gimpel" into *Seize the Day*, the Yiddish all but disappears and the religious phrase *El Molei Rachamim* is reinstated (with a more dignified translation—"Thou God of Mercy") as Jewish civilization loses its bilingual dimension and is transformed in America into Judaism. Bellow's text "remembers" the prayer but in an entirely different context. It remembers what it needs in order to exist in its new cultural landscape, an America dedicated to melting away ethnicity and retaining only religion.

Language as Difference

Bellow's literature of the 1950s both contributes to and critiques the metamorphosis of Jewish culture into Judaism, the third great religion in America. Transforming Jewishness into Judaism served both Jewish and Christian America. For Jews eager to assimilate and to "make it," the shift from urban immigrant neighborhoods where Yiddish coexisted along with English to suburbia and religious affiliation marked by liturgical Hebrew meant acceptance in American culture. As a religion, Judaism becomes a private matter, and the Enlightenment paradigm of the Jew at home and the citizen in the street finds its pristine expression in America just as these Enlightenment principles are bankrupted in Europe, after the genocide of the Jews on racial and not religious grounds. In America of the 1950s Jews could carve out a comfortable place for themselves in the American landscape as white European children of immigrants who practiced Judaism.

Simultaneous with the Jews settling in as mainstream Americans in the 1960s, the melting pot was superseded by the ethnicity movement that paved the way for contemporary multiculturalism. The anxiety and vulnerability experienced by the American Jewish community just prior to the Six-Day War and the vicarious pride in Israel's victory brought about a renewed identification with a people, with a Jewish identity that religion alone could not satisfy. But ethnic identity for Jews in America has been fraught with complications and contradictions. The Old World was never simply one place—a Greek island, a village in Sicily, the shores of Galway. It was more than a score of host countries and as many mother tongues. In order to accommodate themselves to the ethnic revival, Jews needed more than ethnic foods and customs; they needed to create a homogeneous monolingual home, a mother tongue, and this was achieved in part by the reconstruction of a Yiddish shtetl past in cultural work such as Irving Howe's *World of Our Fathers*, Mark Zborowski and Elizabeth Herzog's *Life Is with People: The Culture of the Shtetl* (with an introduction by Margaret Mead), Singer's stories and books, and the musical *Fiddler on the Roof*, to name only a few examples.[17] American Jewish ethnicity, however, deviated from the white ethnic "norm" in that there was no home country to which one could return, nor was there a living language that represented the language of one's grandparents. The eastern European world that had been annihilated in the Holocaust was replaced by another thriving Jewish civilization, Israel, a nation-state whose language was unknown to American Jews (except as liturgy). As a result, American Jewry has found itself in limbo between a homogenized mythical reconstruction of a Yiddish folkloristic world that has no manifestation in contemporary life and a Zionist socialist homeland that elicits allegiance at some level but also remains alien in language, terrain, climate, and to some extent ideology. No one has expressed this in literature more dramatically than Philip Roth whose doppelgänger plots have encompassed both the European Old and Middle Eastern Old/New Worlds. In "Eli, the Fanatic" Eli's secret sharer is a religious Yiddish-speaking Orthodox Holocaust survivor with whom he has no common language, only a common collective history. The legacy that Eli chooses to pass on to his son in the form of the black gaberdine, traditional garb of ultra-Orthodox Jewry, is one of mute darkness and suffering, not an alternative way of life that encompasses language. Years later Roth's Portnoy will find himself emasculated when he returns "home" to the alien beaches of Tel Aviv. In Roth's tour de force, *The Counterlife*, Nathan Zuckerman floats free between the extreme options of Zionist nationalist Hebraic culture and British Christian assimilation. He will choose to circumcise his son in an act that inscribes membership in a collective without any accompanying ritual, language, or collective memories that would give the act itself meaning beyond difference for its own sake.[18]

During the past few decades Hebrew and Yiddish in Jewish-American literature have both increasingly served as signifiers of difference in a cultural landscape that legitimizes and even requires difference. Two almost antithetical approaches can be found in the works of Cynthia Ozick and Grace Paley, who both aim at a split audience while representing "other" languages in radically different ways. Ozick's manifesto is particularism, the self-conscious invocation of motifs from Jewish language, liturgy, and intertextuality, at times expressed in a high modernist, even Jamesian style. She is an intellectual writer, attuned to the cultural significance of German, Greek, Latin, French, Polish, and other languages in the formation of Jewish collective memory and Jewish art as well as to the place of Hebrew incantation, Yiddish folk song, Holocaust memoir, and recurring motifs such as the golem or the tree of life.[19] In her Puttermesser stories she is almost alone among Jewish-American writers in clearing a space on the English printed page for the word *HaShem* (the Holy Name) printed in the Hebrew alphabet. Ozick aims for a reification of Hebrew within the English text which will transform the English into a language suitable for the expression of Jewish experience despite what she identifies as its inherent Christianity.

The very cadence and rhythms of Paley's writing, in contrast, betray the presence of Yiddish without reproducing the language itself on the printed page. Whereas Ozick insists on the bold presence of the other languages, Paley forges a new language, an English imbued with Jewish-American cadence and tone. When Shirley Abramowitz's mother in "The Loudest Voice" says "In the grave it will be quiet," the inverted syntax conveys the Yiddish source language. No translation follows as Paley's style and themes form a new ethnic voice that slips comfortably into pluralistic, multicultural America. When the child kneels at the side of her bed making "a little church of my hands" and reciting "Hear, O Israel . . . " it is not the Shema but the sound of a prayer already transformed into a staple of American Judaism.[20] Paley writes from a universalist concept of America that humorously ridicules Shirley for her naive yoking of Jewish and Christian religious practice but simultaneously applauds her spirit of accommodation.

For a younger generation of Jewish-American writers today, Yiddish is linked with memories of grandparents but has faded as a significant presence. An occasional *nuh* or *feh* peppers the speech of immigrant characters, and by now in many works these are markers of Holocaust survivor characters.[21] The few exceptions are either those whose grandparents played a major role in their upbringing, such as the case of Max Apple, a baby boomer fluent in Yiddish who chronicles his relationship with his grandfather in *Roommates*, or writers who are the product of an Orthodox religious upbringing, such as Rebecca Goldstein, whose *Mind-Body Problem* is sprinkled with Yiddishisms (mainly Hebrew words with Yiddish pronunciations): *yaytzah harah, neshuma, bris, chazzanes, shayva broches, averah, ayshes chayil,* and *shadchan,* to name only a few. Non-Hebraic Yiddish words are also associated with religious practice, as *flayshig and milchik, davening, sheitel,* or *gute voch.* Goldstein's protagonist searches for a universal language that will free her from her traditional Orthodox world, a search that leads her to Western philosophy and to mathematics. Small wonder that her husband Himmel's fame rests on his discovery of numbers termed "supernaturals." But neither of these two spheres frees her from either her Jewish past or her body's demands. Her book ends with a humanistic affirmation that combines Kant's ethical imperative and the memory of her father's chanting of the Kol Nidrei service: "On Rosh Hashanah their destiny is inscribed, and on Yom Kippur it is sealed, how many shall pass away and how many shall be brought into existence, who shall live and who shall die." Her character's response to this chant serves as the motto of many of the Jewish-American writers of her generation: "Long after I ceased believing in these words, the sound of them has caused my spine to tingle and my eyes to tear."[22]

For contemporary Jewish-American writers intent on preserving some linguistic sign of difference, it is the *sound* of either Hebrew or Yiddish and in some cases the sight of the Hebrew alphabet that infiltrates their English texts. Alice Kaplan's *French Lessons* is an interesting case in point, as her passion for French seems to be brought about by her family's rapid shift from Yiddish to impeccable English: "My family had made the transition from diaspora Yiddish to American English in a quick generation. You couldn't hear the shadow of an accent, unless my grandmother was around."[23] Since the languages from her grandmother's past—Russian, Yiddish, and Hebrew—"came up like bile," the only strategy left to the granddaughter to perpetuate the tradition of bilingualism was to turn to another language. "Today I am a French teacher. I think about my Nanny, sliding from Hebrew to English to Yiddish. . . . 'Il n'y avais pas de suite dans ses idees': There was no connection between her ideas. Why does that sentence come to me in French, out of the blue? . . . It's not like my grandmother's switching, but it feels disturbed." After recounting her odyssey toward the French language and culture and her disturbing obsession with Céline, she recognizes that "I'm not writing only about French anymore. French is the mark of something that happened to me, that made me shift into another language."[24]

Unlike Hispanic Americans or Native Americans whose "other" language aspires to legitimacy, whose bilingualism is perceived by many as a threat to English monolingualism in the United States, American Jews for the most part are not actually bilingual with either Hebrew or Yiddish, and certainly they do not seek its legitimacy as an American language. Yet it would be inaccurate to relegate Hebrew to a liturgical language, such as Latin for Catholics, for two simple reasons: Hebrew has always infused diasporic Jewish existence far beyond the limited area of prayer, and since the establishment of the state of Israel Hebrew has become the living language of a Jewish nation, of a homeland. Most American Jews who choose to identify as such are in the paradoxical situation of acquiring two alphabets as children, English at school and Hebrew after school, and of acquiring some familiarity with the sight and sound of another language that connects them with a collective past beyond the bounds of the United States but that also remains alien. Perhaps where Hebrew is understood least it is reified the most, taking on some transcendence or authenticating aura. This strange phenomenon can be illustrated best by the example of the Kaddish with which I began and with which I would like to conclude.

Aleph, Bet, Kaddish

For most American Jews today ethnic difference surfaces at landmark occasions in their lives: at circumcision and naming ceremonies at which they take on a second, Hebrew name; at bar and bat mitzvah where they recite prayers and read from Hebrew scripture; at weddings where part of the rites may still be recited in Hebrew; and at funerals, where they hear the recitation of the Kaddish, a prayer largely in Aramaic characterized by an abundance of praise and glorification of God and an expression of hope for the establishment of peace. The practice of mourners reciting the Kaddish goes back to the thirteenth century, and it is this prayer that seems to have become inscribed into the collective identity of American Jews. It is ironic that the generation writing under the sign of cultural difference and aiming to renew its Jewish identity has focused so heavily on a prayer that marks death.

In 1960 Allen Ginsberg published his poem "Kaddish" dedicated to his mother, Naomi. More of the poem is given over to a Whitmanesque catalog of hers and society's ills and to raging indictments of capitalism as Moloch than to praise of God. Yet it adopts the meter and sound of the Kaddish long before the transliterated second line of the prayer appears on the page, in midchant, the first line taken for granted: "Magnificent, mourned no more, marred of heart, mind behind, married dreamed, mortal changed."[25] The Hebrew prayer blends in with the other sounds in Ginsberg's 1960s America, with the Buddhist Book of Answers and the evangelist's "God Is Love." "I've been up all night, talking, talking, reading the Kaddish aloud, listening to Ray Charles blues shout blind on the phonograph / the rhythm, the rhythm."[26]

Exactly one generation later, in 1980, Johanna Kaplan satirizes the displacement of the traditional Kaddish by the poetry of the Beats and the displacement of traditional Judaism by American culture. In the last chapter of her novel *O My America!* the narrator describes the memorial service of Ezra Slavin, son of Russian-Jewish immigrants, Leftist writer, and intellectual, which takes place in a library in midtown Manhattan. After the eulogies by family and friends, one of his former students reads Pablo Neruda's poem "For Everyone," followed by a song performed by the guitarist who introduced the deceased at an antiwar rally in 1965. Familiar to his audience and to Kaplan's readers as Pete Seeger's "Turn! Turn! Turn! (To Everything There Is a Season)," the words are taken from the book of Ecclesiastes. Just as he repeats the last line without guitar accompaniment, "And a time to every purpose under heaven," presumably the conclusion of the service, Slavin's estranged son Jonathan unexpectedly takes the microphone and "gulps out, 'I'm going to read the Kaddish.'" "Oh! Allen Ginsberg! What a wonderful *idea!*" whispers one of the assembled. "I saw him on the street the other day, and I really didn't think he looked at all well."[27] Jonathan's recitation appears in full in the text, a complete transliterated Kaddish in italics, and it stuns the listeners. "How could you and Dave possibly have allowed something so-so *barbaric!*" charges one of his friends. "It's a *prayer*, dear," assures another.

Recited in part, in full, with errors, or only alluded to, the Kaddish becomes a recurrent sign of collective memory and Jewish identity, a religious text turned marker of ethnic origin. In *Roommates* Max Apple whispers "Yisgadal, v'yisgadash [*sic*]," unable to go on until he hears his grandfather's Yiddish words. "'Shtark zich!' I told myself, and I did . . . my voice steadied, and I made no mistakes. By the last stanza everyone could hear."[28] Robin Hirsch's memoir *Last Dance at the Hotel Kempinski* ends at his father's gravesite, the new rabbi admitting, "Ladies and gentlemen, I didn't know Herbert Hirsch . . ." into which the son splices the words "Yiskadal [*sic*] v'yiskadash."[29] In the memoir *The Color of Water*, African

American writer James McBride's recent tribute to his white Jewish mother who converted to Christianity, he recalls the custom among pious Jews of reciting the Kaddish for a child who left the faith. "I realized then that whoever had said kaddish for Mommy—the Jewish prayer of mourning, the declaration of death, the ritual that absolves them of responsibility for the child's fate—had done the right thing, because Mommy was truly gone from their world."[30] This uncapitalized kaddish whose words are already forgotten along with its alphabet is a stark representation of assimilation into Christian America.

In almost all cases the Kaddish appears in transliteration, perhaps because publishers' policies and budgets don't allow for the printing of the Hebrew alphabet, perhaps because the mere introduction of a foreign language into a text already estranges the reader somewhat and authors fear alienating readers altogether with unfamiliar script, perhaps because the authors know that even Jewish readers may not be able to recognize the Hebrew whereas the sound of the transliterated prayer still has the power to remind and to stir. In light of the tendency to transliterate, when the Hebrew alphabet does appear on the page in an English text it is all the more dramatic, as is the case of Ozick's printing of *HaShem* mentioned earlier. I want to conclude with two powerful instances of such typographical ruptures of untranslated Hebrew, the first in Art Spiegelman's cartoon narrative *Maus* and the other in Tony Kushner's play *Angels in America*.

The child of Holocaust survivors, Spiegelman is haunted by languages other than English, as the German *Maus* in the title testifies along with the heavily accented English of his father, Vladek, narrating his life story to his son. There are only two instances of Hebrew print in the book, neither one translated into English. The first takes place early in the war when Vladek is imprisoned and he recounts: "Every day we prayed. . . . I was very religious, and it wasn't *else* to do."[31] Right above the drawing of three mice in prayer shawls in a concentration camp are the Hebrew words from the daily prayer service: "Mah tovo O'holechah, Ya'akov, mishkenotecha Israel" (How goodly are thy tents, O Jacob, thy dwelling places, O Israel). The painfully ironic juxtaposition of place and language in this frame is available only to the reader literate in Hebrew. In the second instance the actual words of the Kaddish are inserted into the text in what is itself an insert in *Maus*, the section entitled "Prisoner on the Hell Planet," originally published separately, which narrates Art's reaction to his mother's suicide when he was twenty. The words of the prayer are divided between two frames that show Art and his father in front of his mother's coffin, but it is his father who recites the prayer, whereas Art recites from the Tibetan Book of the Dead. Recalling that "I was pretty spaced out in those days," he chooses to document the Kaddish even though he is not the one speaking it.[32]

Throughout *Maus* the reported speech of the Jews during the war is rendered in normative English despite the fact that they were actually shifting between German, Polish, and Yiddish, whereas Art's father's English is heavily accented. This strategy emphasizes the perspective of young Art, American Jew and child of survivors, who feels the lingering effects of the Holocaust on his own life in his father's behavior toward him and his mother. The inadequacy of his father's English to articulate the horrors of his wartime experiences comes to signify the inadequacy of language altogether to convey suffering. In a work in which all of the nations speak a language rendered in the Latin alphabet (even the occasional word in German), it is all the more striking when an untranslated and illegible type surfaces on the page, as if to perversely validate the epigraph to *Maus*, a quotation from Hitler: "The Jews are undoubtedly a race, but they are not human." What could be comforting because it is familiar to Jewish readers, the Hebrew print on the page, has often been perceived in Western culture as alien and menacing.[33]

Tony Kushner's play *Angels in America: Millennium Approaches*, is a multicultural play par excellence. Not only does the play present characters who are WASP, Italian American, African American, Jewish American, Mormon, Eskimo, gay, and straight, but actors cross lines by playing more than one role; one actor plays both rabbi and Mormon, another both Eskimo and Mormon. Yet the work bears Kushner's Jewish-American identity primarily through uncanny eruptions of Yiddish and Hebrew. The play opens with a rabbi in prayer shawl at the funeral rites of the grandmother of Louis Ironson, Sarah Ironson, a Russian-Jewish immigrant whom the rabbi calls "the last of the Mohicans." Encompassing a dizzying array of America's problems, including the ozone layer as one of the last frontiers, religious fundamentalism, racism, and government corruption, the play focuses on the plight of a gay AIDS patient named Prior Walter, a descendant of Mayflower WASPs and Louis Ironson's lover. Louis's New York Jewish upbringing accounts for the few obligatory Yiddish phrases, among them a Yiddish translation from *King Lear* about the ingratitude of children and Louis's recalling that his grandmother once heard Emma Goldman give a speech in Yiddish. All of this lends weight to Yiddish as a defining feature of Louis's ethnicity, his claim to significant difference. But midway through the play Hebrew displaces Yiddish as

Prior's Italian American nurse involuntarily begins to chant excerpts from Hebrew prayers for the dead which have a kabbalistic resonance: "I think that shochen bamromim hamtzeh menucho nechono al kanfey haschino." "What?" asks Prior, and she continues with "Bemaalos k'doshim ut'horim kezohar harokeea mazhirim . . . "[34] Spoken in an automatic trance, unintelligible to both speaker and listener, and never translated for the audience, the lines describe Prior's soul departing the earth on the wings of the Shekhina (the Divine Presence, which in kabbalah is described as a feminine principle). When the nurse takes her leave of Prior, the stage directions magnify the transcendence of this moment by Hebrew erupting literally on the set. "Suddenly there is an astonishing blaze of light, a huge chord sounded by a gigantic choir, and a great book with steep pages mounted atop a molten-red pillar pops up from the stage floor. The book opens; there is a large Aleph inscribed on its pages, which bursts into flames."[35]

As the first letter of the Hebrew alphabet, the "aleph" holds a special place in Jewish tradition. According to one view of the revelation at Mount Sinai, all that the children of Israel heard of the divine voice was the letter aleph with which in the Hebrew text the First Commandment begins, "anokhi," "I." The kabbalists have always regarded the aleph as the spiritual root of all of the other letters, encompassing in its essence the whole alphabet.[36] Moreover, the monotheistic credo, the Shema, ends with the affirmation that "the Lord is One," thereby emphasizing the word *ekhod*, which begins with an aleph as well. It is the first letter of the first creature into whom God breathed life, Adam, and it is the letter whose erasure from the word *emet* saps the golem of life, renders him *met*, dead.

This mystical letter, prior to all others and source of all articulate sound, is revealed to the American Adam named Prior shortly before the ghosts of his ancestors Prior 1 and Prior 2 assemble at his bedside to await his departure from earth, to await what Prior 1 calls "Ha-adam, Ha-gadol," the redemption. At the play's end the Hebrew words uttered by his nurse are literalized on stage; after a blare of triumphant music and light turning several brilliant hues ("God Almighty . . . ," whispers Prior, "*very* Steven Spielberg"), a terrifying crash precedes an angel's descent into the room right above his bed as the book with its blazing aleph rises from the floor. What is this image doing in a play by a Jewish playwright in which a gay dying WASP is surrounded by a Jew, a Mormon, an African American, an Italian American as well as the ghosts of English ancestors? By signifying the anticipated redemption of AIDS victims in what is depicted as a homophobic America, the aleph enlists Jewish sources on the side of transcendence. And by being prior to Prior, it relocates Judaism at the very center of Judeo-Christian America, as it was for the Puritans for whom Hebrew constituted their prior claim to Christianity against the Latin of Catholicism. Prior 1, his thirteenth-century ancestor, is heard chanting words from the kabbalah such as *Zefirot* and *Olam ha-yichud* in contrast with the contemporary Prior who sings lyrics from *My Fair Lady*, a Lerner and Lowe musical. Prior's observation that the arrival of the angel is very Steven Spielberg momentarily shifts the tone of the scene from the sublime to the ridiculous, from the content to the special effects. The inscribed aleph is indeed just that, a special effect, a foreign letter that gives the play a Jewish ethnic marker while simultaneously recognizing that marker as being at the very core of some fundamental American discourse that subsumes all ethnic difference. The aleph is a theatrical special effect that can be claimed by all.

In the sequel to *Millenium Approaches*, entitled *Perestroika*, Louis is asked to recite "the Jewish prayer for the dead" for Roy Cohn, lawyer and power broker who has just died of AIDS. "The Kaddish?" he asks the Gentile who made the request. "That's the one. Hit it." But Louis insists, "I probably know less of the Kaddish than you do," a point he proves by beginning the Kaddish and quickly swerving into the Kiddush and the Shema.[37] A ghost comes to his rescue, softly coaching him through the entire Kaddish—it is none other than the ghost of Ethel Rosenberg, presumably also an Angel of America, another victim of prejudice in a pre-multicultural America. (In an earlier scene Ethel sings "Tumbalalaike" to Roy Cohn in Yiddish.) America's deepest problems and wounds are articulated in this play by means of kitsch and camp. Predictable American-Jewish ethnic markers such as the Kaddish and Hebrew letters such as aleph are paraded before the viewer in that spirit of self-conscious theatricality.

When Bill Clinton recited the last line of the Kaddish it was not only as a sign of respect for Israel's fallen leader and a reminder of his pursuit of peace (the last line is a prayer for peace), it was also for the benefit of American Jews, for in one gesture he recognized both the separateness of their language linked as it is to a spiritual homeland and America's own link to that prior civilization. Even a cursory glance at Jewish-American literature over the past century demonstrates that bilingualism, or at the very least diglossia, has always been one of its features, whether it was on a trajectory toward English mastery or on an opposite path toward recovery of ethnic difference and non-English customs, as is the case today. Diverse strategies for representing the cultural space between languages have yielded diverse and rich works of literature by writers such as Henry Roth, Abraham Cahan, Delmore Schwartz, Isaac Rosenfeld, Saul Bellow, Cynthia Ozick, Grace Paley, and Charles Reznikoff, to name only a few. These authors have drawn on both Yiddish and Hebrew as resonant signs of a Jewish textual and linguistic tradition of which they are a part. In recent years, as Jewish writers are further removed from both immigration and religious practice, their knowledge of these languages fades precisely at a time when multiculturalism requires clear markers of difference and language can provide those markers.[38] At its extreme, the Hebrew alphabet has been inscribed onto the body as tattoo, recently documented on the cover of the provocative San Francisco magazine *Davka*. The recurring motif of the Kaddish ritual in contemporary writing, an extraordinary act of artistic compression, affirms linguistic otherness as part of American Jewish identity. For those who can understand its words, its use as a sign of renewal is apt, for the Kaddish is itself an affirmation of God's glory, of hope for God's kingdom on earth. But for those who hear its sound alone, perhaps it remains a prayer for the dead. In either case, insofar as readers, in the solitary and quiet act of reading, whisper in their hearts the congregational response "brich hoo," it may also be a sign of community.

Notes

1. Shmuel Niger, *Bilingualism in the History of Jewish Literature*, translated from the Yiddish by Joshua Fogel (New York: University Press of America, 1990), 11.

2. Baal-Makhshoves [Israel Isidore Elyashev], "Tsvey shprakhen: Ein eyntsiker literatur," *Petrograder Tageblatt* (Petrograd, 1918). Translated by Hana Wirth-Nesher in *What Is Jewish Literature?* ed. Hana Wirth-Nesher (Philadelphia: Jewish Publication Society, 1994).

3. Mary Antin, *The Promised Land* (1912; reprint, Salem: Ayer Company, 1987), 67.

4. Ibid., 113.

5. Ibid., 117.

6. Ibid., 208.

7. Abraham Cahan, *The Rise of David Levinsky* (1917; reprint, New York: Harper Books, 1960), 254.

8. Ibid., 253.

9. Anzia Yezierska, *Bread Givers* (New York: Persea, 1925), 272.

10. Cynthia Ozick, "Preface," *Bloodshed and Other Novellas* (New York: Knopf, 1976), 9.

11. Henry Roth, *Call It Sleep* (New York: Farrar, Straus, and Giroux, 1991).

12. Cynthia Ozick, "Envy; or, Yiddish in America," in *The Pagan Rabbi and Other Stories* (New York: Schocken, 1976), 82.

13. Isaac Bashevis Singer, "Gimpel the Fool," trans. Saul Bellow, in *A Treasury of Yid-*

dish Stories, ed. Irving Howe and Eliezer Greenberg (New York: The Viking Press, 1953), 413.

14. Irving Howe, *A Margin of Hope: An Intellectual Autobiography* (New York: Harcourt Brace Jovanovich, 1982), 22. Bellow did not translate the story from the printed text but rather from listening to Greenberg's reading it aloud to him; the translation was completed in one session. I am grateful to Ruth Wisse for drawing my attention to this fact and for sharing with me her unpublished essay "The Repression of Aggression: Translation of Yiddish into English."

15. Saul Bellow, *Seize the Day* (New York: Penguin, 1956), 86.

16. For an extensive analysis of the relationship between these two texts, see my essay "'Who's He When He's at Home?' Saul Bellow's Translations," in *New Essays on Seize the Day,* ed. Michael Kramer (Cambridge: Cambridge University Press, 1998).

17. Irving Howe, *World of Our Fathers* (New York: Harcourt Brace Jovanovich, 1976); Mark Zborowski and Elizabeth Herzog, *Life Is with People: The Culture of the Shtetl* (New York: Schocken, 1952).

18. Philip Roth, "Eli the Fanatic," in *Goodbye, Columbus* (New York: Bantam Books, 1973); Philip Roth, *The Counterlife* (New York: Farrar, Straus, and Giroux, 1986); Philip Roth, *Portnoy's Complaint* (New York: Bantam Books, 1970).

19. For a discussion of multilingualism in Ozick's novella *The Shawl,* see my essay "The Languages of Memory: Cynthia Ozick's *The Shawl,*" in *Multilingual America,* ed. Werner Sollors (New York: New York University Press, 1998).

20. Grace Paley, "The Loudest Voice," in *The Little Disturbances of Man* (New York: Viking Penguin, 1959); reprinted in *Jewish-American Stories,* ed. Irving Howe (New York: New American Library, 1977), 470.

21. For a good example of the persistence of Yiddish see Leslea Newman, "A Letter to Harvey Milk," in *America and I,* ed. Joyce Antler (Boston: Beacon Press, 1990).

22. Rebecca Goldstein, *The Mind-Body Problem: A Novel* (New York: Penguin, 1983), 274.

23. Alice Kaplan, *French Lessons: A Memoir* (Chicago: University of Chicago Press, 1993), 9.

24. Ibid., 201.

25. Allen Ginsberg, *Collected Poems: 1947–1980* (New York: Harper and Row, 1984), 212.

26. Ibid., 209.

27. Johanna Kaplan, *O My America!* (orig. ed., Harper and Row, 1980; Syracuse: Syracuse University Press, 1995), 282.

28. Max Apple, *Roommates: My Grandfather's Story* (New York: Warner Books, 1994), 210. There are many other examples of the Kaddish in Jewish-American literature which I do not have the time to discuss in this essay, among them Charles Reznikoff's poem by that name, Woody Allen's short story entitled "No Kaddish for Weinstein," and E.M. Broner, *Mornings and Mourning: A Kaddish Journal.*

29. Robin Hirsch, *Last Dance at the Hotel Kempinski: Creating a Life in the Shadow of History* (Hanover: University Press of New England, 1995), 292.

30. James McBride, *The Color of Water: A Black Man's Tribute to His White Mother* (New York: Riverhead Books, 1996), 222.

31. Art Spiegelman, *Maus: A Survivor's Tale* (New York: Pantheon, 1973), 54.

32. Ibid., 102.

33. See Sander Gilman's extensive work on language and Jewish self-definition in both *Jewish Self-Hatred: Anti-Semitism and the Hidden Language of the Jews* (Baltimore: Johns Hopkins University Press, 1982) and "The Jewish Voice," in *The Jew's Body* (New York: Routledge, 1991).

34. Tony Kushner, *Angels in America: Part 1: Millennium Approaches* (New York: Theatre Communications Group, 1992), 98.

35. Ibid., 99.

36. Gershom Sholem, *On the Kabbalah and Its Symbolism* (New York: Schocken Books, 1969), 30.

37. Tony Kushner, *Angels in America: Part 2: Perestroika.* (New York: Theatre Communications Group, 1992), 125.

38. Uri Nir, "Avant Garde with Bagel" (in Hebrew), *Ha'aretz,* newspaper, August 30, 1996, pp. 42–44.

Modernism and Exile

A View from the Margins

Michael Gluzman

The terms *exile* and *diaspora* have become fashionable tokens in much postmodern and multicultural theory. In his "Imperialism/ Nationalism" Seamus Deane succinctly summarizes the postmodernist view of exile: "[Exile] can lead from belonging nowhere to becoming at home everywhere, a migrant condition that owes something to the old Enlightenment ideal of the Citizen of the World, but also owes much to the contemporary belief that there is an essential virtue and gain in escaping the singularity of one culture into the multiplicity of all, or of all that are available. In such a turn we witness a rejection of nationalism brought to an apparently liberating extreme."[1] This view of exile as privilege has its roots in modernist celebrations of exile. High modernists such as Joyce and Pound repeatedly emphasized the intellectual advantages of being away from home, presenting exile as a vehicle for individuality, freedom, and resistance. As Deane notes, modernist writers' "distance from and disaffection with their home territories has almost always been understood as a paradigmatic refusal of the writer to surrender his or her radical freedom to the demands of an oppressive state or system."[2]

In critical constructions of modernism and exile Jews often occupy a pivotal position. There are, of course, at least two reasons for the Jews' centrality in discussions of modernism and exile. First, Jews have historically been perceived as the paradigmatic diaspora people. Second, modernist Jewish thinkers and writers like Auerbach and Adorno, Celan and Kafka, played a key role in directing critical attention to the ways in which exile yields intellectual freedom and creative power. Given these facts, it is perhaps no wonder that the Wandering Jew has often been invoked as a standing symbol of modernism and modernity.

The three-way correlation between modernism, exile, and Jewishness is brought into focus in David Carroll's introduction to Jean-François Lyotard's *Heidegger and "the jews."* Referring to Lyotard's citation of "Freud, Benjamin, Adorno, Arendt, Celan," Carroll argues that "these are ultimately 'the jews' we all have to read and even in some sense to become, 'the jews' we always already are but have forgotten we are."[3] To be sure, in a number of ways these Jewish writers need to be read as exemplary modernists. As such, Freud, Walter Benjamin, Theodor Adorno, Hannah Arendt and Paul Celan are indeed not only Jews by origin but also by "fate": they all suffered the burden of homelessness and exile.

What we witness here is a common, albeit tacit, double conflation of modernism and exile, of exile and Jewishness. While these conflations are partially grounded in historical facts, it would be grossly inaccurate to assume that all Jewish modernists advocated exile or found it intellectually liberating. In fact, modernist Hebrew writers resisted the idea of exile as a literary privilege or as an inherently Jewish vocation. Their resistance calls into question the very privileging of exile in contemporary theory; it also calls into question the critical tendency to read modernist practices as essentially antinationalist.

Against the backdrop of Anglocentric or Eurocentric views of the modernist canon, the modernist Hebrew canon stands out as somewhat of an oddity. Although Hebrew modernism was often simultaneous with and closely affiliated to European modernisms and although many of its practitioners lived and wrote in the capitals of international modernism, it does not fit neatly into the categories of central modernisms. One way to illustrate the historical specificity of the modernist Hebrew canon is to contrast its rejection of exile as a literary ideology with the glorification of exile and extra-territoriality among high modernists. In what follows I read Hebrew modernism's "Negation of Exile" (*shlilat ha-gola*) as a counternarrative that problematizes and disrupts Eurocentric and Anglocentric constructions of both "home" and "exile." The negation of exile in Hebrew modernism should be viewed, I argue, as an inverted mirror image of the celebration of exile in the writings of Anglo-American and European writers.

The negation of exile in Hebrew modernism involves a striking reversal of the home-exile binary. The "exile" described in modernist Hebrew texts is Europe, the place where the vast majority of Hebrew writers were born and reared; the "home" these writers embrace is Palestine, a new land they continuously portray as unbearably hot, foreign, and forsaken.

Yet the desire for a national sense of place and identity that is untroubled—
as well as the pressures of the canon to fulfill that desire—compels
Hebrew modernists to repress or palliate their sense of exile at "home"
in Palestine. Thus, although they are torn between continents, between
homes, and between languages, modernist Hebrew writers often "deny"
the difficulties inherent in their homecoming. Torn between their Europeanness and their newly fashioned "indigenousness" in Palestine, they
developed a particular way of seeing the home/exile dichotomy.

Referring to Adorno's view that "it is part of morality not to be at home
in one's home," Edward Said notes that "to follow Adorno is to stand
away from 'home' in order to look at it with the exile's detachment."[4] By
contrasting different views of exile—by slapping them one against the
other—I aim to contextualize and historicize various exilic conditions as
well as various canonical representations of exile. I aim, in other words,
to look at exile with a sense of critical detachment: both from outside in
and from inside out.

Exile as Home

The oft-quoted words of Stephen Dedalus in the *Portrait
of the Artist as a Young Man* have long come to emblematize the dominant modernist view of exile as offering unique possibilities for resistance
and freedom: "I will not serve that in which I no longer believe whether
it calls itself my home, my fatherland or my church: and I will try to express
myself in some mode of life or art as freely as I can . . . using for my defence
the only arms I allow myself to use—silence, exile, and cunning."[5] Exile
and freedom become in Stephen Dedalus's formulation almost synonymous. Exile turns out to be not only a mode of life but also a form of art
that, together with silence and cunning, allows for individuality and resistance. Dedalus's words on silence, exile, and cunning are the background
against which Joyce's own exile should be viewed. Exile, for Joyce, is not
decreed from above; it is a creative choice, a modernist form of resistance
which should be cherished and cultivated. Thus Richard Ellman observes
that "whenever [Joyce's] relations with his native land were in danger of
improving, he was to find a new incident to solidify his intransigence and
to reaffirm the rightness of his voluntary absence."[6] Constantly renew-
ing the quarrel with his homeland was a way to remain—both physically
and emotionally—in exile.

The idea that exile is indeed a form of freedom is similarly expressed in Maurice Blanchot's description of Franz Kafka. Describing Kafka as one of those who were "excluded from Canaan," Blanchot sees in Kafka a new sense of elsewhereness. The "error of infinite migration" is for Blanchot nothing less than "the origin of a new freedom."[7]

Joyce and Blanchot were not alone in promulgating exile. Ezra Pound argued that the American genius could not develop in the cultural "Dark Ages" of the United States; it could flourish only in London or Paris. He asserted that "if you have any vital interest in art you sooner or later leave the country."[8] And Gertrude Stein argued that "Americans needed Paris because they could not be artists, they could be dentists at home." In *What Are Masterpieces?* Stein articulated her position as an expatriate writer: "I am an American and I have lived half my life in Paris, not the half that made me but the half that made what I made."[9] In *Paris France* Stein added: "After all, that is, everybody who writes is interested in living inside themselves in order to tell what is inside themselves. That is why writers have to have two countries, the one where they belong and the one in which they live really. The second one is romantic, it is separate from themselves, it is not real but is really there."[10] Stein's words posit exile as a precondition for writing. Although the words "have to have" make exile mandatory for writing, it is noteworthy that the exile Stein describes is one of choice. In Stein's writing exile is in fact a choice, a privileged position, something to be desired; it is a modernist accomplishment, a token of internationalism, an asset rather than a liability. This view is repeatedly expressed in discourses on high modernists. Thus Delmore Schwartz's characterization of T. S. Eliot as an "international hero"[11] whose experiences and words transcended the limits of the national typifies a modernist stance that views exile as a form of resistance to nationalist ideology.

The advent of modernism has come to be perceived as so inextricably entangled with exile that major critics like George Steiner, Raymond Williams, and Hugh Kenner describe exile almost as a necessary condition for membership in international modernism. In George Steiner's words, modernism is an art of "extra-territoriality," whose proponents are poets "unhoused and wanderers across languages."[12] For Steiner, then, exile is the defining characteristic of modernism at large. Describing the "endless border-crossing . . . [that] worked to naturalize the thesis of the non-natural status of language," Raymond Williams notes, in "When Was Modernism?": "Paris, Vienna, Berlin, London, New York took on a new silhouette as the eponymous City of Strangers, the most appropriate locale for art made by the restlessly mobile emigré or exile, the internationally anti-bourgeois artist. From Apollinaire to Joyce to Beckett and Ionesco, writers were continuously moving to Paris, Vienna and Berlin, meeting there exiles from the Revolution coming the other way, bringing with them the manifestoes of post-revolutionary formation."[13] The "restlessly mobile emigré or exile" is, in Williams's view, the new era's protagonist. Continuously moving across borders, creating—through migration—a new international culture, these exiles are emblems of a new, modern world.

In his seminal essay "The Making of the Modernist Canon" Hugh Kenner advances the idea of modernism-as-exile even further. The exclusion of key modernist figures such as Wallace Stevens, Virginia Woolf, and William Faulkner from his construction of "International Modernism" is explained as follows: "The absence of Wallace Stevens from the canon I use has somehow been made to seem notorious. I account for it by his inassimilability into the only story that I find has adequate explanatory power: a story of capitals, from which he was absent. Like Virginia Woolf of Bloomsbury or Faulkner of Oxford, he seems a voice from a province, quirkily enabled by the International Modernism of which he was never a part, no more than they."[14]

The exclusion of Virginia Woolf from the canon ("She is not part of International Modernism; she is an English novelist of manners, writing village gossip from a village called Bloomsbury for her English readers")[15] demonstrates that the narrative Kenner advances is one of exile. It was not enough to be in a European capital, as was Woolf. One had to choose a European city in which one was not at home. Moreover, by arguing that "International Modernism was the work of Irishmen and Americans," although the cities of modernism were in fact London and Paris, Kenner tacitly suggests that the prerequisite for membership in "International Modernism" is exile.

Inasmuch as exile turned into an emblem of modernism, the "Jew" was increasingly perceived as a prototypically modernist figure.[16] Mary McCarthy argues in "A Guide to Exiles, Expatriates, and Internal Emigrés" that the "Wandering Jew . . . is the archetypal exile, sentenced to trail about the earth until the second coming."[17] It is precisely this commonplace that turns the Jew into an emblem of modernity itself. We have already seen how David Carroll, following Lyotard, turns "the jew" into a generic term that represents all forms of otherness, a critical maneuver that turns the readers of "real" Jews into allegorical "jews." We have similarly seen how Blanchot turns Kafka's Jewishness into a modernist quality of homelessness. In the same vein Marina Tsvetayeva writes, in a poem intended for Osip Mandelstam, that "All poets are Jews,"[18] and H. D.

(Hilda Doolittle) draws a parallel between the Jews' wandering and the fate of her Moravian ancestors, who used the term *diaspora* to name their own homelessness.[19]

While modernists like Pound, Joyce, H. D., Eliot, Hemingway, and Fitzgerald often saw "the Jew" as the emblem of both modernism and exile—and in many ways understood their own work as "Jewish"[20]—actual Jews did not quite fit the model. For while European high modernists turned the wandering Jew into an emblem or allegory of the human condition (Joyce's Bloom is a salient example), modernist Hebrew writers were enthusiastic participants in the project of bringing the wandering Jew back home. Hebrew writers resisted the view of exile as a "kind of literary privilege."[21] Moreover, they resisted the view of exile as an "inherently Jewish vocation."[22] The "negation of exile" (*shlilat ha-gola*) thus became a dominant theme or topos in Hebrew modernism. So while Marina Tsvetayeva wrote that "all poets are Jews" and Joyce "Judaized" Ulysses, Hebrew modernists were working to distance themselves from traditional Jewishness, from the "error of infinite migration."

The Negation of Exile

In 1925 Saul Tchernikhovsky, second only to Hayyim Nahman Bialik in the premodernist generation of Hebrew writers who first became active in Odessa of the 1890s, published a long poem entitled "A Man Is Nothing But . . . " The poem celebrates the speaker's emotional attachment to his native Ukraine: "Man is nothing but a little plot of land, / Man is nothing but the image of his native landscape." The poem's celebration of the Ukraine as the speaker's homeland is striking in its deviance from the accepted norms of Hebrew poetry of the day. Unlike Bialik, the designated national poet who described Europe in the wake of the Kishinev pogrom of 1903 as the antithesis of home ("The whole earth is a slaughtering block to me"), Tchernikhovsky evokes the Ukraine as a beloved homeland.

Tchernikhovsky's life embodies the Jewish experience of exile. Born in a village in the border region between Crimea and the Ukraine, he was forced to study medicine in Heidelberg and Lausanne because of restrictions against the admission of Jewish students to Russian universities. After graduating, he returned to Russia but left again for Germany in 1922, for he suspected that there was no future for Hebrew writers in the Soviet

Union. He attempted unsuccessfully to get a medical position in Palestine, the delay resulting in his residence in Germany for nine years. In 1931 he emigrated to Palestine where he resided until his death in 1943. The Poem "A Man Is Nothing But. . . ," which was written in Germany, positions the speaker as the wandering Jew who is relegated to eternal exile. But surprisingly enough Tchernikhovsky celebrates his own exile. Despite the speaker's elegiac tone (the speaker does lament his inability to reach the "Southern Sea"), he does not present exile in negative terms. Unable to ignore the negation of exile in Hebrew letters, he underscores the marginality of his own position:

> And my poem is alien, my poem is stranger to the heart of my nation
> All alone it appeared and all alone it shall leave
> With no one to receive it and with no word
> Like the screech of the lonely eagle, a wild screech.
> And like that wind, which will wander eternally,
> I wandered from sea to sea all the days of my life.
> And when I wanted to reach the Southern Sea
> Mountains blocked my way . . . where should I build my nest?
>
> More wide open space and more roads, where is my walking stick—I shall
>   go . . . [23]

Tchernikhovsky's words are interesting precisely because he markedly and painfully recognizes that the image of the wandering Jew, an image he fully identifies with, has run out of vogue in modern Hebrew letters. The wandering Jew, the emblem of Jewish life in the diaspora, is portrayed in Hebrew texts in extremely negative terms. In most Zionist texts Zionism is continuously portrayed as the cure while exile is identified as the disease. Zionist denunciations of exile were clear and unequivocal. Thus Ben Zion Dinaburg writes in an essay entitled "The Zionist Ideology and Its Principles": "The principle underlying the Zionist conception of Jewish reality was—the Negation of Exile. This negation is the first principle of Zionist ideology. Jewish misfortune has but a single name: exile (*galut*). Exile embodied all the [Jewish people's] disasters and calamities, persecutions and suffering."[24] Against the background of Dinaburg's words, Tchernikhovsky's embrace of the "exilic" Ukraine—and his identification with the wandering Jew—is startlingly iconoclastic. The extent of Tchernikhovsky's deviance from the ideological norms of Hebrew literature becomes clear when we read the uncompromising denouncements of Jewish life in the diaspora. A popular poem by Avigdor Hameiri may be a convenient starting point. Hameiri, a Hungarian-born poet who served in the Hungarian army during World War I (he was taken captive by the Russians and sent to a POW camp in Siberia), emigrated to Palestine in 1921. The following dialogue between mother and son brings to light the ideological and geographical rift between two generations:

> A mother writes with the tear of her eye
> To my good son in Jerusalem
> Your father is dead, your mother is ill
> Come home to the diaspora . . .
> Come home to spring,
> Come home beloved son.
> Come!

And the son replies:

> The pioneer writes with the tear of his eye
> It is 1924 in Jerusalem.
> Forgive me my sick Mother
> I will not return to the diaspora.
> If you truly love me,
> come here and embrace me.
> I shall be a wanderer no more,
> I shall not move from here forever.
> I will not move, I will not move.
> No![25]

Note that from a Zionist perspective the mother's appeal to the son to "come home to the diaspora" is an outright oxymoron. Since "diaspora" and "home" are flagrantly contradictory the son cannot but flatly reject the mother's plea. Moreover, Hameiri rhymes the words "diaspora" (*gola*) and "ill" (*chola*), a rhyme that strengthens the association, prevalent in Zionist ideology, of exile and sickness.

Hameiri's bluntness was not exceptional. The Hebrew poets who took part in the nation building process were eager participants in the cultural war against exile. The most influential Hebrew modernist was the poet Avraham Shlonsky, who was born in Plotov (Ukraine) in 1900. At age thirteen he was sent off by his father to study in Palestine. The outbreak of World War I found him on a visit to Russia, where he was forced to stay through the crucial years of the Revolution and the war. In 1922 he emigrated to Palestine and soon became the leading proponent of the "New" in Hebrew letters. Like other modernist Hebrew poets, Shlonsky was well versed in European culture, and his poetry exhibits a close affinity for and affiliation with the poetics of Russian poets like Alexan-

der Blok and Vladimir Mayakovsky. But while Shlonsky's experimental-
ism and wild imagery — as well as his iconoclastic rejection of tradition —
are couched in and modeled after European examples, his blunt rejection
of exile sets him apart from the European poets he follows. The poetics
of newness advanced by Russian futurism, including the extended use of
neologism, is used by Shlonsky for political means. He advances a utopian
Zionist agenda of newness which calls for a new society, a new language,
and a new homeland. That the new is couched in the rhetoric of return
(to productivity, to Hebrew, to Palestine) renders the utopia just and attain-
able. Shlonsky, who was once characterized as "the poet of the Zionist
revolution," identifies wholeheartedly with the Zionist rejection of exile.
Addressing both his comrades and the homeland ("Listen brethren / and
listen [my] homeland"), Shlonsky describes in "March" the marked
differences between home and exile, past and present:

> hurray
> climb the mountain!
> yesterdays have darkened
> we shall look at the morrow.
> how do the eagle's wings tire?
> indeed we burned,
> we burned the bridge
> who is trying to pull us back to yesterday?
> . . . . .
> we've
> all of us
> known
> that we came
> from a settled land to a forsaken place
> that this is the wasteland
> and that hunger and
> malaria awaited us.
> and in spite of it all
> we do believe
> and we shall believe
> that we will rise
> even if we fall time and again.
> straighten your gaze,
> raise your voice:
> who errs to step right?
> left!
> left!
> left![26]

Although the playful inventiveness of Shlonsky's Hebrew is lost in translation, the ideological identification with the negation of exile remains
fully visible. It is noteworthy that Europe is not even mentioned in Shlonsky's poem. The speaker, whose tone of voice is couched in a revolutionary
European context, ignores Europe altogether, identifying it only indirectly
as "a populated land." Europe is present in the poem only through negation, representing an undesired past. Shlonsky's route in "March" leads
him toward a leftist, socialist vision that is shaped by the Russian Revolution; this vision is imbricated here with a nationalist-cum-modernist
thrust that in turn leads Shlonsky away from Europe. Although Shlonsky presents Palestine as a forsaken place (*erets nidachat*) and as wasteland,
he celebrates it as home and homeland, expressing undiminished
confidence in the imminent success of the Zionist project.

As this example clearly shows, Shlonsky is aware of the harsh conditions in Palestine (hunger, malaria); if Europe looms large in the background as a "populated land" it is only as an emblem of the past. It is
noteworthy that Shlonsky does not deny the difficulties inherent in leaving Europe and immigrating to Palestine, but he accepts the difficulties
with great enthusiasm, as he writes in "Metropolis":

I have loved you my comrades
Among the thorns of the tsabar [prickly pear]
in eagle-clutches of parched-rocky heat;
in rebellion and in peace
let us extend our necks:
Blessed be He who places his heavy yoke on us.
Amen.
Selah.[27]

In Shlonsky's view the newly arrived pioneers cannot but accept the hard-
ship in Palestine wholeheartedly. The modernist desire to negate the past
(Pound's famous exhortation "TO MAKE IT NEW" comes to mind as a salient
slogan) expresses itself in Shlonsky's poem as the negation of Europe.
When Shlonsky claims to have burned the bridge (to Europe, to the past)
and refuses to be pushed back to yesterday, he identifies exile as a chrono-
tope that enmeshes time (past) and place (Europe). Zionism, for Shlonsky, is first and foremost a modernist ideology. Thus he claims: "In my
opinion, every good translation [into Hebrew] as every good [original]
poem is Zionism." And thus the rebuilding of the land and the writing
of modernist Hebrew poetry are perceived by Shlonsky as synonymous.
Consider, for example, the quasi-religious description of the Zionist
rebuilding of the land in his famous poem "Amal" (Toil):

My country wraps itself in light as in a prayer shawl
Houses stand out like phylacteries
And like phylactery straps, the roads that hands have paved glide
    down."[28]

Note that in Hebrew the word *batim,* which is translated above as
"houses," is also the word for stanzas. Thus the modernist/Zionist
poem's stanzas and the newly built houses are synonymous. Consequently
the poet is a full participant in the Zionist project, a "road-building bard
in Israel."

In his diary Shlonsky writes about the relation of Zionism to modernist Hebrew poetry:

What does the sense of a homeland, the fact of a homeland [i.e., Palestine],
bestow on our culture . . . ? It allows an emancipation from the . . . always-
Jewish, only-Jewish—that is from the external and the limiting and bragging
all at once. . . . It is no coincidence that in the Diaspora, our literature—our
art—was specific, and hence *Naturalistic,* since nothing natural, taken for
granted, existent and safe (that is a homeland, a state) gave us a sense of self,
nor did it safeguard our particular characteristics,—and hence our culture
became . . . a substitute for a homeland, for a state. . . . It had to preserve . . .
everything that was Jewish and only Jewish. . . .

In Palestine, I do not need to be only Jewish, always Jewish in order to be a
Jew. In Palestine, I can, I must be a man, first of all a human being, for Jewishness is anyway automatic within the territorial, social and political structures of the homeland. For what does a homeland mean to a people if not a
sense of taken-for-grantedness. It saves a national group from [chauvinistic]
nationalism, and it is the only possibility to base a culture on humanism. It
is no coincidence that Hebrew literature in Palestine is mostly of this kind:
modern, relevant—in its thematics, its mentality, its desires (and also perhaps
in its chances) to take off from a national moment into the international horizon, just as an aeroplane takes off from an airport.[29]

For Shlonsky, Zionism and the emergence of a Jewish homeland are
modernist catalysts that bring about the demise of naturalism. Shlonsky
equates exile and naturalism just as he links the return to Palestine with
modernism. The very possibility of internationalism, which is crucial for
Shlonsky as well as for many other modernists, is based on the existence
of a homeland, metonymically figured through the "airport." As this passage clearly indicates, Shlonsky is not insensitive to the allure of modernist internationalism as a means of resisting "[chauvinistic] nationalism" (*leumanut*). But he acknowledges that in order to resist or criticize
the nation-state structure one must first have a state. The following anec-
dote, told by Palestinian poet Machmud Darwish, may serve to illustrate

Shlonsky's position: "Jean Genet once said that a homeland is a stupid idea, except for those who still don't have one. The Spanish poet Goitisolo then replied: "What about when they get one?" And Genet replied, "Let them throw it out the window."[30] When Shlonsky argues that he wants "to take off from a national moment into the international horizon," he says, in fact, that people have to have a homeland in order to "throw it out the window."

Shlonsky's view of Hebrew modernism is expressed more fully in a historical account of the emergence of a "new poetry" in Palestine. Here too he equates Zionism and modernism: "A new poetry could have arisen only as a result of its identification with a vision, with the beginning [be-reshit] of a new society which is socialist in its form and nationalist in its content."[31] Shlonsky's account of the new Hebrew poetry of which he was part is revealing enough to be worth quoting at some length:

This Hebrew poetry . . . was chronologically and essentially the logical offspring of the Third *Aliya* [immigration wave] in all its manifestations. For better or for worse, its doubts and its achievements—it is the voice and reflection of this glorious story of this *Aliya*. It cannot be located outside this climate, outside the joy of the storming settlers [*mista'arim*], "bare-hearted and labor-driven" of this period. . . . The sites are well known: The Road and the Gilboa, the tent and the commune, Ein-Charod and Beit-Alfa, and *Yachad* Camp. . . . Only in this way, through such an identification with a vision, with the beginning of a different society, "socialist in form and nationalist in content," could a new poetry arise. . . . And so a party of poets came together, who together built the stanzas [*"batim"*—stanzas but also houses] of the new poem. Each one with his particular temperament, but always bearing the collective trait of this newness. [These poets'] roots in the country's landscape are deeper, and the personal biography, of almost all of them, is already that of total identification with the public of *Erets Israel,* whose main essence and glory is the camp of the pioneers.[32]

On reading Shlonsky's account of the emergence of Hebrew modernism it becomes unequivocally clear that he identifies Hebrew modernism with the rejection of exile. In identifying the new Hebrew poetry with the writers of the Third *Aliya* (immigration wave), Shlonsky strictly confines the borders of Hebrew modernism. Delineating clear temporal, geographical, and ideological borderlines to contain the story of Hebrew modernism, mappings like these exclude from the canon writers who did not emigrate to *Erets Israel* (like Lensky), a nativist poet who was born in *Erets Israel* (Esther Raab), and writers who were not politically committed to Zionism (like Fogel).

The story Shlonsky recounts here, perhaps unexpectedly, is one of migration. Not unlike Kenner, Williams, or Steiner, he identifies migration as the only concept that has explanatory power. But as the examples adduced here clearly show, Shlonsky perceives the emigration of Hebrew writers from Europe to Palestine not as exile but rather as a late return, as homecoming. Thus the modernist Hebrew canon, which cannot be separated from the Zionist nation-building process, can be said to have worked to change the *premodernist* norm of exile. As one critic asserted in 1928, "Only someone who is completely blind could fail to see the mutual influence that exists between Zionism and Hebrew literature, [they] arise and succeed together just as they fall and fail together, and God forgive some of our friends, who stubbornly subscribe to the idiocy that Hebrew literature can be built on the basis of a-Zionism or even anti-Zionism."[33] While Kenner excludes writers such as Virginia Woolf, William Faulkner, and Wallace Stevens from the canon of international modernism because they did not live in exile, Hebrew poets who chose to remain in the diaspora or who did not fully negate the concept of exile were excluded from the modernist Hebrew canon or were marginalized by its center. That the exile in which these marginalized Hebrew writers remained included some of the major sites of international modernism is one of the curious ironies of literary history. And while exile seemed like a modernist stance or accomplishment to many European or American writers, most Hebrew writers perceived it as essentially *premodern*, something that needs to be abolished altogether.

Home as Exile

To fully understand a culture one must attend not only to dominant voices but also to the voices that have been silenced, cast out, expelled, or excluded. Although the negation of exile turned out to be the dominant ideology of Hebrew letters, it would be grossly inaccurate to imply that other poetic/ideological positions did not find expression in the textual field we name Hebrew modernism. Indeed almost all Hebrew poets were devout Zionists; but some did voice ambivalence toward or disappointment regarding the "home" they found in Palestine. Since Hebrew criticism demanded full identification with Zionism, poets who continuously expressed ambivalence toward the Zionist project were often rendered minor. Consider, for example, the poetic/political ambivalence of Noach Shtern. Shtern, who was born in Lithuania in 1912, emigrated to Ottawa when he was seventeen; two years later he moved to Cambridge, Massachusetts, to study English literature at Harvard. After graduating, Shtern was offered a scholarship at Columbia University but he decided to emigrate to Palestine. He arrived in Palestine in 1935 but was never at home in his new homeland of choice. Engulfed in ambivalence he describes the orange groves, the emblem of the new land:

> The smell of the heavy oranges
> comes to give pleasure and to torture
> to nurture and strangle as witness
> to the life in this homeland.[34]

Another poet who continuously described Palestine as a disappointing homeland is Alexander Penn. Penn, a Russian-born poet, who was, while still in Russia, a friend of Vladimir Mayakovsky, wrote poems in both Russian and Hebrew. Constantly torn between the USSR and Palestine, Penn wrote in 1929 a poem entitled "A New Homeland." This new homeland he describes in astonishingly negative terms:

> Without faith and direction
> I walk
> your sun in my throat—bronzed heartburn.
> And all the energy of my soul
> You eradicate instantly,
> You so-called New Homeland.[35]

But the most intricate—and ambivalent—poetic rendition of Jewish "homelessness" is to be found in the poetry of Leah Goldberg, who continuously questioned and problematized the notions of home and exile. Unlike Shtern or Penn, who were considered marginal, Goldberg was a leading poet in Shlonsky's coterie. Born in Königsberg, East Prussia, and educated at the universities of Kovno, Bonn, and Berlin, Goldberg was thoroughly familiar with Russian and German literature; she attained native or near-native fluency in many European languages, including Russian, German, French, Italian, and English. Although Goldberg's mastery of Russian was far superior to her knowledge of Hebrew, she decided to write poetry in Hebrew and began doing so at age ten. One of her first poems, entitled "exile," reads:

> How difficult the word how many memories
> of hatred and slavery

and because of it we had shed so many tears:
exile

and yet, I'll rejoice in the fields of exile
which are filled with oats and flax
the hot day and the cool evening
and the dead silence of night

the pale spring and the melting snow
the season which is neither summer nor autumn
when, in the garden, by some miracle
the green turns to gold.[36]

The poem's shift from an ideological negation of exile to an unabashed celebration of the exilic landscape is striking. Goldberg focuses here and elsewhere on the gap or rift between ideology and experience. She begins with a textbook rejection of exile only to find out that the negated site is beautifully familiar. Moreover, a close scrutiny of the text reveals that exile for her, at least here, is clearly textual. It is presented as a "difficult word," a concept in Jewish collective memory ("memories of hatred and slavery") rather than as a concrete experience or fact of life. The speaker's shift from the "difficult word" to the happiness aroused by the fields is undoubtedly surprising. As Goldberg's literary career progressed, however, she became increasingly aware of the problematics of "home" and "exile" and thus gave expression to a particularly complex positionality.

With Goldberg, home is often a function of distance and nostalgia, a place always-already beyond one's grasp and longed for. In a cycle entitled "From the Songs of Zion" Goldberg acknowledges—and indeed problematizes—the relationship between poet and land, immigrant and home. The cycle's first section, entitled "Night," reads:

Does the golden tongue of a bell quiver in the uppermost heaven?
Did a drop of dew fall on the top of the tall cypress tree?
Sing to us of the Songs of Zion!
How shall we sing the song of Zion in Zion's land
And we have not even begun to hear. [37]

Goldberg's poetry becomes increasingly wary of the expectation that Hebrew poetry should be politically committed to Zionism in general and to the negation of exile in particular. The poem echoes the words of the exiles in Psalms 137 who resist their captors' demand that they sing the songs of Zion. Exile, for them, is a state that negates the very possibility of singing. The allusion to Psalms 137, the ur-text on exile in the Jewish tradition, cannot pass unnoticed by Goldberg's readership. Before considering the meaning of Goldberg's iconoclastic allusion, let us look at Sidra DeKoven Ezrahi's reading of the biblical passage:

The theme of exile and homecoming is as old as literature itself, becoming, in its most radical modern readings, virtually synonymous with the literary process. At the source of a long intertextual journey, the 137th Psalm is the canonic moment that generates the poetic vocabulary of exile: "By the rivers of Babylon, *there* we sat and wept as we remembered Zion." The pleonastic "there" in the first and third verses calls attention to itself by its very redundancy; syntactically superfluous, "there" defines exile as the place that is elsewhere. Being elsewhere is the pre-text for poetry.[38]

Note, however, that the biblical passage presents exile as antithetical to poetry. It is interesting that Goldberg expresses the biblical idea that exile negates the possibility for poetry while she is in Palestine. Unlike the exiles in Babylon, she is, in fact, at "home" in the ever-longed-for Zion. This is, no doubt, a bold reversal of the biblical theme. A question of purpose imposes itself: Why can't the speaker in the poem sing "of the Songs of Zion"? Attempting to listen to the land's unheard voices, Goldberg acknowledges her inability to capture poetically the sounds of this unfamiliar homeland.

In "Tel Aviv 1935" Goldberg describes the arrival of a group of immigrants to Tel Aviv in terms of exile and estrangement:

And the knapsacks of the travelers
walked down the streets
And the language of a foreign land
Was plunged into the hot day
like the cold blade of a knife.[39]

Although the poem is clearly about her own immigration to Palestine (she arrived in Jaffa in 1935), Goldberg describes her "homecoming" in strikingly impersonal terms. The experience is collective rather than personal, and the process as a whole is dehumanizing, for the immigrants in the poem turn from subjects into walking knapsacks. As we read these lines, it becomes clear that Goldberg problematizes the notion of "homecoming." Goldberg's double position, simultaneously insider and outsider in both Europe and Palestine, is expressed in the poem through the speaker's visual perspective. The "detached" modernist eye that looks at the "walking knapsacks" from afar seems to be standing on a roof in Tel Aviv. Goldberg describes the immigrants' arrival to a new land as if she is not implicated in the picture she portrays. By looking at a group of immigrants (of which she is part) from outside, with no apparent trace of involvement, she gives succinct expression to her sense of detachment from herself as well as from the collective. Goldberg's double perspective informs the poem in many different ways. For example, one disturbing question remains unsolved: Which is the foreign language that is "plunged into the hot day"? Is it the immigrants' Russian or is it the natives' Hebrew? What, in other words, constitutes the "foreign" in the pregnant moment of homecoming? The question remains unresolved. Moreover, as Goldberg arrives in Palestine, a moment of Jewish wish fulfillment, she instantly thematizes her emotional and spiritual longing for her hometown's architecture, figured through a church at the end of the poem.

In another poem Goldberg's double positionality becomes even more explicit as she acknowledges her sense of "elsewhereness."

> Here I'll not hear the cuckoo's voice,
> Here the tree will not wear a snowy hat
> But in the shadow of these pines
> My entire childhood is revived.
>
> The sound of the conifers: once upon a time . . .
> Homeland I'll name the snowy planes,
> The greenish ice which chains the stream
> The language of poetry in a foreign land
>
> Perhaps only the passing birds know—
> as they dangle between earth and sky—
> this pain of the two homelands.
>
> With you, I was planted twice
> With you, pines, I grew,
> With my roots in two different landscapes.[40]

While Gertrude Stein views the simultaneous affiliation to two countries as a liberating privilege and as a double presence, Goldberg experiences this double affiliation as a tormenting lack or absence. A simple sense of home is untenable for Goldberg, for she perceives her two homelands as mutually exclusive. Having "roots in two different landscapes" is by no means liberating for Goldberg. While contemporary theory advances the idea "that there is an essential virtue and gain in escaping the singularity of one culture into the multiplicity of all, or of all that are available,"[41] Goldberg stresses her inability to feel fully at home in either of her homelands. The multiplicity is experienced as loss. When Goldberg says "I was planted twice," she brings into focus her sense of having been uprooted. Exploring her double positionality, she defines "homeland" in terms of the landscapes she feels close to, as well as in terms of her closeness to texts: thus Russian poetry always remains a homeland.

In 1940 Goldberg expressed herself more fully on the question of exile: "Or perhaps, perhaps only now we have learned to feel that the essence of poetry is not in the combination of harmonies, but in the terrible anxiety which the human heart feels before death, in the human longing for tranquillity and a homeland—which are always beyond our reach?"[42] The question mark at the end of this passage tells the entire story, for the desired homeland is always out of reach. Goldberg's sense of "homelessness"—her having two homelands—could grant her entry into constructions of modernism that valorize the exilic condition. But within Hebrew letters, the position Goldberg held vis-à-vis exile was considered "ex-centric." Consider, for example, Abraham Blat's assessment of her poetry: "Leah Goldberg is a humanist poet. This is her great strength and this is her weakness because her national and social uprootedness left her lonely with her single poem, the love poem (alongside her nature poems). . . . Although we relish great humanist lyrical poetry, we cannot ignore the absence of a specifically Israeli color in her poetry."[43] Blat's description of Goldberg's social and national uprootedness is clearly indicative of the limited range of valued literary topics at a specific historical moment. Reading Goldberg's poetry as excessively personal, he gives succinct expression to a collective literary expectation that poetry participate in the nation-building process. Thus A. B. Yoffe writes: "In 1940 Goldberg's second volume of poetry had been published. It was, undoubtedly, a big step forward in comparison to her first book. The poems became not only less personal and more objective, but the poet exhibited a desire to conquer the landscape of *Erets Israel*."[44]

But the most revealing attack on Goldberg's poems has been advanced by the critic Y. Saaroni, who complains, on reading Goldberg's first book, that "it is hard to believe that this poet lives in our day, in a modern city . . . and not in a medieval monastery, in a dark and solitary chamber. It seems as if she arranges an exile for herself, flapping in the prison of loneliness without finding the gate that would allow her to get out to the wide world."[45] Condemning Goldberg's detachment from the "here and now," Saaroni describes Goldberg as uprooted, as too European; in his view, she is too attached not only to Europe but also to Christianity. Culturally and emotionally immersed in the Old World—wrapped up in an exile of choice—she is viewed as not committed enough to either Judaism or Zionism. As these critical remarks suggest, Goldberg's somewhat ambivalent relation to Palestine as homeland is denounced as irresolute. Her overt longing for the European landscapes of her childhood and her close affiliation with European culture are perceived as evidence of her lack of commitment to the emerging national culture. Although a famous poet who is part of a hegemonic coterie, Goldberg gradually became a liminal figure, an acknowledged poet who was rendered marginal.

Exilic Conditions

By calling into question the Eurocentric/Western view of exile as freedom and by pointing to the ways in which Hebrew writers disrupt the home-exile dichotomy, I do not mean to negate or dismiss the view of modernism as exile. What I want is to reuse the concept of exile in ways that will not gloss over the differences between various exilic conditions.

By juxtaposing two different canons, two opposing views of modernism and exile, I wanted to advance a distinction between various kinds of exile. Taking a step in this direction, Mary McCarthy has already suggested a three-way distinction between exiles, refugees, and expatriates. "Classically," she writes, "exile was a punishment decreed from above, like the original sentence of banishment of Adam and Eve."[46] The expatriate, in her view, is the opposite of the exile: "His main aim is never to go back to his native land, or, failing that, to stay away as long as possible. His departure is wholly voluntary. An exile can be of any nationality, but an expatriate is generally English or American."[47]

Without limiting the expatriate's nationality, I wish to re-deploy McCarthy's important set of distinctions. It is obvious by now that Gertrude Stein's exile was very different from Goldberg's. My sense is that despite the tension between Paris and Oakland, Stein knew where home was—at least in the sense of knowing what she was working against ("what made her" in her terms). Despite the "internationalism" of her literary salon, she was an American writing in English. Paris was a privilege, a perspective that allowed her to transcend national limits. When Stein writes "writers have to have two countries, the one where they *belong* and the one in which they live really," she expresses her sense of belonging to America. American expatriates like Hemingway, Fitzgerald, and Henry Miller also had a very clear sense of where home really was. As Mary McCarthy notes, "When the dollar dropped in value during the thirties, after the crash, the American, by and large, went swiftly home, proving that even those who like Malcolm Cowley (author of a book called *Exile's Return*) had imagined themselves to be exiles were only expatriates."[48]

Exile for Goldberg was something entirely different. To begin with, exile was forced on her as a child, for her family fell victim to the expulsion of Jewish families from Lithuania at the outbreak of World War I. Goldberg described her return to Lithuania in 1919 in her autobiographical novel *Ve'hu Ha-or* (And That Is the Light); in 1938 she retells the traumatic experience. The passage is revealing enough to be quoted in its entirety:

I remember it well: the end of September or the beginning of October, 1919. The days were very cold. The fields were very barren. A stabbing, nasty wind was blowing. At a distance shots were heard. A crossroads. Somewhere on the border between Russia and Lithuania. Most of the column had already crossed the border. We were stopped. Father was arrested and everyday they threatened to execute him. His shoes were yellowish-reddish and the Lithuanian troops announced that such shoes were a clear sign of belonging to the Communist party. . . . One day the hope glimmered that we would be allowed to continue our journey. Mother went to beg the officers for mercy. I remained to watch over the suitcases. Alone. In the field. It was very cold. A few "fingers" in my gloves were missing. My hands were freezing. No one was around. Barren fields. Every once in a while soldiers passed by. They didn't touch me. Continued on their way. Many hours passed and it started getting dark. My feet also froze. A terrible fear emerged from the fields. And I didn't cry. I wasn't afraid of wild animals. I was afraid of human beings and from the absence of human beings in the surrounding. I was already eight years old, and I knew that evil comes from man and from desertion. My feet froze and my head was burning. Later it became clear that I had high fever. Over thirty-nine degrees. Rubella. Once the stars had been turned on in the sky my mother appeared—found me alone in a field at a crossroads. Sitting and watching over the suitcases. I still remember from the thread of those days: a huge, transient wooden hut that was built in the fields. Babies were crying. Mothers wept at night. Tortured men wept as well. Someone rebuked. The column did not move from that spot. For ten days nothing, nothing has come into my mouth except for water, and once every three days—a tiny slice of bread. I do not recall the distress of hunger, nor the dread. I mainly remember a wide field and cornflowers among the aging spikes. And I still remember a well at the edge of the village, and a day after the rain. A little greenish frog leaped out of the well. I sat on a big stone and spoke to it. Who knows what I said to it but [life] was almost good. I don't remember the distress of hunger.[49]

Edward Said has already noted that "exile is strangely compelling to think about but terrible to experience."[50] And indeed, against the background of Blanchot's construction of exile as freedom or against the background of Stein's privileged exile in Paris, Goldberg's description is troubling and disruptive. Goldberg's description fractures the immateriality of allegorical readings of both Jewishness and exile. Moreover, it throws into some question the whole privileging of exile in modern literature and theory. However disturbing the description is (it definitely explains the appeal of Zionism for Goldberg) one must not forget that Goldberg did not feel fully at home in Palestine either. Although Goldberg identifies herself as Zionist, it is noteworthy that in her homeland of choice she felt uprooted from her Europeanness, from the landscapes of her childhood. The only option left for Goldberg was to thematize her ever-growing sense of uprootedness. From a constantly problematized positionality, Goldberg was able to question and rewrite the home-exile binary. But her perspective—although typically, even prototypically modernist—has rendered her minor in the Hebrew canon, a canon whose constellations of inside/outside, home/exile are diametrically opposed to the constellations Kenner posits for international modernism. Writers like Goldberg, who refused to fully participate in the construction of nationness as a form of social and textual affiliation, were gradually rendered minor. In a modernist movement that celebrated Jewish nationalism, the "cosmopolitan," exilic, anationalist constructions of "elsewhereness" were construed as violations of social and poetic codes.

Notes

I would like to thank Chana Kronfeld as well as the editors of this book for helpful criticisms and suggestions.

1. Seamus Deane, "Imperialism/Nationalism," in *Critical Terms for Literary Study,* ed. Frank Lentricchia and Thomas McLaughlin (Chicago: University of Chicago Press, 1995), 367.
2. Ibid.
3. Jean-François Lyotard, *Heidegger and "the jews,"* trans. Andreas Michel and Mark S. Roberts (Minneapolis: University of Minnesota Press, 1990), xxiv. For a critique of Lyotard's universalization of "the jew," see Daniel Boyarin and Jonathan Boyarin, "Diaspora: Generation and the Ground of Jewish Identity," *Critical Inquiry* 19 (1993): 693–725.
4. Edward Said, "Reflections on Exile," in *Altogether Elsewhere,* ed. Marc Robinson (New York: Harcourt Brace, 1994), 147.
5. James Joyce, *Portrait of the Artist as a Young Man* (New York: Vintage, 1973), 246–247.
6. Richard Ellman, *James Joyce* (New York: Oxford University Press, 1965), 113.
7. Maurice Blanchot, *The Space of Literature,* trans. Ann Smock (Lincoln: University of Nebraska Press, 982), 70, 71.

8. Ezra Pound, *Selected Prose, 1909–1965* (New York: New Directions, 1973), 122.

9. Gertrude Stein, *What Are Masterpieces?* (New York: Pitman Publishing, 1970), 62.

10. Gertrude Stein, *Paris France* (New York: Liveright, 1970).

11. Delmore Schwartz cited in Susan Stanford Friedman, "Exile in the American Grain: H.D.'s Diaspora," in *Women's Writing in Exile,* ed. Mary Lynn Broe and Angela Ingram (Chapel Hill: University of North Carolina Press, 1989), 89.

12. George Steiner cited in Malcolm Bradbury, "A Nonhomemade World: European and American Modernism," in *Modernist Culture in America,* ed. Daniel Joseph Singal (Belmont, Calif.: Wadsworth, 1991), 36.

13. Raymond Williams, *The Politics of Modernism,* ed. Tony Pinkney (London: Verso, 1989), 34.

14. Hugh Kenner, "The Making of the Modernist Canon," in *Canons,* ed. Robert von Hallberg (Chicago: University of Chicago Press, 1984), 373.

15. Ibid., 371.

16. For an interesting conflation of Jewish textuality, extra-territoriality, and modernity, see George Steiner, "Our Homeland, the Text," in *Salmagundi* 66 (1985): 4–25.

17. Mary McCarthy, "A Guide to Exiles, Expatriates, and Internal Emigrés," in *Altogether Elsewhere,* ed. Marc Robinson (New York: Harcourt Brace, 1994), 49.

18. Marina Tsvetayeva, *Selected Poems,* trans. Elaine Feinstein (Harmondsworth: Penguin, 1974), 3.

19. Bryan Cheyette, *Constructions of 'the Jew' in English Literature and Society* (Cambridge: Cambridge University Press, 1993), 267.

20. Bryan Cheyette argues further that "the Jew" became a standing symbol of modernism. Tracing the abundance of "semitic representations" in modernist texts, Cheyette argues that "the acceptance, within a modernist aesthetics, of the impossibility of fully 'knowing' anything, made 'the Jew' an ideal objective correlative for this lack of absolute knowledge. There is, in short, a coincidence of interest between 'the Jew' as an unstable cultural signifier and a modernist style which refuses to be reduced to a settled narrative." Cheyette also believes that it is precisely this congruence between "Jewishness" and modernism that produced T. S. Eliot's anti-Semitism: "It was Eliot's repressed fear of being Judaized that resulted in an extreme racialization of 'the Jew' in his 1920 *Poems.*" See Bryan Cheyette, *Constructions of "the Jew" in English Literature and Society* (Cambridge: Cambridge University Press, 1993), 267.

21. The words are those of Sidra DeKoven Ezrahi. See "Our Homeland, the Text . . . Our Text the Homeland: Exile and Homecoming in the Modern Jewish Imagination," *Michigan Quarterly Review* 31, no. 4 (1992): 468.

22. Ibid. Edmond Jabe's words — "Gradually I realized that the Jew's real place is the book" — exemplify the view of exile as an "inherently Jewish vocation."

23. Saul Tchernikhovsky, *Collected Poems* (in Hebrew) (Tel Aviv: Schocken, 1950), 469.

24. Ben Zion Dinaburg, "The Zionist Ideology and Its Principles," in *A Collection of Hebrew Essays* (in Hebrew) (Tel Aviv: Gazit, 1945), 552. Explicating the negation of exile in Zionist ideology, Anita Shapira argues: "The concept Negation of Exile was one of the dominant components in Labor ideology in Palestine. A revolutionary movement's need to repudiate everything that had preceded it, to burn bridges to the past in order to gather together the necessary psychological strength for a revolutionary shift, was expressed in the total rejection of Jewish pattern of life in the Diaspora." See Anita Shapira, *Land and Power* (Oxford: Oxford University Press, 1992), 321.

25. Hameiri's popular poem is cited in Amos Elon, *The Israelis* (in Hebrew) (Tel Aviv: Schocken, 1971), 128.

26. "March," in Avraham Shlonsky, *Collected Poems,* Vol. 1 (in Hebrew) (Tel Aviv: Sifriyat Po'alim, 1954), 302.

27. "Metropolis" in Avraham Shlonsky, *Collected Poems* (in Hebrew).

28. "Toil," in ibid.

29. Avraham Shlonsky, *Notes from the Diary* (in Hebrew) (Tel Aviv: Sifriyat Po'alim, 1981), 59.

30. Machmud Darwish, "Exile Is So Strong within Me, I Might Bring It to the Land" (in Hebrew), *Chadarim* (1996), p. 176.

31. Avraham Shlonsky, *Selected Critical Writing* (in Hebrew) (Tel Aviv: Sifriyat Po'alim, 1960), 56.

32. Ibid., 57.

33. Moshe Kleinman, *Characters and Levels: Notes on the History and Evolution of the New Hebrew Literature* (in Hebrew) (Paris: Voltaire Press, 1928), 208.

34. Noach Shtern, *Amid Fogs* (in Hebrew) (Tel Aviv: Hakibuts Hameuchad, 1973), 100.

35. "A New Homeland," in Alexander Penn, *Nights without Roof* (in Hebrew) (Tel Aviv: Hakibuts Hameuchad, 1985), 54.

36. Leah Goldberg, "exile," in Tuvya Ruebner, *Leah Goldberg: A Monograph* (in Hebrew) (Tel Aviv: Sifriyat Po'alim, 1980), 10.

37. "From the Songs of Zion," in Leah Goldberg, *Collected Poems*, Vol. 2 (in Hebrew) (Tel Aviv: Sifriyat Po'alim, 1970), 219.

38. Sidra DeKoven Ezrahi, "Our Homeland, the Text . . . Our Text the Homeland," 465.

39. "Tel Aviv 1935," in Leah Goldberg, *Collected Poems*, Vol. 3 (in Hebrew) (Tel Aviv: Yachdav, 1970), 14.

40. Leah Goldberg, *Collected Poems*, Vol. 2 (in Hebrew) (Tel Aviv: Yachdav, 1970), 14.

41. Seamus Deane, "Imperialism/Nationalism," 367.

42. Cited in A. B. Yoffe, *Leah Goldberg: An Appreciation of the Poet and Her Work* (in Hebrew) (Tel Aviv: Reshafim, 1994), 6.

43. Abraham Blat, *In Writers' Path* (in Hebrew) (Tel Aviv: Menora, 1967), 107.

44. See A. B. Yoffe, *Leah Goldberg*, 241.

45. See ibid., 228.

46. Mary McCarthy, "A Guide to Exiles, Expatriates, and Internal Emigrés," in *Altogether Elsewhere*, 50.

47. Ibid., 51.

48. Ibid., 52.

49. Cited in A. B. Yoffe, *Leah Goldberg*, 17–18.

50. Edward Said, "Reflections on Exile," 137.

CHAPTER 12

Fag-Hags and Bu-Jews

Toward a (Jewish) Politics of Vicarious Identity

Naomi Seidman

The question of how Jews as a group fit into American multiculturalism is a vexed enough one. But Jews participate in the multi-culture not only as Jews, that is, not only from within a group identity or politics. Jewish academics and activists have stood on various multi-cultural fronts by virtue of their commitment to progressive causes, but they have done so more commonly as feminists, as historians and critics, as leftists than as Jews. For these Jewish participants, multiculturalism has created its own set of complications: multicultural practice invites the proud articulation of ethnic or racial identity, but it does so as part of the political program of increasing the visibility of minorities and struggling to reverse discrimination. Not so long ago Jews might still have comfortably marched under the double banner of multiculturalism—the celebration of diversity and the struggle for group self-determination. But given the implicit link between these two agendas, on the one hand, and the horrors of modern history, on the other, Jewish insistence on representation in the multiculture is inevitably interpreted as a bid for the status of victim. Many progressive Jews who might be attracted to the invitation to identify their "subject position" are nevertheless reluctant to do so for fear of appearing to make a claim that, given American Jewish success, might well seem like special pleading.

The traces of this dilemma are everywhere, but they are particularly close to the surface in feminism and gender studies, where strong multi-cultural currents and the ubiquity of Jewish participants often combine to uncomfortable effect. The peculiarities of the dilemma I have outlined,

with its contradictory demands to articulate and keep silent, require a reading of the footnotes and parentheses of recent texts. Thus, in *Bodies That
Matters*, for instance, Judith Butler takes issue with bell hooks' critique
of the documentary filmmaker Jenny Livingston (*Paris Is Burning*) as a
woman who "does not oppose the way hegemonic whiteness 'represents'
blackness."[1] Butler insists on adding a qualification to hooks' description
of the filmmaker as white: "Livingston is a white lesbian (in other contexts called 'a Jewish lesbian from Yale,' an interpellation which also impli-
cates this author [Butler] in its sweep)."[2] Butler challenges hooks' critique
of Livingston by arguing that the filmmaker, as a lesbian, "maintains some
kind of identificatory bond with the gay men in [*Paris Is Burning*]"; but
Livingston's Jewishness plays no part in qualifying her whiteness, except
in a parentheses that is never expanded into an argument. The form of
this qualification, the parentheses, is crucial here. Butler strikes the precise note she needs, one that will assert a shade of difference in the characterization of Livingston—and herself—as white, but without making
an overt political claim for the significance of that difference; in contrast,
she does argue for the significance of Livingston's "lesbian gaze." If anything, the additional attribution "from Yale" suggests that however Jewishness may complicate one's identity, this complication is not one that
involves exclusion from the Ivy League. Jewishness, then, only parenthetically qualifies whiteness.

Just such a scene of ambivalent avowal of Jewishness occurs in a passage by the feminist critic Nancy Miller. Acknowledging the political pressure to situate herself within her own work and more specifically to "frac-
ture the simplified profile of straight white woman," Miller records her
desire to place herself in a work she was writing "as a Jew."[3] The attempt
fails, Miller confesses, because "I have not found a way to assume that
rhetoric of identity (although I am both, I cannot lay claim to 'Jewish
feminist'): it is not a ground of action for me in the world, nor the guarantee of my politics—my writing."[4] What is striking about Miller's parenthetical (dis)avowal is her sense that however strongly she theoretically
supports the grounding of discourse in a specific and contingent "subject position," saying that she is who she says she is cannot in good faith
be counted as such a grounding. Jewish feminist identity, that is, either
does not have or has lost the power of "fracturing the simplified profile
of straight white woman," and to pretend otherwise would be dishon-
est. Laura Levitt, in a critique of Miller's position, rightly charges Miller
with "making 'Jewish feminist' into a single absolute term" and argues
that Miller "does not allow for instability" or "contradictions within these

identities," since she first reifies and then rejects what Jewish feminism might mean.[5] What this analysis fails to take into account, though, is that Miller is utterly uninterested in constructing a postmodern, multicultural definition of Jewishness or Jewish feminism. It is precisely her rejection of these categories as meaningful which would have to be included in any definition of Jewish feminist that could conceivably encompass Miller's position. And that is a more difficult proposition.

We do not have a vocabulary to describe the Jewishness of Butler, Miller, or (in an example I will discuss later in this piece) Eve Kosofsky Sedgwick. Yet it seems to me that there is something about their similar positions in the multiculture that *is* particularly Jewish, not only in the passages where they discuss their Jewishness but even—perhaps especially—in their reluctance to do so. By its nature, a stance like Miller's evades categorization as Jewish; it is not illuminated by such concepts as "hyphenated" identity. The Jewish claim in the passages I quoted above occurs only parenthetically or under erasure, as it were. It is nevertheless true that Miller's stance can, paradoxically, be described as Jewish, exposing its "Jewishness" not only in the repudiation of Jewish particularism but also in the adoption and championing of another marginality. For each of the writers I analyze here is known as a theorist of some other "difference" than the Jewish one. Miller writes about third world women's literature, Judith Butler has analyzed the subversive potential of drag, and Sedgwick's most powerful work focuses on homosexual men. It is no accident that a film like the recent *Zebrahead* (1992) portrays a Jewish adolescent in the role of would-be African American or that Woody Allen's *Zelig* (1983) wryly describes its protagonist as a Jewish man who "is able to transform himself into a Negro or an Indian." Just as important to multiculturalism as spokespersons for Jewish identity, it seems to me, is this subterranean tradition of Zeligs and Zebraheads, parenthetical Jews and identifiers with an "other" identity.

It may be perverse to claim as Jewish a stance distinguished precisely by its reluctance to make this claim for itself. If I do so, it is first of all on historical rather than polemical or apologetic grounds. The prevalence of Jewish participation in "other" political struggles has been explained through the discourse of pathology as false-consciousness or assimilation; it has been defended through the apologetic discourse of Jewish altruism and sympathy for the underdog. I prefer to trace the route by which Jews have started down what would seem to be such a difficult road. Moreover, it is worth pointing out that however oblique or opaque the desires that drive vicarious identifications may seem, they are no less operative for that. My analysis here is an attempt to locate what I see as a budding but hidden tradition of Jewish vicarious identification and render its submerged desires transparent. As I see it, the parenthetical Jews I discuss in this essay are as logical and coherent an expression of contemporary Jewish identity—given both Jewish history and the demands of American multiculturalism—as more straightforwardly identified Jews.

If indeed one can point to the coherence of a Jewish politics of the vicarious, this coherence is a sign of both the persistence and the dialectical transformation of what Hannah Arendt and Isaac Deutscher identified as a "hidden tradition" of secular Jewish experience. In her 1944 essay "The Jew as Pariah," Arendt traced the importance of Jewish thinkers in a number of fields to the status of the Jews as a "pariah people" who, like poets and revolutionaries, could never be quite at home in the world. For the Jews of Germany in particular, the promise of equality held out by emancipation turned out to be both treacherous and ambiguous; but the very conditions that kept Jews from growing comfortable in the majority culture also granted them a critical perspective closed to those inside it. The "pariah Jew," who had abandoned Jewish practice or community and was marginalized in the majority culture, revolutionized disparate cultural arenas; nevertheless, Arendt wrote, connections could be drawn between these isolated figures over time, since "for over a hundred years the same basic conditions have obtained and evoked the same basic reaction."[6] For Arendt, Jews had no choice about their outsider status; the only options for Jews were to become social-climbing parvenus—submerging their Jewishness (whatever that happened to be) in exchange for the hollow promise of social acceptance—or conscious pariahs, participants in a proud, subterranean form of modern Jewish experience.

In his famous essay of 1958 Isaac Deutscher described and championed a similar modern phenomenon in "the non-Jewish Jew," a Jew who had no particular ties to the Jewish community or religion, no Jewish "consciousness," even, but who could be nonetheless identified as a distinct product of Jewish history, as a Jewish "type." Deutscher distanced himself from the racialism of nationalists, as had Arendt before him. What was important in creating this kind of Jew wasn't the content of Judaism or racial characteristics but the position of Jews outside their own religion, on the one hand, and on the sidelines of various European cultures, on the other. Living on the margins of Christian society, Deutscher argued, granted Jews an epistemological advantage, the ability to view systems of belief with a skepticism history had made a Jewish characteristic. Thus, a marginal Jew like Marx "rose above German philosophy, French socialism, and English political economy; he absorbed what was best in each of these trends and transcended the limitations of each." Rosa Luxemburg, Trotsky, and Freud had in common "that the very conditions in which they lived and worked did not allow them to reconcile themselves to ideas which were nationally or religiously limited and induced them to strive for a universal *Weltanschauung*."[7]

Arendt and Deutscher drew different conclusions from examining much the same material. For Arendt, the utter failure of German-Jewish coexistence pointed in the direction of (a far from mainstream) Zionism, since it was Jewish "worldlessness" that had rendered their position so precarious.[9] Deutscher felt otherwise: Since it was the Jewish position outside what was "nationally or religiously limited" which had created the conditions for the radical universalism of the non-Jewish Jew, Deutscher lamented the Jewish embrace of the nation-state in his own time, just when this form of political organization had begun to decline. Deutscher ends his essay with the rousing hope that Jews will "ultimately become aware— or regain the awareness—of the inadequacy of the nation state and find their way back to the moral and political heritage that the genius of the Jews who have gone beyond Jewry has left us—the message of universal human emancipation."[8]

Deutscher, of course, turned out to be hugely wrong. The ringing universalist note on which Deutscher ends dates his essay unmistakably. Things have gone, for Jews among others, in the direction of the particularism Jews were supposed to be especially brilliant at abandoning. Even Deutscher's Zionist critique is rarely echoed precisely in his terms: the leftist problem with the Jewish "nation-state" is not that Jews ought to be citizens of the world rather than citizens of the Middle East but rather that this case of Jewish particularism happens to have intruded on prior claims whose particularism no "non-Jewish Jew" would dream of deprecating. So what would Deutscher make of the Jews beyond Jewishness who populate the multiculture? Where do these Jewish energies go, when progressive thought walks under the banner of cultural diversity? Back to a Jewish particularism now invested with the postmodern glamour of ethnic identity? Well, yes, for some Jews, though even that return is complicated by a contemporary self-consciousness and a politics of comparison, one effect of the historical Jewish embrace of the universalist position. What lies beyond Deutscher's non-Jewish Jew, however, is just as likely to be a multicultural particularism refracted through the traditional Jewish universalist prism (if traditional can be applied to the belated construct Deutscher describes) to land elsewhere, as it were. Thus, what I call a Jewish politics of vicarious identity emerged from conditions as basically Jewish as those Arendt unearths for the conscious pariah.

The dissolution of a politics of universalism in which Jews could participate was complicated by the fact that this universalism was, from one point of view, an expanded form of Jewish particularism. It has often been noted that Jews were more passionately committed to the Enlightenment than any other group because they had the most to gain from the adoption of its principles of tolerance. As the sociologist Gordon Lafer remarks, Jewish universalist credos gained the dominance they did because, for periods preceding our own, they lived in easy harmony with Jewish particularist interests. Thus, "while Jews were commonly excluded from educational and social organizations, efforts to advance their own career opportunities meshed seamlessly with the more general struggle for the triumph of meritocracy over chauvinism; and later, when Jews were victims of Nazism, the struggle against fascist anti-Semitism could easily be understood as part of the larger struggle against all assertions of national superiority."[10] The tradition of Jewish universalism was then threatened in two directions: by the unraveling of what Lafer calls the "easy marriage between liberal universalism and Jewish particularism" which followed on the Jewish rise out of the working class, and by the more general dissolution of liberal universalist institutions. By this logic, then, American Jews were invited to pursue a particularist politics at precisely the period of Jewish entry into the mainstream, the moment, that is, when Jewish particularism could no longer be confused with a wider ethical commitment.

It would be wrong, then, to see Jews who participate in such numbers in non-Jewish particularist struggles as direct heirs of Arendt's and Deutscher's subterranean Jewish tradition. When American Jewish scholars speak of Jewish marginality, as often as not they are borrowing from Europe and the European past. (Thus, a scholar of French Jewry like Elaine Marks sets out her own "subject position" by speaking of "the belonging sickness" she and others "seem to share with Jacques Derrida.")[11] The American-Jewish position cannot be easily explained, however, by recourse to models set up in very different European contexts. Jews, in Arendt's and Deutscher's essays, are the privileged models for marginality; thus, Jewish experience is a metonym for both oppression and revolution which is easily carried into more general struggles. For American Jews, this entire cultural perception has both receded in historical immediacy and solidified into a banal rhetoric of ethnic pride; the spread of this Jewish self-definition, that is, has roughly coincided with its obsolescence. In contemporary American-Jewish culture Arendt's "hidden tradition" has not

so much ended as become (as has been said of modernism) both dominant and dead. And as this hidden tradition increasingly becomes an open
secret, its dialectical continuation is driven further underground. There
are many routes out of this dissonance, but one of them has certainly been
to retain in some form the legacy of Jewish marginality while seeking its
"truer" expression in particularist, non-Jewish models. The price has been,
for some, the awkwardness of championing particularisms while avoiding one's own, or, alternatively, to feel one's self-identification as a Jew as
somehow in bad faith.

However untidily American-Jewish experience fits the multicultural paradigm, the problematics of Jewish participation is at the very heart of its
development. If the founding moment of American multiculturalism
is in the shift from the liberalism of the civil rights movement to the identity politics of Black Power in the mid- to late 1960s, then multiculturalism, from the beginning, signaled the expulsion of Jews from a comfortable home on the left. More than that, African American experience,
as Michael Rogin points out, indirectly provided both the Jewish blackface vaudevillian and the civil rights worker with a path toward integration, a way to be white in a society where African Americans, not Jews,
were the dominant Other.[12] No wonder multiculturalism and the Jews
has so often turned out to be a traumatic conjunction. For the Jews, particularism began not in a return to ethnic celebration but in a radical dis-
location of what had become a not-so-hidden tradition of Jewish universalist secularism. The Jewish civil rights worker, after the expulsion of
whites from the movement, has been an ambivalent and overdetermined
figure, a figure made superfluous in the first surge of black nationalism
and whose reincarnation has haunted the political scene since then. The
Jewish pariah, in the multiculture, leads a shadowy political existence
untouched by a rhetoric of pride. What distinguishes the Jew in the multiculture from Deutscher's Jewish universalist is an unstable translata-
bility run amok. Where "the [Jewish] jazz singer Americanized himself
through blackface,"[13] the Jewish would-be participant secures herself/
himself a place in the multiculture through a different kind of blackface,
lifting a marginality wholesale from elsewhere and making it serve other
(and Other) interests.

To compound the Jewish/multicultural problem, what prevented the
widespread Jewish adoption of Jewish ethnic particularism was, in a way,
Jewishness itself, in the form of the tradition of universalism that came
closest to articulating modern Jewish hopes and pride. Rodger Kamenetz,
in trying to account for the prevalence of American Jews in Western Bud-

dhist circles, has suggested a similar etiology for Jewish rejection of Jewish practice. Kamenetz addresses the tendency of secular Jews to be more open to other religions than their own, acknowledging that "the Hasidim represented everything [Allen] Ginsberg's family had run screaming from for two generations."[14] But Kamenetz's most powerful insight is his recognition that the rejection of one kind of Jewish tradition is also, from another perspective, another kind of Jewish tradition: "I began to suspect that Jewish identity, as it has evolved in the West today, could be a real barrier to encountering the depths of Judaism. In other words, being Jewish could keep you from being a Jew."[15] Kamenetz's analysis is directed to secular Jewish interest in non-Jewish religious traditions, but the same could be said for the rejection of the politics of Jewish particularism by a certain portion of this group. In the absence of a particularist Jewish political affiliation that could also satisfy the progressive universalist agenda with which Jewish politics has been historically linked, adopting the particularist position of another group paradoxically becomes a distinctively Jewish act.

Eve Kosofsky Sedgwick's 1990 *Epistemology of the Closet* is the most revealing text I have found on the phenomenon I am tracing here. Sedgwick's classic work of queer theory focuses not so much on the political contexts and consequences of homosexual self-disclosure—though these are always at hand—as on the play of knowledge and identity across the charged borders of the "coming-out" scene. Gay coming out, for Sedgwick, is primarily an epistemological drama, in which all participants are necessarily implicated and which threatens all identities in a heterosexist culture. It is important for Sedgwick to argue that she is speaking specifically of the gay dramas of self-disclosure; other such scenes leave the identities of the participants intact. The book begins with Sedgwick's attempt to contain the discursive spread of the model of the closet to other forms of self-concealment/disclosure—for which Jewish identity rapidly becomes the privileged example. Sedgwick enlists Racine's reworking of the Esther story (which plays an important part in her discussion of Proust, the subject of her final chapter) as a counterexample of the gay closet, although she acknowledges that it is only a particular, and literary, construction of the Jewish coming-out narrative.

The telling moment comes at the very end of Sedwick's analysis of how gay and Jewish identities differ, an analysis that includes the claim that there is no uncertainty in either Esther's or Ahasuerus' identities to complicate the matter of disclosure. Ahasuerus will not wonder whether he too is really a Jew, while Esther, as Sedgwick argues, "knows who her people are." Unlike gay people, "Esther has intact and to hand the identity and history and commitments she was brought up in."[16] It is only at the end of her argument that Sedgwick extends her claims beyond the Racinian view of the Bible to that of contemporary Jewish culture and her own Jewish origins. The last point of comparison Sedgwick draws between Jewish and gay identity is that "Esther's avowal occurs within and perpetuates a coherent system of gender subordination." The passage, with the crucial parenthetical closet (by contrast, gay identity is not parenthetical), is worth citing in its entirety:

Esther the Jew is introduced onto this scene [of Vashti's gender insubordination] as a salvific ideal of female submissiveness, her single moment of risk with the king given point by her customary pliancy. (Even today, Jewish little girls are educated in gender roles—fondness for being looked at, fearlessness in defense of "their people," non-solidarity with their sex—through masquerading as Queen Esther at Purim; I have a snapshot of myself at about five, barefoot in the pretty "Queen Esther" dress my grandmother made [white satin, gold spangles], making a careful eyes-down toe-pointed curtsey at [presumably] my father, who is manifest in the picture only as the flashgun that hurls my shadow, pillaring up tall and black, over the dwarfed sofa onto the wall behind me.) . . . If the story of Esther reflects a firm Jewish choice of a minority politics based on a conservative reinscription of gender roles, however, such a choice has never been able to be made intelligibly by gay people in a modern culture (although there have been repeated attempts at making it, especially by men). Instead, both within and outside of homosexual-rights movements, the contradictory understandings of same-sex bondings and desire and of male and female gay identity have crossed and recrossed the definitional lines of gender identity with such disruptive frequency that the concepts "minority" and "gender" themselves have lost a good deal of their categorizing (although certainly not of their performative) force.[17]

As a coming-out scene, this is remarkably complex and fiercely beautiful. It appears as the very last of the catalog of ways in which Jewish identity is not as radical or disruptive as gay identity. The catalog, we should recall, begins by positing Jewish identity as one in a list of other ethnic and other identities potentially comparable to gay identities; by the end of the argument, however, Jewish identity has become the sole point of comparison. Thus, while only the coming-out scene in the passage I quoted is actually in parentheses, the entire progression of the argument contributes to what could be called the parenthetizing of Jewish identity, first as one among other possible substitutions for gay experience, then as an inaccurate analogy to gay experience, and finally, as (incidentally) something very close to the opposite of gay experience. Putting Jewish identity in parentheses, then, is apparently very important business.

Making her Jewish identity parenthetical thus has implications for Sedgwick's subject position not only as Jew but also as theorist of homosexual culture. It is this aspect of her work that the "Jewish choice of a minority politics based on a conservative reinscription of gender roles" both threatens and opposes. In Sedgwick's reading of Esther's relation with the Persian king, Jewish identity reveals itself as the political counterweight to feminist and gay identity. Esther's avowal of her Jewishness never disrupts her status as pliant wife to Ahasuerus and faithful cousin to Mordechai. Sedgwick's coming out as a (Jew) neatly reverses Esther's: while Esther's coming out as a Jew leaves both the gender and ethnic order intact, Sedgwick's presentation and disavowal of her own image as a nice Jewish girl turn niceness, Jewishness, and girlishness into transparently fictional theater.

Ethnicity, then, can also be a kind of drag, an inversion that says "appearance is an illusion."[18] But if that is true, then Sedgwick's own performance of a Jew pretending to be a Jew gives the lie to the solidity of Jewish identity. As Judith Butler describes it, "[Drag] reveals the distinctness of those aspects of gendered experience which are falsely naturalized as a unity through the regulatory fiction of heterosexual coherence. *In imitating gender, drag implicitly reveals the imitative structure of gender itself—as well as its contingency.*"[19] If Eve in the guise of Queen Esther is in drag, masquerading in a dress sewn for her by her grandmother, hamming it up with a curtsey, her image preserved only in a half-reliable vortex of memory and aggressive technology, then so is Queen Esther, in all of her various manifestations. Extrapolating from Butler's theorem that "gay is to straight *not* as copy is to original, but, rather, as copy is to copy" leads to only one possible conclusion: both Eve-Esther and Queen Esther are simulacra, (Jewish) drag queens. The parentheses that communicate that Jewishness can sometimes be inessential do not separate Eve's ethnic identity from Esther's to the extent that Sedgwick seems to think: what else is Esther's avowal than a carefully crafted performance, in the Bible, in Racine, and in Sedgwick's own representation? It's no coincidence, after all, that Purim is the holiday in which both gender and ethnic roles are subjected to parodic subversion and revelers are enjoined to drink until they can no longer tell the difference between the villain Haman and Mordechai the Jew.

Something of this blurriness appears already in the semidisclosure that is the name of the author of *Epistemology of the Closet*. Eve Kosofsky Sedgwick invites the traditional guessing game of Jew/not-Jew, in which the American "non-Jewish Jew" is the prototypical subject. Kosofsky Sedg wick might signify a Jewish name, either her own or, more old-fashionedly, her mother's, covered and legally superseded by one with a Mayflower stamp—the absent *e* after the *g* looks particularly British to my eye. If the name doesn't come from the man who wielded the Jewish "flashgun," then it must belong to a presumably non-Jewish husband. How does this man, whose non-Jewish name leaves a larger patriarchal shadow than her father's does, fit into her story of repudiating a heterosexist ethnic affiliation in the name of the higher identifications of feminism and homosexuality? Does Sedgwick's signature strengthen or weaken the connection between her and Ahasuerus's wife? I don't pose these questions to find out their answers, but rather to point out that there is a double tension in this coming-out scene: Sedgwick simultaneously does and does not come out as Jewish and, less explicitly, she almost but doesn't quite come out as not-heterosexual. Whatever else you can say about this scene, it hardly involves a simple, "non-disruptive" identity.

Sedgwick's parenthetical and ambivalent Jewish self-presentation is itself the strongest argument against the stability of Jewish identity and the relative straightforwardness of the Jewish coming-out scene. To make such an argument, though, is to risk trivializing the gay closet by falling into the trap Sedgwick is trying to avoid: making Jewish experience the model for all marginality. My intention in shifting the focus of Sedgwick's discussion from the gay closet to her Jewish self-disclosure is not to insist that, despite Sedgwick's argument, Jewish identity is as painful, as meaningful, as difficult as gay identity. The parenthesis is not a closet, and Sedgwick's parenthetical disclosure is intended to register precisely that point. My interest in highlighting Sedgwick's affirmation-by-negation is not to claim, where she does not, that her Jewish identity is important or coherent in some way she is unwilling to acknowledge. The extent of my ambition here is to register the pattern and subtlety of such a parenthetical Jewish identity alongside that of Nancy K. Miller's parenthetical refusal to claim the status of "Jewish feminist" and to read this grammar within the "hidden tradition" of postmodern (Jewish) identity. To remove the parentheses, to insist unequivocally on the Jewishness of such a position as Sedgwick's, is to be deaf to the political desire that motivates and shapes it.

There is one other moment in *Epistemology of the Closet* when Sedgwick speaks of these desires and how they contribute to her work in gay theory. Describing herself as a woman and, "in some regimes, a Jew," Sedgwick meditates on how this multiple identity contributes to her "ability to keep generating ideas about 'the closet'": "May it not be influenced by the fact that my own relation, as a woman, to gay male discourse and

gay men echoes most with the pre-Stonewall gay self-definition of (say)
the 1950s?—something, that is, whose names, where they exist at all, are
still so exotically coarse and demeaning as to challenge recognition, never
mind acknowledgment, leaving, in the stigma-impregnated space of
refused recognition, sometimes also a stimulating ether of the unnamed,
the lived experiment."[20] This is as close as Sedgwick comes to articulating her "subject position" as heterosexual woman who is also a pioneer-
ing queer theorist. Her affinity for the closet then derives from her operating from within a still unbreached "stigma-impregnated space of refused
recognition." It would be useful to set these two moments of self-disclosure
together: the one an identification of who one is "by birth and history"
through a mechanism of disavowal, the other a confession that one has
impossibly, unreciprocally embraced the desire of the Other. Sedgwick is
right then. It is not the Jew who resembles the homosexual. The figures
who turn out to be the most similar, at least in her own oblique self-dis-
closures, are the (Jew) and the fag-hag, the heterosexual woman who loves
gay men. If the parenthetical Jew and the heterosexual queer theorist—
and it's no accident that they should be one and the same—are connected
by an impulse to vacate what would necessarily be a conservative politics
of self-interest, the radical movements they join are not so radical that
they can embrace this move. The culture that easily champions hybridity
and marginality still wraps the (Jewish) fag-hag in the stigma of arrested
desire and incoherent identity.

Among the range of homophobic insults, we might note, "fag-hag"
has been particularly resistant to reclamation. Cassell's *Queer Companion*,
for instance, defines "faggot" as a "slang term for a gay man. Originally
pejorative, the word has been adopted by gay men to describe themselves";
the entry for "fag hag" is far more tentative and ambivalent: "Slang term
for a heterosexual woman who spends the majority of her time with gay
men. Used pejoratively, the term can indicate the misogyny that exists
within gay male communities, and the mistrust of women's motives in
wanting to socialize with gay men. However, the term can show the understanding that can exist between gay men and straight women."[21]

There is still almost no context in which "fag-hag" is not a dirty word,
code for a figure who provokes both derision and pity. It isn't immediately clear why this should be, given the unpredictable friendships and
alliances recorded in the stereotype. Yet "fag-hag" names no emancipatory movement, no transcendence of stigma or pathology. Even the diagnoses of her condition fail to reach intelligibility: the fag-hag is both
masochist and narcissist, parasite and self-hater. The fag-hag is a category

mistake, a structural deviation. What resists the incorporation of the fag-hag in a liberatory political discourse is, from this point of view, the ambiguity of her position. In a queer culture that unites sexual realization with political liberation, the woman whose sexual satisfaction seems at odds with her social investments opens herself to the contradictory diagnoses and rehabilitative interventions. Within the cult of identity, it is the fag-hag's love that dare not speak its name.

It is the position of the fag-hag in queer culture, I would argue, that is the best analog to a certain characteristically Jewish position in the multiculture, although I can think of no comparable insult that would encode the absurdity and impropriety of this Jewish stance. In a culture that equates the battle for representation and rights with political progressivism, the Jew who resists a straightforward identity politics in exchange for participation in the struggle of "someone else" opens herself up to the charges of assimilationism, self-hatred, and parasitism. The very absence of any apparent ethnic self-interest becomes cause for suspicion, revealing itself as the symptom of an apparently Jewish pathology. In an environment that celebrates marginality, the Jewish politics of the vicarious is a marginal position that has yet to find its champion.

Yet if the drag-queen is the subversive who demystifies the "natural" coherence of sex, gender, and sexual orientation, the fag-hag is the marginal figure who demystifies the equally naturalist assumptions of contemporary queer culture: that social investments will embody sexual orientation, that sexual orientation is predictive of political affiliation, and that all of these can find a unified mode of satisfaction. The drag-queen thus primarily threatens gender conservatives; the fag-hag threatens both the gender order and the emancipatory vision of its overthrow. If I am right that Jews like Miller and Sedgwick are the fag-hags of the multiculture, then their unintelligible identity politics throws the multicultural vision into anxious question.

It is no accident, then, that the founding queer theorist is (not really) Jewish (and not really gay). Like Al Jolson, who put on blackface to sing to his Jewish mother, the Jew beyond even the non-Jewish Jew requires and solicits other faces in order to see her own. If Jacques Lacan is right, the self is always grasped externally, through the mirror of the Other. The time is past when we could confidently grade the authenticity and depth of a Jewish identity, as if ethnicity were not always constituted within the laws of performance and intelligibility. There is no Jewishness that avoids the logic of specularity, that has found a "natural" unity of past and present, politics and identity. But such unity is always an illusion. If we are to imagine a progressive politics capable of exceeding the limitations of a reifying multiculturalism, this identity-that-is-not-one may be a good place to start.

I do not mean to suggest that Jewish advocacy for non-Jewish causes is necessarily radical in itself. Michael Rogin's analysis of Jewish participation in civil rights culture as, to some degree, a continuation of immigrant Jewish blackface should warn us of the deeply conservative potential of soliciting other faces in order to see your own. Political and ethnic drag is a luxury unavailable to all ethnicities in America, we should remember; blackface was the very tool, in Rogin's argument, by which Jews transformed themselves into white Americans.[22] The Jewish adoption of marginal identities in an attempt to participate in the multiculture is not in the final analysis different enough from the jazz singer's blackface. There is something, even for unaffiliated Jews, in multiculturalism's demand for the identification of one's position as a subject; tactfully bracketing one's Jewish identity in the presence of "real" marginality can lead, as it does in Sedgwick, to an unconsciousness of how even this bracketed Jewishness shapes who we are.

But there is no easy way out of Jewish political drag either. The straight road of Jewish self-identification in the multiculture is only apparently so. Without coalition partners with similar goals, without a sense that one's particularist struggle contributes significantly to a greater American good, Jewish group participation in the multiculture becomes itself a form of charade, a mimicking of other, probably more crucial American struggles. Jews may be postmodern models of fractured identities, demystifying the apparent unities of self and politics, social position, and political desire. But multiculturalism has more pressing interests than the demystification of identity. In either case then, whether as (Jews) or as Jews, we are at best only stepchildren of the multiculture. But that will have to be enough.

Notes

1. bell hooks, "Is Paris Burning?" *Z*, June 1991, p. 61. Quoted in Judith Butler, *Bodies That Matter: On the Discursive Limits of "Sex"* (London: Routledge Press, 1993), 133–134.

2. Butler, *Bodies That Matter*, 133.

3. Nancy Miller, *Getting Personal: Feminist Occasions and Other Autobiographical Acts* (New York: Routledge, 1991), 95. Quoted in Laura Levitt, "Rethinking Jewish Feminist Identity/ies: What Difference Can Feminist Theory Make," in *Interpreting Judaism in a Postmodern Age*, edited by Steven Kepnes (New York: New York University Press, 1996), 368.

4. Miller, *Getting Personal,* 97, in Levitt, "Rethinking Jewish Feminist Identity/ies," 369.

5. Levitt, "Rethinking Jewish Feminist Identity/ies," 370.

6. Hannah Arendt, "The Jew as Pariah: A Hidden Tradition," in *The Jew as Pariah: Jewish Identity and Politics in the Modern Age,* ed. Ron H. Feldman (1944; New York: Grove Press, 1978, 68).

7. Isaac Deutscher, "The Non-Jewish Jew," in *The Non-Jewish Jew and Other Essays* (1958; Oxford: Oxford University Press, 1968, 30).

8. Ibid., 41.

9. Arendt's argument is developed in her section on anti-Semitism, in *The Origins of Totalitarianism* (New York: Harcourt Brace Jovanovich, 1951).

10. Gordon Lafer, "Universalism and Particularism in Jewish Law: Making Sense of Political Loyalties," in *Jewish Identity,* ed. David Theo Goldberg and Michael Krausz (Philadelphia: Temple University Press, 1993), 180.

11. Elaine Marks, *The Marrano as Metaphor: The Jewish Presence in French Writing* (New York: Columbia University Press, 1996), 151.

12. Michael Rogin, *Blackface, White Noise: Jewish Immigrants in the Hollywood Melting Pot* (Berkeley: University of California Press, 1996).

13. Ibid., 147.

14. Rodger Kamenetz, *The Jew in the Lotus* (San Francisco: Harper San Francisco, 1994), 241.

15. Ibid., 156.

16. Eve Kosofsky Sedgwick, *The Epistemology of the Closet* (Berkeley: University of California Press, 1990), 72.

17. Ibid., 82.

18. Esther Newton, "Mother Camp: Female Impersonators in America," as quoted in Judith Butler, *Gender Trouble* (New York: Routledge Press, 1991), 137.

19. Butler, *Gender Trouble,* 137. Emphasis in the original.

20. Sedgwick, *Epistemology of the Closet,* 63.

21. William Stuart, *Cassell's Queer Companion* (New York: Cassell Press, 1995), 58.

22. Rogin, *Blackface, White Noise,* 73–112.

Notes on Contributors

Robert Alter is Class of 1937 Professor of Hebrew and Comparative Literature at the University of California at Berkeley. He has written on the European and American novel, on modern Hebrew literature, and on literary aspects of the Bible. His most recent books are *Hebrew and Modernity* (Indiana University Press, 1994) and *Genesis: Translation and Commentary* (Norton, 1996).

David Biale is Koret Professor of Jewish History and director of the Center for Jewish Studies at the Graduate Theological Union in Berkeley. He is the author of *Gershom Scholem: Kabbalah and Counter-History* (Harvard University Press, 1974), *Power and Powerlessness in Jewish History* (Schocken, 1986), and *Eros and the Jews* (University of California Press, 1997). He is currently editing a three-volume cultural history of the Jews.

Mitchell Cohen is co-editor of *Dissent* magazine and professor of political science at Baruch College and the Graduate School of the City University of New York. He is the author of *The Wager of Lucien Goldmann* (Princeton University Press, 1994) and *Zion and State* (Columbia University Press, 1992), and has edited *Princeton Readings in Political Thought* (Princeton University Press, 1996, with Nicole Fermon) and *Rebels and Reactionaries: An Anthology of Great Political Short Stories* (Dell, 1992).

Michael Galchinsky is the author of *The Origin of the Modern Jewish Woman Writer* (Wayne State University Press, 1996) and, as Visiting Skir-

ball Fellow at the Oxford Centre for Hebrew and Jewish Studies, is editing an anthology of Anglo-Jewish women's writings. His other scholarly
interests include the relation between American Jews and popular culture.
He teaches English literature and women's studies at Millsaps College in
Jackson, Mississippi.

Michael Gluzman teaches comparative literature at Tel Aviv University.
His book *The Politics of Canonicity: Lines of Resistance in Modernist Hebrew
Poetry* will be published by Stanford University Press. He is co-editor (with
Naomi Seidman) of *Israel: A Traveler's Literary Companion* (Whereabouts
Press, 1996). He is currently working on a book-length study of Zionist
masculinity entitled "The Zionist Body."

Cheryl Greenberg is an associate professor of history at Trinity College,
Hartford, Connecticut, where she teaches African American and twentieth-
century American history; she was also a Fellow at the W. E. B. Du Bois
Institute for Afro-American Studies at Harvard University. Her first
book, *"Or Does It Explode?" Black Harlem in the Great Depression,* was published in 1991 by Oxford University Press. Her current project, a political history of black-Jewish relations in the twentieth century, is tentatively
entitled "Troubling the Waters: Black-Jewish Relations from Leo Frank
to Louis Farrakhan."

Susannah Heschel holds the Eli Black Chair in Jewish Studies at Dart-
mouth College. She is the editor of *On Being a Jewish Feminist: A Reader*
(Schocken, 1983) and co-editor, with Rachel Biale, of a forthcoming anthology of feminist readings of classical Jewish texts (University of California Press). She is also the author of a monograph on *Abraham Geiger and
the Jewish Jesus* which will be published by the University of Chicago Press,
and co-editor, with Robert Ericksen, of the forthcoming *The German
Churches under Hitler* (Fortress Press).

Sara R. Horowitz is director of the Jewish Studies Program and associate professor of English literature in the Honors Program at the University of Delaware. She is the author of *Voicing the Void: Muteness and
Memory in Holocaust Fiction* (New York: SUNY Press, 1997) and is currently completing a book called "Gender, Genocide, and Jewish Memory." She has published on Holocaust literature, women survivors, Jewish-
American fiction, and pedagogy. She is founding co-editor of *KEREM:
A Journal of Creative Explorations in Judaism* and has served as fiction advi-

sory editor for *Jewish American Women Writers: A Bio-Bibliographical and Critical Sourcebook,* edited by A. Shapiro, S. Horowitz, E. Schiff, and M. Glazer (Greenwood Press, 1994).

Amy Newman teaches philosophy at Philadelphia College of Textiles and Science. She has recently published essays in the *Journal of the American Academy of Religion* and *Hypatia.*

Naomi Seidman is an assistant professor of Jewish culture at the Center for Jewish Studies of the Graduate Theological Union in Berkeley. She is the author of *A Marriage Made in Heaven: The Sexual Politics of Hebrew and Yiddish* (University of California Press, 1997).

Michael Walzer is a professor of social science at the Institute for Advanced Study in Princeton, New Jersey. He is the co-editor of *Dissent* magazine, a contributing editor of the *New Republic,* and the author of *Just and Unjust Wars* (Basic Books, 1977), *Spheres of Justice* (Basic Books, 1983), *Company of Critics* (Basic Books, 1988), and, most recently, *On Toleration* (Yale University Press, 1997).

Hana Wirth-Nesher is an associate professor at Tel Aviv University and head of the Department of English. She is the author of *City Codes: Reading the Modern Urban Novel* (Cambridge University Press, 1996) and essays on American, British, and Jewish fiction. She is also the editor of *What Is Jewish Literature?* (Jewish Publication Society, 1994), *New Essays on Call It Sleep* (Cambridge University Press, 1996), and the Sheila Carmel Lectures.

Index

Aaron, David, 168

Academy: Christianity controls, 103, 104–105; Jewish studies in, 118–121, 123–124, 127–129; multiculturalism in, 106, 117–121; other histories in, 106–107

Acculturation, 65. *See also* Assimilation

Adorno, Theodor, 1, 233

Adotevi, Stanislaus, 78

Affirmative action programs: African Americans and Jews disagree on, 72–75; Jewish women benefit from, 6, 60

Africa, memory of, 151

African Americans, 27; on affirmative action, 72–75; as anti-Semitic, 66, 67–68, 71, 72; assimilation by, 23, 63, 65, 70–71; civil rights movement of, 28, 63–64, 65–66, 68, 69–70, 71, 260; class tensions of, 66–67, 68, 72, 76, 79–80; diaspora of, 191, 193, 196; on discrimination, 65–66, 68, 72–75; as feminist, 121; on integration, 57, 59, 63–64, 65, 70, 74–75; and Jews, 4–5, 23, 55, 62–87, 92, 122, 123, 124, 125, 193, 260; as militant or nationalistic, 57, 71–72, 75, 76, 193; particularistic, 71; on pluralism, 63–64, 65, 69–70, 72, 74–75, 80; on race, 64, 66–67, 68–69, 70–71, 74, 75, 76, 78, 80, 122, 123, 124, 125

African-American Teachers Association, 72

Afrocentrism: feminists disagree with, 174–175, 176; on integration, 59; on Juda-

ism, 152–160, 174–175; on monotheism, 174; race defined by, 58–59; on social organization originated in Africa, 175–176

Aleph, 226–227

Allen, Woody, 156

America: anti-Semitism in, 66, 67–68, 185, 252 n.20; assimilation in, 2–3, 23, 57, 63, 65, 70–71, 213–214, 215, 216, 218–219; cultural pluralism in, 39–40, 57; economic inequality in, 51; emigration to, 17–18, 20, 38; identity in (American-ism), 21–22, 38, 39, 40, 42–43, 44, 190; Jews in/Jews at home in, 17–18, 19–24, 61, 62, 165–166, 199, 212, 213–220; as melting pot, 18, 19–24, 42, 43, 57; mul-ticulturalism in, 56–58; passing in, 69; racism in (*see* Racism); as shaatnez, 43; transnationalism in, 38–39, 40–42, 43

American Jewish Committee (AJC), 61, 62, 65; on African American-Jewish tensions, 75–76; on discrimination, 68, 76

American Jewish Congress, 61, 68

Anderson, Benedict, 208; on diaspora, 192–193, 196

Anglo-conformity, 57, 60

Ani, Marimba, 152–154

Anti-Defamation League (ADL), 61, 62, 63, 65, 66, 68; on anti-Semitism, 72; founded, 91

Immigration: assimilation after (*see* Assimilation); in multiculturalism, 38, 56–57; xenophobia follows, 61–62

Insider: African Americans on, 66–67, 68, 75, 76, 78, 80; as imperialist, 60; Jew as, 5, 60, 66–67, 68, 75, 76, 78, 80, 103, 104, 119–120; in multiculturalism, 60, 103, 104

Institute for American Democracy, 66

Integration: African Americans on, 57, 59, 63–64, 65, 70, 74–75; Afrocentrism on, 59; civil rights groups on, 63–64, 65; multiculturalism as barrier to, 61; political v. social, 3, 5; Zionism on, 61

Intermarriage, 22–23, 30, 31–32. *See also* Assimilation

Israel: American Jews on, 200, 201–202, 208; as center, 198, 199, 200 (*see also* Homeland, Palestine as); defined, 199–200; interdependence of, 198, 199; as state, 193, 204

Jabotinsky, Vladimir, 34–36, 51
Jeffries, Leonard, 45, 50
Jesus, 107–108, 109, 111
Jewish Labor Committee, 61
Jewish studies, 45; in academy, 118–121, 123–124, 127–129; on Christianity, 102–103, 107, 109–110, 111; as counter-history, 101–115, 126–127; defined, 123–124; direction of, 109; v. ethnic studies, 6–7; in Germany, 102, 104; in multiculturalism, 103–104, 118–130; nineteenth-century, 101–115; postcolonialism on, 101–102; radicalism in, 101, 103, 104; role of Jesus in, 109, 111; self-definition in, 109

Jews: on affirmative action programs, 72–75; African Americans and, 4–5, 23, 55, 62–87, 92, 122, 123, 124, 125, 193, 260; in America, 3, 17–18, 19–24, 61, 62, 165–166, 185–186, 187, 198–207, 212, 213–230; assimilation by, 19, 20, 21, 22, 62, 65, 102, 213–214, 215, 216, 218–219; as black, 23; Buddhist, 260–261; canon of, 10, 121, 131, 132–133, 134–136, 137, 139, 140, 141, 145, 147, 161, 194, 197; civil rights agencies of, 27, 28, 61–62, 63–64, 65–66, 68, 72, 92; in civil rights movement, 62–63, 64, 92, 260, 267; as colonial peoples, 127; diaspora of, 76–77, 185–186, 187, 193, 194–197, 198–

207, 208–209; on Enlightenment, 5–6, 7, 259; in exile, 194, 198, 199, 231–232, 235–236, 237; on exile, 236–243, 244–249; in Germany, 102; language defines, 213–214, 215, 216, 218–222; as marginal/minority, 27–28, 59, 60, 124, 257–258, 259–260, 264, 266, 267; in modernism, 232–233, 236, 238–243; and multiculturalism, 4–5, 45, 51, 59–60, 61, 78, 103, 104, 113; as multilingual, 212–213, 214, 215, 220, 221–222, 227–228; nationalism of, 41–42 (*see also* Zionism); neoconservative, 45–48, 51, 75, 77; on other minorities, 61, 62; as outsider, 78, 79, 80, 82, 128, 257; pass as white, 69; in pluralism, 59, 60, 62, 65, 72, 73–74, 80; plural loyalties of, 36; politics of, 96; in postcolonialism, 186; as race, 125; racial attitudes of, 61, 68–69, 76, 81; reject Jewishness, 260–261; secular, 260–261; Sephardic, 20; in slave trade, 156–157; social networks of, 93; as victim/as vulnerable, 60–61, 82, 96, 254; as white, 2, 4, 26–29, 31, 69, 112, 122, 123, 124, 125, 255; women, 6, 60, 113, 200, 255, 264

Job, Book of, 132, 135, 136
Joyce, James, on exile, 233, 236
Judaism: v. Afrocentrism, 152–160, 174–175; in capitalism, 165–166; as chauvinsim, 153; Christianity reformed / reinterpreted/ cleansed, 105, 108, 109–110, 111, 112, 120, 122, 157–158, 161, 162; deity in, 161, 163, 169–171; diversity within, 167–169; feminists on, 121–122, 152–160, 169–170, 174–175; German view of, 152; as history, 102–103, 161–162, 171–172; Jewish culture becomes, 168, 218; law as basis of, 158–159, 161, 167–168; as monolithic, 167–168; as monotheistic, 173, 174; as oppressive, 157, 174; as original religion, 102, 108; particularism v. universalism in, 258–259, 260, 261; as patriarchal/sexist, 121–122, 154–155, 156–157; and Puritanism, 166; racism in, 155–156, 168; as religion of retribution, 163; taboos in (*see* Shaatnez); texts of, 10, 123, 125–126, 128, 129, 132 (*see also* Bible, as Jewish canon)

Kabbalism, 226

Designer:	U.C. Press Staff
Compositor:	Integrated Composition Systems
Text:	10/13 Galliard
Display:	Galliard
Printer & Binder:	Haddon Craftsmen, Inc.